ONE LORD, ONE PLAN, ONE PEOPLE

One Lord, One Plan, One People

*A Journey through the Bible from
Genesis to Revelation*

Rodger Crooks

THE BANNER OF TRUTH TRUST

THE BANNER OF TRUTH TRUST

3 Murrayfield Road, Edinburgh, EH12 6EL, UK
PO Box 621, Carlisle, Pennsylvania, USA

© Rodger Crooks 2011
First published 2011
Reprinted 2013

ISBN: 978 1 84871 137 2

Typeset in 11/14.5 Minion Pro at
The Banner of Truth Trust, Edinburgh

Printed in the USA by
Versa Press Inc.,
East Peoria, IL

In memory of my parents,
Mervyn and Florence Crooks,
who first taught me the Scriptures
which made me wise for salvation;
and my mother-in-law,
Sarah Hamilton,
who knew the Scriptures
which made her wise for salvation.

It is dedicated to
my congregation, Belvoir Presbyterian Church, Belfast,
who listened to all the sometimes-longer-than-usual sermons
that formed the basis of this book
(your good-humoured patience is incredible!);
my younger daughter, Elizabeth Crooks,
who first suggested that I write this book
(that is her story and she's sticking to it!);
my father-in-law, David Hamilton,
who asked constantly if I had finished this book
(well, finally I have);
and my wife of thirty years, Joan Crooks,
who supported me throughout the writing of this book
(your love has continually blessed and enriched my life).

Contents

Preface

It was a Wednesday morning, and during Key Stage 2 assembly in a south Belfast primary school, the children were asked 'How many of you have a mobile phone?' A forest of hands shot up. It was easier to count the children who did not own one than those who did. The follow-up question soon arrived: 'And how many of you have a Bible at home?' Less than those who did not have access to a mobile phone. My snapshot of the religious life of eight to eleven year olds in south Belfast is not very scientific, but I suspect that it is accurate enough. Secularism has made rapid and massive inroads into Northern Ireland's society, and one of the sad consequences is that the level of biblical literacy has fallen off a cliff. I am encountering more and more people of all ages and backgrounds who have little or no knowledge of the Bible. When they are converted, as many of them are, and are urged to read the Bible, they struggle. They do not know where to begin or what the Bible is all about. They also have huge problems with preaching because most sermons they listen to assume a knowledge of basic Bible facts which they do not possess. The Bible still remains a problematic and even a closed book to them because of their underlying level of biblical literacy. If this is true of you, then this book is designed to help you gain access to the Bible's contents so that you can significantly increase the extent of your Bible knowledge. As you read it, just imagine that I am sitting down with you over coffee – I like mine strong and black with no sugar – and doing a one-to-one Bible study with you, in which I take you on a journey from Genesis to Revelation, pointing out the main features of each book.

'Did they check the date on your birth certificate?' was the reaction of one of my friends when he heard that the Youth Board of my denomination, the Presbyterian Church in Ireland, had invited me to take part in Route 66, a Bible conference for young adults. They obviously had not, because for the next eight years I spent the August Bank Holiday weekend as the oldest member of the Route 66 speaking team. As most of the Route 66ers were from a church background, their knowledge of the Bible's main stories was pretty solid. However, lots of them were decidedly unsteady when it came to the question of how all these stories join together. They knew that all the individual pieces should interconnect, but how did they? This situation could be due to the way the post-modern given, that there is no 'meta-narrative', had influenced their thinking much more than they realised; but after chatting to many of them, I think it was due to the fact that no one had ever shown them how all the Bible's constituent parts fit together. If this describes you, someone who is aware of the fact that the Bible is not just a collection of random stories, then this book is designed to help you see what – or more correctly *who* – is the Bible's focal point. As you read it, you will see that all the Bible's sixty-six books focus on Jesus, the one Lord who is the terminal point of God's promises. It is Jesus' life, death, resurrection, ascension, reign and coming return which is the Bible's big story. It is seeing the Bible through that lens which will enable you to grasp the way the Bible's individual parts interlock.

Then in September 2004, after returning home from that year's Route 66, I thought that my congregation, Belvoir Presbyterian Church, would benefit from something similar. So I started to preach one sermon on each book of the Bible at our evening service, in which I would not only give an outline of the book's storyline but more importantly show how it pointed to Jesus. Two and a half years and sixty-seven sermons later, we had travelled from Genesis to Revelation and, in the spring of 2007, our journey was over. Those sermons formed the basis of this book because somewhere about Obadiah – I cannot remember exactly because, like my knees, my memory is not what it used to be – my younger daughter, Elizabeth, suggested that these sermons should be made available to a wider audience by being put into print. Surprisingly, others agreed. So a copy of the handouts that I produced to accompany each sermon were sent off to the Banner of Truth to see if they would be interested in publishing the material. Even more surprisingly, they replied that they would be, and the rest, as they say, is history. You are holding the end result of all their positive encouragement in your hands today.

In the feedback from my congregation on these sixty-seven sermons, many admitted that they had seen for the first time how important the Old Testament was in preparing the ground for the coming of Jesus into our world. Before that, apart from a few quick excursions in the book of Psalms, they had stuck pretty much to reading the New Testament. If this is you, then this book is designed to help you see that the Bible actually begins with *Genesis* and not Matthew. Every good stand-up knows that a good joke must have a good story leading up to a good punch line. Any joke that does not have both will bomb spectacularly. *Only* reading the New Testament is like a joke with *only* a punch line, and *only* reading the Old Testament is like a joke with *no* punch line. As you read this book, you will make the discovery that many have made, that not only do we need the New Testament to make sense of the Old, but we also need the Old Testament to provide the framework for the New. For there is only one plan of salvation that runs through both the Testaments of the Bible, as God calls out one people to belong to him and to live under the rule of one Lord.

Apart from those mentioned in the dedication, many others have contributed to the publication of this book, and I must say a quick thanks to them. The fellowship, 'craic', and spiritual stimulation I enjoyed as part of the working group for Route 66, which was chaired by Roz Stirling, was a real blessing. My fellow elders, Brian Dunwoody, Gilbert Anderson and Norman Mannis, were hugely supportive and gave me space to write. All preachers stand on other preachers' shoulders, benefiting from their insights, and I am no exception. The eagle-eyed among you will detect the input of men like Martyn Lloyd-Jones, Alec Motyer, Stuart Olyott, John Stott, Don Carson, Edmund Clowney, Desi Alexander, and Dale Ralph Davis into what I have written and even how I have written it. If I have not acknowledged their influence as often I should, forgive me. This book began life as a series of sermons, and busy preachers are not as copious with their footnotes and citations as they perhaps ought to be. Catherine Riddell proofread lots of this material until its bad grammar and split infinitives nearly drove her crazy. Douglas Taylor's skilful editing turned my sermon scripts into readable book chapters. Jonathan Watson's encouragement helped me keep going with this writing project, especially at the time of my father's death. Above all, I want to express my gratitude to God for all his grace. It is a constant source of amazement to me that not only should I be on the receiving end of all his covenant promises, but that he should call me to be a preacher of 'the unsearchable riches of Christ' which are to be found in all the Scriptures.

RODGER CROOKS
Belfast
May 2011

The 'W5' of the Bible

At the *Odyssey* entertainment complex in Belfast, the city in which I have worked for the past twelve years, there is an interactive discovery centre called *W5*. The five Ws stand for Who? What? When? Where? and Why? Before we set out on our journey through the sixty-six individual books of the Bible, I want us to pause and take a look at the Bible itself, using the W5 template.

WHO WROTE THE BIBLE?

On one level, the Bible was written by human authors like Moses, David, Isaiah, Ezra, Luke, Paul, Peter and John. Many of them openly attached their names to what they wrote, so we do not have to guess who some of the Bible's human authors were. Even when others wrote anonymously we can still work out who they were through hints in the text and references in other parts of the Bible. As it was written by different authors from a variety of backgrounds, when we try to get to grips with the Bible's message, we have to take into account the authors' individual styles, interests and vocabulary. So, for example, if we think that John wrote Revelation in just the same way Ezra wrote 1 and 2 Chronicles, and so they can both be interpreted in exactly the same way, we may come up with some pretty ingenious but off-the-wall results, miles out of line from what Revelation and 1 and 2 Chronicles are really saying.

While all this is undeniably true, the Bible's dominant message is that behind all the human authors lies one divine Author, God himself. Fundamentally the Bible comes to us, not primarily from people like Samuel, Jeremiah, Mark and James, but from God. Historically this idea that God himself is the principal author of the Bible has been described theologically as 'The Inspiration of Scripture'. A key statement in trying to get our heads around this idea is the opening part of 2 Timothy 3:16. In older translations of the Bible, Paul's statement has been translated, 'All Scripture is given by inspiration of God' (AV), or, 'All Scripture is inspired by God' (RSV), which is where the term 'Inspiration of Scripture' comes from. This is the only time Paul uses the Greek adjective translated 'inspired by God'. It is a hybrid word meaning 'breathed out from God's mouth', which is why the NIV scores more points out of ten than the older translations for its rendering, 'All Scripture is God-breathed.' To affirm that the Bible comes from God and that he is its principal author, Paul could not have used a stronger expression than this one. He wants us to be absolutely clear that the Bible was not an already-existing collection of religious writings which God looked at and, thinking it would do the job as an inspiration to people to live better lives, gave it his stamp of approval. Paul is underscoring the fact that the Bible is from God, spoken by him and breathed out by him. In affirming this, Paul is not coming up with any ground-breaking suggestion, but is simply underpinning what was taught over and over again in the Old Testament about God's mouth speaking out his word (*Deut.* 8:3; *Isa.* 1:20; 40:5; 55:11; 58:14).

What Paul says about the Bible being from God is backed up by Peter in 2 Peter 1:21. It is true that he refers to the Bible's human authors when he writes that 'men spoke'. However, he reminds us very graphically that this dual authorship of the Bible is not 'a partnership . . . of equals.'[1] He informs us that 'prophecy never had its origin in the will of man'. In other words, men like Ezekiel or Luke did not wake up one morning and say, 'What will I do today? It's a bit chilly for a walk, so I will make myself some coffee and do a spot of Bible writing.' The Bible's human authors only wrote when God, the principal author, spoke to them, giving them the word he wanted them to communicate. Just as the wind gets up and fills the sails of a yacht, so that it moves power-fully across the sea, so the Bible's human authors 'spoke from God as they were carried along by the Holy Spirit'.

[1] Dick Lucas, *The Message of 2 Peter and Jude* (Leicester, England: Inter-Varsity Press, 1995), p. 83.

I need to add a few riders to what I have just said, not to give myself some wriggle room, but just to clarify the Bible's teaching. All the Bible, and not just the bits we like because they fit into our preconceived ideas, is from God, but, by the inspiration of the Bible, I do not mean that every bit of the Bible is equally inspiring and will enthuse us to get up and live for God in a passionate way. If you have ever worked your way through all the laws of Leviticus, or the list of names at the start of 1 Chronicles, or the details of Ezekiel's vision of the temple, you will know that some bits of the Bible are, at least on the surface, less inspiring. But they are breathed out by God, and we must be prepared to work hard to arrive at their meaning.

Also the process of inspiration was not a mechanical one, in which God, like a company executive dictating to his secretary, gave the words of the Bible to the human authors. As they wrote, they wrote as individuals, using their own styles and vocabularies, yet the Holy Spirit so controlled them that they did not distort God's message in the slightest. Their words were really their own words, but they were, and still are, also God's words, so that what the Bible says, God says.

The extent of the Bible's inspiration is the full, original text of Scripture. The fact is, however, that nothing of the original autographs survives today. In his providential care of his Word, God did not permit any of the original texts to survive. What we do possess are copies of the originals. These copies are wonderfully accurate, and they are also very numerous. Their accuracy and abundance means that we today can read the very Word of God.

Inspiration also extends to the very words which the Bible's human authors used (*1 Cor.* 2:13). God's control of the process of inspiration ensured that the words of men would convey the truth of God. Some people, feeling uncomfortable with the idea that the very words are inspired by God (that is, the doctrine of 'verbal inspiration'), suggest that, while the words the Bible's human authors used might be error-prone, the ideas they conveyed were not – that God inspired the 'message', not the actual words. But that is not what the Bible says about itself. Inspiration extends to the very words of Scripture, as originally given, and not merely to the 'ideas' or 'message'.

Like a planet with four moons revolving around it, each controlled by the planet's gravitational pull, the idea of the Bible's inspiration controls four other ideas. The first is the Bible's *authority*. When I was a small boy, my granny had a calendar, on which was written a bit of homespun advice such as, 'An apple a day keeps the doctor away', for each day of the year. Is the Bible like my granny's calendar, just dispensing nice platitudes which we can take or leave depending on what mood we are in? If the Bible is – as it claims to be – God the Creator, Saviour and King speaking to us, then we have no option but to do what it says and to allow its teaching to control every area of our thinking and behaviour. Irrespective of how much inconvenience it might cause to our comfortable lifestyles, and even if doing what God says will involve our going against our culture's received wisdom and acceptable behaviour, something each of us naturally hates doing, we have to submit to the Bible's authority because behind it lies the authority of the God from whom it comes, who breathed it from his mouth. Submitting to Jesus' lordship means doing what the Bible says (*Luke* 6:46; *John* 13:13, 17), and being filled with the Spirit is the same as being controlled by the Bible's teaching (*Eph.* 5:18–19; *Col.* 3:16–17).

Another area over which the Bible's inspiration exerts its influence is the Bible's *inerrancy*. Because it comes from a God who is incapable of lying (*Num.*23:19; *Titus* 1:2), has as its focus Jesus who is the Truth (*John* 14:6), and was controlled in its writing, compilation and preservation by the Spirit of truth (*John* 16:13), it is impossible for the Bible to contain mistakes. When people point out apparent inconsistencies in the Bible it usually says more about them than the Bible. It reflects a hostile prejudice against the God of the Bible which inevitably leads to a faulty and jaundiced interpretation of the Bible. It is amazing how often something which critics of the Bible trumpet as a glaring contradiction or mistake, when more evidence and information become available, actually highlights the Bible's accuracy and correctness. When God spoke he did not stutter or deceive or talk out of both sides of his mouth at once. He spoke the truth, and nothing but the truth, and because what comes from God to us is inerrant, we can trust the Bible and the God it tells us about totally and without reserve.

The Bible's inspiration also pulls within its orbit the issue of the Bible's *sufficiency*. The Bible is complete, needing no new messages to supplement what it says. God has nothing more to add to it by way of bolt-ons because, in the Bible, he has given us everything we need to experience his salvation, to grow spiritually, and to serve Jesus effectively (*2 Tim.* 3:16–17; *2 Pet.* 1:3). When it comes to living for Jesus, the Bible is the only show in town, and it is the only thing we need, as it is 'the *only* authority for glorifying and enjoying [God]'.[1]

One final issue that the Bible's inspiration draws within its sphere of influence concerns the Bible's *clarity*, or, if you like the old theological term, its *perspicuity*. The overall thrust of what it teaches is plain and obvious, so that we do not need to be cryptic code breakers or specialists with insider expertise to understand what God is saying in his Word. Instead, relying on the Holy Spirit to illuminate our minds (*Psa.* 119:18), whether from what is explicitly stated or from what can logically and reasonably be deduced from its principles, every Christian can know what the Bible is primarily about. Having said that, not all parts of the Bible are equally clear. What do we do when we hit one of those less clear parts? We start with the bits we do understand, and, by comparing the less clear section of the Bible with the clearer one, we can, with God's help, arrive at a better understanding of what God is saying to us in the more difficult parts of his Word.

You might be wondering if I am ever going to get to the other four Ws, as I have spent so long on the first one. However, I am totally unapologetic, because the Bible's inspiration is so important to everything else that it is vital that I spend time on it. If we go wrong here, we will go wrong everywhere else.

WHEN WAS THE BIBLE WRITTEN?

The Bible is not, strictly speaking, one book but a library of sixty-six separate books. It was written by over forty different human authors over a period of approximately 1500 years. The earliest book in the Bible is thought to be Job, which may have been written down as early as 1450 BC, while the smart money is on Revelation being the last Bible

---

[1] *The Shorter Catechism in Modern English*, Question 2.

book to be written, probably around AD 95. In spite of the length of time it took to complete its writing, the number of human authors involved, and the wide variety of styles in which they wrote, one of the amazing things about the Bible – one of the subsidiary indicators that it is from God – is, as we shall see, that it has a unified, single theme: everything is about Jesus.

WHERE DID OUR ENGLISH BIBLE COME FROM?

The Bible, which was originally written in Hebrew, Greek, and a dash of Aramaic, has been constantly translated so that people can have God's Word in their own language. The two most famous early translations are the 'Septuagint', which is a translation of the Old Testament into Greek undertaken in the third century BC in Egypt, and the 'Vulgate', which is a translation of the Bible into Latin carried out in the late fourth century AD by Jerome.

As far as the English Bible is concerned, the first significant date is 1384, when John Wycliffe produced an English version of the Bible. However, the real breakthrough for the English Bible came in 1526 with the publication of William Tyndale's translation of the New Testament. The crucial difference between Wycliffe and Tyndale was that Tyndale based his on the original Greek, while Wycliffe based his on the Vulgate. Tyndale's translation became the benchmark, in terms of style and accuracy, for all subsequent English translations. Then, in 1611, came the watershed moment for the English Bible with the appearance of the Authorized Version. It was commissioned by King James I, who was a very shrewd political operator, as a compromise between two competing versions: the 'Bishops' Bible' of 1568, which was the official Bible of the Church of England, and the 'Geneva Bible', which the Puritans favoured. After a little opposition, the Authorized Version established itself as the premier English Bible and held on to its top spot for several hundred years.

However, developments in the English language, advances in biblical scholarship and the discovery of new Bible manuscripts led to a challenge to the Authorized Version's supremacy; so, from the 1950s through to the present, a glut of English translations has burst on to the scene, each of them setting out its stall as to why it is a worthy successor to the Authorized Version. At the risk of over-simplification, each newer English Bible can be categorized by its pedigree and its translation philosophy. Some stand in direct line to the Authorized Version and appear to be revisions, modernizations and tweakings of it, while others claim to stand in a completely different tradition, with less reliance on the Authorized Version and a more direct translation from the original Bible languages. Some use what is known as 'Formal Equivalence' when they translate the Bible languages, attempting a word-for-word approach to the original languages' lexical and grammatical forms. Others use what is called 'Dynamic Equivalence', attempting to convey what they think the text would have conveyed to the original readers, irrespective of its original form.

In the English-speaking world, we have a bewildering number of different Bible translations available to us. We even have the luxury of being able to debate about and – sadly – fall out with each other over which one is the best, the most accurate, and the soundest. We need to remember that there are many thousands of our Christian brothers and sisters who, even if they can read, do not have access to a Bible, or even part of a Bible, in their own language. This should make us a little less aggressive and argumentative in our debates, and instead cause us to be more committed in our prayers for and generous in our support of those who are working extremely hard, often in very dangerous situations, to make sure people can hear God's Word in their own languages.

WHY ONLY SIXTY-SIX BOOKS IN THE BIBLE?

Dan Brown's *The Da Vinci Code* and the media interest in alternative versions of the story of Jesus such as *The Gospel of Judas* has raised the status of the question of the canon of Scripture from a bit of an in-house debate among obsessive theologians to an important apologetic issue. Nothing could be further from the truth than the line pushed by Brown and his fellow-travellers that the make-up of the Bible is a sordid and long-running conspiracy by the church to suppress some potentially embarrassing truths about Jesus and to sell a particular image of him.

The canon of Scripture, those sixty-six books which are recognized as God's authoritative Word, was not something imposed on the church from the outside, nor was it something the church itself decided. Instead, it was a matter of Christians, under the Holy Spirit's guidance, recognizing these sixty-six books as being God's Word.

As far as the Old Testament canon is concerned, the first Christians already had an accepted list of the books which made up the Old Testament, and they regarded these as Scripture. The matter of which books should be included in the New Testament canon is a bit more complex. Even as the New Testament itself was being written, some letters were already recognized as part of God's Word and on a par as regards authority with the Old Testament (2 Pet. 3:15–16). Certain criteria were applied to see if a book should be in the New Testament. Jesus had commissioned his apostles to define and pass on the gospel (John 14:26; 16:12–13), so to be accepted a book had to be written either by an apostle, such as Paul, Matthew and John, or by someone closely associated with an apostle, such as Mark, Luke and James. Since God's truth is consistent, another criterion for inclusion was that the teaching of the book should be in harmony with the contents of the other books already recognized as Scripture. A final consideration was whether there was a consensus in the church as a whole that a book should be included. This criterion did not prevent some prolonged discussion about certain books, but ultimately there was agreement over which books should be in and which books should not. In AD 397, the Council of Carthage recognized the sixty-six books which had met these three criteria and placed them in the order in which we find them in our English Bibles.[1]

WHAT IS THE MAIN THEME OF THE BIBLE?

The Bible is not a disjointed series of random stories, instructions and ideas with nothing in common. It has a unifying theme, and that

[1] This did not exclude debate about the status of the Apocrypha. These writings, not part of the Jewish canon, are accepted by the Roman Catholic and Eastern Orthodox churches, but rejected by Protestants. Neither Jesus nor any New Testament writer ever quoted from them.

theme is not an idea but a person – Jesus. That is what Jesus himself taught (*Luke* 24:27, 44; *John* 5:39). The Old Testament sets the scene for his coming and the New Testament gives us the facts about and implications of his coming. In the Old Testament God's promise of Jesus is made and in the New Testament God's promise of Jesus is kept. In the Old Testament God's covenant – which centres on Jesus – starts to be unwrapped and in the New Testament God's covenant – which centres on Jesus – reaches its climax.

Some of my nephews used to be keen on the *Where's Wally?* books. On each page of the book was a picture and somewhere in that picture Wally was hidden. Your task was to find him. Jesus is on every page of the Bible, either explicitly or implicitly, either in shadow or reality, either in anticipation or fulfilment, and so, no matter where we are in the Bible, the question we should always be asking is this: 'Where is Jesus?'[1]

---

[1] C. H. Spurgeon once quoted the advice of an old Welsh preacher: 'From every little village in England—it does not matter where it is—there is sure to be a road to London. Though there may not be a road to certain other places, there is certain to be a road to London. Now, from every text in the Bible there is a road to Jesus Christ, and the way to preach is just to say, "How can I get from this text to Jesus Christ?", and then go preaching all the way along it.' *Metropolitan Tabernacle Pulpit*, 25, No. 1503.

2

Genesis

As we set out on our journey through the Bible, we begin with Genesis, the first book of a five-volume sub-section of the Old Testament known as the 'Pentateuch'. You will not find that label for the books of Genesis, Exodus, Leviticus, Numbers and Deuteronomy in the Bible itself, but you will see them referred to as 'The Book of the Law' (*Josh.* 1:8) and 'The Law of Moses' (*Josh.* 23:6; *1 Kings* 2:3; *Ezra* 7:6; *Dan.* 9:13). This last description of the first five books of the Bible really should close the sterile debate about who wrote them. Jesus clearly believed Moses did (*Matt.* 8:4; 19:8; *Mark* 7:10; 12:26; *Luke* 24:27, 44) and that should decide the matter.

Reading Genesis is like watching the highlights of an event on television. Because Genesis covers such a long period of human history, Moses does not give us a blow-by-blow account of everything that went on but only the most significant moments. This should remind us right away that, in the Bible, God does not tell us everything that we, in our curiosity – and often our sinful curiosity – might demand to know; he only tells us what we need to know, so that we can experience his salvation and live for his glory (*Deut.* 29:29; *2 Tim.* 3:15–17).

The highlights of the first half of Genesis, which covers Genesis 1-11, are FOUR DEFINING EVENTS.

The first of them is *creation* (1:1–2:25). Before anything else existed, God was (*Psa.* 90:2), being eternally present as Father, Son and Holy Spirit. But then, this God began to make all things (1:1). He spoke (1:3, 9, 14, 20, 26, 29), initially into nothingness, and, out of what was 'formless and empty' (1:2), in six days, he created something ordered and beautiful. In the first three days of creation, God formed three different environments out of what was formless: light (1:3–5), waters and sky (1:6–8), and ground and vegetation (1:9–13). Then, during the last three days of creation, God filled what was empty, creating inhabitants for each of these three environments: the sun, moon and stars for the light (1:14–19), fish and birds for the waters and sky (1:20–23) and animals and humans for the ground and vegetation (1:24–31). After six days of stunning creative activity, God was delighted with all he had done (1:31). Then, on the seventh day, God rested, and, in doing so, established the principle of sabbath, a one-day-in-seven time to rest in order to worship and be refreshed.

The pinnacle of God's creative work was human beings, made, in contrast to the rest of creation, in God's image (1:26–27). Jesus is 'the image of the invisible God' (*Col.* 1:15) and 'the last Adam' (*1 Cor.* 15:45). This shows that being made in God's image means that, like Jesus, human beings enjoy a relationship with God of love, expressed in obedience. This makes creation, not only an act of awesome power and enormous wisdom, but also an act of extraordinary grace. Although he did not need to, because he eternally existed as a perfect community of Father, Son and Holy Spirit, God created human beings to join in that relationship of love and to share in the life of the triune Godhead.

If only things had stayed that way! Tragically they did not, because the next defining event is the *Fall*, which is recorded in Genesis 3. Although all the earth was very good (1:31), God created the Garden of Eden to be a special place of beauty, provision, security and, above all, friendship with God for human beings to enjoy (2:8–9). In Eden, Adam had a royal role (1:28) – he reigned over the rest of creation as God's co-regent (2:19–20) – and a priestly function as he cultivated and maintained the garden (2:15). His rule was not an absolute one, because he was under God's authority, and he expressed his submission to God by obeying the command to enjoy the fruit from all the trees in Eden except one – the tree of the knowledge of good and evil (2:16–17).

Then the turning point of history took place. Satan, in the form of a snake, deceived Adam, and Eve, his wife, into questioning the trustworthiness of God's Word (compare 3:1, 4 with 2:17) and the motives behind God's generosity (compare 3:1 with 2:16). Once he had got them to do this, and to start to look at things from their own perspective rather than God's (3:6), it was easy for Satan, and soon Adam and Eve were helping themselves to fruit from the tree of the knowledge of good and evil. Not only had they rejected God's authority to tell them what to do, but from now on they would decide what was right and wrong. In an act of high treason, they rebelled against God and hijacked his position, and, in an act of self-centred independence, they started to be 'like God', setting the agenda for their own lives. We know that the original sin involved rebellion against God's legitimate rule and blasphemy in 'playing God', not just from Genesis 3, but supremely from Jesus' death. When Jesus died for his people's sin, he was treated as the Original Sinner, crucified for the twin crimes of blasphemy and rebellion (*Mark* 14:61–64; 15:26), put to death for the very sins of which we are essentially guilty.

The next defining event is the *Flood*, which is described in Genesis 6–9. This devastating act of judgment, which becomes the template of God's judgment throughout the Bible, did not come without good reason. The Fall had catastrophic consequences, not just for Adam personally, but also for all humanity. Instead of God's blessing, there is now God's curse, which affects the environment, makes work tedious, causes childbearing to be a painful experience, and leads to gender conflict (3:16–19). Instead of life, there is now death, as humanity is cut off from the tree of life. Although humans beings did not die straight away, decay that leads inevitably to death became part and parcel of human experience (5:1–32, with the exception of Enoch). Instead of harmony, there is now hostility, as first Adam and Eve play the 'blame game' with each other as to whose fault the original sin was (3:12), and then as Cain murders Abel, his brother (4:8). Instead of friendship with God, there is now alienation, as Adam and Eve try to hide from God rather than running out to meet him as they had always done (3:8).

Like an aggressive cancer, sin spread and spread until every part of human life was polluted by it. God was so pained over the extent of sin that he decided to wipe humanity from the earth with a cataclysmic worldwide flood (6:5–7). However, in an act of grace, God preserved Noah and his family, together with representatives of all animals. When the floodwaters had subsided, he made a promise never again to use a similar flood to judge the earth (9:1–17).

Humanity failed miserably to make good use of the new start God had given them. The next defining event is the *Tower of Babel*, which we find in Genesis 11:1–9. The proposed construction of a city with a tower showed that nothing much had changed, for it was a calculated attempt by humans to derail God's purposes. God's plan was to give Jesus an enduring and supreme name (*Psa.* 72:17; *Phil.* 2:9), and that the nations should spread throughout the whole earth (1:28), but in their anti-God pride and rebellion, the builders of Babel wanted to make a name for themselves, and to keep people together (11:4). In a clear signal that no challenge to his purposes would be ignored, God judged human blasphemy and rebellion by multiplying their languages so that they could not understand each other. Thus they were forced to fulfil his purpose that they should spread throughout the earth. This judgment was reversed on the day of Pentecost (*Acts* 2:5–11) and will be completely removed in heaven (*Rev.* 5:13; 7:9–10).

The first half of Genesis ends with humanity under God's judgment, yet this provides the background against which the rescue mission that God was to carry out through his Son is to be seen. We have all turned against God and are under his judgment, but, in Genesis 3:15, God gives the first indication of his plan to send the Saviour we desperately need. The Saviour will be the second Man, a real human being, who, at great personal cost, will succeed where Adam, the first Man, failed. By his obedience, which led to his death on the cross, Jesus, the last Adam, will overturn all Satan's evil work in the Garden of Eden (*1 John* 3:8), so that, on the basis of the righteousness of his sinless life and sin-bearing death, friendship between God and his people will be restored.

The highlights of the second half of Genesis, which covers Genesis 12–50, are FOUR DEFINING PROMISES.

A soap-opera scriptwriter, given the outline of Genesis 12–50, would be overjoyed, for that storyline traces the comings and goings of four generations of the same family and is crammed full of promising plots. What scriptwriter would not delight to describe how Abraham, who had migrated from Ur, in what is now Iraq, to Canaan, in modern Israel and Palestine, struggled, not just to establish himself as an immigrant in a new country and to protect his considerable assets in times of crisis – such as famine, land and water shortages, and civil unrest – but primarily with the fact that he and Sarah, his wife, had no son and heir? Although such a situation causes heartache to western couples, in a Middle Eastern cultural context it was almost unbearable. The goings-on within the family of Isaac, Abraham's son, would be an additional fertile source of script material. Isaac and Rebekah had twin boys, but the family was split down the middle by parental favouritism. Isaac favoured Esau, the crude, unspiritual elder son, while Rebekah, Isaac's manipulative wife, favoured Jacob, their sly and scheming younger son. An episode based on the incident in which Jacob, with his mother's collusion, duped his blind father into blessing him instead of Esau would be compelling.

Jacob is the most colourful of Abraham's family. When he had cheated Esau out of his inheritance, his brother swore revenge, so Jacob fled back to present-day Iraq, his mother's birthplace. There he encountered Laban, his uncle, and it is hard to say which of them was the more devious. Jacob's wedding did not go according to plan. Laban made him work seven years without wages for the hand of Rachel, his beautiful younger daughter, but then, on the wedding night, switched her for Leah, the older but not nearly so attractive daughter. Then, when Jacob protested, Laban made him agree to work another seven years for Rachel, although to Laban's credit he gave Jacob his 'wages' in advance. However, Jacob's behaviour became just as underhand, as he manipulated the breeding process in Laban's flocks to make himself a very wealthy man. The sibling rivalry between Leah and Rachel would delight the scriptwriter. Leah conceived with no difficulty, but Rachel was infertile, and her sister's super-fertility infuriated her. Unsympathetically, Jacob reminds Rachel that the problem must be hers since he has fathered four sons already. What follows is chaotic, but the outcome is that Rachel has a son, Joseph, whose story is told in the last section of the book.

The way Jacob treated Joseph seemed to repeat the family-dividing favouritism Isaac showed for Esau. This, coupled with some prophetic dreams Joseph related to his family, so irritated his brothers that they vowed to kill him. However, greed trumped hatred, so they sold Joseph as a slave to some traders heading for Egypt. Through his personal integrity and his God-given ability to interpret dreams, Joseph rose to become Egypt's second-in-command. When a devastating famine engulfed the whole region for seven years, the economic plan Joseph had put in place not only saved Egypt from starvation but his own family as well. Genesis ends with Jacob reunited to his son whom he had thought dead, the reconciliation of Joseph and his brothers, and the migration of Jacob's extended family to Egypt where they enjoyed the protection of the country's ruler.

Obviously, though it does make an enthralling story, this is not why Moses was guided by the Holy Spirit to include these incidents in Genesis. What is the connecting factor linking all these larger-than-life incidents? What links them is God's promise to Abraham in Genesis 12:2–3, restated in Genesis 15 and 17. God enters into a covenant with Abraham and makes him four promises, which define the outline of Genesis, if not the whole of the Bible. God promises *a people,* 'I will make you into a great nation'; *protection,* 'I will bless those who bless you and curse those who curse you'; *a place,* 'to your offspring I will give this land' (12:7); and *a programme,* in which 'all peoples on earth will be blessed through you'. As we look at Genesis through the lens of these four defining promises, we see at least one of them in every story.

When God called Abraham, while he was living in Ur, to leave and head for a land about which he undertook to tell him (12:1), he promised him a *place,* an inheritance of land (12:7). But when Abraham died he did not possess any of the land, except for a field at Hebron which he bought as a family burial plot (chapter 23). All that Isaac owned was the same small piece of Canaan he had inherited from his father. This hardly seems the fulfilment of God's promise. In fact, Genesis ends with Jacob, who was also given the promise of a place of blessing by God (28:13), not actually in Canaan at all, but in Egypt. All this seems to indicate that there is more to this promise than meets the eye. It seems to involve something more than physical real estate, and Moses is in effect telling us to wait and see how these things unfold.

If God's promise of a *people* too numerous to count (15:5; 22:17; 26:4; 28:14) was to come to pass, Abraham, Isaac and Jacob needed to have sons. This is why Moses devotes a seemingly disproportionate number of column inches to telling us about the births of Isaac, Jacob, and Jacob's twelve sons. At the end of Genesis, the family – now a nation – has seventy members (46:27), and we see God's promise of a people taking shape. Yet Sarah, Rebekah, and Rachel, all had trouble conceiving. God did not make it easy for his promise to be fulfilled. He did this to demonstrate that his purposes would be accomplished, not through human achievement and ingenuity, but only through his own power and grace. His promise of a people was also to be fulfilled despite the mess caused by human sin. This is what lies behind the strife of Genesis 29–30. Amidst all the conflict between Leah and Rachel, God's promise of a people is taking shape: after all, between them they had eleven sons. Does this mean that God approved of all that happened? No, the fact that God is working out his promise does not excuse human sin. Nevertheless, in the midst of the strife, God's work is going forward: the people are becoming numerically stronger. This is what makes God's control of his world so amazing: he takes the refuse of human twistedness and sin and turns it into the compost in which his promises grow.

If God's promise of a people was to work out, his promise of *protection* had to be fulfilled, because God's people were constantly under threat. Sometimes the threat came from outside factors, such as the famine recorded in Genesis 41–47. It threatened to derail God's promise of a people, as Jacob and his family faced extinction through starvation. But God was already at work to protect his promise by raising Joseph to the rank of second-in-command in Egypt. Through Joseph's intervention, Jacob and his family migrate to Egypt, where they are not only saved from being wiped out (45:7; 50:19–21), but also prosper (47:27). However, God frequently had to protect his promise from the very people he had given it to. For example, not just once but twice, through a lack of faith, Abraham tried to save his own skin by passing off Sarah, his wife, as his sister, thereby placing God's promise of a people in jeopardy (12:10–20; 20:1–18). Later on, Isaac repeated his father's faithless and cowardly act (26:1–11). On all three occasions, God stepped in to make sure neither Sarah nor Rebekah were molested, and in doing so protected his promise.

While the other three were important, the most significant promise concerned a *programme*, in which God would bless all nations through one of Abraham's descendants. In the storyline of Genesis, this promise worked itself out on a material level. For example, Joseph's presence brought God's material blessing to other groups of people – to Potiphar's household (39:5), to the prison in which he was interned after being falsely accused (39:20–23), and on the land of Egypt as a whole through his economic policies (41:41–49). However, this promise does not focus on material blessings for all nations, but on spiritual blessings. In Genesis 3:15, God promised that someone would come to rescue humanity from the catastrophic consequences of the Fall. The genealogies of Genesis 5 and 11:10–32 link Abraham to Adam, and indicate a focusing of God's promise of a programme. The Saviour who was to bring spiritual blessings to all humanity would be a descendant of Abraham. This is why God acted to protect his promise of a people; it was to keep his promise of a programme moving ahead.

Looking at the story of Genesis in the way we have done helps us see Jesus. Luke's account of Jesus' birth reminds us of the story of Isaac's birth. John the Baptist, Jesus' forerunner, was the late child of Zechariah and Elizabeth, an elderly and until then infertile couple like Abraham and Sarah (*Luke* 1:5–7). When Mary asked how she, a virgin, would conceive (*Luke* 1:34), Gabriel's reply (*Luke* 1:37) has exactly the ring of Genesis 18:14. Jesus' career is anticipated by the Genesis account of Joseph's. Joseph's career had a 'son stage', in which he was loved by his father and sent by Jacob to his brothers, and this is paralleled in Jesus' career (*Matt.* 3:17; *John* 1:11). Then Joseph went through a 'servant stage', in which he was hated and conspired against by his brothers, sold as a slave, and yet remained strong when tempted, in the most trying of circumstances. Jesus travelled along a similar path (*Psa.* 35:19; *Mark* 3:6; *Matt.* 27:3; *Heb.* 4:15). Finally Joseph enjoyed a 'sovereign stage', receiving and exercising sovereignty, just as Jesus did (*Phil.* 2:9; *Heb.* 1:3). When God tells Abraham to sacrifice his only son, whom he loved

(22:2), we see, in faint outline, what would happen centuries later when another Father offered his only Son, whom he loved, as a sacrifice. The crucial difference, however, was that Isaac was spared but Jesus was not (*Rom.* 8:32), so that we might experience the blessings of salvation.

Where we see Jesus most clearly in Genesis is as the fulfilment of the four defining promises. Jesus is the descendant of Abraham through whom God's programme to bring blessing to all nations is implemented (*Gal.* 3:6–4:7). Jesus is the focal point of God's promise of a people. As Abraham's response to this promise indicates (15:6), God's people are not those who share Abraham's DNA but those who share Abraham's faith in Jesus and, as a result, are justified by God through faith alone. Jesus is the location of the promise of a place of blessing, because it is in him we experience salvation (*Eph.* 1:3) and find rest (*Matt.* 11:28–30). Jesus is the ultimate protector of his people (*John* 10:28), because, through his death and resurrection, he has defeated all the enemies which threatened our security.

3

Exodus

I n the four hundred years which had elapsed between the end of Genesis and the start of Exodus, everything had changed for the Israelites. A new dynasty, which owed nothing to Joseph's disaster-averting policies (*Gen.* 41:46–57; 47:13–26), had come to power in Egypt (1:8), and the big losers in the political shake-up were the Israelites. Previously they had enjoyed the support of the Pharaohs, but now their rapid population growth was seen as a security threat (1:9-10). So the Israelites were forced into back-breaking hard labour, working on the Pharaohs' grandiose building projects (1:11). However, piling more and more work on them did not stop the Israelite baby boom. With Plan A obviously not achieving the desired outcome, Pharaoh put his more sinister Plan B into action – genocide (1:15–16, 22). As Exodus opens, the Israelites have their backs to the wall: they are brutalized, crushed and in danger of extinction. However, in another sense, the four hundred years which had elapsed had changed nothing. The Israelites were still the recipients of the Genesis 12:2–3 promises, and it is God's commit-ment to his covenant, the umbrella term for these four promises, which underpins everything that happens. God remembered his promises to Abraham (2:24; 6:4–5) and took action to do what he said he would do in Genesis 15:13–14. All that happens in Exodus relates to one of the four covenant promises of a *people*, a *place*, *protection* and a *programme*.

The first main section of Exodus, chapters 1–18, focuses on THE GOD WHO DELIVERS. It is the events of this opening part of the book which give it its name. 'Exodus' means 'departure' or 'going out', and the story of these chapters is that of God liberating the Israelites from slavery in Egypt and bringing them to Mount Sinai, the first stage on their journey to Canaan.

The scene is set for God's rescue mission in Exodus 1–2. In keeping with his promise of protection (*Gen.* 12:3), when he sees Pharaoh not only treating the Israelites brutally but trying to wipe them out, he is not idle but starts off the process of deliverance with the birth of Moses, his human instrument in bringing freedom to his people. Although he was an Israelite by birth, and so should have been drowned at birth in line with Pharaoh's genocide policy, Moses received divine protection. God had him rescued by one of Pharaoh's own daughters, who brought him up in the Egyptian court. During that time, Moses did not forget his Hebrew roots or faith, and, when he grew up, he deliberately opted to side with the Israelites (*Heb.* 11:24–26). However, his premature attempts to help his people failed (2:11–14), and he had to flee into exile in Midian (2:15). God was teaching Moses that *his* plan must be carried out in *his* way according to *his* timetable.

In Exodus 3–11, we see the obstacles to God's rescue mission, and the first one, strange as it may seem, is Moses' reluctance. God called Moses by means of a bush that was burning but not being burnt up, revealing himself as 'I AM' (3:14), the God who is going to keep his promise of a place (*Gen.* 12:7) by freeing the Israelites from slavery in Egypt and bringing them to Canaan. He called Moses to be the Israelites' leader (2:6–10), but perhaps the memory of the last time he had tried to help was still too painful. Moses made excuse after excuse as to why he was not the man for the job. But God was having none of his reluctance, and countered each of Moses' excuses, giving him the promise of his presence and help.

There are no prizes for working out that Pharaoh would be the most formidable obstacle to God's rescue mission. He not only treated Moses' request to let the Israelites go with contempt, but he also increased their workload, to put any thoughts of freedom out of their minds. Pharaoh's strategy not only made the Israelites' miserable existence even more miserable, but it drove a wedge between Moses and the people he wanted to lead (5:1–21). But if it was God's gracious presence that overcame Moses' reluctance to lead his rescue mission, it was his fierce judgment that swept aside Pharaoh's resistance to it. God launched a series of ten devastating plagues against Egypt: plagues of blood, frogs, gnats, flies, livestock disease, boils, hail, locusts, darkness and the death of the firstborn (7–11). While undoubtedly the plagues were designed to bring Pharaoh to submission, there was something even more significant going on. These ten acts of judgment were not simply natural disasters, but a confrontation between God and the gods of Egypt, to see who was supreme. The targets God chose were not random but specifically chosen to show him to be the sovereign God. So, for example, the Nile, which the Egyptians held sacred because its waters brought fertility to the nation, was turned into blood, bringing death instead of life (7:14–24). The Egyptians worshipped the sun, but God turned its light into pitch darkness (10:21–29). Even Pharaoh was regarded as divine, but he was crushed as God killed his firstborn son (11:1–8; 12:29). This showdown with the gods of Egypt was really no contest: God triumphed decisively, showing himself to be the invincible Lord. As plague after plague hit Egypt, Pharaoh's heart became more and more resistant, but following the tenth and most catastrophic plague, his resistance crumbled. He freed the Israelites (12:31–36), thus fulfilling God's promise to Abraham centuries before (*Gen.* 15:13–14).

The Israelites' experience of their rescue is recorded in Exodus 12:1–15:21. On the night when the tenth plague struck, God let loose his destroying angel upon Egypt to kill the firstborn in each family. However, beforehand he had told the Israelites how they could escape the cataclysmic consequences of this plague. They were to kill an unblemished year-old lamb and daub its blood on the doorframes of their homes, and then they were to roast the lamb, eating it along with bread containing no yeast, and bitter herbs. When the angel of death saw the blood on the doorframes of a home, he would leave the firstborn in that house alone and not kill him. There was a death that night in every home in Egypt: either the firstborn son or a substitute lamb. Sheltering under the protection of a slaughtered lamb's blood, the Israelites were kept safe from God's judgment, and, when that night of death was over, they left Egypt as a freed people. This event was so central to the Israelites' life and faith that they were to commemorate it each year in a meal called 'The Passover', which remembered what happened that night (12:14–20).

No sooner had Pharaoh let the Israelites go than he changed his mind, and, mobilizing his elite troops, set off in hot pursuit of them (14:4–9). As they saw this deadly fighting machine bearing down on them, the Israelites were terrified. But God stepped in, placing himself as a pillar of fiery cloud between the Israelites and their pursuers. At God's command, Moses stretched out his hand over the Red Sea and God opened up a path of dry ground in the middle of the sea, through which the Israelites went until they reached the other side. When the Egyptian army tried to follow them, God threw them into confusion and caused the sea to come crashing in on them so that they were all drowned. This was the mother of all military upsets! Granted they had God on their side, but, on the face of it, the Israelites, a crowd of escaping slaves with no training in battle, had dramatically overcome the most formidable army in the world at that time. No wonder that, from the safety of the east bank of the Red Sea with the washed-up corpses of the shattered Egyptian army at their feet, they sang a magnificent hymn of thanksgiving to God, praising him for his salvation, guidance, care and rule (15:1–21).

The focus on the God who delivers continues from Exodus 15:22 to 18:27. This section could be dubbed God's ongoing rescue, because God's deliverance is not a one-off event but a day-to-day experience. Instead of taking them along the northerly trade routes between Egypt and Canaan, God led the Israelites south to Mount Sinai. Their journey took them through one of the most inhospitable environments on earth to test their willingness to trust in his promise to protect them. Sadly, in a foretaste of things to come, they did not come through this test with much credit. They complained about the poor quality of the water at Marah (15:22–24); the lack of food (16:1–3); and the lack of water at Massah and Meribah (17:1–3). God graciously made the bitter water sweet (15:24); brought them to the oasis of Elim (15:27); provided them with quail and manna (16:13–16); and gave them water out of a rock (17:4–7). On top of all this, they were attacked by the Amalekites, but, through Moses' intercession and Joshua's military expertise, God gave them victory. Throughout this journey to Sinai, the Israelites were learning to trust in God on a daily basis.

Then, in Exodus 18, we learn of the visit of Jethro, Moses' father-in-law, to the Israelites' camp. This incident is not in chronological order in Exodus. When Jethro arrived at Sinai, the Israelites were already there, and, as their arrival at Sinai is mentioned in Exodus 19:1–2, Exodus 18 must have taken place chronologically after Exodus 19. Also, Jethro witnessed Moses' near exhaustion because of the way he administered God's laws (18:13–16), whereas Moses only received the law in Exodus 20–23. Why was this story brought forward from when it chronologically took place? This seems to be done to highlight God's faithfulness to his promises. God protected Moses' sanity and health through Jethro's wise counsel. Another of the promises in Genesis 12:2–3 concerned the bringing of God's blessing to all nations, and we find Jethro, who was a Gentile, trusting in God, as his praise indicated (18:1, 8–12). Gentile Jethro's confession of his faith in God as the supreme, saving God is a signal of what will happen when God's promise of a programme to bless all nations really gets underway, later in the Bible's storyline.

Three months after leaving Egypt, the Israelites arrived at Mount Sinai, and, in the central section of Exodus, which runs from Exodus 19 to 24, we discover THE GOD WHO DEMANDS. Until now, the Exodus drama has been dominated by God's promise of protection, with the promise of a place playing a significant supporting role. But now the promise of a people takes centre stage. That promise, summarized in the words, 'I will be your God, and you will be my people', involved a relationship in which God committed himself to his people and, in response, his people committed themselves to God. In the Exodus event, God had shown his commitment to his people, and now, at Mount Sinai, his people were coming to express their commitment to him. They were to do so by pledging themselves to obey God's law. This is the reason he brought them to Sinai (6:2–8).

The scene is set for this binding act of commitment to God by the thunder, lightning, smoke and fire of Exodus 19. But why does God not simply speak to the people instead of terrifying them with this display? God wants the people to understand from the start that this is not a relationship of equals. The setting of the scene in Exodus 19 is to stress that God is in charge. He has come to Mount Sinai as the great King, fresh from his victory over the gods of Egypt, and it is as the sovereign King that God calls on the Israelites to commit themselves to him in obedience. Their commitment was to be seen in their obedience to the Ten Commandments (chapter 20) – which set out the essence of their relationship with God (Commandments 1–4) and with man (Commandments 5–10) – and to the detailed working out of the principles of the Commandments in Israelite society (21–23). This central section of Exodus ends with a ceremony involving sacrifices, the reading of the law, vows, the eating of a meal, and the sprinkling of blood on the people. In this the Israelites formally committed themselves to be God's people, a commitment which was to be seen in their obedience to his law (chapter 24).

God's law was given to a *redeemed* people, not *to redeem* people. This is clear, not only from Exodus 20:2, but also from the fact that the section focusing on God's law comes after the story of God's deliverance. The law was given to people who had already experienced God's salvation. God's grace precedes God's law. What God has done comes before what he demands. He gave redemption before he imposed requirements. He sets free, and only then does he show how a freed people are to live. Obeying God's law was never meant to be a device for obtaining God's grace. It was always meant to be a loving response to grace already received. If that is first settled in our minds, the whole of the Bible, and the dynamic of living for Jesus, will make sense. People never were, are, or will be saved by keeping God's law. It was not a Plan A, which went horribly wrong, forcing God to come up with an alternative Plan B in Jesus. The law is only opposed to the gospel if people mistakenly see it as a means of salvation, instead of as a pointer to a greater than Moses, and a greater Exodus.

The third major portion of the book is Exodus 25–40. This zeroes in on THE GOD WHO DWELLS, as thirteen chapters (25–31; 35–40) detail the construction of the Tabernacle, a movable sanctuary for God. The Tabernacle had three distinct sections. There was an enclosed rectangular courtyard, within which stood the Tabernacle itself, in the shape of a tent with two rooms in it. Entered from the east, the Holy Place was the first room inside the Tabernacle. In it was the *Menorah*, or seven-branched candelabrum, the table on which was placed the Bread of the Presence, and the Altar of Incense. Separated from the Holy Place by embroidered curtains was the Holy of Holies, the second room within the Tabernacle, and it housed the Ark of the Covenant.

The reason why this meticulous record of the dimensions and materials to be used for the stakes, curtains, skins, and various pieces of furniture comes last is to signal the fact that neither the Passover, nor the Red Sea, nor even Sinai, is the climax of Exodus: the Tabernacle is! The reason for the Passover, the Red Sea, and the bringing of the Israelites to Sinai is so that God might dwell among them (29:45–46) and he does so in the Tabernacle (25:8). Also, if the Genesis 12:2–3 promise of a people is the driving force of this part of Exodus, there must be a relationship in which God and his people come close to each other. It is a mistake to get lost in the details of the Tabernacle's furnishings and the materials from which it was constructed. God told the Israelites to build the Tabernacle so that he might come near to his people and be among them. Just as a bridegroom wants to be with his bride, so God wants to be with his people.

But the Israelites almost threw away this privilege of God's presence among them when they forsook their commitment to worship God alone by putting pressure on Aaron to make a substitute god of gold in the shape of a calf (32:1–6). This act of astonishing betrayal – for it was as bad as a bride committing adultery on her wedding night – made them candidates for destruction as a nation (32:9–10). However, after a process lasting for one agonizing paragraph after another in which Moses pleaded with God to have mercy on the fickle Israelites (32:11–34:45), God restored them as his people and reassured them that he would after all dwell with them again.

What does Exodus, with its focus on God's power, will and presence, tell us about Jesus? Like all Old Testament symbols, the Tabernacle was only temporary. It pointed forward to the way in which Jesus came as God in human flesh and 'made his dwelling [literally, *tabernacled*] among us' (*John* 1:14). There are several parallels between the Tabernacle and the Garden of Eden: both were entered from the east and guarded by cherubim (*Gen.* 3:24; *Exod.* 26:31); the *Menorah* in the Tabernacle was a representation of the tree of life (*Gen.* 2:9; *Exod.* 25:31–35); and gold, which is mentioned in Genesis 2:11–12, was used extensively in the Tabernacle. In this we see that the Tabernacle ultimately looks forward to the restored Garden of Eden in heaven, in which Jesus' glory will be seen in all its magnificence and splendour (*Rev.* 21–22).

At the start of Exodus, God announced that Israel was his firstborn son (4:22), and this too is where Matthew begins his gospel account (*Matt.* 3:17). There are striking parallels between Jesus, God's one and only Son, and Israel, God's firstborn son. The very existence of both was threatened by those in power. Like Israel, Jesus made the journey into and out of Egypt (*Matt.* 2:13–15). Just as the Israelites left Egypt and came to the Red Sea, Matthew follows up his account of Jesus' return from Egypt with the story of his baptism (*Matt.* 2:23; 3:1). Just as Israel emerged from the Red Sea to go into the desert, so Jesus went from the Jordan and his baptism into the Judean Desert to be tempted (*Matt.* 4:1). The Israelites experienced a lack of water and food, as did Jesus during his first temptation (*Matt.* 4:1–4). At Massah and Meribah, the Israelites put God to the test, something which Jesus refused to do in his second temptation (*Matt.* 4:7). In the Golden Calf incident, Israel turned away from God to worship an idol, but, by contrast, Jesus insisted that God alone is to be worshipped (*Matt.* 4:8–10). On the one hand, Israel, the firstborn son, needs salvation, because of failure at every point of testing. On the other, Jesus, the one and only Son, brings salvation (*Matt.* 1:21) because he is perfect and righteous, and succeeds at every point of testing.

When, in his desperate attempt to escape his call, Moses asked God what his name was, the reply came back 'I AM' (3:14). John's Gospel contains seven statements made by Jesus in which he reveals his identity, each beginning with the phrase, 'I am . . . ' (*John* 6:35; 8:12; 10:7; 10:11; 11:25; 14:6; 15:1). Jesus is aligning himself with this Exodus name for God, to show that he himself is God. Some of the 'I am' statements have even stronger Exodus connections. When Jesus says, 'I am the bread of life', he is taking his audience back to the time when God fed his people with manna as they travelled from Egypt to Canaan. When he says, 'I am the Light of the world', he is claiming to be the fulfilment of the pillar of cloud and fire which guided God's people through the desert. When he says, 'I am the Good Shepherd', he is looking back to the time when God led his people through the desert as a shepherd leads his sheep (*Psa.* 80:1). Even his statement, 'I am the True Vine', has, as its backdrop, the Exodus period (*Psa.* 80:8).

The Passover became so embedded in Israelite thinking that it became the template for all God's acts of salvation. So, when the New Testament writers – whose minds were steeped in Old Testament thought – came to describe Jesus' death, God's greatest act of salvation, it is no surprise that they did so using Passover terminology. Right at the start of his ministry, John the Baptist showed that Jesus was going to be the fulfilment of the Passover by announcing him to be 'the Lamb of God' (*John* 1:29). Just as the ten plagues, which culminated in the Passover, were designed to show who God was (6:6–7; 7:5), so Jesus' miracles were pointers to who he was (*John* 2:11). In spite of the scheming of the Jewish religious authorities (*Matt.* 26:3–4; *Mark* 14:1–2; *Luke* 22:13), Jesus died at the Passover (*Matt.* 26:19; *Mark* 14:16; *Luke* 22:13). The meal Jesus established to help Christians remember his death began as a Passover meal (*Matt.* 26:20–23; *Mark* 14:17–26; *Luke* 22:14–20). So widespread is Passover imagery in the New Testament's description of Jesus' death that Paul refers to him as 'our Passover lamb' (*1 Cor.* 5:7). The main difference between the death of Jesus, the ultimate Passover Lamb, and the original Passover lamb is that Jesus *achieved* spiritual liberation for his people. By sheltering under his blood, through faith in him alone, we are set free from sin's control and placed under his gracious rule (*Col.* 1:13–14). Through his death he rescues us from God's wrath and judgment and brings us near to God as his children (*Eph.* 2:3, 13).

4

Leviticus

I t was the start of my second year at theological college and the first class of a module on the book of Leviticus. The lecturer opened with the statement, 'Leviticus was the first book Jewish children studied in the synagogue.' He paused and waited for a reaction. It was not long in coming, as one student asked, 'You are joking, aren't you?' But he was not. For most western Christians, Leviticus is one of the least accessible books in the Bible, so the idea that it would be the first book in a child's religious education curriculum seems bizarre. Its language, style and concepts place it in a time and a cultural setting a million miles away from western religious culture at the start of the twenty-first century.

It is not that the STRUCTURE of the book is difficult. If we could make an aerial survey of Leviticus, we might find the terrain unusual, but we would still notice three distinct zones in the landscape. The first concerns instructions about *sacrifices* (1:1–7:38). The five main types of sacrifices are listed: the *burnt offering* (1), the *grain offering* (2), the *fellowship or peace offering* (3), the *sin offering* (4:1–5:13) and the *guilt offering* (5:14–6:7). The instructions on making the sacrifice differ from offering to offering, providing clues as to the function of each. Although the burnt offering primarily carried with it the idea of acceptance with God on the basis of an atoning sacrifice, also contained within it was the idea of consecration: the worshipper holds nothing back from God, as the entire sacrifice is consumed. The grain offering was technically not a sacrifice, since no blood was shed. Its main component was flour, which was combined with oil and incense when offered to God. From the way the term 'grain offering' is often translated as 'tribute' (*Judg.* 3:15, 17–18; 2 *Sam.* 8:6; 1 *Kings* 4:21), we can say that in the grain

Leviticus

offering the worshipper presented a gift to God in which he acknowledges his loyalty to him as his covenant Lord. The fellowship or peace
offering celebrated the restoration of a good relationship with God after
his wrath had been appeased. The sin offering secured forgiveness for
those who had sinned unintentionally. The guilt offering has a lot in
common with the sin offering, but it introduces a human-to-human
element into the forgiveness equation. The offender had to compensate
the offended party by means of restitution. 'The central thrust of this
sacrifice was the total satisfaction of every claim that sin might exercise
upon the sinner: every offence to God and to people was covered.'[1]

The second distinct zone concerns instructions about *the priesthood* (8–16). If there are to be sacrifices, there must be priests to offer
them. We therefore read in Leviticus 8–9 of how Aaron and his sons
were consecrated to be Israel's priests. The seriousness of everything
being done as God commanded is underlined in Leviticus 10 in the
account of how Nadab and Abihu, two of Aaron's sons, were struck
dead because they offered 'unauthorized fire before the LORD, contrary
to his command'.

Apart from performing the sacrifices, the priests also had the
important task of maintaining the purity of the camp. This explains
why laws about cleanness and uncleanness (11–15) occur in the section dealing with the priesthood. These regulations about cleanness
and uncleanness have nothing to do with hygiene: they are all about
purity. Leviticus focuses on three related categories: *holy, clean* and
unclean. This is reflected in the layout of the camp. The Tabernacle, at
the centre of the camp, is a holy area, set apart for God. The rest of the
camp is clean, while outside the camp is unclean. This is also reflected
in the status of the people linked with each of these areas: the priests
are holy, as they are set apart for God; the Israelites are clean; and
non-Israelites are unclean.

The purity of the camp and the Tabernacle can be spoiled by the presence of those who have eaten certain unclean foods (11); experienced
various bodily discharges (12:1–8; 15:1–33); contracted various skin
diseases (13:1–46; 14:1–32); or been in contact with mildew (13:47–59).

[1] Alec Motyer, *The Story of the Old Testament* (London: Candle Books, 2001), p. 37.

It was the priest's function to protect the Israelite camp from threats to its purity by identifying what was unclean (10:10). They were also to take steps to restore the camp's purity through sacrifice, through removing the unclean person from the camp for a period of time and then ensuring that the appropriate purification rites were carried out, and, in extreme cases, through the destruction of what was impure. The priests also acted as a buffer between the holy and the clean, since the priests alone were allowed into the Tabernacle. Even clean Israelites were excluded since they were not holy, set apart by God for himself.

Yet even within these three broad categories, there are sub-divisions. While the Tabernacle is holy, the Holy of Holies where God dwells, is especially holy. While the priests are holy, the High Priest, by virtue of his title, his clothing and the much stricter rules regarding his marriage, his purity and even the way he is to mourn a death, is even holier. So the instructions about the priesthood finish with the regulations concerning the Day of Atonement (16). After very careful preparations, once a year, on the most holy day of the Israelite religious calendar, the High Priest, the most holy of the priests, went into the Holy of Holies, the most holy room in the Tabernacle, and there performed a unique act of atonement which not only cleansed the people of their sin but also purified the Tabernacle, maintaining its holiness.

The third distinct zone in Leviticus' landscape is concerned with instructions about *holiness* (17–19). It is easy to get bogged down in the details of these chapters, but, if we take a few steps back from them, we can see that they are designed to show how God's people can reflect God's character in the way they live. The people were to be holy just as God himself is holy (11:44; 11:45; 19:2; 20:7). There was cleansing, forgiveness and renewed fellowship when people sinned, but prevention is always better than the need of a cure. So these instructions about how to live a holy life were intended to encourage behaviour that minimized the need for atonement, cleansing and forgiveness.

These regulations cover a wide spectrum of issues, with no distinction made between the secular and the sacred. Holiness is not a private matter. It is to be lived out in the public square, in the details of everyday life. While the instructions might appear quite specific, the topics covered indicate that holiness is not abstract. It impacted on the way God's people were to use their time, to behave sexually, to treat outsiders and the marginalized, to care for their animals, to interact as a community, to relate to one another within family life, and even on what they were to eat. These closing chapters of Leviticus proclaim loudly that holiness is practical and down to earth.

If our difficulty with Leviticus is not due to its structure, could it be due to its MESSAGE? In one sense, Leviticus' message is not hard to understand. The key to discovering it is its place in the Old Testament. The storyline of Leviticus, like that of the last section of Exodus, is driven by the promise in Genesis 12:2–3 of a people who know God. If that promise is to come true, God must come near to his people, and this is what is happening in the last chapters of Exodus, as the Tabernacle is built and placed in the midst of the camp. But there must also be a people who come near to God, and this is where Leviticus comes in. The message of Leviticus concerns a people living in close proximity to a holy God, so as to enjoy fellowship with him.

The book explains that those who desire to draw near to God must be holy. Only those who avoid certain sinful patterns of behaviour and practise certain godly virtues can come near to a holy God. Centuries later, in language clearly borrowed from Leviticus, David would state that they had to have clean hands and pure hearts (*Psa.* 24:3–4; *Psa.* 15). But the Israelites found keeping all these regulations impossible. Again and again they failed to do what God told them to do, and deliberately opted for what he had forbidden. If they were to draw near to God, they needed a mediator to bring them to God, and a sacrifice to deal with the offence to God caused by their failure and disobedience. This is where the activity of the priests in general, and the High Priest in particular, came in. Through their mediation, as they offered sacrifices which would atone for sin, cleanse from sin, secure forgiveness for sin, and appease God's wrath against sin, the people could come near to God. The message of Leviticus is clear: in order to draw near to God, people need to live a holy life and they need the mediation of a priest who will offer a sacrifice on their behalf. Then and only then can they draw near to God.

But therein lies our difficulty with Leviticus: it is not that its message is unclear and hidden, but that it is too clear and hard-hitting. Instead of standing against the rampant consumerism in our culture, large sections of the western church have embraced it and allowed it to affect the way we look at all aspects of our lives, including our approach to God. God becomes like a commodity, accessed on our terms, because in consumerism the customer is always king. But the opening section of Leviticus, with its emphasis on sacrifices that enable sinners to approach God, collides with this way of thinking, reminding us that it is God, and not we, who determines the rules of engagement. Leviticus asserts as strongly as possible that there is a way to come near to God, but it is God's way, not ours. It is God, not man, who is king, and the only basis upon which he can be worshipped is through sacrifice.

Consumerism encourages us, in order to get the best deal possible, to 'cut out the middleman'. This way of thinking has been imported into some forms of Christian spirituality. These tell people that they can go straight to God themselves without any mediator. So, for example, the Bible is sidelined. After all, who needs the Bible, which is so old-school, when we can have the excitement of being spoken to directly through so-called prophetic words, or in visions, or by hearing voices in our thoughts? But the middle section of Leviticus, with its emphasis on the priesthood, challenges this kind of spirituality. We must have a mediator to take us to God. We cannot approach him directly. We must have mediated instruction to know what is right and wrong. We cannot make up the rules ourselves as we go along. If we have no priestly mediation, we cannot come near to God, irrespective of what we might think or how sincere we may be.

Relativism – with its absolute claim that there are no absolutes! – dominates the landscape of our post–modern culture, and large sections of the church have taken it up. Their favourite colour is grey. They hate black and white because they reject the idea that actions are right or wrong. But the closing section of Leviticus, with all its regulations about what is right and what is wrong, opposes these grey-loving Christians. Leviticus is unashamedly black and white, stating unambiguously that behaviour is either right or wrong, clean or unclean.

It is this clarity which makes Leviticus one of the least frequented books of the Bible. It is not too difficult to understand, but too uncomfortable when understood. It challenges our pathetic sell-out to our culture, condemning our idolatry of worshipping at the shrine of consumerism and relativism. We shy away from it because its message leaves us uneasy. We want to be left alone to go our own way, and because Leviticus refuses to let us, we keep it at arm's length.

But we should not do this, because 'Leviticus is good news,'[1] as it finds its fulfilment in Jesus. The opening section focuses on the sacrifices, and the New Testament writer who explores most clearly how Jesus' death fulfils the Old Testament sacrificial system is the writer of Hebrews. Although Jesus' death was better than the sacrifices offered by the Old Testament priests because Jesus offered up himself and not an animal, what really highlights the superiority of Jesus' sacrificial death is its effectiveness. Five times the writer of Hebrews underlines the 'once for all' nature of Jesus' sacrifice (*Heb.* 7:7; 9:12; 9:26; 10:2; 10:10). This stands in stark contrast to the repetitive way in which the Old Testament sacrifices were performed day after day, month after month, year after year. These animal sacrifices could not deal radically and effectively with sin. However, the once-for-all sacrifice of Jesus *really* dealt with sin (*Heb.* 9:26, 10:10).

The effectiveness of his sacrificial death is also underlined by the way the writer of Hebrews states four times that Jesus 'sat down' at God's right hand (*Heb.* 1:3, 8:1, 10:12, 12:2). Only when a task is finished does one sit down, but the Old Testament priests never sat down, because their work was never completed. Jesus sat down because he had completed his work: his death had dealt radically and effectively with sin. The Old Testament sacrificial system, as set out in the opening section of Leviticus, was fulfilled in Jesus' death. Because he died in our place, our acceptance with God is secure. God's justified anger against us has been turned away and our sins have been forgiven, so that we now enjoy peace with God. On the basis of Jesus' death, we can come near to God.

---

[1] Derek Tidball, *The Message of Leviticus* (Leicester: Inter-Varsity Press, 2004), p. 1.

The instructions about the priesthood in the middle section of Leviticus anticipated the coming of Jesus as God's great Priest. In the New Testament accounts of his life, what Jesus did is often portrayed in priestly terms. His baptism may be seen as his ordination to the role of God's great Priest as it fulfilled all the necessary conditions for a valid ordination. He involved himself in priestly activity such as cleansing people of leprosy (*Mark* 1:40–45), healing those whose illnesses had made them ceremonially unclean (*Mark* 5:25–34), arbitrating on what was clean and unclean (*Mark* 7:14–19), and purifying the Temple from defilement (*Mark* 11:15–18). In John 17, as Jesus prays before his death, there are parallels with the way the Old Testament High Priest prepared himself before taking part in the rituals of the Day of Atonement. This connection is underlined by the way the curtain which separated the Holy of Holies from the rest of the Temple was torn in two when he died (*Mark* 15:37–38). By his death, Jesus, God's great Priest, had not only fulfilled the rituals of the Day of Atonement but had introduced an altogether better way of approach to God. As a result of his death, access to God was opened up to all, not just to one man; and this was valid for all time, not just on one day of the year.

Once again it is the writer of Hebrews who explores in most detail the implications of the fact that Jesus is God's great Priest and the fulfilment of the Old Testament priesthood. He deals with the question of Jesus' non-Levitical ancestry, showing that Jesus was of the order of Melchizedek and therefore superior to Levitical priests (*Heb.* 7:1–25). He also stresses Jesus' sympathy as our great Priest: he understands exactly what we go through in life because his humanity is real, and he was really tempted – though he was sinless (*Heb.* 2:18; 4:15). This means that Jesus can help us to handle life's pressures and temptations in a way that honours God (*Heb.* 4:16). When we fail, he pleads our cause with the Father (*Heb.* 7:25) and secures our forgiveness by highlighting what he achieved by his death (*1 John* 2:1b–2a).

Having our sins forgiven, however, is not enough. If we are to come near to God, and stay near him, we need a positive righteousness, as Psalm 24:3–4 and Psalm 15 remind us so clearly. There is absolutely no possibility of our perfectly keeping the laws outlined in the last section of Leviticus, but if someone came and did it for us, that would completely alter the picture. The good news of the Christian message is that Jesus has done just that. He has done everything perfectly on our behalf, not only dying the death we should have died but also living the life we should have lived. Imagine that you are deeply in debt, owing the bank a sum that you will never be able to repay. But imagine you have a friend who is a multimillionaire. If he wrote off all your debts, you would be tremendously relieved. However, you would still have nothing in your account. If you checked your balance online, it would read zero. But just suppose your friend went to your bank manager and said, 'I want you to transfer everything in my account into my friend's account and everything in his account into mine.' That would be unbelievably wonderful, for not only would you be debt free, but you would be fabulously rich. That is what God has done for us in Jesus. On the cross, a great exchange took place as God took our law-breaking and transferred it to Jesus (*2 Cor.* 5:21), treating him as he should have treated us and punishing him for our sins (*Isa.* 53:3–6). Then God took Jesus' perfect obedience to his law and transferred it to us, treating us as he would have treated Jesus, as those who had never broken his law. Now we have that perfect righteousness we need to come and stay near a holy God. The final section of Leviticus, with all its rules, points us to Jesus, reminding us that God has graciously given us in him the righteousness we need to live in his holy presence.

In hindsight, my friends and I were too quick to pour cold water on the idea that Leviticus should be the first book in a Jewish child's religious education curriculum. Having revisited it on several occasions since then, the wisdom of teaching Leviticus to children becomes increasingly obvious. It contains the fundamentals of the gospel, telling us how God's promise in Genesis 12:2–3 that there will be a people who know him can be fulfilled. It reminds us how sinful people like us can have a personal relationship with a holy and just God through the sacrificial death, the mediation, and the obedience of Jesus. Rather than marginalizing it, we need to place Leviticus' teaching right at the centre of our thinking and live on the basis of its teaching day by day.

5

Numbers

E ven a quick scan of Numbers reveals the rich variety of different
types of literature used by Moses in its compilation, including
poetry, speeches, songs, travelogues, tribal listings, camping directives, priestly regulations, religious calendars, prophecy, a diplomatic
letter and military records. This wide assortment of literary genres
has led some to dismiss the book as the Old Testament equivalent of a
lumber room. The book's English title gives us a truer characterization
of the book. It refers to the two censuses (1, 26), one at the beginning
and the other at the end of the book, in which the numbers of men of
military age among the people who left Egypt and among their children
are recorded. These two censuses highlight how and why the Exodus
generation, those people who were rescued from Egyptian slavery,
failed, with the exception of two men, to inherit God's covenant promise
of a place, and how it fell to their children to inherit God's promise of
a land of blessing. Numbers tells the story of the dying out of the old
generation and the emergence of the new. This process took roughly
forty years – a long and sad funeral march.

NUMBERS' STORYLINE falls into three main sections. The first covers
chapters 1–10 and tells of the Israelites' *setting out*. The book opens with
the Israelites still camped at Sinai, prior to their departure for the place
promised to them by God. However, before they set out for Canaan,
preparations had to be made. The first was to draw up a register of
every male of military age (1:3). On the basis of this census, it has been
estimated that the nation totalled approximately two million people.
Instead of trying to minimize the numbers recorded in the two censuses, we should see them as a testimony to the way God miraculously
fed, watered and kept alive so many in one of earth's most challenging

environments, in order to be graciously true to his covenant promise, to bring them to the promised land of blessing, and to protect them every step of the way.

After the census was completed, various instructions were given as to how the Israelites were to organize themselves. They were told how to set up the camp (2), where each tribe was to pitch, and the place of the Tabernacle right at the centre, symbolizing God's presence with his people. There then follows a whole series of commands about how the purity of the camp was to be maintained (5); about the special commitment to God of certain men, called Nazarites (6:1–21); and about how God was to be worshipped (6:22–9:14). Finally, directions were given concerning when the Israelites were to break camp, when they were to set up camp again (9:15–23), and how the tribes were to march, with Judah leading the way and the Ark of the Covenant in the middle (10). After about two months of preparation, everything was in place and the order came to strike camp (10:11). Then, no doubt full of anticipation at the thought of going to the place promised to them by God, the Israelites departed for Canaan.

The second and longest section of Numbers is chapters 11–25. It is all about the Israelites' *marking time* as they made a forty-year detour, wandering in the desert until the Exodus generation died out and a new generation took its place. When the Israelites left Sinai, apparently in a positive frame of mind, there was no reason to believe that things would go as badly wrong as they subsequently did.

But the people very soon started to complain about how hard their journey was (11:1), and then about the lack of variety in their diet (11:5–6). God saw their complaints for what they really were – a personal rejection of him (11:20), and it was not long before his judgment fell upon the Israelites in the form of a firestorm (11:1) and a plague (11:33). However, not even God's fierce judgment could cure their murmuring, and soon it surfaced again as Miriam and Aaron challenged Moses' right to speak on God's behalf, accusing him of arrogance (12:1–3). Once again God's judgment was swift and sharp, as he underlined how he had chosen to speak through Moses (12:4–8) by striking Miriam with leprosy (12:10).

The Israelites' rebellion reached an all-time low at Kadesh Barnea on the southern border of Canaan (13–14). When they arrived there, before they launched their invasion, twelve spies, one man from each tribe, were sent to carry out a forty-day reconnaissance mission. When they returned, the majority recommendation was to put any invasion plans on hold due to the military superiority of Canaan's inhabitants. The ten spies might have balked at the giant size of their enemies, but their real problem was that they had forgotten God's promise of a place and his assurance that he would be fighting for them to give them the land of blessing. But Joshua and Caleb brought in a minority report. Though they did not deny the toughness of the assignment, they urged the Israelites to trust in God, to remember his promises, and to launch the invasion. The Israelites rejected their plea and refused to invade, treating God's promise of a place of blessing with disbelief. God's reaction to their unbelief and refusal to carry out their covenant obligations was fierce. No one from the Exodus generation, apart from Joshua and Caleb, would set foot in Canaan, and they would wander in the desert for forty years, one year for each of the days the spies took to scout out the land, until everyone had died (14:28–35).

After the catastrophe of Kadesh Barnea, the Israelites headed back into the desert. The chapters that record this forty-year detour follow a pattern that is already familiar. There are periodic revolts against Moses and Aaron's leadership, the most infamous being that led by Korah and his associates Dathan and Abiram (16). The Israelites still grumble constantly about having no water (20:1–13) and about the monotony of the manna (21:4–9). On top of this, they begin to feel pressure from kings who are worried about such a big group of migrants coming too near their territory. So the king of Arad attacks them (21:1–3), as does Sihon, king of the Amorites, and Og, king of Bashan (21:21–35). Though they do not deserve it, God remembers his covenant promise of protection and enables the Israelites to defeat these three kings.

The most serious external threat to Israel came from Balaam, a non-Israelite prophet, who was called in by Balak, king of Moab, to curse Israel (22–24). However, much to Balak's annoyance and Balaam's growing frustration –since Balak was willing to pay him handsomely if he cursed Israel – Balaam ended up blessing Israel instead. God's promise of protection had intervened once more. But Balaam did secure a victory over them. He managed to seduce the Israelites to commit sexual immorality as they worshipped Baal at a place called Peor (25:1–3). The inevitable result of all this rebellion, complaining and sexual immorality was God's judgment. Korah's revolt terminated when the ground opened and swallowed him up. The Israelites' complaints about the manna ended abruptly when poisonous snakes attacked them. The immorality at Peor led to a plague sweeping through the Israelites camp.

All these fair yet fierce acts of God's judgment – scattered with frightening regularity throughout this section of Numbers – are not pleasant reading, but we must not lose sight of what is going on. Through his judgment, brought about by the Israelites' persistent complaints and disobedience, God is doing what he said he would do. The Exodus generation is being removed, often violently, since few of them die peacefully in their sleep. They will not inherit the covenant promise of a place of blessing because of their unfaithfulness to the covenant. So, when the second census is conducted in Numbers 26, no one who was included in the first census, with the exception of Joshua and Caleb, is mentioned. God had been true to his word, and the Exodus generation had died out under his judgment. His promise of a land of blessing still stood, but it would be inherited by the new generation, whose fighting men were recorded in the second census.

When we reach Numbers 26, the opening chapter of the final section of the book, everything is different. When we encounter the Israelites *getting ready* in Numbers 26–36, we find ourselves in a different location. They have moved out of the desert and camped on the plains of Moab on the east bank of the Jordan. We also sense a different atmosphere in the Israelites' camp. The Exodus generation might have gone, but God's covenant promise of a place endured. So, under Moses' direction, the new generation get ready to invade Canaan. They are not going to be shut out of God's inheritance through a lack of trust in him. There was a determination that there would be no repetition of Kadesh Barnea.

A rapid survey of this final section of Numbers highlights the variety of preparations the Israelites made on the plains of Moab. A second census was carried out (26). Joshua was appointed to succeed Moses as the new Israelite leader (27:12–23), because God had disqualified Moses from leading the Israelites into Canaan (20:2–13). The various daily, monthly and yearly religious festivals which the Israelites were to observe were enumerated (28–29). Permission was given and arrangements made for two and a half tribes, the tribes of Gad and Reuben and half of the tribe of Manasseh, to settle on the east side of the Jordan, but only after their fighting men had helped the other Israelite tribes to conquer Canaan (32). The laws of inheritance were settled (27:1–11; 36) and cities of refuge – in which people who had committed manslaughter but not murder could find sanctuary – were established (35:6–34). All the death, unrest and negativity of the desert years was gone, replaced by a new positive, forward-looking atmosphere in the Israelites' camp.

As we consider NUMBERS' LESSONS, what can this story, which started so well but ran literally into the sand in the middle, though making a more positive comeback at the end, teach us about Jesus? To begin with, in his night-time conversation with Nicodemus Jesus used the Numbers 21:4–9 incident involving the bronze snake to explain his mission (*John* 3:14–15). Just as the bronze snake was lifted up on a pole so that undeserving Israelites might look at it and be healed, so would he be lifted up on a cross so that undeserving sinners might look to the crucified Jesus in faith and experience salvation.

We come across some pointers to Jesus in the chapters concerning Balaam (22–24). A *theophany* is an appearance of Jesus before his incarnation, and we have one in the story of Balaam and his temporarily-talking donkey. The angel of the LORD, who turned out to be God himself (22:35), blocked Balaam's path as he set out to go to Balak. But only Balaam's donkey saw the angel of the LORD, and it is not until the donkey speaks to him to rebuke him that Balaam's eyes are opened to see him too.

Later on, in Numbers 24:17, Balaam gives a prophecy about Jesus in which he links together the concepts of kingship and a star. The same two ideas are connected in Matthew's story of the *magi* or wise men coming to search for Jesus (*Matt.* 2:1–2).

In the fallout after Korah's rebellion, Aaron's authority is questioned (16:41). However, God vindicated his High Priest by causing Aaron's staff to sprout, bud, blossom and produce almonds (17; see also *Heb.* 9:4). Jesus, God's great and definitive High Priest, claimed that, as a result of his sacrificial death, he would secure salvation for his people. But when he was crucified, this claim was dismissed as ridiculous and outrageous. However, by raising him from the dead, God vindicated Jesus and made it clear that Jesus' priestly activity on the cross achieved what he had said it would achieve. In Numbers 20:22–29, we find the account of Aaron's death. It must have been a very moving moment for Israel as the only High Priest they had known died. But in contrast with Aaron's high priesthood stands the eternal and permanent high priesthood of Jesus, our great High Priest (*Heb.* 7:16, 24–25).

In Numbers we get a very stern warning from Jesus. Through his authorized apostles, Jesus used this period of Israelite history as a red flashing light to alert us to the hazard of having wonderful outward spiritual privileges but remaining hardened in sin and unbelief (*1 Cor.* 10:1–13; *Heb.* 3:7–19). Professing Christians are in constant danger of travelling along the same spiritual route as the Exodus generation. If we think we are standing firm, we should be careful that we do not fall (*1 Cor.* 10:12)!

6

Deuteronomy

The long funeral march had come to an end. Camped on the plains of Moab, on the east bank of the Jordan, the Israelites were ready to launch the invasion of Canaan. Over the past forty years, the Exodus generation, apart from Joshua and Caleb, had died under God's judgment for their unbelieving failure to carry out their covenant obligations. Moses knew that he too was about to die, disqualified from entering the place of promise for his failure to treat God with holy reverence before the people (*Num.* 20:12). His final act as leader was to gather the nation together and renew the covenant with God. In that act of covenant renewal, Moses was challenging the new generation to embrace their obligations in a way that the previous generation had failed so miserably to do.

It is this act of covenant renewal which gives Deuteronomy ITS NAME. The word 'Deuteronomy' combines two Greek words which together mean 'second law' or 'repetition of the law'. The book's name comes from the fact that the centrepiece of this act of covenant renewal was Moses' placing before the Israelites the Ten Commandments for a second time. It was not that the Ten Commandments, originally given at Sinai four decades previously, had been forgotten. They were still very much in effect, controlling Israel's social, political and religious life. It was simply that this new generation needed to hear them for themselves to be clear concerning their covenant obligations.

This act of covenant renewal also gives Deuteronomy ITS STRUCTURE. The book bears a marked resemblance to the peace treaties which powerful nations in the ancient middle east sometimes imposed on smaller conquered nations. These peace treaties had a set pattern. There was a preamble, beginning with the phrase, 'These are the words

. . . ', followed by a historical prologue outlining all the events that led up to the signing of this treaty. Then came a section stating some general rules the small nation had to keep, and after that another section setting out some specific obligations it had to carry out. Next came a list of various 'gods' who were supposed to be witnesses to this treaty. Finally there would be a catalogue of blessings and curses, specifying all the good things that would come the smaller nation's way if it carried out the treaty's general and specific regulations and all the harm that would come crashing down on them if they did not. Although there are also many differences, it can be argued that Deuteronomy is structured like one of these treaties. God had rescued the Israelites from slavery by defeating the Egyptians and their gods in battle. He had been with his people for the past forty years, protecting and looking after them. Now, as they stand poised to take God's purpose for them to a new level by invading Canaan, the Israelites commit themselves afresh to God, acknowledging him to be their covenant Lord and submitting to his rule and control.

Deuteronomy 1:1–5 resembles the classic *preamble* to such treaties. This is followed by the *historical prologue* (1:6–4:49), in which Moses reviews Israel's history so far, skilfully weaving together two themes: God's faithfulness to his covenant promises in defeating Israel's enemies and providing for all Israel's needs, and Israel's unfaithfulness to its covenant obligations. After this comes a section dealing with *general covenant obligations* (5:1–11:32). It begins with the restatement of the Ten Commandments (5:6–21), setting out in broad-brush terms how God wanted his people to live. Then come various general encouragements to love God, warnings not to repeat the sins of the past, and appeals not to be sucked into adopting the worldview and behaviour of the surrounding nations.

These general covenant obligations are backed up by a whole series of *specific covenant requirements* (12:1–26:19), which cover Israel's civil and ceremonial life and are an application of the principles outlined in the Ten Commandments. There are instructions about worship, religious institutions and practice (12–16; 18; 23); the operation of a future Israelite legal system (17–19); the conduct of warfare (20); and family life (21–25). Next comes the most significant section of the book, apart from the Ten Commandments: the list of *blessings and curses* (27:1–28:68). The alternatives could not be clearer. If the Israelites are faithful to their covenant obligations, God will keep his covenant promises of Genesis 12 and bless them with material prosperity and national security. But if the Israelites are unfaithful to their covenant obligations, the covenant of Genesis 12 will go into reverse and all kinds of horrible disasters, similar to the plagues God inflicted on Egypt, will overtake them, ultimately resulting in expulsion from the place of promise (28:15–68). Deuteronomy finishes by invoking *witnesses to the covenant* between God and Israel: heaven and earth (30:19–20), the song of Moses (31:19), and the words of the law itself (31:16). Parts of Deuteronomy do not fit neatly into this treaty template, for example Deuteronomy 34:1–12, which records Moses' death and ends with a short obituary note on his life.

It is this act of covenant renewal which gives Deuteronomy ITS IMPORTANCE for understanding the rest of the Old Testament. Even if you are not a theological student, here is a question to put to yourself: Is Deuteronomy the most important book in the Old Testament? Being able to answer that question will help you make sense of the storyline of the rest of the Old Testament. Why might we see Deuteronomy as the most important Old Testament book? With Deuteronomy, God's covenant moves to a different level. Up to this point, the emphasis, by and large, has been on the unconditional side of the covenant as the focus has been firmly on God's promises of *a people, a place, protection* and *a programme*. But now in Deuteronomy the conditional aspect comes to the fore. The phrase 'if . . . then' crops up again and again. Deuteronomy's stress on the conditional side of the covenant gives us a lens through which to see what is going on in the rest of the Old Testament.

This stress on the conditional explains the success of the conquest of Canaan under Joshua's leadership. This comes out in the battle orders God gave Joshua in the run-up to the invasion. God would give the Israelites the land as he had promised (*Josh.* 1:3, 6), but victory would also depend on Israel's faithfulness to the covenant (*Josh.* 1:7–8). This also shows why the Israelites, after mounting a successful invasion, failed to occupy Canaan totally. They were not able to dislodge all Canaan's inhabitants, with all the adverse spiritual side-effects that brought, due to their disobedience to God (*Judg.* 2:1–5).

The weight Deuteronomy gives to the conditional side of the covenant sheds light on why the Old Testament regards David as the ideal Israelite king. It was not because he had exceptional military prowess, although he had (*2 Sam.* 8:1–14). It was not because he was morally perfect, because he committed some horrendous sins and had many glaring weaknesses. David was Israel's ideal king because he loved God and was faithful to the covenant, seeking to reflect in his rule the way God ruled his people. He was 'a man after [God's] heart' (*1 Sam.* 13:14).

This emphasis on the conditional side of the covenant also accounts for the division of the kingdom after Solomon's death. Although he started off well, Solomon's reign ended badly as he became increasingly unfaithful to the covenant. The catalyst for this was his inability to control his taste for politically advantageous marriage alliances, so that he married many pagan wives (*1 Kings* 11:1–10). God's judgment on Solomon for his covenant unfaithfulness was that, after his death, the kingdom which his father David had worked so hard to unify split in two (*1 Kings* 11:11–13). Ten tribes broke away to form a new kingdom in the north called Israel, with Samaria as its capital. Judah and Benjamin, the two remaining tribes, formed the kingdom of Judah in the south, with Jerusalem as its capital.

Deuteronomy's emphasis on the conditional side of the covenant sheds light on the constant clashes between kings and prophets after the split. Although a few of Judah's kings were good, all of Israel's kings and most of Judah's were bad, some particularly so, pursuing their own agenda and refusing to reflect God's rule in their own rule. So God sent prophets like Elijah, Elisha, Isaiah, Jeremiah, Ezekiel and nine of the twelve 'Minor Prophets' to act as covenant enforcers. They confronted the kings about their covenant unfaithfulness and called the people back to God's ways as set out in Deuteronomy. You can see immediately that there is going to be trouble. The prophets' passion to put God's agenda into effect in the face of royal rebellion and royal stubbornness explains the sharp exchanges between Elijah and Ahab, Elisha and Ahab's successors, and Jeremiah and Jehoiachin and Zedekiah.

Finally, Deuteronomy's focus on the conditional side of the covenant explains the exile of Israel and Judah. Israel was the first to go, in 722 BC, when Samaria was taken by the Assyrians. Judah lasted a little longer, but, in 586 BC, after a horrific siege, Nebuchadnezzar flattened Jerusalem and transported its inhabitants into exile in Babylon. Although Israel and Judah disappeared at different times, both fell for the same reason – God judged them for their covenant unfaithfulness (2 *Kings* 17:7–23).

Therefore everything that took place in Israelite history from the Conquest to the Exile only makes sense in the light of the conditional aspect of the covenant. This is why the act of covenant renewal is so important in the Old Testament's storyline.

This act of covenant renewal also gives Deuteronomy ITS VALUE as a pointer to Jesus. Renewing the covenant was Moses' last act as Israel's leader. After he had finished delivering Deuteronomy, Moses ascended Mount Nebo, from which God gave him a panoramic view of the land of promise (34:1–4). After seeing the land, Moses died, and God buried him (34:5–6). Part of his impressive obituary reads, 'Since then, no prophet has risen in Israel like Moses' (34:10). However, in Deuteronomy 18:15, Moses predicted that, at a future time, God would raise up a final Prophet who would supersede him and be in a class of his own. When Jesus was transfigured (*Mark* 9:2–8), God's voice which spoke from the cloud that enveloped Mount Hermon identified Jesus as that final Prophet. Mark 9:7 reverberates with the sound of Deuteronomy 18:15. Other New Testament writers saw Jesus as this Prophet *par excellence* about whom Moses spoke (*Acts* 3:22; 7:37; *Heb.* 1:1–2).

At the heart of keeping the covenant was obedience to the Ten Commandments, and the New Testament presents Jesus as the substance of the Ten Commandments, the one we honour when we obey them. The first commandment teaches us to worship Jesus as the only Saviour and Lord (*Acts* 4:12; *1 Tim.* 2:5). Jesus is God's perfect image (*Col.* 1:15; *Heb.* 1:3), and it is our devotion to him that precludes the worship of any other image, as the second commandment requires. The third commandment tells us to revere Jesus, who, as the eternal Son and the crucified but risen Saviour, has been given the supreme name in the entire universe, to which every knee will bow (*Phil.* 2:10–11). Jesus is our Sabbath rest, and in his presence we break off from our legitimate daily activities to worship and listen to him (*Luke* 10:38–42). In the fifth commandment we honour Jesus who has brought us as his 'sons' to glory (*Heb.* 2:10), and, in the sixth, as the one who is the life (*John* 11:25; 14:6) and who died that we might live (*Mark* 10:45). In the seventh commandment we honour Jesus as our bridegroom, who gave himself for us to cleanse us and to make us his pure bride (*Eph.* 5:22–33). As a loving response to what he has done for us, we only have eyes for him and love him as no other. In the eighth commandment, we honour Jesus as our inheritance (*Eph.* 1:11), and, in the ninth, as God's truth (*John* 1:17; 14:6), in whom all God's promises are complete (2 *Cor.* 1:20). Finally in the tenth commandment, we honour Jesus as completely capable of meeting all our external needs and the renewed desires of our hearts (2 *Cor.* 12:9; *Phil.* 4:10–20). Christians can become nervous when talk of obeying the law is in the air, suspecting that it smacks of legalism. However, when we see Jesus as the substance of the Ten Commandments, keeping our covenant obligations takes on a completely different meaning.

We do not have to go too far into William Shakespeare's *Romeo and Juliet* to sense that too much has passed between the Montagues and the Capulets for there to be a happy ending. We get the same uneasy feeling when we arrive at the end of Deuteronomy. It is caused by the tension between God's covenant with Abraham in Genesis and the Deuteronomy act of covenant renewal. Deuteronomy emphasizes the conditional: if Israel did this, then God would do that, but if Israel did not do this, then God would do the very opposite. Everything seemed to ride on Israel's faithfulness to God's covenant. However God's covenant with Abraham was totally unconditional. We do not find the word 'if' at all in Genesis 12:1–3. Instead, impressively, God speaks seven times in three verses of what *he* will do. Everything in God's covenant with Abraham depended upon God. Our sense of unease is compounded as we listen to Moses spelling out Israel's covenant obligations. We are constantly saying to ourselves, 'This is impossible. There is absolutely no way that the Israelites will keep all their covenant obligations.' This sense is intensified by the fact that in Deuteronomy 28 Moses uses far more space to warn of the curses which will follow disobedience than he does in encouraging them with the blessings which will follow obedience. And our sense of unease reaches its peak in Deuteronomy 31:16 where God himself predicts that Israel will break the covenant.

How can this tension between God's covenant with Abraham in Genesis and the act of covenant renewal in Deuteronomy be resolved? Not by saying, as some do, that God had various plans of salvation for various times in history, because that would fly in the face of all the biblical data. God only has a Plan A: no Plan B, Plan C, or Plan D. The resolution of this tension is found in Deuteronomy 32, in a section referred to as 'The Song of Moses'. This follows hot on the heels of God's prediction of Israel's covenant-breaking. The dominant image Moses uses for God in this song is that he is a Rock (*Deut.* 32:4, 15, 18, 30, 31). This image of God as the Rock did not appear out of thin air but was drawn from one of the defining moments in Moses' experience as leader of the Israelites (*Exod.* 17:1–7).

Shortly after their escape from Egypt, the Israelites started to complain that they had no water to drink, and challenged God to prove himself by doing something about it. In despair, Moses asks God, 'What am I to do with these people?' (*Exod.* 17:4), to which God replies: 'Walk on ahead of the people. Take with you some of the elders of Israel and take in your hand the staff with which you struck the Nile, and go. I will stand there before you on the rock at Horeb. Strike the rock, and water will come out of it for the people to drink' (*Exod.* 17:5–6). Moses' staff was the instrument of God's judgment with which he had struck the Nile, bringing down God's curses upon Egypt. Now Moses must wield that instrument again, but not in judgment against the Israelites, who deserved to be cursed for their unbelief, rather to strike the rock upon which God stood. God himself would bear his own judgment, and, when Moses struck the rock with the instrument of God's judgment, water gushed from the rock to bless the undeserving people.

And so the image of God as the Rock brings hope of a resolution to the tension between God's promises of blessing to his people and his judgment on them for their sin. If God could take the judgment on himself then, could he not do it again? Moses' hope was not misplaced, for, in 1 Corinthians 10:4, Paul informs us that the rock which Moses struck pointed to Christ. On the cross, he experienced the horrors of God's curses as he died for our covenant-breaking so that we might experience the blessing of God's salvation. As one of the Roman soldiers drove his spear into Jesus' side, water, the symbol of God's blessing and salvation, flowed from it (*John* 19:34). Here is how the tension is resolved – in the death of Jesus, the Rock of Ages.

That Jesus' death is the resolution to this tension is underlined by something he said in Luke 7:33–35. John the Baptist had sent some of his disciples to Jesus to find out if he really was the promised Messiah. When they had left with a strongly positive answer, Jesus started to talk about John the Baptist. The religious leaders rejected John's ministry because no-one could please them. John did not socialize and kept himself to himself, so they said he was demon-possessed. Jesus mixed with all sorts of people to show that God's salvation was for all and not the exclusive preserve of the religious, so they wrote him off as 'a glutton and a drunkard'. That derogatory label did not come from nowhere but is an allusion to Deuteronomy 21:18–21, one of Deuteronomy's laws that make us feel uncomfortable. What the Jewish religious leaders were saying by calling Jesus 'a glutton and a drunkard' is that he was a rebellious son of Israel who deserved to be put to death. But there is a double irony here: First, Jesus is, in fact, the faithful son of Israel, while it was the religious leaders who were the stubborn and rebellious ones, deserving death. When Jesus says, 'But wisdom is proved right by all her children' (*Luke* 7:35), He is saying, 'We will see who really is the faithful child.' Jesus is the faithful son who perfectly fulfils the terms of the covenant so that covenant-breakers who trust in him alone are considered faithful covenant-keepers by God. Second, Jesus did die the death of a rebellious son of Israel; but not for his own covenant-breaking; rather for the covenant-breaking of his people. The very next verses in Deuteronomy 21 are these: 'If a man guilty of a capital offence is put to death and his body is hung on a tree, you must not leave his body on the tree overnight. Be sure to bury him that same day, because anyone who is hung on a tree is under God's curse' (21:22–23a). That last statement is quoted by Paul in Galatians 3:13–14 in connection with Jesus' death. Do you see what Paul is saying? As he, the faithful son, dies in the place of the rebellious son, Jesus resolves the tension, bearing the covenant curses so that we might experience the covenant blessings.

The same point is made in a dramatic way in Genesis 15:9–21. God had just restated his covenant to Abraham, but Abraham was unsure if God could deliver what he had promised. So God told Abraham to take various animals and birds, kill them, cut them in half, and arrange their dismembered carcases in two rows. This sort of thing was common practice in the ratification of ancient peace treaties of the second millennium BC. When the two parties making the treaty walked between the two rows of carcases they were saying symbolically, 'May the same thing happen to me as happened to these animals and birds if I do not deliver my side of the treaty.' But God did something unexpected. He put Abraham to sleep so that he was totally inactive and could not walk between the carcases. Instead God appeared in the form of fire and he alone walked down the middle of the two rows of death (*Gen.* 15:12, 17). By doing that, God was accepting responsibility for both sides of this covenant – the obligation-keeping side, as well as the blessing-delivery side. Everything, blessing and judgment, promise and curses, depended on God. On the cross, the macabre drama of Genesis 15 is fulfilled. As Jesus dies a horrible death in our place for our covenant-breaking, God judges himself, in the person of his Son, and brings all the curses associated with breaking his covenant down on himself. But Jesus' death is not only the way of escape from God's curses; it is also the way of salvation, activating all the promises of God's blessing. In Jesus' death, as the hymn says, 'the curse to blessing turns', for he gets what we deserved in order that we might get what he deserved.

All Deuteronomy's emphasis on the need to obey the covenant obligations and the awful curses that will crash down on those who fail to carry out the conditions of the covenant seems totally at odds with God's unconditional promises of Genesis. But the tension is resolved in Jesus, who bore the Deuteronomy curses so that we might experience the Genesis blessings. He lived the life we should have lived and died the death we should have died. Jesus, who did not deserve to be cursed, because he had perfectly carried out his covenant obligations, was cursed for us, who did deserve to be cursed, because we had failed miserably to carry out our covenant obligations. The Bible has one word for this. It is 'grace'!

7
Joshua

In our journey through the Bible, we have arrived at Joshua, and you will immediately notice that we are travelling through different terrain. We have left behind the Pentateuch – Genesis to Deuteronomy – and with Joshua we have arrived at the start of the historical books of the Old Testament, which will take us all the way to the end of Esther. Although the book is named after its main character, the leader of this group of second-generation freed slaves, it would be a mistake to imagine that Joshua is the dominant figure in the book. The main player is God himself, and the storyline emphasizes the fact that the Israelites' success was not due to their military prowess or their leader's tactical brilliance or their high moral values, but to God keeping the promise of a place of blessing which he had given centuries before (*Gen.* 12:7). Joshua is not a book about remarkable human achievement but about a remarkable God who is true to his word.

Joshua's STORYLINE falls into four sections of unequal length, and the first one is *invading the land* (1:1–5:12). As Israel's D–Day approached, Joshua received his battle orders from God (1:1–9), in which he was reminded that the key factor in the campaigns which lay ahead was that the land the Israelites were about to invade was God's gift to them. God would give them Canaan to fulfil his promise to Abraham, and, although they would have to engage in some savage fighting, God would be with them. In the light of this, Joshua was to carry out his covenant obligations. Success in the invasion of Canaan would depend primarily on God's faithfulness to his promise, and this would be backed up by Joshua's faithfulness to his responsibilities.

Encouraged by what God told him, Joshua began to prepare the Israelites for their D–Day (1:10–11). Specifically he sent two spies on a reconnaissance mission to Jericho (2:1–24). There Rahab, a prostitute, not only hid them from Jericho's police, but told them what they wanted to hear: Jericho's inhabitants had heard what God had done for the Israelites and were terrified (2:9–11). After abseiling down the city walls and lying low for three days, the spies reported back to Joshua and urged him to advance the invasion plan because God was going to give them the land. This was not going to be Kadesh Barnea all over again.

There was one more major obstacle to be negotiated before the Israelites actually stood in Canaan: a river in flood. Joshua 3–4 tells the story of how the Jordan was crossed. As soon as the priests carrying the Ark of the Covenant set foot in the fast-moving waters, the river stopped flowing. When they reached the middle of the river, they paused and allowed the rest of the nation to cross. While the Israelites were hurrying over, twelve men, one from each tribe, were to pick up a stone from Jordan's dried–up riverbed and carry it to the other side. On the Jordan's west bank these twelve stones were to be erected into a memorial to how God's power had stopped the river flowing so that Israel could cross over. After everyone had reached the safety of Jordan's west bank, the priests carrying the Ark of the Covenant came out of the river, and it began to flow in flood as before. What a boost all this was to the Israelites' faith! They were now actually standing in the land God had promised them, having experienced God's awesome power for themselves in what was almost an action replay of the crossing of the Red Sea.

Joshua set up his base camp at Gilgal, and there all Israelite males were circumcised (5:2–9) and the Passover was celebrated (5:10). As they observed the two Old Testament 'sacraments', which recalled God's covenant promises and God's redeeming grace, the Israelites were reminded that what they were engaged in was primarily a spiritual mission, rather than a military campaign or a migratory movement of a displaced people.

Invading the land was only the beginning. The next section of Joshua focuses on *conquering the land* (5:13–12:24). Joshua needed to secure a bridgehead in enemy territory, which is why he set his sights on

Jericho. But Jericho had formidable defences and the Israelites had no experience of siege warfare. How was it to be captured? As Joshua considered this, the mysterious 'commander of the army of the LORD' – a preincarnate appearance of the Son of God – told him how it was to happen (5:13–6:5), and what a strange method it was! It involved armed men, seven priests blowing rams'-horn trumpets, the Ark of the Covenant, and a rearguard, marching around Jericho once for six days, then, on the seventh day, doing so seven times. On the seventh day, after they had completed their seventh circuit, when the people heard the priests give a blast on their trumpets, they were to shout, and the walls of Jericho would collapse, allowing the Israelite army to storm into the city. These tactics may not be found in a military manual, but they worked. Jericho fell, not because Joshua fought the battle of Jericho, but because God, whose presence was symbolized by the Ark of the Covenant, fought for his people. The victory at Jericho would be the pattern for the conquest of Canaan. This was God's war, and he would fight against Israel's enemies, but success was dependent on Israel's obedience to God.

This pattern is reinforced by what happened subsequently at Ai, the next city on Joshua's list. Its capture should have been easy, but Israel's initial attack was repulsed (7:2–5). When a distraught Joshua asked God what had gone wrong (7:6–9), he was told that Israel – in the person of Achan – had failed to obey God during the assault on Jericho. That was the reason for the setback (7:1, 11–12). After the sin was dealt with through Achan's execution (7:13–26), Ai was defeated and destroyed. Following Ai's destruction, in order to comply with Moses' instructions in Deuteronomy 11:29 and Deuteronomy 27:11–14, Israel renewed its covenant with God at Mount Ebal and Mount Gerizim (8:30–35). This further underlined the conditions for success in the campaign. Victory depended completely on God's faithfulness to his promises, and their faithfulness to his covenant.

After establishing a bridgehead, the next thing any invading force must do is break out from it. The way Joshua did this shows his genius as a military tactician. From his secure bridgehead, he launched a three-pronged strike against his enemies. First, he attacked the centre of the country (9:1–10:28), thus driving a wedge between his enemies and robbing them of the possibility of fighting against the Israelites as one huge army. Then he turned south and defeated Israel's opponents there (10:29–43). After that, he headed north and crushed all opposition there (11:1–23). Undoubtedly Joshua was a brilliant general. This is seen in his all-night march to launch a surprise attack against a five-king alliance at Gibeon (10:9), and in the way he engaged the northern coalition of kings led by the King of Hazor in the hilly terrain around the Waters of Meron (11:17) to neutralize the threat of the coalition's chariots (11:4). But again and again the account stresses the fact that Israel was victorious because God fought for them (10:11, 42; 11:6).

The section recording the conquest of Canaan ends with a look into Israel's trophy cabinet: a catalogue of all the defeated kings. But we are invited to view this, not to applaud Israel's prowess or Joshua's military genius, but to celebrate God's faithfulness to his covenant promise in Genesis 12 of a place of blessing.

After their military conquest, the Israelites set about *occupying the land* (13:1–22:34). At first sight, the lists of strange place names might appear dull to us. But as each tribe receives its inheritance as a gift from God, these lists are shouting at us that God has kept his word (*Gen.* 17:7–8; 22:17). There is nothing dull about that!

After repeating the fact that the tribes of Gad and Reuben and half the tribe of Manasseh were to settle on the east of the Jordan (13:8–32), the account focuses on Caleb and the tribe of Judah (14:6–15:63), and then on the tribe of Ephraim and the other half of the tribe of Manasseh (16:1–17:18). These three tribes are going to play a leading role in the nation's subsequent history. In Joshua 18–19 the land allocated to the other seven tribes is recorded. Benjamin's inheritance is mentioned first because Israel's first king will be from that tribe. The record concludes with Joshua's allotment (19:49–51). Caleb and Joshua, the only survivors from the Exodus generation, are therefore the bookends of this section. At the end of the distribution record are two important land matters: the designation of the cities of refuge (20:1–9) and the provisions made for the Levites (21:1–45), who do not inherit any territory in Canaan. God himself is their inheritance (13:33).

The final section of Joshua's storyline deals with *retaining the land* (23:1–24:33). Towards the end of his life, Joshua was becoming concerned that the Israelites were slackening in their bid to destroy what was left of the Canaanites. Perhaps in their increasing battle weariness, they were becoming more open to coexistence as opposed to confrontation. Twice Joshua gathers the people to voice his concerns. In both speeches Joshua reminds them of all God has done for them, especially in giving them the land as a gift (23:3–5; 24:2–13). In response to God's faithfulness to his covenant promise of a place of blessing, the Israelites must be faithful to their covenant obligation to obey God (23:6–11; 24:14). He warns them that if they evade their covenant responsibilities, disaster will overtake them, and they will be removed from the land, in line with the curses of Deuteronomy 28 (23:12–13, 16). He also challenges them to follow his example and consciously commit themselves to serving God (24:15). Only in this way will the land which they have conquered and are occupying be retained.

But there is an elephant in the room which cannot be ignored – an issue which everyone sees, but no one wishes to deal with. It is the THORNY ISSUE of Israel's treatment of the Canaanites. All war is barbaric, but what the Israelites did hardly complies with the Geneva Conventions. It savours of genocide. How are we to regard what is referred to as *cherem*, the devotion to destruction of everyone and everything in a city? The most common escape route is to say that, although the Israelites thought they were doing what God wanted, they were not. All they were doing was reflecting the primitive times in which they lived. But that way out is a dead-end because the annihilation of the Canaanites *was* God's will, sanctioned by his clear commands (10:40; *Deut.* 20:16–17).

Here are a number of factors we need to take into consideration as we struggle with this issue. First, *cherem* was not to be the norm for the Israelites. Normally an enemy would be asked to surrender, and only if they refused to do so were they to be attacked. When victory was secured, only male combatants were to be killed: everyone and everything else was plunder (*Deut.* 20:10–15). The fact that *cherem* was not to be used indiscriminately but only against the inhabitants of Canaan (*Deut.* 20:16–17) indicates that there was a purpose in it, and protection was part of it (*Deut.* 20:18). The annihilation of the Canaanites was designed to remove everything that might seduce the Israelites away from faithfulness to God.

Another purpose of *cherem* is to execute God's judicial condemnation of the inhabitants of Canaan. In Genesis 15:16 God explained to Abraham that his descendants would not inherit Canaan immediately but would come back in the fourth generation, 'for the sin of the Amorites has not yet reached its full measure'. The implication of what God said is that he was being patient with the Canaanites; but, when their sins had reached the limit, he would use Abraham's descendants to bring his judgment on them. The Canaanites were notorious for their sexual perversions (*Lev.* 18:24–25) and their pursuit of sorcery and other dark arts (*Deut.* 18:9–12). The Israelites were to be God's instruments to carry out his punishment of the Canaanites, just as centuries later he would use the Assyrians and Babylonians as his instruments to punish Israel and Judah. The fact that everyone and everything in a city was subject to *cherem* shows that the Israelites cannot be stigmatized as land-grabbing marauders seeking to enrich themselves. Something else is going on in this act of judgment. God's judgment of the Canaanites is a pointer to his final judgment, when those who have rejected the Saviour will be punished in hell.

A final factor that we must consider is that, in the middle of all this destruction, God's grace is still evident. Rahab, along with her family, was saved from the destruction of Jericho because she had helped the two spies (2:8–14; 6:25a). And, in fulfilment of God's covenant promise that he had a programme to bring the blessings of his salvation to non-Jews, Rahab is also incorporated into the Israelite community (6:25b). Even when he discovered that the Gibeonites had tricked him into signing a non-aggression pact with them, Joshua did not exterminate them in line with Deuteronomy 20:16–17. Instead he forced them to work as wood cutters and water carriers at God's sanctuary (9:27). Sheer drudgery might now be their lot, but at least they were still breathing (9:26). While these factors may not stop us feeling uncomfortable with the idea of *cherem*, they may at least help us to understand it.

What is Joshua's MESSAGE? Let me first point out that it has nothing to do with political and economic liberation. Neither has it much to do with death and dying, in spite of the way in which well-known hymns and books use the image of crossing the Jordan as a symbol for leaving this world and entering heaven.

Joshua challenges us to be loyal to Jesus. The book's pivotal passage is Joshua 21:43–45. This gives the book a 'before' and an 'after'. The 'after' is a challenge to carry out our obligations under the First Commandment, which is another way of saying that we should be loyal to Jesus, since he is the substance of that commandment. We are to serve him alone – not to desert him and give ourselves to substitute gods. But how can people like us, who are more prone to sin than we could possibly imagine, remain loyal to Jesus? We have to look at what precedes the pivotal passage to find an answer to that question. The 'before' is a celebration of God's grace. It is displayed in the gracious assurances God gave to Joshua as he stepped into the position of leader of the Israelites after Moses' death; in the gracious way God drew Rahab to faith in himself and gave her a place in Israel and in the ancestry of Jesus (*Matt.* 1:5); in the gracious exercise of his power as he enabled Israel to defeat their enemies; in the gracious working out of his wrath that led Israel to repentance and restoration after Achan's sin; and in his gracious gift of the land to the Israelites. By placing this celebration of God's grace before the challenge to be loyal to Jesus, Joshua is saying to us that the dynamic which will enable us to carry out our covenant obligations of being faithful to Jesus is *grace*. We cannot be loyal to him in our own strength, but by God's grace we can.

Joshua tells us insistently that God keeps his word. His commitment to deliver his covenant promises leaps out from every page of the book. This is made clear at the start of the book in God's battle orders to Joshua (1:1–9), and we find the same point being made right at the end of the book. We are taken to the graves of Joshua, Joseph and Eleazar (24:29–33). The aim of this tour of cemeteries is to hammer home for the final time the truth that God is faithful to what he has said. Joshua and Eleazar might be dead, but look where they are buried – in the land of promise! Joseph's bones, which were first buried in Egypt (*Gen.*

50:26), have been reinterred, in line with his wishes (*Gen.* 50:24–25) in Shechem, in the territory given by God to Ephraim, one of his sons. 'Every promise has been fulfilled; not one has failed' (23:14). This is the message of Joshua.

With all this in mind, we need to realize that the conquest of Canaan was not the true fulfilment of God's covenant promise of a place of blessing. The writer of Hebrews informs us that Joshua could not give real rest (*Heb.* 4:8); so the true fulfilment of the promise of a place of blessing still remained open after the conquest (*Heb.* 4:1). Where can its true fulfilment be found? It is not found in a physical place, because God's ultimate purpose for his people is not a strip of land at the eastern end of the Mediterranean Sea. Its true fulfilment is found in a person – the Lord Jesus Christ. When Jesus says, 'Come to me, all you who are weary and burdened, and I will give you rest' (*Matt.* 11:28), he is deliberately aligning himself with God's covenant promise of a place of blessing, stating that he is its true fulfilment. This verse is not primarily to make us feel good. It is an announcement that Jesus offers what Joshua, his namesake, could not offer. Joshua could not give real rest, but Jesus definitely can, as he offers – to the spiritually crushed and ground-down – a place of blessing.

8

Judges

A friend of mine who had had a number of collisions with the law before he became a Christian told me of his immense relief when he was told as he read the Bible for the first time that the Judges in this book were not the legal officials he was familiar with but warrior-rescuers who had saved the Israelites from their oppressors. Although 'Saviours' might be a better term for the main characters of the book, I will keep the traditional label.

The events described in Judges cover perhaps three hundred and fifty years, but coming up with a neat chronology is notoriously difficult, because the judges mentioned did not judge all the twelve tribes or operate throughout the whole of Israel. In fact, some judges judged at the same time as others, though in different parts of the country.

According to later Jewish tradition, Samuel was the author of Judges. That is pure conjecture, but there are hints in the text that the author was writing in the time of Samuel. The last verse of the book (21:25) informs us that Judges describes the period before the monarchy was established. The implications of that verse are that, when the author wrote, there was a king ruling over Israel, and that, if there had been one at the time of the book of Judges, the nation would not have been in such a spiritual and moral mess. However, in Judges 1:21, we are also told that, at the time of writing, the Jebusites still occupied Jerusalem. When he became king, one of the first things David did was to capture Jerusalem from the Jebusites in a daring special-forces-style raid through the city's water system and then make it his capital (2 *Sam.* 5:6–9). So Judges' author was someone who wrote when Israel had a king but before David captured Jerusalem. That is all the text tells us. It does not actually say who wrote the book.

While there may be some uncertainty about Judges' author and chronology, there are no arguments about its main emphasis. Judges describes Israel's Dark Ages. It traces the nation's spiritual deterioration and moral decline, so that, by the time we reach Judges 17–21, things have sunk to an all-time low. As we read of how one tribe completely departs from God in favour of deviant idol worship, not to mention the sickening events described in Judges 19–21, we are surprised that they are in the Bible at all and we almost need to lie down in a darkened room to regain our moral composure after reading them!

Let me give you a bird's-eye view of the structure of Judges before we examine its storyline in more detail. Judges opens with a double introduction (1:1–3:6). The first part (1:1–2:5) highlights the *development* of Israel's spiritual and consequently moral deterioration. The second (2:6–3:6) is a description of the *pattern* of Israel's spiritual and consequently moral deterioration. The book ends with a double conclusion (17:1–21:25), which parallels the double introduction. The first part (17–18) describes Israel's *spiritual* mess, and the second (19–21) focuses on Israel's *moral* mess. Sandwiched between in the main part of Judges is a double presentation of the exploits of the various judges (3:7–16:31). There are twelve judges mentioned in this section, but six of them – Shamgar (3:31), Tola (10:1–2), Jair (10:3–5), Ibzan (12:8–10), Elon (12:11–12) and Abdon (12:13–15) – are minor judges with only minor roles in the story. The exploits of the six other judges – the main players in Judges – are recorded in two parts. The first, which tells of what Othniel, Ehud and Deborah did (3:7–5:31), tends to be positive, while the second, which records the activity of Gideon, Jephthah and Samson (6:1–16:31), has quite a number of negative things to say about them.

As we zoom in on Judges' structure, we discover that the book's first section deals with *the development of Israel's spiritual and moral deterioration* (1:1–2:5). Joshua had shattered Canaanite resistance to the Israelites' invasion by launching a rapid attack on the centre of the country, then on the south, and finally on the north. After this, the land was parcelled out to the various tribes, who were supposed to clean up their own areas. This section of Judges shows how the Israelites increasingly failed to do this. At first things went according to plan, with Judah's relative success in the south (1:1–20), but then things started to unravel because of the northern tribes' failure to follow up the conquest (1:21–36). Instead of driving out the Canaanites, the northern tribes allowed them to coexist with them. That might not have seemed to matter, but the next thing we know is that the northern tribes are cosying up to the Canaanites, buying into their culture, religion and values. Through his repetition of the verb 'not to drive out' we can sense the writer's growing anger at what he is describing. But God was also angry at the Israelites' covenant unfaithfulness. So the Angel of the Lord appears at Bokim (or Bochim) and announces God's judgment on the Israelites for what they had not done (2:1–5). God will not drive out the remaining nations, but will allow them to stay to pose a spiritual hazard to his people. Because of the Israelites' unfaithfulness to their covenant obligations, the land is no longer a place of blessing but a place of threat.

Several years ago I visited Bannockburn, the site of the famous victory by Robert the Bruce and his Scottish army over proud Edward II and his English army. Before touring the battle site, I went to the Visitor Centre and watched a multimedia presentation, which gave an overview of what went on during those fateful days in June 1314. The next section of Judges, which records *the pattern of Israel's spiritual and moral deterioration* (2:6–3:6), is Judges' 'Visitor Centre'. It gives us a framework through which to look at what will be described in Judges 3:7–16:31. At the 'Visitor Centre' we come across the 'Four Rs Cycle', which occurs six times in the book:

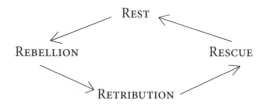

At the top of the cycle is REST, when the Israelites enjoyed a period of peace and security. Then they turned their backs on God, and, in a blatant act of covenant unfaithfulness, worshipped Baal (2:10–13), so entering the REBELLION phase. God did not abandon his people to the worship of Baal but punished them by sending a foreign power to oppress and terrorize them (2:14–15a). This is the RETRIBUTION part of the Cycle. But then God had pity on his people and sent a judge to defeat the enemy and save the Israelites from their oppression (2:15b–16). We have reached the RESCUE stage of the sequence. Notice that there is no indication of Israel repenting. They are in trouble and pain, and cry out to God. But, apart from perhaps Judges 10:10, there is no sign of Israel being sorry for worshipping Baal. God rescues them, not because Israel has repented, but because he is gracious. The 'Four Rs Cycle' has come full circle and we are back to REST, with the people once more enjoying peace and security. Even here, however, there is a cautionary rider. The rest they enjoyed was only temporary, lasting as long as the judge who had saved them lived. Once he was out of the picture, the Israelites not only went back to their old unfaithful and idolatrous ways, but they did so with greater energy than before (2:18–19).

The main portion of Judges is *a record of God's salvation* (3:7–16:31), as the 'Four Rs Cycle' is repeated six times. The table below shows this.

Cycle	Passage	Enemy	Judge(s)
1	3:8–11	Mesopotamians	Othniel
2	3:12–31	Moabites	Ehud, Shamgar
3	4:1–5:31	Canaanites	Deborah
4	6:1–10:5	Midianites	Gideon, Tola, Jair
5	10:6–12:15	Ammonites	Jephthah, Ibzan, Elon
6	13:1–16:31	Philistines	Samson

A few years ago, I had to conduct a small-group Bible study with a group of ten thirteen-year-old boys, mostly from Christian backgrounds. Boys of that age have not made up their minds whether they are children or adults, but they had made up their minds on one thing: the Bible studies they were meant to do were boring. I abandoned those studies and took them through the stories of how the six main judges saved Israel. We eased our way into Judges with how Othniel, Caleb's nephew and son-in-law, saved Israel by sorting out Cushan-Rishathaim (3:7–11), as his story illustrates clearly the 'Four Rs Cycle'. Then we moved on to the 'good stuff', looking at how Ehud, the Benjamite lefthander, rescued Israel by assassinating Eglon, the obese king of Moab (3:12–30).

Their favourite part of Judges was how Deborah rescued Israel from a Canaanite coalition led by Jabin, king of Hazor, and under the command of Sisera, Jabin's chief of staff (4:1–5:31). From the way Deborah had to cajole and bully Barak into attacking Jabin's forces near Mount Tabor, they labelled Barak 'a bit of a wimp'. The story of how Jael struck a hammer blow for Israel by driving a tent peg through Sisera's skull had the boys' undivided attention. They were amazed at how Gideon defeated a huge Midianite army with only three hundred troops (6:1–8:21), and then were shocked by the way Gideon let success go to his head and led himself and his family astray (8:22–9:57).

My group of boys admired Jephthah's dash and panache in defeating the Ammonites (10:6–12:7). They thought the way he was prepared to put to one side all the personal hurt he felt at being disinherited and ostracized by his family and community to help them in trouble was awesome. But they concluded that his vow was just stupid, especially when it led to him offering up his only daughter as a human sacrifice.[1] We finally looked at Samson's life (13:1–16:31). He was a man of enormous potential who threw away his spiritual heritage for a self-indulgent lifestyle. Yet, in spite of his personal weaknesses, and in particular his inability to control himself, God used him to begin to rescue Israel from the Philistines. Because most adults get queasy at the sight of tomato juice, we find Judges' violence a bit too much, but not these thirteen-year-old boys: they loved Judges. When one asked if there was more stuff like this in the Bible, I suggested that he should read through and find out for himself.

[1] Not all commentators agree that Jephthah carried out his vow literally. See, for example, A. R. Fausset, *Judges*, 1885 (repr. Edinburgh: Banner of Truth, 1999), p. 203.

If you thought Judges 3:7–16:31 was a bit gruesome, brace yourself for Judges 17:1–21:25. In this *picture of a people in chaos*, we find the Israelites wallowing at the bottom of a spiritual and moral cesspit. It is a time of religious meltdown, with illicit shrines served by renegade priests (17:1–13). It was a period of social unrest and violence (18:1–31), during which the theological basis for land tenure was ignored (*Lev.* 25:23), and what the disaffected wanted, they grabbed. It was an era of moral collapse (19:1–30), for in this ghastly episode it looks as if Sodom is in Israel. It was an age of national division (20:1–21:25) as disputes were settled by the sword, solutions fudged, and the vulnerable exploited. All this chaos was happening at ground level, and was a result of the Israelites' covenant unfaithfulness. The lesson of Judges is clear: disobeying God's Word by going after substitute gods is a road that only leads to spiritual and moral disaster.

Where would you begin when it comes to SEEING JESUS in all the dreadfulness of Judges? We can see Jesus in the concept of the judge. The judge was raised up by God to rescue his people from their enemies, to restore the relationship between God and his people, and to bring peace to God's people. The judge was a saviour, and this is the first time in the Bible that this concept is clearly spelt out. So when, centuries later, it was announced that Jesus was the promised Saviour (*Luke* 2:11), those with any spiritual awareness knew something of what was involved in his saving activity (*Luke* 1:68–75).

Pointers to Jesus' saving activity can be picked up from the exploits of certain judges. In the Deborah story, God used an unusual instrument to save his people. No one expected God to save through Jael, a woman, driving a tent peg through Sisera's skull. In the same way God choosing to save through the cross was totally unexpected (*1 Cor.* 1:18–25). In the Gideon story, God brings about victory through weakness as he whittles Gideon's army down to its bare bones of three hundred men. Similarly God achieved his greatest victory through the weakness of the cross. The conclusion of the Samson story informs us that Samson saved Israel by his death, killing more when he died than when he lived (16:30b). Centuries later Jesus was to do the same as he saved his people through his death, destroying his enemies when he died.

The Israelites' problem was that they were in the grip of sin, so they fell back into a state of spiritual and moral deterioration again and again. They found it impossible to walk away from sin as it had them in its stranglehold. They needed a Saviour who would rescue them, not only from the consequences of their sin, but also from sin's control. None of the judges could do this, but, in Jesus, we have a Saviour who can. By his death, he sets us free from sin's grip over our lives (*Rom.* 6:17–18), and, by the gift of his Spirit, he enables us to live lives that please God (*Rom.* 8:4). In Judges the point is repeated, almost *ad nauseam*, that Israel enjoyed peace as long as the judge lived, but when the judge died, the people returned to their old rebellious Baal-worshipping ways. What was needed was a Saviour who would not die but would continue to lead God's people in righteous ways. In Jesus, we have such a Saviour (*Heb.* 7:25).

The behaviour of some of the judges creates a longing for Jesus. Take Jephthah, for example. He won a stunning victory over the Ammonites, but it is totally overshadowed by the tragic events surrounding his foolish vow and the sacrifice of his daughter. We are left wondering where we are going to find a leader who will not tarnish victory with tragedy and who will be consistently righteous. Jephthah's defects put us on the lookout for a Saviour of whom it can be said 'he has done everything well' (*Mark* 7:37).

The awfulness of Judges' final chapters makes us ask if there is any hope. But there is a light shining in the pitch blackness, and it comes in the form of the phrase which is repeated four times: 'Israel had no king' (17:6; 18:1; 19:1; 21:25). People were thinking that there must be something better than this, that what was needed was a strong leader to unite them and keep them right. This paved the way for David and his royal line, from which Jesus, our true king, would come. 'As a king, Christ brings us under His power, rules and defends us, and restrains and conquers all His and all our enemies,'[1] so that we no longer do what is right in our own eyes, but submit to his rule and live in a way that is pleasing to God and faithful to his covenant.

[1] *The Shorter Catechism in Modern English*, Question 26

9
Ruth

How to classify the book of Ruth is a matter of debate. Many would regard it as a romantic story because the marriage of Ruth, a Moabitess immigrant, and Boaz, Bethlehem's most eligible bachelor, is central to it. The compilers of the Hebrew Bible placed the book in the 'Writings' section, focusing on its lessons rather than its storyline. In the English Bible, Ruth is found somewhere else: in the 'History' section, sandwiched between Judges and 1 Samuel, forming a bridge between them. The narrative begins by setting it in the same time period as Judges (1:1), and it ends by emphasizing the fact that Ruth was David's great-grandmother, so leading us into 1 Samuel, the book which begins to tell the story of David, Israel's greatest king.

The book is full of surprises, and the first is its title. The Bible's culture is generally quite masculine, but here is a book named after a woman, and, what is more, Ruth was not even Jewish; she was a Gentile outsider. Here in the book's title there is more than a hint that God's promise in Genesis 12 of a programme to bring the blessings of his salvation to all nations will feature highly in Ruth's story.

Let me take you through RUTH'S STORYLINE. What a gem of a story it is! It begins with *Ruth leaving Moab* (1:1–22) and ends happily in a way that could not have been easily foreseen. We are first introduced to an Israelite family: Elimelech, Naomi, his wife, and their two sons, Mahlon and Kilion (or Chilion). They live in Bethlehem, which literally means 'house of bread', but the town is not living up to its name since famine's hand has gripped the land and food is very scarce. So, presumably to give his family a 'better life', Elimelech takes them to Moab. The writer does not comment on the rightness or wrongness of the move, but, as they were distancing themselves from the land of

God's blessing, we are probably meant to give the family a disapproving glare as they depart for Moab. They stay there roughly ten years, but Elimelech dies, and Mahlon and Kilion marry Moabite girls, Orpah and Ruth. Then tragedy strikes. Both Mahlon and Kilion die, leaving Naomi on her own with only her two daughters-in-law and no male relatives for support.

News reaches Moab that the famine in Israel is over, so Naomi decides to head back home to Bethlehem (1:6). She tries to persuade her daughters-in-law not to come with her but to make new lives for themselves in Moab (1:8–13). Ruth refuses, and, in a wonderful statement of loyalty, she articulates her determination to stick with Naomi through thick and thin (1:16–17). So, destitute and not a little embittered (1:20–21), Naomi arrives in Bethlehem with her foreign daughter-in-law, just as the barley is about to be harvested (1:22). Naomi's arrival in town, after an absence of ten years, causes quite a stir (1:19).

Several features of Naomi's faith stand out in chapter 1. God has made her life very bitter (1:20–21), but she does not abandon faith in him. She may be complaining, but she is complaining to God. She does not believe that God is a localized tribal deity, restricted in his activity to Israel. She wants Orpah and Ruth to experience blessing in Moab, and invokes God's name (1:8). In the religious ideas of the time, Moab was considered to be the territory of the god Chemosh, but that is not what Naomi thinks. God is still God in Moab, for he is the God of all the earth. Naomi still believes that God is a kindness-showing God (1:8), and this conviction is reinforced by what is happening when Naomi and Ruth arrive back in Bethlehem. The barley harvest is beginning. When she left Bethlehem ten years previously, there was no barley harvest: only famine. But now, thanks to God's direct intervention (1:6), there is a harvest. Naomi is still experiencing pain, but there is a glimmer of hope. If God is showing kindness to his people generally, may he not begin to show kindness to her specifically? Naomi's faith must have been attractive to Ruth because her statement of loyalty is couched in covenantal phraseology, especially, 'Your people will be my people and your God my God.' Ruth has learnt this from Naomi. She has come to trust in God through Naomi's witness.

The story moves on with *Ruth catching Boaz' attention* (2:1–23). With no male relatives to provide for them and in a culture where there was no such thing as social security, how were two desperately poor widows to feed themselves? But God has already provided for such a situation in Leviticus 19:9–10. Harvest fields were not to be reaped to their edges, nor was fallen grain or fruit to be picked up by the harvesters. These scraps could be collected by the poor for food. So, with Naomi's approval, Ruth goes out to gather up the barley harvest leftovers (2:2). Now, she 'just happened' to glean in a field belonging to Boaz, who has already been introduced to us as a relative of Elimelech (2:1). By mentioning Boaz before he actually appears in the story, the writer is telling us to keep an eye on this man: he is going to be a major player in all that happens.

Although Boaz has heard about Ruth (2:11a) – Bethlehem is a small town, and Naomi's return has attracted attention – he does not know what she looks like and has to rely on the foreman of his harvesters to point her out to him. When he is told of how hard Ruth has worked, Boaz gives her permission to glean in his field (2:8). But he is a generous man, going beyond what God's law specified, and so Boaz offers Ruth protection from any harassment she might experience on account of being a foreign woman, and tells her to help herself to water (2:9). Later on, he invites her to share in a meal (2:14).

Ruth is overwhelmed by Boaz' generosity (2:10). Perhaps this was the first genuine kindness she had experienced in Bethlehem, as small towns are not only notorious for gossip, but also for being unwelcoming to incomers. Then Boaz explains why he has acted in this way (2:11) and blesses her for what she has done (2:12). Boaz' statement is remarkable because it resonates with Genesis 12:1. He is saying that Ruth is like a female Abraham because she has responded in faith as Abraham did. But this female Abraham is a Moabitess outsider. God's covenant promise of a programme is in the wings once more.

Thanks to Boaz' instructions to his harvesters to 'accidentally' leave some grain stalks lying around for Ruth to gather (2:15–16), she arrives home with quite a lot of grain, roughly twenty-two litres, enough to feed her and Naomi for a month. After quizzing Ruth and finding out that she worked in Boaz' field, Naomi's spirits lift because he is a relative of her late husband (2:20). What a difference a day's gleaning in a barley field can make! The tone of Ruth 2:20 is a million miles away from that of Ruth 1:20–21. Hope is beginning to return. Everything in Naomi's tough situation is not sorted out, but God has given a signal that he has not abandoned her and may be about to turn things around. This is typical of how God works. When our lives are tough, he does not take away our stress and make everything wonderful, but he does give us tokens of his kindness, that he has not forgotten us.

There seems to be a time lapse between chapters 2 and 3, during which Ruth continues to work in Boaz' fields to take care of Naomi (2:23). But after this the story resumes with *Ruth requesting redemption* (3:1–18). Before we look at this chapter, we need to see the background to what is going on. When someone sold his property, his next of kin, a person known as the 'kinsman-redeemer', had both the right and the responsibility to buy it back in order to keep the land within the family (*Lev.* 25:25). Also, when a man died childless, his brother, or kinsman-redeemer if the brother was dead, had the responsibility to marry the widow and give her a son who would be legally considered the dead man's son and so inherit his property and keep his name going (*Deut.* 25:5–6). This last bit of legislation was known as 'levirate marriage' from *levir*, the Latin for 'brother-in-law'.

Naomi forms a plan, based on the levirate marriage legislation, to have Boaz fulfil his obligations as kinsman-redeemer. She thought, mistakenly as it turns out, that Boaz was Elimelech's closest relative, so she tells Ruth to wash, anoint herself, and put on her best clothes, go to Boaz, and follow his instructions carefully (3:3–4). It was a high-risk strategy, but the stakes were high. After a hard day's work and ample food and wine, Boaz was asleep on the threshing floor. Ruth tiptoed in and lay down at his feet (3:7).

In the middle of the night Boaz woke to find Ruth lying at his feet (3:9), and, before he had time to work out what was going on, Ruth asked Boaz to 'spread the corner of [his] garment', literally to 'spread his wing', over her. What Ruth was doing was asking Boaz, as her kinsman-redeemer, to marry her, since spreading the corner of one's garment over someone is a metaphor for marriage (*Ezek.* 16:8). Boaz himself had used similar language in Ruth 2:12 when referring to Ruth coming under the shelter of God's wings. Now Ruth wants Boaz to be as God to her and take her under his protection in marriage.

It is not that Boaz does not want to marry Ruth. He has clearly admired and loved her since he first saw her (3:10–11). But there is a problem – he is not Elimelech's closest relative (3:12). However, he promises Ruth that, if the man will not act as kinsman-redeemer, he will (3:13). Ruth slips home with her shawl filled with barley and tells Naomi everything that went on. Apart from one unforeseen hitch, Naomi's plan is working well, and she knows that Boaz will not rest till he has resolved the matter (3:18).

Naomi was right. Boaz wastes no time in hastening matters and it is not long before we see *Ruth receiving redemption* (4:1–17). At the town gate, where legal business was publicly transacted, and in the presence of ten of Bethlehem's leading citizens who would act as witnesses, Boaz raises with Elimelech's closest relative the matter of buying Elimelech's land. The man, who was probably keen to add to his property portfolio, was initially very interested in the deal. But then Boaz says something unexpected: he tells the man that, along with the property come Naomi and Ruth, and, if he buys the land, he will have to marry Ruth and have a son by her, who will inherit the property. This is completely different. The land would not be part of his inheritance to pass on to his children, and he would have a number of extra mouths to feed. So he speedily backs out.

With Elimelech's closest relative out of the picture, Boaz closes the deal in short order. He gets the land and, more importantly for him, marries Ruth. Then God enables Ruth to conceive and give birth to a son (4:13). Along with Ruth 1:6, Ruth 4:13 is the only time in the book that we read of God's direct intervention in events. These two verses bracket the story, and between them God operates indirectly through his providence. So the sad story which started with three funerals concludes with a wedding and soon a birth. What began with an embittered widow ends with a joyful grandmother cradling her grandson, so that they said, 'Naomi has a son.'

But Ruth is not in the Bible to give us happy feelings; it is there to teach us. So what are RUTH'S LESSONS?

For one thing, Ruth reminds us that *God brings good out of evil.* Ruth's wonderful statement of faith in 1:16–17 would not have been made if 1:1–5 had not taken place. Elimelech's action in taking his family down to Moab is indefensible, but, if he had not done what was wrong, Ruth would never have come to trust in God. God brought good out of evil. This principle is supremely seen in Jesus' death. Out of the most evil act ever carried out by human beings, God, in his gracious sovereignty, brought the greatest good human beings can ever experience (*Acts* 2:23).

The time setting of Ruth informs us that *God always has a people who love him.* The story happens during Israel's Dark Ages (1:1) when things were spiritually and morally grim. Yet, even in the middle of the general defection from God, there were still some people of integrity, like Boaz, who allowed their covenant obligations to shape how they lived. This is the first appearance in the Bible of the 'remnant motif'. Even in the most horrible times, God always has a people who love him and seek to follow him. This remnant motif finds its fulfilment in Jesus (*John* 15:1).

The inclusion of Ruth, a Moabite, into Israel points out that *Gentiles are not beyond the reach of God's love.* God's plan of salvation might come through the Jews, Abraham's descendants, but it was not their exclusive franchise, since God's programme extended to all nations (*Gen.* 12:3). This international and multiethnic scope of God's plan of salvation was achieved through Jesus' death (*Eph.* 2:11–13).

The genealogy (4:18–22), which sets the scene for *the appearance of David and the Davidic royal line*, is the climax of the book. God's promised Saviour would not only be a real human being (*Gen.* 3:15) and a Jew (*Gen.* 12:3), but also one of David's descendants (*2 Sam.* 7:12–16). All this hope of a Saviour is here in embryo form with this snapshot of David's family tree, for Obed, son of Boaz and Ruth, was David's grandfather, and, as a result, one of Jesus' ancestors.

In Ruth we see God working out his programme to bring the blessing of salvation to all nations through the death of Jesus the Messiah. But

God's programme is not like an out-of-control juggernaut, crashing through history unconcerned about the collateral damage it causes. Although he used Naomi's pain to further his programme of salvation – for redemption is always costly, as Jesus' death attests – *God is constantly caring for the individual*. In Ruth, God is operating on two tracks. He is not only concerned for his programme, but he is also concerned for Naomi. At the end of each chapter, the storyline comes back to Naomi and some provision God has sent to encourage her. In chapter 1, Ruth was Naomi's provision, even though her circumstances had blinded her to that fact. In chapter 2, it was twenty-two litres of barley. In chapter 3, it was what Ruth told her after she returned from the threshing floor, and, in chapter 4, it was Obed. God never gets so wrapped up in his immense programme that he forgets individuals.

Finally, Ruth introduces us to the idea of the kinsman-redeemer, and the Bible informs us that *Jesus is our ultimate Kinsman-Redeemer*. The Old Testament kinsman-redeemer had to be a relative, financially able to redeem, willing to do so, and also willing, as in Ruth 4:5, to take a bride. Jesus fulfils all this. He could redeem because he was one of us (*Gal.* 4:4–5), As a result of his total obedience, Jesus is able to redeem, and he was willing to bear the full fury of God's judgment against us because of our sin in order to redeem us. And to top it all, Jesus was willing to take us, in spite of all our wrinkles, spots and blemishes, to be his bride (*Eph.* 5:23).

10

1 Samuel

With 1 Samuel, we arrive at the first of three 'double' books: 1 and 2 Samuel, 1 and 2 Kings, and 1 and 2 Chronicles. In the Hebrew Bible, 1 and 2 Samuel formed one book, because, thanks to Hebrew's compactness, it was able to fit on to a single scroll. However, when the Hebrew Bible was translated into Greek, a translation called the 'Septuagint', the translators found that they needed two scrolls, since Greek is a much bulkier language to write down than Hebrew. So they split the original single book into two, leaving us with the double books of 1 and 2 Samuel. The same thing happened with Kings and Chronicles.

Some suggest that, as well as being named after Samuel, because he is the first major character mentioned in the narrative, the book was partly written and edited by him (see *1 Chron.* 29:29). This might be true, but we just do not know. What is important to us is the text which the Holy Spirit has, in his sovereign wisdom, preserved for us. There is no dispute about its outline: the book tells the story of the transition from the era of the judges to the era of the kings, and from theocracy – when leadership was periodic and need-driven – to monarchy – when leadership was institutional and hereditary. The remarkable transformation from a loose confederacy of tribes to a united kingdom was possible because there was a superpower vacuum in the wider region during this period. This left the door open for a local Israelite leader to bring the various tribes together, which is what Saul tried to do, and David eventually accomplished.

However, we are running ahead of 1 Samuel's storyline. We must go back to the beginning and see how 1 SAMUEL'S PLOT develops. The most straightforward way is to focus on the three main players as they emerge chronologically. The first is *Samuel, the kingmaker* (1:1–10:27). As the book opens, things are not looking good in Israel. Eli, the high priest, is an old man, and Hophni and Phinehas, his two sons, who score minus marks for morality and respect for God's law, are taking advantage of their father's softness towards them to do all sorts of evil (1:3; 2:12–17, 22). However, in the grimness of the situation there is hope because we have seen earlier that God tends to make hopelessness the starting point for something new. And this hope is reinforced by the fact that Hannah, Samuel's mother, was, before God's intervention, infertile. We have previously come across infertile women whose children have become major players in bringing forward God's purposes: Sarah and Isaac, Rebekah and Jacob, Rachel and Joseph, and Manoah's wife and Samson. So, when we read of Samuel being born to the previously childless Hannah in response to prayer, we make a mental note to follow this child's career. God is at work again, and Samuel is certain to be part of the action.

Hannah had promised that, if God gave her a son, she would dedicate him to the Lord's service (1:11), so, when Samuel was weaned, she did what she had said she would do and took Samuel to live with Eli in the Tabernacle, which was located at Shiloh, to act as his companion and apprentice. It was there that God one night commissioned Samuel to be his prophet (3:1–21). As he prayed Samuel was given God's message to speak (3:10–14), and this set the pattern for his ministry. His very name, 'Heard by God', reminded everyone that God answers prayer. Through prayer, Samuel brought about spiritual renewal in the nation's life (7:5–6) and achieved victory over the Philistines, Israel's nemesis (7:7–11). People knew that when Samuel prayed, things happened (12:16–18). He saw praying for them as one of the most important ways in which he could serve the Israelites (12:23). Alongside of his reputation as a man of prayer, Samuel had the name of being a man of God's Word: everyone knew from an early stage in his ministry that God spoke through him (3:20–4:1). It was as he prayed that Samuel received the prophetic word from the Lord to pass on to others (8:6–7, 21–22; 15:11–16). The depth of Samuel's spirituality is seen in the way he ended his ministry as he began it, something that not all great

Christian leaders do, with the twin commitment to prayer and God's Word (3:10–18; 12:1–25).

Samuel's ministry was conducted against the backround of ongoing Philistine aggression against Israel. The Philistines had settled in the south-western coastal strip of Canaan around 1200 BC, and their superior military technology of iron chariots and weapons gave them the edge over the Israelites in battle. From their bases in Ashkelon, Ashdod, Gath, Ekron and Gaza, they expanded their influence deep into Israelite territory. Samson, and then Samuel, had had some success against them, but like a nagging toothache the Philistine threat never went away. It was to solve the Philistine problem that senior Israelite figures came to Samuel to ask him to appoint a king over the nation. Samuel was too old for fighting and his sons had neither the competence nor the trust of the people to lead Israel against the old enemy (8:5).

Samuel was unhappy with the request. It is often said that this was because he saw the request as a rejection of God and his rule (see *1 Sam.* 8:7). But there was another reason. It had always been God's plan for Israel to be ruled by a king. Even in the Garden of Eden God ruled his creation through a human king – Adam. His promise to Abraham that some of his descendants would be kings (*Gen.* 17:6) would not have made sense if God had not always planned that there should be an Israelite king. Even before Israel invaded Canaan, God had given instructions as to how future Israelite kings should behave (*Deut.* 17:14–20). It was not the request for a king that angered Samuel but the kind of king they were asking for. God wanted a king whose rule would reflect his own. The human king was to reflect the divine King's good, positive, beneficial, life-affirming and peace-bringing rule. But that was not the kind of king Israel wanted. They wanted a king 'such as all the other nations have' (8:5). One of the disastrous consequences of the Fall was a redefinition of the idea of rule. The people hankered after a secular type of king. Samuel saw their request as a rejection of God's idea of rule, and a sell-out to Satan's twisted view of kingship. Samuel warned the people that if they went for the kind of king they wanted, he would exploit them (8:11–18), but they paid no attention. Samuel was, in their estimation, a throwback to a bygone age, standing in the way of progress. So reluctantly, but in obedience to God, Samuel complied with the people's request.

The people's desire for a king paved the way for the appearance of *Saul, the first Israelite king* (11:1–35; 28:3–25; 31:1–13). Because they wanted a king to lead them into battle against the Philistines, Saul measured up. He was the sort of person everyone looked up to, literally (9:2). When he was anointed king, nearly everyone was enthusiastic and approving (10:24–27). But soon the Ammonites attacked Jabesh Gilead and imposed some nasty surrender terms on its inhabitants (11:1–2). Saul rushed to its rescue and won a spectacular victory (11:4–11). In doing so he repaid a long-standing debt that his tribe, Benjamin, owed to Jabesh Gilead for saving it from dying out (*Judg.* 21). Saul's success at Jabesh Gilead brought even the sceptics on board. He enjoyed the total loyalty of the whole nation (11:12–15). Victories over the Philistines at Michmash and over an Amalekite raiding party (13:23–14:48) reninforced his position.

Nevertheless, after this promising start, Saul's reign began to collapse. He mustered his troops for a big offensive against the Philistines, but, when Samuel failed to arrive when he said he would because a Philistine counter-offensive had delayed him, Saul panicked and offered a sacrifice (13:6–13), which he should not have done. Then, in attacking the Amalekites, he deliberately chose not to carry out God's command to destroy them totally (15:1–9). God intended this attack to enact his judgment on the Amalekites for their sin. Everything and everyone was to be slaughtered. But instead Saul spared the Amalekite king and the best of the rest. Instead of divine retribution for sin, it now looked more like a grubby smash-and-grab reprisal raid. As a result, Samuel announces God's judgment on Saul: the kingdom is going to be taken from him and his family and given to someone who would reflect God's rule (13:14; 15:22–23, 26–29). Samuel's worst nightmares had come true in Saul: his rule reflected human ideals of kingship and not God's.

Saul's reign splutters on for many years, unravelling all the time, and it reaches a tragic and bloody conclusion when the Israelite army, under his command, is cut to ribbons by the Philistines at Mount Gilboa (31:1). Saul commits suicide rather than be captured, and his sons, including

Jonathan, are among the Israelite fatalities (31:2–4). The next day the Philistines mutilate Saul's body, decapitate it, strip off the armour and fasten his headless carcase to the walls of Beth Shan. This is a dark, dark day for God's kingdom. The gory head paraded through Philistine territory belonged to the Lord's anointed king. The corpses scattered all over Gilboa belonged to soldiers in the Lord's army. If the king and his army were disgraced, so was their God. There is deep sadness throughout Israel that Saul is dead, but there should be even deeper sadness that God is being ridiculed. This is why the Bible's verdict on Saul is so damning: if kingship in Israel was designed to reflect God's rule and bring applause to him, Saul was an abject failure. When his reign ended in humiliating defeat, God's glory was tarnished.

God's rejection of Saul meant that a new king had to be found and it is against that backdrop that we are introduced to 1 and 2 Samuel's main character. In 1 Samuel 16:1–30:31, we come across him as *David, the king in waiting*. At the start of 1 Samuel 16, God told Samuel to stop mourning over Saul and go to Bethlehem to anoint one of Jesse's sons as the new king. When Jesse's boys were paraded in front of him, Samuel was about to use the same criterion for choosing a king as he had done with Saul, thinking that Eliab, the most physically impressive, was the ideal choice. But God overruled him (13:14; 16:7). David was the Lord's surprise choice. As Samuel emptied his horn of oil over David's head, God's Spirit entered him, equipping him for the task that lay ahead. But what lay ahead was conflict because, as with Jesus (*Mark* 1:9–13) and with Christians (*Gal.* 5:16–17), the coming of the Spirit quickly leads to conflict.

Things were never the same again for David. Soon he entered Saul's service as an armour-bearer (16:21), and a music therapist whose skill on the harp brought Saul relief when he was tormented by an evil spirit (16:23). But what brought David into the public gaze was the confrontation between Israelite and Philistine forces across the Elah Valley (17:1–3). Twice a day for forty days, Goliath of Gath, the imposing champion of the Philistine army, challenged any Israelite with enough courage to single combat in which the winner took all (17:4–10; 16). Only David grasped the real issue. Goliath was not just defying men; he was challenging the God of Israel (17:26). David would, with God's help, put a stop to his blasphemy (17:36–37). After jettisoning Saul's armour, David advanced against Goliath clothed in the armour of God. The actual combat did not last long, as Goliath's state-of-the-art military hardware was no match for David's divinely-directed and propelled slingshot. His first shot stopped Goliath dead in his tracks and his massive bulk came crashing to the ground. David quickly used the giant's sword to chop off his head. A famous victory had been won.

From that moment David became the rising star of Saul's army (18:5). Not only did he gain rapid promotion, he forged a deep-seated and life-long friendship with Jonathan, Saul's son (18:1); he married into the royal family (18:20–27); and he saw his popularity with the public soar (18:6–7). While David was upwardly mobile, it was obvious that Saul was on the slide, and it seemed clear that David would become king sooner rather than later. But once again events took an unexpected turn. Saul's suspicion and jealousy of David erupted into attacks on him. Twice Saul tried to pin David to the wall with a spear, but missed (18:10–11). Saul sent David on an almost-suicidal military raid, hoping the Philistines would do his dirty work for him (18:24–25). When that scheme backfired, Saul ordered his servants to kill David (19:1).

David had to go on the run, and the final chapters of 1 Samuel record how Saul relentlessly hunted him down all over the southern part of the country. Things became so threatening that David slipped across the border into Philistine country, where he and his men signed up as mercenaries in the service of Achish, one of the Philistine overlords (27). Yet, throughout this period, in all the near-misses with Saul and actions driven more by fear than by faith, David could not have been safer than he was. He was in the Lord's hands, under his protection, and there was no way that God was going to let his promise to David fail. During this challenging time, David enjoyed the friendship, spiritual encouragement and advocacy of Jonathan. Jonathan knew that David would be king and not he, but his gracious humble submission to God's purposes stands in stark contrast to his father's embittered raging against what God had decreed. Jonathan is one of 1 Samuel's heroes, laying aside a kingdom he could not have to enter a kingdom he could not lose. On two occasions, David had the opportunity to kill Saul (24:1–22; 26:1–25) but he refused to lay a finger on him because he was the Lord's anointed (24:6; 26:9). David was not only committed to God's plan for his life, but also to God's timing in his life. God's time for David finally arrived with Saul's death on Mount Gilboa. The king in waiting could finally ascend to his throne.

Throughout the book there are clear POINTERS TO JESUS. It is in 1 Samuel that we come across the motif of prophet, priest and king. Judges has already familiarized us with the idea of warrior–judges who were kings in all but name. However, in 1 Samuel, we encounter Eli who, as well as being Israel's high priest, is also Israel's judge (4:18). Samuel was the last of Israel's judges (7:15), but also universally recognized as a prophet (4:1). If we trace the prophet, priest and king motif to its terminal point, we find that they merge together in Jesus, whom the New Testament writers depict as carrying out at the same time the function of God's final prophet (*Mark* 9:7; *Heb.* 1:1–2), God's great High Priest (*Heb.* 4:14) and God's ultimate king (*Psa.* 2:6–7; *Mark* 1:11).

The main pointer to Jesus comes in the way the biblical text presents David, not as an ordinary man, but always as the Lord's anointed. If we view what 1 Samuel says about him through this lens, we find ourselves face to face with Jesus, who is the culminating point of the Bible's concept of the Lord's anointed (*Psa.* 2:1–2; *Acts* 4:25–27). Seeing David's victory over Goliath through this lens keeps us from missing the point of the story. Often it is understood as encouraging us to stand firm in God's strength against all the 'Goliaths' which invade our lives. But that is not what this incident is about. As the Lord's anointed, David represents his people. If he wins, they win, but if he loses, they lose. David triumphs and the Israelites share in the consequences of his victory – freedom, at least for a while, from Philistine oppression. We need to skip forward about a thousand years from the Elah Valley to the Hill of the Skull outside Jerusalem. On the cross, Jesus, the Lord's definitive Anointed, dies, not as an ordinary individual, but as the representative of his people. In his death, he wins a crushing victory over Satan, sin and death, and, as a result, we share, by faith in him alone, in the benefits of his achievement (*Rom.* 5:12–21).

During the fugitive phase of David's life, Saul was so fixated with killing him that he neglected his duty to look after his people. While he was rampaging all over the place trying to hunt David down, Saul was failing to guard the Israelites from being attacked by enemies. Into this security vacuum stepped David. If Saul would not protect the Israelites he would, and he gathered around him a group of formidable fighters who gave the Israelites the protection Saul should have given them (23:1–6; 24:4–7; 27:8). There are parallels to this in Jesus' ministry. The Jewish religious authorities were so set on getting rid of Jesus that even old traditional divisions were put on one side (*Mark* 3:6, 11:18, 12:12, 41:1). But in their diabolical obsession with destroying Jesus, they were neglecting their duty to give the people spiritual leadership. Jesus filled this spiritual void by gathering people around him to teach them God's ways, something the Jewish religious authorities should have done (*Mark* 4:1; 6:6, 34; 11:18; 12:37).

It is in David as the king in waiting that we see another pointer to Jesus. Although he was the Lord's anointed king (16:1–13), David had to wait many years before he actually ascended to the throne over all Israel (2 *Sam.* 5:4). During that period, some, like Jonathan and Abigail (25:30), recognized his kingship, but most did not, especially if they were connected with Saul or were trying to gain his favour. Throughout his time on earth, Jesus was the king in waiting. He was anointed king at his baptism, but it was not until after his death and resurrection that he ascended to his throne (*Phil.* 2:9–11). During this time, Jesus' claim to be God's king was recognized by some, usually those who were on the margins or even outsiders (*Matt.* 2:11; *Mark* 10:46–47; 15:39). However, the major players rejected Jesus' kingship, and their rejection of him reached rock bottom when they clamoured for his death (*John* 19:13–16).

11

2 *Samuel*

This book's English title, 2 Samuel, is rather misleading as it has nothing to do with Samuel. This reminds us that the English Bible's two books of 1 and 2 Samuel were originally one in the Hebrew Bible, and that single book was called *Samuel* after its first main character. The focus of 2 Samuel is David, Israel's second and greatest king. David is one of the Bible's major figures. Sixty-one chapters (1 Samuel 16–1 Kings 2 and 1 Chronicles 11–29) are allocated to telling the story of his career and reign. The Bible software package I use records 1,127 mentions of his name in the Bible, fifty-eight of which are in the New Testament. In addition he is the human author of a large segment of the Bible with seventy-three out of the 150 Psalms directly attributed to him, although it is likely that he also composed other Psalms which do not bear his name.

The story of David's reign opens with the record of THE KING'S TRIUMPHS (1–10). When news of the military disaster at Gilboa reaches him, far from being ecstatic that the waiting is over and he can now become king, David is distraught. Saul and Jonathan are dead, and, worst of all, God's name is disgraced with the destruction of the Lord's army (1:11–12). Using his musical talents, David composes a moving lament for Saul and Jonathan (1:17–27). After securing God's approval, David's initial move is to set himself up as king of Judah in Hebron (2:1–7).

Although God's consent signalled the legitimacy of David's kingdom, not everyone recognized that, and Ish-Bosheth, one of Saul's surviving sons, set up a rival kingdom, so that, for several years, the nation was engulfed in a civil war. Victory for David was guaranteed when Abner, Ish-Bosheth's chief of staff, switched sides, but, whatever political gain Abner hoped to secure by the move did not materialize because Joab,

David's chief of staff, assassinated him in revenge for Abner having killed Asahel, Joab's brother. The tide moved further in David's favour when Ish-Bosheth was murdered (2:8–4:13), and it was not long before representatives came to David in Hebron, asking him to become king over the whole nation (5:1–2). When David accepted and was anointed king (5:3–5), God's promise to him had finally become a reality.

The next two chapters describe three events which, on the surface, could be seen as smart moves on David's part to consolidate his rule over the nation and unite Israel; but, as we shall see, they are much more than this. Hebron, his current base, was too far south: he needed a more central location for his new administration. So, using the city's water system to gain entry into what seemed an impregnable stronghold, David captured Jerusalem from the Jebusites (5:1–6). It became the nation's new capital and was known as 'The City of David'. David's rise to power sent alarm bells ringing throughout Philistia. The Philistines knew from bitter experience how formidable an opponent David was, and, with him as king, they saw their control over Israel slipping away. So they mobilized a large army to crush David before he had time to settle. However, the Philistines were thoroughly defeated in two battles (5:17–25), and David was able to put an end to Philistine interference in Israel's affairs. After the Philistine threat was removed, David brought the Ark of the Covenant to Jerusalem (6:1–23). All Israel joined together in the celebrations and the sense of unity in the nation was almost tangible, although David's enthusiasm did result in a domestic row in the palace.

To see these events as just politically astute ways of bringing a disunited people together is to miss the whole point of what was going on. In each case David was bringing God's promises to realization and carrying out God's commands to perfection. In Genesis 15:18–21, as part of the covenant promises he made to Abraham, God said that he would give 'the land of the . . . Jebusites' to his people. The capture of Jerusalem was part of the fulfilment of God's covenant promise. In the time of Samson, God promised that he would begin to rescue his people from Philistine oppression (*Judg.* 13:5). This was continued through Samuel and Saul, but it was not until David decisively crushed the Philistines twice in the Valley of Rephaim that God's promise was finally fulfilled. In Deuteronomy 12:1–14, 20–25, God comanded that, when his people had settled in the land of promise and were at peace, his worship should be centred at one place. In bringing the Ark of the Covenant to Jerusalem, and in his plans to build a temple for God in Jerusalem (7:1–2), David was simply carrying out God's commands. So we should view the events of 2 Samuel 5–6 as a display of David's love for God, a love expressed in joyful obedience to God's commands and wholehearted trust in God's covenant promises.

Then, in 2 Samuel 7, David's story takes a giant leap forward. David was concerned that he was living in a palace while the ark of God was still housed in a tent. So he planned to build a temple, a more permanent residence for it. However, God had other plans for David, something more significant than building a temple. God entered into a covenant with David that from one of his descendants he would raise up a king who would rule over God's people for ever (7:12–16). If you compare 2 Samuel 7:12 with Genesis 15:4, you will immediately see that God's covenant with David was connected to his covenant with Abraham, which, in turn, was linked to Genesis 3:15. The promised Saviour would not only be a real human being (*Gen.* 3:15) and a descendant of Abraham (*Gen.* 12:3), but also a direct descendant of David. David wanted to build a house, a temple, for God, but instead God promises to build a house, a dynasty, for David, which will last for ever because out of it will come the promised Saviour of the world.

This section of 2 Samuel recording the king's triumphs ends with a list of David's achievements. Through military conquest (8:1–14; 10:1–19) and competent administration (8:15–18), David ruled over a small empire that stretched from the Euphrates in the north to the Gulf of Aqaba in the south. But the record of David's achievements reaches its peak in 2 Samuel 9 in the gracious way he treated Mephibosheth, one of Jonathan's sons. God's king not only does what is 'just and right' (8:15); he supremely rules in grace, reflecting God's covenant generosity towards his people.

Unfortunately the story of David's reign does not end on this high note because the next section records THE KING'S SIN (11–12). Sadly, the story reads uncomfortably like the front page of a Sunday tabloid, but this is God's king, not some pagan philanderer. Questions about what David was doing stack up in our minds. Why was he not leading his army? Why was he pampering and indulging himself? Did he not know that the devil finds work for idle hands to do? But what happened next is truly horrifying. He broke the tenth commandment by coveting his neighbour's wife (11:2–3); the seventh by sleeping with Bathsheba (11:4); the eighth by robbing Uriah of his wife and Bathsheba of her dignity (11:4); the ninth by trying to cover up his sin (11:6–13); and, most sinister of all, the sixth because when the honourable and loyal Uriah would not do as David hoped he might, David engineered his death (11:14–17). When the despicable deed was done and Uriah dead, and after a respectable period of mourning, David took Bathsheba as his wife, and she gave birth to their son (11:26–27a). David must have thought that he had got away with it as the only person in on the sordid affair was Joab, and he had too many skeletons in his own cupboard to accuse David. But, as the end of chapter 11 points out, someone else knew exactly what was going on, and he was not pleased, nor was he going to ignore the situation.

God sent Nathan to confront David by telling him a story which would rouse David's anger and sense of justice. Nathan's tale of a rich man who would not use any of his considerable assets to feed an unexpected guest but took a poor man's pet lamb and barbecued it instead made David explode with rage (12:1–6). When God, through Nathan, had David exactly where he wanted him, he delivered the decisive stroke: 'You are the man!' (12:7). David's sin was out in the open. He poured out his heart to God in prayers of repentance, which he recorded in Psalms 32 and 51 for our instruction, and for our use too, as we are all sinners who need to repent daily.

In his grace, God answered David's prayers and forgave him. But David's sin had consequences for the rest of his life. It was like the effects of throwing a stone into a pond: the stone may be retrieved, but the ripples cannot be. So the final section of the story of David's reign records THE KING'S TROUBLES (13–24). As God had said through Nathan (12:10), the repercussions of David's appalling actions spread far and wide, affecting more than the immediate participants. The first to feel the effects was the baby boy, who died after a week-long illness (12:15–19). But worse was to come: Amnon, David's eldest son (3:2), raped Tamar, his half-sister (13:1–20). David was furious (13:21), but his sin with Bathsheba tied his hands. Then Absalom, another of David's sons and Tamar's brother, took matters into his own hands. On Absalom's orders, his servants murdered Amnon in revenge for the rape of his sister. Then Absalom escaped for fear of reprisals (13:23–39). Absalom need not have worried, for David had a soft spot for him; and Absalom soon took advantage of David's lenient attitude towards him to mount a full-scale rebellion against his father which came very close to succeeding (15:1–18:33). Later Sheba, a Benjamite, led another rebellion (20:1–26). Israel's peace and cohesion had been shattered as a result of David's sin.

The final chapters of 2 Samuel (21–24) are more than a miscellaneous appendix. They are carefully structured – an atonement story, a warrior list, a song, another song, a warrior list and an atonement story – and this should alert us to their significance. These chapters show us how we are to view God's kingdom as it was ordered by David. The two atonement stories, the avenging of the Gibeonites (21:1–14) and the census (24:1–25), are often labelled barbaric and senseless, but this must be challenged. The avenging of the Gibeonites reminds us that covenant-breaking is serious (*Josh.* 9; 21:2) and that atonement is bloody and ugly, truths displayed supremely in Jesus' death as he bore the penalty of our covenant-breaking. When David, against the advice of Joab, conducted the census, the wrath it provoked in the form of a devastating plague was only dealt with by an atoning sacrifice. We know that the place where God's wrath was ultimately felt in all its fury was not far from Araunah's threshing floor. There, enveloped by the darkness of God's judgment (*Mark* 15:33), Jesus bore the penalty, made propitiation, and, with his cry of desertion, brought the darkness to an end (*Mark* 15:34).

David's claim to fame in the unfolding of the Bible's storyline is not as a military genius, a gifted singer-songwriter, or a charismatic leader behind whom a disunited nation could rally. His significance lies in his being the Lord's anointed, a theme which crops up again and again in 1 and 2 Samuel. It is as the Lord's anointed that David POINTS TO JESUS, the Lord's Anointed. As the Lord's anointed, David constantly battled against the enemies of God's people. As the Lord's Anointed, Jesus, the ultimate warrior (*Isa.* 9:6), engaged in constant warfare with Satan and the powers of darkness, culminating in the fiercest of all battles on the cross. While David had a formidable military machine backing him up, spearheaded by his brave warriors (21:15–22; 23:8–39), it was in the weakness of his death that Jesus broke the power of all his enemies (*Col.* 2:15). At the opposite end of the spectrum from his successes, David's failures also point to Jesus. Even Israel's greatest king was flawed. His sin with Bathsheba left a nasty stain on his reign. This gave rise to the longing: when would there be a king over God's people who would be just and right always, with no skeletons in the royal cupboard? This could only happen when Jesus appeared in Galilee, announcing that God's kingdom had burst on the scene of history, because he, God's just and righteous king, had come (*Mark* 1:14–15).

Jesus is the embodiment of God's promises to David. It is in this way that David points us to Jesus. Over and over again the New Testament presents Jesus as the king who is the fulfilment of God's covenant with David. The announcement of Jesus' birth suggests the proclamation of a royal birth (*Matt.* 2:2; *Luke* 1:31–33; 2:11). From a human perspective, Jesus can trace his family tree directly back to David (*Matt.* 1:1–17). He is born in Bethlehem, David's home town (*Luke* 2:1–7). Jesus' preferred self–designation was 'Son of Man', which, from its roots in Daniel 7:13–14, is a royal title as well as a divine one. The central theme of his preaching was the kingdom of God. Jesus' miracles were windows into the blessings that would abound where he, the king, reigned. His parables were parables of the kingdom, explaining its operating principles.

The way Jesus entered Jerusalem on the Sunday before his death not only sent shock waves through the Jewish political and religious establishment but fulfilled the Old Testament prophecy about God's king riding into Jerusalem on a donkey (*Zech.* 9:9). He was executed for being a king, as the notice which Pilate had fastened to his cross indicated (*John* 19:19). Yet the cross was the battlefield on which he won his most spectacular kingly victory, crushing sin, death and Satan. The cross was also the throne from which he reigned as the victorious king (*John* 19:30). He rose in kingly triumph from the grave, having conquered all his enemies. Jesus ascended back to heaven and sits at God's right hand in the position of supreme authority in the universe (*Psa.* 2:6–9; 24:7–10; *Phil.* 2:9–11; *Rev.* 5:5; 7:17). He sends his church to announce everywhere his kingly victory and to summon everyone to surrender to his authority (*Matt.* 28:18–20; *Acts* 17:30). One day, Jesus will return as the King of kings and Lord of lords (*Rev.* 19:16) to judge the living and the dead, and, on that day, everyone will realize beyond a shadow of doubt that Jesus is the Lord's Anointed, God's ultimate king (*Rev.* 1:7).

12

1 Kings

I have two confessions to make. The first is that I am one of those annoying people who often read the last chapter of a novel to see where the story ends. If you do that with 1 Kings, you will find that it finishes at a seemingly random point. Most of Elijah's story is told in 1 Kings, but some of it spills over into 2 Kings, and, while Ahaziah's reign is recorded in 2 Kings, his accession to the throne is mentioned in the last three verses of 1 Kings. This apparently arbitrary divison reminds us that our 1 Kings and 2 Kings originally was one book in the Hebrew Bible. It had to be divided in two when it was translated into Greek because it was too big to fit on one scroll.

My second confession is that I used to be a history teacher. Somebody had to do it! As I look at 1 and 2 Kings with my history teacher's glasses on, I find the material included in these two books fascinating. They cover roughly three hundred and seventy years, from the transition of power to Solomon in about 931 BC (1:1–2:12) to the release of Jehoiachin from prison during the Exile in about 562/561 BC (2 *Kings* 25:27–30). While not every single event and character can be covered, some get lots of space and others are just noted in passing. The author of 1 and 2 Kings, whose name we do not know, is interested in *chronology*, which is the backbone of historical writing. We see this from the attention he gives to telling us how long each king reigned and who his contemporary in the other kingdom was. Even Zimri, the seven-day king, has the same treatment as others who ruled for much longer (16:15). But chronology was not his main interest: *theology* was. He has another criterion for the weight he gives to various people than the fact that they were there. The crucial factor was the impact they had on the worship of God. We can see this in the book's storyline if we take a quick look at the reigns of Omri, Israel's sixth king, and Ahab, his son. From a secular perspective, Omri's reign was successful. He built a new capital city in Samaria, exerted so much political influence that for the next one hundred and fifty years the Assyrians referred to Israel as 'the land of Omri', and established a new dynasty, so that his son succeeded him, something that not many kings of Israel achieved. But his reign only gets eight verses in 1 Kings (16:21–28) because, judged by the author's theological criterion, Omri was a minor player. By contrast, Ahab, who was, from a secular perspective, a poor ruler, hardly deserving a footnote, has more than five chapters devoted to him. The reason is the impact his reign had on the worship of God. This pathetically weak man allowed Jezebel, his bossy Phoenician wife, to bully him into replacing the worship of God with the worship of Baal, her god, as Israel's state religion. As you read through 1 and 2 Kings, remember that, while you are looking at events that really happened and people who really lived, the story is being told through a theological lens.

The material which the author includes in 1 Kings falls into three main parts. The first could be labelled the record of A PARTIAL KING-DOM (1–11). The transition of power from David to Solomon was not smooth and seamless. Adonijah, David's oldest son, seeing his father's increasing frailty, tried to grab power. He was ambitious (1:5a), had style (1:5b) and the right image (1:6), and was supported by leading figures within the military and the religious establishment (1:7, 9). But Nathan, loyal to David, heard of Adonijah's coup and told Bathsheba, Solomon's mother, and David. David still had enough of his wits about him to grasp what was going on, and he ordered that Solomon should immediately be anointed king, thus keeping his promise to Bathsheba (1:29–40). Although now king, Solomon's hold on power was in doubt as Adonijah and his co-conspirators were still around. But, when Adonijah foolishly made another play for power – which is what his request to marry Abishag was all about – and when Shimei broke his conditions of bail, Solomon pounced. With a ruthlessness which makes us wince, he had Adonijah, Joab and Shimei executed, and Abiathar, one of Adonijah's close supporters, had his death sentence commuted to banishment (2:13–46a). The upshot of all this retribution is that all with the potential to undermine his rule were eliminated and Solomon's position as David's successor was secure (2:46b).

When this bloody succession crisis was over, Solomon embarked on a reign that turned out to be the high watermark of the Israelite monarchy. David's military victories ensured that during Solomon's time the nation enjoyed a period of unprecedented peace (4:25). The peace dividend was considerable. Israel's population exploded (4:20), and political stability resulted in a trade boom. The wealth generated by it led to an affluence never experienced before (10:27). Solomon brought greater cohesion to the nation by putting into place a new administrative structure (4:7–19), which he hoped would sort out the old north/south tensions that still simmered beneath the surface, tensions that Absalom had used when he rebelled against David (2 *Sam.* 15:1–16). Solomon now expanded his empire until he ruled over an area which extended from the Euphrates to the north and east, and the Mediterranean in the west, to the Egyptian border in the south (4:21). Just in case any of his dependent territories stepped out of line, Solomon kept a large standing army. He made Israel an international player by forging alliances with the surrounding nations, alliances that he usually sealed by a marriage (3:1).

The author of 1 Kings applauds Solomon for his economic, political, administrative and diplomatic achievements, but what he concentrates on is his flair as a builder. He built many impressive structures such as the Palace of the Forest of Lebanon, which took him thirteen years to complete (7:1–12). But the most important of Solomon's building works – and remember the lens through which the author looks – was the Temple. The author spends four chapters (5–8) describing its planning, construction, decoration and dedication. The Temple was important because of what God wanted in terms of the centralization of his worship (*Deut.* 12:5). As Christians, we should note that the Temple was designed by God himself to anticipate Jesus' saving activity. This was where God dwelt with his people, and, in Jesus, God dwells with us as Immanuel (*John* 1:14). The Temple sacrifices foreshadowed Jesus' death on the cross, and its priesthood, particularly the office of High Priest, pointed forward to Jesus' high-priestly activity.

The author of 1 Kings is very clear that everything Solomon had and achieved was a gift from God. After telling us how he secured his grip on power, the author recounts the crucial incident in Solomon's life (3:1–15). In a dream God promised to give him whatever he wanted. What a blank cheque of a promise! Solomon wisely asked for wisdom rather than power, wealth, health or security. His choice so pleased God that he also gave him the things he did not ask for. Solomon soon displayed his wisdom, one example being the rather unorthodox but effective way in which he settled a custody dispute between two prostitutes (3:16–28). His reputation for wisdom soon attracted visitors from abroad (4:34), including the Queen of Sheba (10:1–13), who found all she saw and heard massively impressive. At the end of Matthew 12 Jesus praises this lady for the way she listened to Solomon's wisdom. Then he contrasts her with his own generation's careless treatment of him (*Matt.* 12:42). On the day of judgment her avid attention to Solomon's wisdom will condemn those who fail to submit to the authority of Jesus, a person greater by far than Solomon.

The prosperity of Solomon's reign probably fuelled speculation that Israel was witnessing the fulfilment of God's Genesis 12:2–3 promises. The statement of 1 Kings 4:20 definitely refers back to Genesis 32:12. God was with his people at the Temple. His blessing was obviously upon the country. Nations were coming to listen to Solomon's wisdom. The way the boundaries of Solomon's empire are outlined in 1 Kings 4:21 sounds similar to Exodus 23:31. It seemed that God's covenant promises of people, presence, protection and a programme were becoming a reality. Unfortunately Solomon's reign was only a partial kingdom because, just when people were wondering what could possibly go wrong, everything began to go wrong. Solomon set a pattern that was repeated in the lives of the good kings who followed him: he started off well, but finished poorly. Cracks began to appear in Israel due to the crippling level of taxation and the forced labour needed for his grand building projects. But the wives Solomon took were his real downfall (11:1, 3). His actions were in direct violation of God's commands (11:2; *Deut.* 7:3–4) and they brought coldness into his relationship with God (11:4). If that was not disastrous enough, Solomon began to worship these idols (11:5–10). The author of 1 Kings does not mince his words. Solomon's marital adventures led to spiritual apostasy, and this sounded the death-knell for his kingdom (11:11–13).

With 1 Kings 12 we come to the second section of material. It is short, but we should not be fooled by its size. It records a key moment in the history of the Israelite monarchy, the appearance of A SPLIT KINGDOM. The closing years of Solomon's reign saw several rebellions against his rule (11:14–40), but Rehoboam, Solomon's son and successor, was so politically inept that he could not see the reasons for the discontent. When he arrived at Shechem to be made king (12:1), he expected it to be a formality, but Jeroboam, son of Nebat, had other ideas. He had returned from exile in Egypt where he had fled after an unsuccessful revolt and now asked the new king to ease the burdens Solomon had imposed (12:4). Rehoboam consulted with Israel's grandees, his father's advisors. They suggested some concessions, which would end the complaints and win popular support (12:6–7). But that was not what Rehoboam wanted to hear, so he consulted his contemporaries, who advised a very hard line (12:8–10).

When Rehoboam spat out his vulgar, arrogant reply to the people's request, the plan to create a new breakaway kingdom fell into place (12:16). Ten northern tribes split away from Judah and Benjamin to form a new kingdom, called Israel, with Jeroboam as the first king. Rehoboam continued to rule over the two southern tribes. His kingdom was called Judah and was centred on Jerusalem. What ultimately caused the split? The author of 1 Kings is in no doubt. It came about because of the word of the Lord (12:15). God was behind it. The arrogance and ambition of both Rehoboam and Jeroboam were used to bring about his purposes. Human pride and selfishness might seem to prevail, but God is in charge. It is this truth which keeps Christians sane when sin seems to be running amok: behind the scenes, God is in control.

Understandably, there were tensions between the two kingdoms, which often erupted into border skirmishes and sometimes war. But the most terrible consequence of the split was not the political division of the nation, but the religious rupture that took place. Jeroboam was afraid that, if his subjects continued to go to Jerusalem to worship at the Temple, their loyalty to him would fade. So for purely political reasons Jeroboam set up a whole new religious system, based on the worship of two golden calves – one in Dan and the other in Bethel (12:26–33). Jeroboam returning from Egypt might have looked like a new Moses, but he turned out to be a new Aaron, for what he did has Exodus 32 written all over it. The author of 1 Kings, whose concern is the worship of God, is indignant at Jeroboam's sham religion (12:30). None of Israel's subsequent sixteen kings did anything to put an end to it but continued to use it to further their political ends. So they are written off by the author as following in 'the sins of Jeroboam'. Even Zimri, who was only king for a week before Omri killed him, does not escape condemnation (16:19).

The final part of 1 Kings runs from chapter 13 through to chapter 22, and could be called DETERIORATING KINGDOMS. Reading through this section can be confusing. The author adopts the 'baseline rally' approach by switching from one kingdom to the other, alternating between the kings of Judah and the kings of Israel. To add to the potential confusion there are two Jeroboams in one kingdom, a Rehoboam in the other who is a contemporary of one of the Jeroboams, and a Jehoram, or Joram, in both kingdoms at about the same time, not to mention two Ahaziahs.

Let me try to make things a little less complex by taking the kings of Judah and Israel separately. The 1 Kings' *kings of Judah*, the southern kingdom, were Rehoboam, Abijam, Asa and Jehoshaphat. They were very different personalities, but they were all – and this is important for the author of 1 Kings – Davidic kings. Yet although all four could trace their family tree back to David, only Asa and Jehoshaphat were said to have shared David's faith (15:11; 22:43).

While the kings of Judah were a mixture of good and bad, the 1 Kings' *kings of Israel*, the northern kingdom – Jeroboam I, Nadab, Baasha, Elah, Zimri, Omri, Ahab and Ahaziah – were all bad. However, the worst was Ahab, and the closing chapters of 1 Kings focus on his calamitous reign. He married Jezebel, an outright pagan from Phoenicia, modern Lebanon, and sitting quietly in the background, doing nothing but smiling sweetly, was the last thing on her mind. Not only did this domineering woman bulldoze Ahab into worshipping Baal, she also got him to make Baal worship the official state religion (16:31–33). God's answer to this swaggering, high-handed, government-sponsored paganism was Elijah, who suddenly appears and announces God's judgment on the nation for its covenant unfaithfulness: God is suspending rainfall until further notice (*Deut.* 28:22). Ahab searches high and low for Elijah, hoping that he might find him and get him to reverse the curse, but God protects him, hiding him, first of all, in the isolation of the Kerith (or Cherith) Ravine, where he is fed by food-carrying ravens (17:2–6), and then in the last place Ahab would think of looking for him, in Jezebel's backyard, where a widow from the Phoenician village of Zarephath provides him with food from a flour jar that miraculously never runs out (17:7–24).

After three and a half years of the most severe drought, God told Elijah that he was going to send rain, but not before he had demonstrated that he alone was God (18:1). Elijah organized a contest between himself and Jezebel's prophets of Baal at Mount Carmel. It was very straightforward: both sides would prepare a sacrifice but not light it, and the God who sent fire from heaven would be shown to be the true God (18:23–24). No matter what the prophets of Baal did to get Baal to send fire, there was not even the flicker of a spark (18:26–29). After they had exhausted themselves, it was Elijah's turn. He rebuilt God's altar, prepared the sacrifice, and then to make sure no one would think that chance was involved, he poured gallons of water over the sacrifice until it was extremely soggy and totally incombustible (18:30–35). Then Elijah prayed (18:36–37), and God sent fire to incinerate the sacrifice (18:38). Everyone knew that there was only one God in Israel, and it was not Baal (18:39). To underscore God's total victory over Baal, Baal's prophets were slaughtered (18:40) and God – not Baal – sent rain in response to Elijah's prayer (18:41–46). The drama on Mount Carmel may not have altered the religious situation much, because, after all, Ahab was still king, but it put down a marker that God was still in control and that, if his people continued to turn their backs on him and their covenant obligation to worship him alone, judgment was not far away.

As for POINTERS TO JESUS, we can see a pencil sketch of Jesus' kingdom in Solomon's golden age – the peace, blessings and presence of God all foreshadow Christ's glorious reign. However, even the great Solomon was flawed. Under the influence of his pagan wives he drifted increasingly from God's ideal for kingship. In Deuteronomy 17:14–17, God set out three criteria for kingship, and, if we compare them with 1 Kings 10:14–11:3, we find Solomon failing in all of them. At the end of his reign, he was doing everything a king should not do: acquiring many horses and going to Egypt to get them; marrying many wives; and amassing huge stockpiles of gold. If Solomon was not God's model king, who was? The hope of a future king who would embody God's ideal for kingship, one who would fulfil God's covenant with David, began to develop. This hope was only realized when Jesus, the greater than Solomon, appeared.

The way the author tells the story makes the same point. All the jumping backwards and forwards is so that we will always have both kingdoms in our field of vision at the same time. The kingdoms display two different types of kingship. In Israel, kingship was based on political flair and military muscle. Men often seized power by assassinations and coups. Down south in Judah, kingship was based on being related to David, with son following father in an orderly line. But neither produced God's ideal for kingship. A conviction began to take shape that neither human ability and power, nor simply being part of David's gene pool could result in the appearance of God's model king. Something more and someone special, such as God himself coming to rule over his people, would be required if God's ideal for kingship was to be realized (*Ezek.* 34:23–24). This hope was only fulfilled when Jesus, God himself in human flesh, appeared.

The rejection of God's ideal for kingship, which started with Solomon, accelerated after the split. All of 1 Kings' kings of Israel and half of the 1 Kings' kings of Judah failed to reflect God's rule in the way they behaved. How were the people to know what God's rule was like? Into the vacuum stepped the prophets. They were not spiritual innovators, but men who saw their role as enforcing the covenant. They went back to the covenant obligations as set out in God's law, showed the meaning of God's kingly demands, and applied them to the contemporary situation. You can immediately see that there are storm clouds on the horizon. If the prophets were attempting to enforce God's agenda and the kings were trying to pursue their own, it would not be long before prophets and kings clashed. We see this most sharply in Ahab's reign because he was the king with the most blatantly anti-God agenda. So Elijah challenges him, not only about his spiritual apostasy, but for his murder of Naboth in order to get his soiled hands on the man's vineyard (21). But Elijah is not the only prophetic thorn in Ahab's side. An unnamed prophet condemns him for the lenient way in which he treated Ben-Hadad, the Syrian king (20), and Micaiah predicts Ahab's defeat and death in the battle of Ramoth Gilead (22).

These clashes between prophets and kings would only be brought to an end when God's king appeared to demonstrate God's rule. Several hundred years later, on a mountain top in northern Israel (*Mark* 9:2–8), we find Elijah standing before another king, just as he used to stand before Ahab, only this time there is no word of condemnation and no declaration of God's disapproval. Here finally we have a king in whom God delights (*Mark* 9:7; *Psa.* 2:7) and about whom the prophets, represented by Elijah, have no complaints because he rules in righteousness and grace. And who is that model king, this embodiment of God's ideal for kingship? You are right first time: it is Jesus.

13

2 *Kings*

etween 1776 and 1789, the English historian Edward Gibbon published a landmark six–volume work called *The History of the Decline
and Fall of the Roman Empire*, in which he traced the disintegration
and eventual collapse of the once all-conquering Roman Empire. If
we alter the title a little, we can characterize what 1 Kings and 2 Kings
are about. They are the history of the decline and fall of the Israelite
monarchy from its peak during the reigns of David and Solomon to its
disappearance in 722 BC, in the case of Israel, the northern kingdom,
and in 587 BC, in the case of Judah, the southern kingdom.

In spite of the somewhat random place, in which the English Bible
divides the originally single book, both 1 Kings and 2 Kings follow a
similar pattern: they move from the generally positive to the horribly
negative. 1 Kings begins with the blessing experienced during Solomon's
reign (*1 Kings* 1–10), but is followed by the folly of Solomon himself
and those who succeeded him, especially in the case of Jeroboam's
bootleg religion and Ahab's raw paganism (*1 Kings* 11–22). 2 Kings
travels along the same route, opening up with Elisha's ministry, a pause
in the downward spiral, in which God displays his grace (1–8), but,
when that grace is despised, the process of judgment gathers pace until
God consigns Israel and Judah to the 'tender mercies' of the Assyrians
and Babylonians (9–25).

In 2 Kings, the author continues to use the same method of storytell-
ing as he did in 1 Kings: the 'baseline rally' approach. As he records
the decline and fall of the Israelite monarchy, he switches back and
forth between Israel and Judah. As this may induce a state of mental
confusion, I am going to deal with each kingdom separately, beginning with ISRAEL.

The twelve 2 *Kings* kings of Israel – Ahaziah, Jehoram, Jehu, Jehoa-haz, Jeroboam II, Zechariah, Shallum, Manahem, Pekahiah, Pekah and Hoshea – are all labelled as bad by the author. That is not a reflection on their political know-how, military prowess or administrative competence, but an indictment on them for allowing Jeroboam I's counterfeit cult to continue as an alternative to the Jerusalem Temple. This perspective is seen in the way Jehu's reign is recorded in 2 Kings 9–10. Although the methods of the original 'boy racer' (9:20) are not for the squeamish – I doubt if the stories of how he disposed of Jezebel, butchered Ahab's family, slaughtered Baal's priests, and desecrated Baal's temple by turning it into a public toilet (9:30–10:28) find their way into many children's Sunday School lessons – he is commended for carrying out God's instructions to wipe out Ahab's legacy by re-moving Baal worship (10:30). But all that amounts to nothing as far as the author is concerned because he allowed Jeroboam's counterfeit religion to go on unchecked (10:29, 31).

Into the vacuum created by these kings' failure to pursue God's ideal of kingship stepped the prophets who gave the nation the spiritual direction it was not receiving. Their function was to act as God's spokesmen, warning the nation about its covenant unfaithfulness, especially in not worshipping in the way and in the place God had specified. Elijah was the first and greatest of these covenant enforcers, but his ministry is mostly recorded in 1 Kings. Only his declaration of God's judgment on Ahaziah, Ahab's son and a chip off the old pagan block, continues into 2 Kings (1:1–18). Then 2 Kings 2:1–18 records the story of Elijah being taken up into heaven in a whirlwind. What was going to happen now that Israel's spiritual defence system was no longer there? The same as before: God's servants might come and go, but God's cause went on. Elijah had anointed and trained Elisha to be his successor in the struggle for truth and true worship in Israel (*1 Kings* 19:16, 19–21). When Elijah was gone, Elisha literally and sym-bolically picked up Elijah's mantle and continued to give the spiritual leadership that the nation desperately needed (2:8, 13–14). In this, he was aided by groups of men known as 'the company of the prophets' (2:3, 5, 7, 15; 4:1, 38; 5:22; 6:1; 9:1), whom Elijah gathered around him to teach them the principles of biblical prophecy. It seems that Elisha continued what Elijah had done, building on his legacy. Towards the end of the nation's political existence as an independent state, God sent Jonah, Amos and Hosea to be his prophetic voice to Israel. Although Amos was not from the company of the prophets (*Amos* 7:14), Jonah and Hosea might have been. The dominant theme of the prophets God sent to Israel was judgment, yet their appearance was also a sign of God's grace, because behind their warnings was the call to turn back to God and the assurance that, if they did, God would forgive.

God's grace in sending prophets to Israel is seen most clearly in Elisha (2:1–8:15). Judgment is present too. When a mob of youths from Bethel, one of the centres of Israel's false religion, confronted him as he made his way past their town, deliberately insulting and abusing him because he was God's prophet, Elisha caused one of the curses for covenant unfaithfulness (*Lev.* 26:22) to fall on them (2:23–25). And when Gehazi, his servant, tried to cash in on Naaman's gratitude for being cured of his leprosy (5:20–24), Elisha announced God's judgment on him (5:25–27), not primarily because Gehazi was a gold-digger but because his greed had obscured God's gracious character. God's grace was free, which is why Elisha was adamant he would take no payment for curing Naaman (5:15–16), but Gehazi's grubby request had suggested that God was like the petty gods of the region – greedy, and doing everything for a price. Another example of God's judgment through Elisha comes in 2 Kings 6:24–7:20 with the harrowing story of how Ben-Hadad, the Syrian king, mobilized a massive force and laid siege to Samaria. Conditions inside the city were so dire that some were driven to cannibalism to stay alive. Rather than accepting all this as God's judgment on Israel for its covenant unfaithfulness (*Lev.* 26:27–29; *Deut.* 28:52–57), the king rashly blamed God and decreed that Elisha, God's representative, should suffer. Elisha's response was to announce that, within twenty-four hours, the siege would be lifted. But, when the king's aide scoffed at the suggestion, he was told that, even though he would see the relief of Samaria, he would not benefit from it. Sure enough, the next day, when news spread that the enemy army had gone and the starving population piled out of the city to grab supplies from the abandoned Syrian camp, the king's aide was trampled to death in the stampede.

But the keynote of Elisha's ministry was not judgment but grace. We see this in what he did when he returned to Jericho after witnessing Elijah's departure into heaven (2:19–22). Joshua had put Jericho under a curse (*Josh.* 6:26), but during the dark days of Ahab's reign, when few cared about God's word, Hiel the Bethelite rebuilt the city. The graves of his oldest and youngest sons became monuments to Hiel's choice to play fast and loose with God's threats (*1 Kings* 16:34). The new residents of Hiel's city regretted the day they moved in because Jericho's water was lethal, causing fatalities among livestock and humans. But Elisha took a new bowl, filled it with salt, threw the salt into the spring, and declared that God had healed the water, making it wholesome and life-giving. This action is loaded with symbolism. Salt was a component of sacrifice (*Lev.* 2:13; *Ezek.* 43:24) and an unexplained covenant symbol (*Lev.* 2:13; *Num.* 18:19; *2 Chron.* 13:5). Elisha was bringing Jericho out of the sphere of curse into that of covenant blessing.

This action was a foretaste of the grace that would characterize the rest of Elisha's ministry. Miracle followed miracle. Not only was Jericho's water supply purified but a widow was provided with enough oil to pay off her late husband's debts (4:1–7); a well-to-do woman from Shunem had her son restored to life (4:8–37); a pot of poisonous stew was made edible (4:38–41); twenty barley bread loaves fed one hundred men (4:42–44); Naaman, the Syrian chief of staff, was cured of leprosy (5:1–27); a borrowed axe head floated so that it could be recovered from the Jordan (6:1–7); and Syrian soldiers who had been sent to capture Elisha were struck blind, restored to sight, and repatriated, after being fed and watered (6:8–23). So strong was the connection between Elisha and the miraculous that a miracle took place at his tomb after he was dead (13:20–21).

Like all Bible miracles, Elisha's were to be like windows through which people could see the kind of salvation God gives to those who trust him. As the Shunammite's son was raised to life, so God will give resurrection life to his people, and death will not be able to separate them from his love in Christ (*Rom.* 8:38–39). As Naaman was cured of leprosy when he followed Elisha's instructions, so God will cleanse us from our sin – but only if we trust in Jesus alone (*John* 14:6; *Acts* 4:12). As the widow was rescued from debt, so God will free us from the spiritual debt arising from our sin on the basis of Jesus' death (*Col.* 2:13–14). As Elisha's servant was given spiritual sight when the Syrian force attacked Dothan (6:16–17), so the Holy Spirit gives us spiritual sight to see and enter the kingdom (*John* 3:3, 5). Elisha's miracles also highlight who will receive God's salvation: the helpless who have no one to turn to but God, and the undeserving who have neither done nor can do anything to make God bless them. Apart from Naaman, we are not told the names of those who received God's grace through Elisha's miracles. The one person whose name we are told, along with the Syrian soldiers, is an outsider. This gives us more than a hint that God's programme for the nations is not to destroy them but to bless them through his Son's death (*Gen.* 12:3; *Eph.* 2:11–13). Elisha's miracles show us that God's grace does exactly what it promises: it brings God's mercy, kindness and compassion to the weak, despised and undeserving (*Luke* 1:50–55).

The New Testament writers draw attention to the parallels between Elijah and Elisha on the one hand and John the Baptist and Jesus on the other. John the Baptist certainly resembled Elijah, even in his dress (*Matt.* 3:4; 2 *Kings* 1:7–8). Both Elijah and John faced royal opposition, and their main antagonists were women: Jezebel in Elijah's case (1 *Kings* 19:2, 10, 14) and Herodias in John's (*Matt.* 14:3–12). Elijah was the forerunner of Elisha, just as John was of Jesus (*Mark* 1:2–3). Both marked out their successors in the area of the River Jordan. Just as Elisha's keynote of grace contrasts with Elijah's message of judgment, so Jesus' message of grace (*John* 3:17) contrasts with John's preaching of judgment (*Matt.* 3:7–12). What pinpoints Jesus as the new Elisha, however, is his miracles. No section of the Old Testament is as full of miracles as the story of Elisha in 2 Kings. In the same way, no portion of the New Testament is so full of miracles as the story of Jesus himself, in which God, through Jesus' many miracles, not only shows what his salvation is like but validates his Son's claims about himself and the benefits of his death (*Heb.* 2:3–4).

Elisha's miracles were not designed to make him popular, but to draw people to trust in God. However, that did not happen on a large scale, and Israel's downward spiritual spiral continued. In 793 BC, Jeroboam, son of Jehoash (Jeroboam II), came to the throne. His forty-year reign in some ways masked Israel's deep-seated state of covenant unfaithfulness for, while Jeroboam II was king, Israel experienced a national renaissance. The king's expansionist foreign policy put Israel's enemy Syria in its place, gave him control of the regional trade routes, and brought about an economic boom. In the new prosperity people bought second homes (*Amos* 3:15), expensive furniture and interior decorations (*Amos* 3:15; 6:4), and excessive pleasures (*Amos* 4:1; 6:4–5). But this was only a small minority of Israel's society, the already-wealthy upper class. The poor sank deeper and deeper into poverty. Affluence bred smugness, complacency, self-indulgence and social heartlessness.

Israel paid a high price for Jeroboam II's expansionist foreign policy. To the east lay the Assyrian Empire. Until now, Syria had acted as a buffer between Israel and Assyria, but, by weakening Syria, Jeroboam II had brought Israel more directly up against Assyria than before. This fact was to shape events in the final years of the northern kingdom's existence. When Jeroboam II died, political instability returned. Six kings occupied the throne in only thirty years. Israel was like a rotten tree: the next big storm would see its collapse, and that big storm came from Assyria. Pekah, Israel's penultimate king, decided to bring Assyrian interference in Israel's affairs to an end by making an anti-Assyrian alliance with Syria. This was not the cleverest move, because Tiglath-Pileser, the Assyrian king, savagely attacked Syria, capturing Damascus in 732 BC, and absorbing Syria into his empire. He also annexed parts of Israel and deported their inhabitants to Assyria (15:29). Hoshea, Israel's last king, was only an Assyrian lackey whose sphere of influence did not extend much beyond Samaria and its hinterland. Israel's rush to oblivion reached the end of the road when, relying on Egypt, Hoshea rebelled against Assyria. In response Shalmaneser, the new Assyrian king, attacked Samaria. After a terrible three-year siege, Samaria fell in 722 BC, and the remaining population was taken into exile in Assyria (17:3–6).

Perhaps you feel a sense of optimism as we turn the spotlight on to JUDAH, the southern kingdom. Do not be too hopeful. Although it lasted longer than its northern neighbour, Judah suffered a similar fate in 587 BC. The book opens with Jehoshaphat on the throne, and he is followed by fifteen others – Jehoram, Ahaziah, Joash, Amaziah, Azariah (or Uzziah), Jotham, Ahaz, Hezekiah, Manasseh, Amon, Josiah, Jehoahaz, Jehoiakim, Jehoiachin and Zedekiah. You might imagine that, with the Temple on their doorstep, Judah's kings would be rated more highly by the author than Israel's. Sadly, this was not the case. Judah had its equivalent of Jeroboam's shrine at Bethel: the high places, where idols were worshipped as alternatives to the true God. The kings' attitude to the high places became the standard by which they were judged. Only Hezekiah and Josiah had a perfect record here: they were not only faithful worshippers of God, but they also removed the high places. Another five – Jehoshaphat, Joash, Amaziah, Uzziah and Jotham – were personally faithful to God and his worship, but they took no action against the high places. The other nine kings not only refused to worship God but actively participated in the idolatry of the high places. The worst was Manasseh, the Ahab of the south, who rebuilt the high places his father Hezekiah had destroyed and took part in some stomach-churning religious activities at them (21:1–9, 16). His sins were the cause of God declaring that he would do to Judah and Jerusalem as he had done to Israel and Samaria (21:10–15).

Jehoshaphat arranged the marriage of Jehoram, his son, to Athaliah, daughter of Ahab and Jezebel (8:18), to shore up an anti-Syrian alliance with Israel (*1 Kings* 22:44). This was to result in a very dark period in Judah's history. When Ahaziah, her son, died, Athaliah seized power, and one of her first actions was to murder the royal family (11:1). God's promise of a Saviour was linked to David's line, so if Satan could destroy Judah's royal family, God's plan of salvation would fail. But Jehosheba, Ahaziah's sister, rescued baby Joash from the massacre and hid him in the Temple complex for six years (11:2–3). When Joash was seven, Jehoiada the priest staged a coup and reinstalled the Davidic king on the throne of Judah (11:4–16). God's plan of salvation, which, from a human perspective, was hanging by a thread, was on course again.

Judah was in spiritual decline, and God graciously sent prophets to alert the nation to this and to call them back to himself. Joel, Obadiah, Isaiah, Micah, Nahum, Habakkuk, Zephaniah and Jeremiah all exercised their ministries during this period. Some kings heeded God, and are applauded by the author. One is Joash who repaired the Temple after Athaliah's reign of terror (12:4–16), but he failed to remove the high places (12:3). He also preferred bribery to battle and stripped the newly-renovated Temple of its resources to buy off Hazael, the Syrian king, who had attacked Jerusalem (12:17–18).

Hezekiah also receives high praise for the religious reforms that re-established the worship of God and smashed the influence of the high places (18:3–4). But he receives the greatest praise for his trust in God (18:5–6). This was stretched almost to breaking point, but ultimately triumphed when the Assyrian came down like a wolf on the fold. Faced with Sennacherib's shock tactics, Hezekiah's faith initially wobbled as he tried to buy Sennacherib off (18:13–16) and as he relied on the Egyptians (18:24). But then he turned to God (19:14–19); and his trust was vindicated when the angel of the Lord destroyed vast numbers in the Assyrian camp, causing Sennacherib to withdraw back to Nineveh (19:35–36), where he was later assassinated by two of his sons (19:37).

The author also gives high praise to Josiah, whose story is told in chapters 22–23. Although he inherited a nation in spiritual chaos after nearly sixty years of paganism, Josiah set about re-establishing the worship of God and destroying the high places. This involved repairing the dilapidated Temple, and amidst the rubble a copy of Deuteronomy was discovered. When it was read to Josiah he was distraught at the extent of Judah's covenant unfaithfulness, and tried to put God's law back at the centre of national life, renewing the nation's covenant with God and reintroducing the Passover celebrations. However, all Josiah's reforms were too late, since the die of judgment had already been cast.

The end came about in this way. Babylon was in the process of replacing Assyria as the current superpower. In a desperate attempt to halt Babylon, Assyria asked Egypt for help. When Pharaoh Neco marched north to support Assyria, Josiah attacked him at Megiddo, but tragically Josiah's army was defeated and Josiah killed. Jehoahaz, his son, succeeded him as king, but not for long, since Pharaoh Neco deposed him and installed Jehoiakim as his puppet king (22:29–35). When power in the region shifted in Babylon's favour in 605 BC after Nebuchadnezzar's victory over Egypt at Carchemish, Jehoiakim was caught in the crossfire and became Babylon's vassal (24:1a). The cream of Judah's rising generation were then taken off to Babylon (*Dan*. 1:1–4). After three years Jehoiakim rebelled against Babylonian rule (24:1b), but it was his son Jehoiachin who bore the brunt of the Babylonian retribution for his father's rebellion. Jehoiachin surrendered to Nebuchadnezzar and was deported to Babylon along with the best of Judah's remaining inhabitants and the treasures which the Babylonians had looted from the Temple and the royal palace (24:8–16). Nebuchadnezzar installed Zedekiah as king, but he too rebelled. The Babylonians again besieged Jerusalem and after a ghastly eighteen-month siege the city was captured in 587 BC. Nebuchadnezzar's revenge was terrible. Those not executed were marched off into exile in Babylon. But what the author of 2 Kings concentrates on is the destruction of Jerusalem, and especially the Temple, which was reduced to a smoking ruin.

The contrast between the opening of 1 Kings and the end of 2 Kings is stark. In Solomon's golden age the promises of God seemed close to fulfilment. Solomon had succeeded David as God's king in Jerusalem. The promises made to Abraham seemed to be ripening fast. God's people were in his place of promise, enjoying his presence in the worship of the Temple, and living under his protection. Foreign rulers came to Jerusalem to listen to the wisdom of God's king. But the nightmare conclusion to 2 Kings (25:51b) seemed to suggest that all God's promises had gone wrong. There was no longer any Davidic king reigning in Jerusalem. Foreign kings lined up to attack Jerusalem, and, as a result of all these wars and sieges, the numerical strength of God's people was greatly reduced. God's promise of protection seemed to have failed, as the Babylonian army trampled all over the armies of Judah. As for God's presence, the Temple had been destroyed. Home was no longer in the place of promise. For most it was hundreds of miles away in Babylon, while others ended up where the nation had started centuries before – in Egypt (25:26).

In the emphasis of his narrative the author shows that God's faithfulness to his promises is not in question. The reason for the Exile was not any failure on God's part but Judah's covenant unfaithfulness, and especially the unfaithfulness of Judah's kings. This is why he devotes so much space to Hezekiah and Josiah. If only the kings had trusted God, as Hezekiah did, God would have rescued them from their enemies. If only the kings had repented, as Josiah did, God would have had mercy on them and a Davidic king would still be reigning in Jerusalem. But Judah's kings failed and, as an inescapable result, God's judgment overtook them.

Deuteronomy, particularly the blessings and curses section of chapter 28, explains the downfall of Israel and Judah (17:7–23; 22:14–17). What had happened was exactly in line with what God had warned would happen if the people were unfaithful to him (*Deut.* 28:58–68). The events of 587 BC demonstrated God's ability to do what he had said he would do. He had warned that, if his people were unfaithful to the covenant, he would remain faithful to it, even if that meant carrying out the threats the covenant contained.

Amid the darkness of the covenant curses, there is a glimmer of hope. In Deuteronomy 29, Moses warned the Israelites of the disaster that would overtake them for covenant unfaithfulness. But then, in Deuteronomy 30, he went on to say that judgment would not be his final act. If the people turned back to God, he would restore them and begin to bless them again. Also, 2 Kings does not end with 2 Kings 25:21b, but with the story of Jehoiachin, who by this time was being shown kindness by Evil-Merodach, Babylon's new king (25:27–30). Amidst all the noise of battle, the crash of demolition and the wails of defeat, look carefully and you will see a chink of light: one of David's descendants is being shown special favour. It may be only a chink, but at least it hints that God has not finished with David and his family. As Matthew points out in Matthew 1:1–17, and especially verses 12–16, that chink of light would not be extinguished but would burst into a blaze of glory with Jesus' coming, for it is in him that all God's promises to Abraham and David find their fulfilment.

14

1 & 2 Chronicles

O nce you have made your way through the list of names at the start of 1 and 2 Chronicles, you may begin to get a distinct feeling of *déjà vu*, thinking that a lot of the ground has already been covered in 1 and 2 Samuel and 1 and 2 Kings. You might suspect that the Chronicler (as we call the author of 1 and 2 Chronicles), has not heard of plagiarism. But you can relax, for although there is common ground with Samuel and Kings, there is less than some suggest. The Chronicler has not stolen someone else's work and claimed it as his own; instead he is making his own distinctive contribution to the story. When the translators and compilers of the Septuagint split the single book into two, they also shifted its location, placing it after 1 and 2 Kings. However, in the Hebrew Bible, Chronicles is the final book, reflecting the fact that it was probably the last Old Testament book to be written, and it is the book's late date that enables us to understand the Chronicler's distinctive contribution.

When Jerusalem fell in 587 BC and those who had survived the siege were taken to Babylon, the question everyone was asking was, How could this tragedy have happened? The response of the author of Kings is to point out that God had not failed but had carried out his threats in Deuteronomy 28, as he brought on the nation the ghastly consequences of their covenant unfaithfulness. Rather than calling God's faithfulness and power into question, the Exile demonstrated God's commitment to the covenant and his ability to deliver the covenant curses. Writing roughly one hundred and fifty years after Jerusalem's capture and the people's deportation, the Chronicler is addressing a completely different issue. The Exile was over, but the initial enthusiasm which had accompanied the return to Judah, had faded, and spiritual apathy had set in, as parts of Ezra and Nehemiah and the books of Haggai and Malachi indicate. The Chronicler was concerned that the same covenant unfaithfulness which had led to the Exile was rearing its head again. So, in order that there will be no repeat of 587 BC, he writes a history book – but more than a history book – in which he chronicles the main events in Jewish history from Adam (*1 Chron.* 1:1) to Cyrus' edict in 539 BC that brought an end to the Exile. He does not give us a blow-by-blow account of everything that happened but is selective in what he includes – and especially in what he leaves out. Only about forty-five percent of his material is found in the other two books. Everything he includes is designed to drive forward the purpose of his book, which is to help a spiritually sluggish people recover from their apathy and avoid a repetition of the judgment of God on the nation.

When we analyse the structure of 1 and 2 Chronicles, we can see that the book breaks down into three large sections and one tiny section. The first is occupied by THE GENEALOGIES (*1 Chron.* 1–9). These chapters are full of lists of difficult names. As we make our way through them, we may well wonder why they are in the Bible.

In the spiritually apathetic environment in which the Chronicler was working, a common view was that God's covenant with his people had collapsed, buried under the rubble of Jerusalem after the Babylonian conquest. So he records these genealogies to challenge the myth that God had abandoned his people and his promises to Abraham and David and left them to their own devices. By getting the returned exiles to look back on their history and see that God's dealings with them went right back to Adam, the Chronicler is pointing out that God has not written off his people.

The genealogies bear witness to God's grace in loving his people and sticking with them through thick and thin – and it was mostly thin – and his power in protecting and preserving them. He is reassuring them that, if God has invested so much of his power and grace in them, it is quite out of the question that he should now toss them aside.

While the genealogies are not exhaustive, their clear focus is on Abraham and his descendants, because it was with them that God entered into covenant (*Gen.* 17:7). But then, in 1 Chronicles 9, we find what is not strictly speaking a genealogy but an inventory of the Chronicler's contemporaries. Why this switch from listing the dead to listing living people? The Chronicler is tying God's people in the present tightly to God's people in the past to remind the returned exiles that they too are still involved with God's covenant.

Within this focus on Abraham and his descendants, the Chronicler underlines Judah's place in the scheme of things, not because he was Jacob's eldest, but because out of Judah came David, to whom God made the promise that one of his descendants would rule over God's people (2 *Sam.* 7:12–17). This is why a whole chapter (1 *Chron.* 3) is given over to David's family tree. But God's promise to David seemed to have died out when the Babylonians burnt Jerusalem and marched Jehoiachin and Zedekiah, the last Davidic kings, off to Babylon. Why did the Chronicler continue listing the royal line after the Exile (1 *Chron.* 3:17–24) when there was no Davidic king reigning in Jerusalem and the chances of any of those listed in these verses ever being king was less than zero?

Could he not just accept the fact that God's promises to David had failed? Absolutely not! The Chronicler continued to live in the expectation of a coming king, believing that God would do as he had said, and that a descendant of David *par excellence* would appear to rule over God's people. The Chronicler's insistence on continuing to trace David's royal line even after the Exile was a clear reminder that God's promise to David was still alive and active. Far from being a sentry who denies us access to Chronicles, the genealogies are like a host who invites us into the rest of the book.

But while the genealogies assured the returned exiles of their continuity with God's promises to Abraham and David, the Chronicler is concerned to show them that that is not enough. So he draws the reader away from the reassurance of the genealogies into the obligations implied in the rest of the book. He wants them to see the implications of the covenant promises they have received for their own lives. So, after the genealogies, we find ourselves in the second main section of the book which is all about THE UNITED MONARCHY OF DAVID AND SOLOMON (1 *Chron.* 10–2 *Chron.* 9).

Some who read what the Chronicler has to say about David and Solomon are less than happy with what they read. They accuse him of whitewashing these men's reputations. Neither of them, they think, was as pure as he makes them out to be. Such readers need to remember why the Chronicler put pen to paper. He was not a tabloid journalist, poking around for the sensational and the sordid, but was preaching a sermon on covenant faithfulness, expressed in devotion and loyalty to God. What he does is zero in on certain events from the reigns of David and Solomon which reinforce his argument.

The Chronicler begins his record of David's loyalty to God by contrasting his conduct with Saul's suicide on Mount Gilboa (*1 Chron.* 10). Saul is given his place as Israel's first king, but David's covenant faithfulness is highlighted, because the Chronicler tells us that the reason Saul died was his unfaithfulness to God (*1 Chron.* 10:13). David is the opposite of Saul. Because of his total commitment to God, he is able to consolidate his rule. The whole nation falls in behind his leadership (*1 Chron.* 11–12), and he enjoys phenomenal military success as all his enemies are crushed (*1 Chron.* 14:8–17; 18:1–20:8). David's devotion to God is highlighted in the way he brings the Ark of the Covenant to Jerusalem amidst euphoric celebrations (*1 Chron.* 13:1–14; 15:1–16:43), and his passion to build a temple to house the Ark (*1 Chron.* 17:1). But God has other plans for David: one of his sons will build the Temple, and, as the story progresses, we discover that that son is Solomon (*1 Chron.* 22:9–10). Yet David's 'consolation' for not being allowed to build the Temple is beyond his wildest dreams. David's plan was to build a house, a temple, for God, but God's plan is to build a house, a dynasty, for David (*1 Chron.* 17). The Chronicler continues to draw our attention to David's loyalty to God by cataloguing the extensive preparations he made for the Temple's construction: drawing up plans, organizing the workforce, and gathering the necessary finance and materials (*1 Chron.* 22:2–29:20). The one negative story about David – in which he counts the fighting men (*1 Chron.* 21:1–22:1) – still relates to his commitment to the construction of the Temple because Araunah's threshing floor, where all the action connected with the ending of the plague takes place, became the site of the Temple.

Though he refuses to give us a warts-and-all picture of David, the Chronicler is not deceiving us. What he writes about David actually happened. But he does want us to see David in a certain light: David was loyal to God, and his devotion brought blessing. For the Chronicler, this is the only way forward, and the only way to avoid a repetition of the Exile.

The same approach continues in the Chronicler's record of Solomon's reign (*1 Chron.* 29:21–2 *Chron.* 9:31). The bulk of what he says focuses on how Solomon built the Temple. The wisdom he received from God was specifically for that purpose (2 *Chron.* 2:12). Solomon made maximum use of this wisdom, and 2 Chronicles 3:1–7:10 – the centrepiece of the whole book – informs us about the preparations for and the building and dedication of the Temple. These chapters provide the explanation of Solomon's achievements (2 *Chron.* 8:1–9:31) as they illustrate the point that the Chronicler wants to drive home, namely that when people are committed to God, he blesses them.

The Chronicler continues to underscore the same truth as he moves the storyline on into another section of his book. This one deals with THE SPLIT KINGDOM AFTER DAVID AND SOLOMON (2 *Chron.* 10:1–36:21).

Unlike the earlier books, there is no switching back and forth between Israel and Judah. In fact, after recording the story of Jeroboam's rebellion and the subsequent rupture (2 *Chron.* 10:1–11:4), the Chronicler's focus is entirely on Judah. The only time Israel is mentioned is when what it does has some impact on Judah.

In spite of having been recently ousted from its position as the best-known verse in Chronicles by the prayer of Jabez (1 *Chron.* 4:10), 2 Chronicles 7:14 is still the statement which controls the Chronicler's presentation of the history of the kingdom after the split. If the king exhibits humility in terms of seeking God, repentance in terms of turning away from idolatry, and trust in God in terms of commitment to his worship at the Temple, then God will bless him. But, if the king travels in the opposite direction by relying on his own know-how and ability, continuing in idolatry, and failing to trust in God as he forges alliances with other nations to get himself out of trouble, God will punish him. So the Chronicler speaks of good kings who, despite their flaws, basically follow 2 Chronicles 7:14, and evil kings, to whom this whole approach is foreign.

The good kings are loyal to God and express it through a positive attitude towards the Temple and its worship. The Chronicler inserts into his history stories of kings such as Joash, Hezekiah and Josiah repairing the Temple after it had fallen into disrepair (2 *Chron.* 24:4–14; 29:1–36; 34:8–13). Along with this came the reinstatement of God's worship at the Temple and, in the case of Hezekiah and Josiah, giving the Passover a central place in the nation's religious life (2 *Chron.* 30:1–27; 35:1–19). In keeping with 2 Chronicles 7:14, these acts of religious devotion and covenant obedience on the part of the good kings resulted in God's blessing: economic well-being (2 *Chron.* 32:27–30); victory in battle, sometimes in the face of overwhelming odds (2 *Chron.* 14:8–15; 20:2–30; 32:1–22); the provision of heirs to succeed them (2 *Chron.* 11:18–22; 13:21; 21:1–3); and popular support (2 *Chron.* 15:10–15; 19:4–11; 30:13; 34:29–32). These are not random blessings but are in line with God's covenant promises to Abraham and David, and they reverberate with the covenant blessings promised in Deuteronomy 28:1–14. On occasions God's blessings moved into extraordinary territory as, in five instances, during the reigns of Asa, Jehoshaphat, Joash, Hezekiah and Josiah, God graciously sent revival, so that the nation's spiritual life was renewed and taken to a new level.

Also in keeping with 2 Chronicles 7:14, the acts of idolatry and disobedience committed by the evil kings led to God's judgment. The nation suffered military defeat (2 *Chron.* 28:4–8, 16–25; 36:15–20); there were rumblings and expressions of popular dissatisfaction with the king (2 *Chron.* 25:27–28; 33:24–25); and kings were struck down with disease (2 *Chron.* 21:18–19). Once again these punishments were not random, but part of the penalty for covenant unfaithfulness set out in Deuteronomy 28:15–68.

By using 2 Chronicles 7:14 to control his presentation of the kingdom's history after the split, the Chronicler is pressing home his point that the only way to avoid repeating the Exile is faithfulness to covenant obligations. He had learnt from Deuteronomy that obedience is the route to blessing, and disobedience the road to judgment. Conditions were far from ideal. Those who returned were dependent on the Persian Empire. There were more Jews still in Persia than there were in Judah. Their neighbours all around hated them. But if they were loyal to God and devoted to his worship, God would bless them, just as he blessed Hezekiah when the odds were heavily against him.

The account of the split kingdom after David and Solomon ends where it must – with the capture of Jerusalem by the Babylonian army, the destruction of the Temple, the demolition of the city, and the deportation of the people into exile (2 *Chron.* 36:17–21). The Chronicler and the author of Kings both emphasize that the reason for the disaster of 587 BC was the refusal of the people to let go of their idols (2 *Chron.* 36:14) and their rejection of God's words through his prophets (36:16). However, the Chronicler has not finished. He has one more lesson to teach, and it comes in the final section of the book, which is so short that we could easily miss it. It has to do with THE RETURN FROM EXILE (36:22–23).

God had punished them with seventy years of exile, but he has not finished with his people. In accordance with his Word, God uses Cyrus, the Persian king, to facilitate a return to Judah to build a new temple for God's worship. If we thought God's promises concerning his people, in his place, under his protection, and experiencing his presence, had failed, we need to think again. With Cyrus' proclamation, the promises are on track again, and the Chronicler is strongly advising us to keep an eye on how they develop.

The way in which the Chronicler points us in THE DIRECTION OF JESUS is by the twin themes of his book. They are flagged up in the genealogies which function like the overture of a symphony, introducing the ideas which will be developed later. The first theme is *God's king*. This explains why the tribe of Judah, from which God's king would come (*Gen.* 49:10), is given so much prominence. But God's king has to be a descendant of David, with whom God entered into covenant (2 *Sam.* 7:12–17; 2 *Chron.* 17). So the Chronicler quickly dispenses with Saul's reign and gives the kings of Israel no space at all, except when they affect the kings of Judah: they are not Davidic kings.

Judah's good kings have more than their fair share of trouble because, when they have put in place reforms which renew the nation's life, they are often attacked by enemies determined to destroy them. That was certainly true for Asa, Jehoshaphat and Hezekiah. However, because a good king was leading them, God's people experienced God's blessing in these situations. God's promises of a people in his place under the rule of a Davidic king remained intact, since the enemies were unable to wipe out the people, overrun the land, or depose the king. For the followers of Jesus, blessing is not measured by freedom from trials and crises, but rather by being enabled to live as 'more than conquerors' in the crises which inevitably occur.

The Chronicler makes the point that blessing is experienced when God's king rules over his people. But, unlike his portrayal of David and Solomon, his presentation of Judah's good kings after the split does not conceal their faults. All of them are flawed, and their reigns generally end in disappointment. To see this, we need look no further than Asa, Joash, Uzziah, Hezekiah and Josiah. The Chronicler is alerting the reader to the fact that God's promise to David has yet to be fulfilled: God's king has yet to appear on the stage of history. But when Matthew follows the Chronicler's example and produces a genealogy that traces the Davidic line after the Exile, he finishes with Jesus (*Matt.* 1:12–16). He is announcing that, in Jesus, God's king has arrived. It is as we come under Jesus' righteous rule and obey him that God's blessing is truly known (*Rom.* 6:22–23).

The Chronicler is also keen to remind us that it was descendants of David who led the return from exile (*1 Chron.* 3:17–19; *Ezra* 2:1–2). This concept was fully realized centuries later when Jesus, David's ultimate descendant, by his death led God's people out of an even greater exile – the exile from God on account of sin (*Eph.* 2:13).

The Chronicler's other theme is *God's temple*, and this is indicated not only by the central position given to Levi's family tree in the genealogies (*1 Chron.* 6), but also by the dominant place given to the Temple in the rest of the book. Great swathes of the book focus on the preparations for building the Temple during David's reign, the actual construction and dedication of the Temple during Solomon's reign, and the various restorations of the Temple by Asa, Joash, Hezekiah and Josiah after periods of neglect. The main criterion for deciding whether a king was to be labelled 'good' or 'evil' had to do with his attitude to the Temple and its worship. The Chronicler is emphasizing the idea that devotion to the Temple leads to blessing while neglect and negativity toward it result in judgment.

The Chronicler stresses the role of the Temple as the only place to approach God. There alone God dwells with his people, and there alone faith in God can be strengthened. In Jesus, all these lines of thought finally converge. The only way in which God can be approached is on the basis of Jesus' death (*Heb.* 10:19–22). It is in Jesus alone that God himself has come to be with us (*John* 1:14). If we want to be empowered to live a life of faith, glorifying God and experiencing his grace in the midst of all life's problems and crises, we have to go to Jesus (*Heb.* 4:14–16; 12:1–3). When we look at what the Chronicler is saying about devotion to the Temple through the lens of the New Testament, we see that its true fulfilment is in faith in the Lord Jesus Christ.

How can we experience God's blessing and not leave ourselves exposed to his judgment? That is the question the Chronicler has been tackling. In his answer, he is completely clear: God graciously blesses those who live under Jesus' rule and who are passionate in their loyalty to him. This is expressed in loving, enthusiastic obedience to his kingly Word. Some two thousand years on from the Chronicler, probably the most spiritually-minded and theologically-competent body of men ever to meet under one roof – the Westminster Assembly – would make the same point. It is as God's people glorify him that they enjoy him (see the *Shorter Catechism*, Q. and A. 1).

15

Ezra

When he retired, my father enjoyed nothing better than reclaiming a piece of broken furniture and restoring it to its former glory. He would take it back to his workshop and, after a lot of hard work, it would be as good as new. The books of Ezra and Nehemiah are about a restoration project, not the reconstruction of a broken piece of furniture but of a broken nation. They tell the story of how Ezra and Nehemiah rebuilt not only Judah's physical infrastructure, but also its religious life and morale. In the Hebrew Bible, the two books were treated as one, but, in the English Bible, they are split in two. Since I am following the English Bible's running-order, I will deal with them separately.

Ezra is a book of two halves: the first half, Ezra 1–6, describes events that took place between 539 and roughly 516 BC, and concentrates on the REBUILDING OF GOD'S TEMPLE.

In a letter to the exile community in Babylon, Jeremiah had informed them that God would end the Exile when seventy years had passed (*Jer.* 29:10–14). By the opening of Ezra, the time had come. So, in 539 BC, to fulfil his promise, God turned the whole of ancient Middle Eastern politics on its head. With hardly a blow being struck, the once invincible Babylonian Empire was conquered by Cyrus and his Persian army. This regime change also brought about a major shift in policy towards conquered nations. The Babylonians, like the Assyrians before them, herded off defeated peoples into exile away from their homeland, but the Persians did the exact opposite: they allowed deported people to go back home. This enabled the Persians to represent themselves as liberators, in contrast with the brutal Babylonian oppressors. While Cyrus' decree (1:2–4) can be seen as part of a wider Persian policy, that is not how Ezra sees it. He shows us that it is God who is orchestrating events and policies to fulfil his word through Jeremiah (1:1).

There was a mixed response to Cyrus' edict (1:5–11). Only about fifty thousand Jews decided to go home, out of an estimated two to three million Jews living in the Persian Empire at the time. But they were returning for the right reason. Just as he had done with Cyrus, God had moved the returning exiles' hearts (1:5) to grasp that their future lay in Judah and with God's promises. Also the return was like a second Exodus since, as in Exodus 12:35–36, God saw to it that the exiles did not leave empty-handed (1:6). Even the spoils ransacked from Jerusalem (2 *Kings* 24:13; *Jer.* 52:17–19; *Dan.* 1:1–2) were handed back to the exiles to help refurnish the new Temple (1:7–11). Another positive aspect of the return is that it was headed by Zerubbabel, a descendant of David (1 *Chron.* 3:19).

Like the exile, the return happened in stages, and in chapter 2 there is a directory of the first group to return. While this list contains the names of those who will form the nucleus of the reborn nation, its focus is elsewhere. If the mandate for heading home was to rebuild the Temple, then it was essential that there were those suitably qualified to serve in it, so the list concentrates on priests and Levites who could prove their right to serve. After their safe arrival in Jerusalem (2:68) and before they dispersed (2:70), some of the exiles brought gifts for the rebuilding of the Temple (2:68–69). This act of spontaneous giving reinforces the parallel with the Exodus since it echoes Exodus 25:2–9, where gifts were brought to help build the Tabernacle.

The exiles were soon back in Jerusalem (3:1), with the rebuilding of the Temple as their top priority. The leaders realized that the worship of God could restart without the Temple structure, so the altar was built and sacrifices recommenced (3:2–3). The Feast of Tabernacles was celebrated again, as Moses had stipulated in Exodus 23:14–17 and Leviticus 23:33–42 (3:4–6). That festival reminded them of how God had kept his covenant promises of protection and a place by bringing their ancestors safely from Egypt through the desert to Canaan. It must have been particularly moving for the returned exiles. They too had experienced the benefit of these covenant promises as God brought them safely back from exile to Judah. After the reinstatement of the sacrifices and the celebration of the Feast of Tabernacles, the hard work of rebuilding the Temple started in earnest. Foundations had to be laid, and, as in the construction of Solomon's Temple, the building materials were obtained from Lebanon (3:7). When the foundations were in place, a service of worship was held in which there was a deliberate attempt to recapture the joy experienced at the dedication of Solomon's Temple (2 *Chron.* 5:12–13; 7:3). Some of the very old men who remembered Solomon's Temple wept when they thought of what had once been (3:12–13).

But opposition to the work of rebuilding soon appeared. Ezra 4 records the launch of the enemies' counter-offensive. There had been signs of this gathering storm. The returned exiles knew that the people already in the land saw their arrival as a threat, yet 'despite their fear of the peoples around them', God's altar had been constructed and sacrifices restarted (3:3). It was only after the Temple foundations were laid, however, that the opposition gathered strength. The enemies initially came with an offer of help (4:2), but the leaders saw through all the sweetness and light and turned it down (4:3). Things now turned nasty as counsellors were hired to make a case against the Jews at the Persian court. In Ezra 4:6–23, we have a letter to the king, together with his reply, which show the kind of misinformation that was being put out about what the Jews were doing and why. The upshot of all the intimidation and pressure was that, in 534 BC, work on the Temple came to a standstill for fifteen years (4:24).

This was not the end of the story, because, in 520 BC, the work began again. The driving force behind the restart was God's word preached by the prophets Haggai and Zechariah (5:1–2). Urged on by their preaching, the workers got back on site (5:2) and the work began again (5:8). The renewed activity soon came to the attention of Tattenai, the governor of the province of Trans-Euphrates, which included Judah. He was worried that all this Temple building would upset the *status quo* and lead to unrest, something with which Darius, the Persian king, would not be happy. So, after questioning the Jewish leaders about what they were doing (5:3–4), Tattenai filed a report to Darius and asked for guidance as to what he should do (5:6–17). Meanwhile, back at the Temple site, the work continued (5:5). Darius' answer to Tattenai's communication could not have been better: not only were the Jews given permission to go on with their work without interference – and anyone opposing them was to be treated severely – but the project was to be funded from the government exchequer (6:1–12). With official backing for rebuilding the Temple set out in black and white, morale among the returned exiles was restored, the work progressed rapidly, and Haggai and Zechariah's continuing ministry of God's word maintained the forward momentum (6:14). In 516 BC the work was completed (6:15), the new structure dedicated, and everything put in place for worship to start in earnest (6:16–18). The first feast celebrated in the rebuilt Temple was Passover (6:19–22). For people who had so recently experienced a second Exodus, this Passover must have been very special.

The second half of the book, Ezra 7–10, tells of another type of reconstruction which was needed if the broken nation was to be restored. These chapters focus on the REBUILDING OF GOD'S RULE. In them, we finally meet the man from whom the whole book gets its name and whose memoirs are the source of the information contained in them.

One way in which 'Christ executes the office of a king' is by 'powerfully arranging all things . . . for [his people's] good'.[1] If we look at Ezra 7–8 from that point of view, we will discover that these chapters – which contain a family tree (7:1–5); an official imperial memorandum (7:11–26); a prayer (7:27–28); a catalogue of names (8:1–14) and a narrative extract from Ezra's journal (8:15–26) – are all about people *experiencing God's rule*. The phrase, 'after these things' (7:1), bridges a sixty-year gap between the events of Ezra 1–6 and those of Ezra 7–10. During this time the action described in the book of Esther took place, as God intervened to prevent the genocide of Jews in the Persian Empire. Another example of God's rule at work was in Ezra's personal background (7:1–6a). The problems he would encounter when he went back to Jerusalem were formidable, requiring a man of considerable

[1] *The Larger Catechism*, Q. and A. 45.

spiritual strength and wisdom to tackle them. In Ezra, God had been preparing such a spiritual champion. While Ezra had respectability because he could trace his family tree back to Aaron (7:1–6a), his authority and wisdom stemmed from his intimacy with God in prayer (9:5–15) and his thorough grasp of the meaning and application of God's law (7:10). We can also see the way in which God's rule was in action in the change in the imperial government's attitude towards the Jews (7:11–26). Initially Artaxerxes, the Persian king, was negative towards them (4:17–22), but security concerns had brought about a change. He now issued a decree which allowed Ezra to return to Jerusalem and to go about his work with royal endorsement.

Although the second wave of returning exiles was much smaller than the first, it is obvious that God was with them too. When Ezra registered the people returning with him he made the unwelcome discovery that there were no Levites among them, something which would have a detrimental effect on the Temple's ability to function properly. After a search carried out by men hand-picked by Ezra (8:16–17), not only were enough Levites found but a gifted leader was also discovered. Ezra was quick to attribute all this to God's control of the situation (8:18–20). Before the expedition set out from their camp beside the Ahava Canal, they did two things. First Ezra counted out how much money they were taking with them for the Temple, entrusted it to twelve leading priests to look after during the journey, and instructed them to count it again when they arrived in Jerusalem (8:24–30). On their arrival at the Temple, the figure was the same as at the Ahava Canal (8:33–34). This financial transparency highlighted the way in which God had blessed the second wave of returning exiles with leaders of integrity. The second thing they did at the Ahava Canal was to pray for a safe journey (8:21). Not only were they about to set off on a demanding nine-hundred mile trip through rugged terrain, but all the money they had with them would make them a prime target for bandits, and, having boasted to the king about the way God protects his people, Ezra felt that he could not ask for a military escort (8:22). God answered their prayers and, after a four-month journey, they arrived tired but safe in Jerusalem (7:8–9; 8:31).

This experience of God's control was the way in which God put in place all the pieces for something greater, the *establishing of God's rule* (Ezra 9–10). Ezra's attention was drawn to the way many Jews, and in particular community leaders, had married non-Jews (9:1–2). He was horrified (9:3), because, as his prayer of confession in Ezra 9:5–15 indicates, he saw this practice as a rejection of God's rule (9:10–12). Marrying outside the bounds of Israel was forbidden in God's law (*Deut.* 7:3–4). This prohibition was not driven by national prejudice, but was designed to maintain covenant faithfulness among God's people. Intermarriage with non-Jews always went hand in hand with idolatry, a turning away from God to paganism, and exposure to God's anger (9:14).

Ezra's passionate reaction to this rejection of God's rule stung the people into action. They admitted their responsibility for the mess and proposed a mass meeting to sort the matter out (10:1–8). When it took place, the weather reflected the sombre mood of the occasion (10:9). After spelling out their culpability in rejecting God's rule by marrying non-Jews, Ezra called on them to repent of their covenant unfaithfulness and accept God's rule over them by divorcing their non-Jewish partners (10:10–11). The meeting concluded by arranging procedures to deal with the legal practicalities of doing what Ezra said (10:12–17). The fact that these legal proceedings took three months to complete indicates how widespread the problem was among the returnees and how deep-seated their rejection of the rule of God's law was.

Ezra ends with a 'name and shame' list of those who had married non-Jews (10:18–44). This might seem a strange way in which to end the book, but we must remember that, in the Hebrew Bible, the book of Nehemiah follows straight on from Ezra 10:44. The Ezra story is therefore not over, and we have to read on into Nehemiah to see how matters develop. There is also a positive way to look at the list. If God's rule had not been re-established, the sin of marrying non-Jews would not have been exposed and the list would never have seen the light of day. The fact that it was written down at all is testimony to Ezra's success in rebuilding God's rule, as expressed in his law, back into the fabric of the restored community.

The events described in Ezra signal *the relaunch of the covenant*. With the Exile it seemed as if God's covenant with his people had come to nothing, but, with the return from exile and the arrival of Ezra in Jerusalem, God was announcing that his promises to Abraham of a people, a place, protection, and a programme, and his promise to David of a king, had not been abandoned. Through their participation in a second Exodus, the nation was reconstituted as God's people and could begin to see themselves once more as being in a unique relationship with God, expressed in a distinct lifestyle. This is why Zerubbabel turned down the offer of outside help with the rebuilding of the Temple (4:1–3) and why Ezra took such robust action against those who had married non-Jews (9–10). Nothing must be tolerated which might dilute the distinctiveness of God's people. The covenant promise which was most obviously restored was that of a place of blessing. Once again, after seventy years, God's people were back in the Promised Land.

Another covenant promise which plays a leading role in Ezra is that of protection. Scattered through the book are instances of how God provided for his people, keeping them safe from their enemies and even from themselves. With the reconstruction of the Temple, God's promise to be with his people came once more to the fore. His promise of a programme reappears in Ezra only in a negative way. The nations are portrayed as constantly trying to block God's plans, especially concerning the Temple. But they cannot stand in the way of God's purposes because – despite all the nations can do – these plans move forward. The clearest example of the nations' opposition to God's programme is not in Ezra but at the cross of Christ. There the nations conspire against the Lord's Anointed to destroy him (*Psa.* 2:1–3), but God uses their hostility to bring his plan of salvation to its fulfilment (*Acts* 2:23; 4:27–28).

Even the promise to David of a king returns in Ezra, but in an unexpected way. Before the Exile, God ruled his people through a human king, a physical descendant of David, but now, there was no chance of a Davidic king ruling over God's people since they were part of the sprawling, cosmopolitan Persian Empire. But God still kept his promise to rule over his people, only now he did so through his Word.

This is why Ezra's role as a teacher of God's law is so important. He re-establishes God's rule over his people by re-establishing the authority of God's Word. The way God's authoritative voice is heard is in the words of a written document. Ezra rebuilds God's rule by putting God's written Word at the centre of the nation's life. This relaunch of the covenant reminds us that the promised coming of Jesus, the ultimate fulfilment of these promises, was getting nearer.

The return-from-exile motif gives *a picture of what God's salvation is like*. We are in exile because of our sin, but, when God saves us, on the basis of the shedding of the blood of Christ, he brings us back to himself (*Eph.* 2:13). The same motif also explains what will happen when Jesus returns. In Ezekiel 37:12–14, there is the picture of the opening of the people's graves and the giving of new resurrection life in order to bring God's people home. Paul clearly had the fulfilment of this picture in mind when he wrote about the Second Coming: graves will be opened, new resurrection life will be given, and God's people will go home to heaven (*1 Thess.* 4:14–17).

16

Nehemiah

Whether it is undertaken after the devastation of war, or after an earthquake or a tsunami, reconstruction is a long-term activity, and this was certainly true of the rebuilding of the Jewish nation, as described in the books of Ezra and Nehemiah. If we do some cross-referencing, we will find that the events of Ezra 1–6 took place between 539 BC (*Ezra* 1:1) and 516 BC (*Ezra* 6:15); but then there is a sixty-year gap in the narrative because the action in Ezra 7–10 all happened in 458 BC (*Ezra* 7:8). Then there is another gap of thirteen years until 445 BC when the opening chapter of Nehemiah picks up the story once more. The next significant date is 433 BC (13:6), when, after more than a decade as governor of Judah, Nehemiah is recalled. However, he returned to Jerusalem 'some time later' (13:6) during Artaxerxes' reign, though we are not told exactly when. Since Artaxerxes died in 423 BC, Nehemiah's second period in charge at Jerusalem took place some time between 433 BC and 423 BC. If my calculations are correct, the reconstruction of the nation took perhaps as long as 116 years, from 539 BC until, at the very latest, 423 BC.

Before we look at Nehemiah's storyline, let us remind ourselves of what has happened so far. Ezra 1–6 told us of how, after some delays, God's Temple was rebuilt. Then, in Ezra 7–10, we learned how Ezra rebuilt God's rule among the returned exiles as he tackled the issue of intermarriage with non-Jews. But there is still reconstruction work to be done as we arrive at Nehemiah 1–6: the account of the REBUILDING OF GOD'S CITY.

When we first meet Nehemiah, the book's main human player, he has just received bad news about the state of affairs in Jerusalem (1:3). Morale among those who have returned is extremely low because the work of reconstruction is proceeding so slowly. The walls of Jerusalem are still just piles of rubble. This is not just devastating to national pride, reminding the Jews of their humiliating defeat in war and subsequent subservience to various foreign powers. Jerusalem is God's city (*Psa.* 48:2). Its ruined walls bring great dishonour to God.

Nehemiah's reaction to the news is to engage in serious prayer (1:4–11). As he prayed, Nehemiah formed a plan that would exploit his position as the Persian king's cupbearer (1:11). In Nehemiah's time, being cupbearer was an influential position. It involved protecting the king from poisoning. The cupbearer had regular access to the king, and the two of them could develop a relationship of trust. This seems to have been the case with Nehemiah and Artaxerxes. One day, the king noticed that Nehemiah was not himself and he asked why he was sad (2:2). Artaxerxes' question made Nehemiah's heart pound. He had deliberately broken court etiquette in order to raise Jerusalem's predicament with the king. Nehemiah had been planning for this moment for months. He prayed, then said his well-rehearsed piece. He asked for leave of absence to go to Jerusalem and rebuild the city, and, by the way, could he also have some imperial backing and resources to carry out the construction work? (2:3–8). Not only did Artaxerxes give Nehemiah what he wanted, but he also provided him with a military escort for the journey to Jerusalem (2:9).

It might seem that Artaxerxes was short-sighted in giving a vassal city permission to rebuild its walls. Might that not encourage rebellion at some stage? But Artaxerxes was no fool. His large sprawling empire stretched from India in the east to Egypt and the eastern Mediterranean in the west. The Egyptians were in revolt and the independent Greek states, led by Athens, were making constant incursions along the Empire's western fringes. Perhaps a rebuilt Jerusalem could be part of a buffer zone protecting the Empire from threats originating in the west. But the real reason for the king going along with Nehemiah's plan had nothing to do with military strategy: God was behind Nehemiah's success (2:8b). It was *his* will that his city should be rebuilt.

The rest of the first half of the book, 2:10–6:19, records the story of how Jerusalem's walls were rebuilt and its gates replaced. It only took fifty-two days to complete the task (6:15), which was a remarkable feat of engineering, administration and management. It is even more amazing because of the odds stacked against the Jews. The task itself was a daunting one, as Nehemiah discovered during a night-time reconnaissance shortly after he arrived from Persia (2:11–16). He must have wondered if he could pull off such an undertaking. But, as well as rock-solid confidence in God, Nehemiah had a clear plan. As he explained it to the community leaders, they accepted what he said (2:17–18). The whole community was motivated by Nehemiah's inspirational leadership to carry out the project. This list of who repaired what and where includes all sorts of people from all walks of life. Some were so enthused that they built two sections of the wall.

In reconstructing the wall, Nehemiah had to overcome internal obstacles. Some of the nobles thought manual labour was beneath them (3:5), and their attitude may have caused discontent among the people. But that was nothing compared with the morale-sapping actions of some wealthy Jews. In a time of economic pressure, they were lending money to fellow Jews at crippling rates of interest, something God's law prohibited (*Exod.* 22:25). When people defaulted on their loans, they were selling them as slaves to foreigners to get their money back (5:1–5). Nehemiah took firm action to stamp out this practice (5:6–13), and then shored up the people's damaged morale by his personal example of generosity: buying back Jewish slaves (5:8); arranging interest-free loans (5:10); minimizing his expenses as governor by not using his position to line his own pocket (5:14–16); and always having plenty of guests for meals (5:17–18).

But the greatest barrier to rebuilding the walls came from external opposition in the shape of Sanballat the Horonite, Tobiah the Ammonite, and Geshem the Arab, who tried everything to halt the work. After ridiculing what was going on (2:19; 4:1–3), they turned nasty and threatened to attack the workers (4:7–8); but, through a combination of organizational skills, serious prayer, courageous faith and practical action, this threat of violence was neutralized (4:9–23). The opposition soon realized that their only chance of stopping the work was to remove Nehemiah. They tried to persuade him to come to talks aimed at ending the dispute (6:2). But Nehemiah knew that once they got him out of Jerusalem, they were going to assassinate him. When their scheme was foiled, the opposition resorted to blackmail (6:5–7) and tried to lure Nehemiah into doing something which would discredit him (6:10–13). Nehemiah's replies are superb (6:3, 8, 11) and show that he was not going to allow anything to sidetrack him from his God-given work.

In spite of the scale of the task, the internal problems, and the external opposition, Jerusalem's walls were rebuilt, as we have seen, in only fifty–two days. This remarkable feat put an end to the enemies' swaggering and forced them to recognize that God was with the Jews (6:16).

Even though the walls had been rebuilt to the glory of God, the restoration of the broken nation was not complete. So, in Nehemiah 7–13, we find the REBUILDING OF GOD'S SOCIETY.

Until now, people had been reluctant to settle in a defenceless city, but with the walls in place, Nehemiah saw no reason not to live in it. He unearthed the list of the first wave of returning exiles and repopulated the city with their descendants (7:4–73; 11:1–12:26). But the people who lived in God's city had to be God's people, committed to his rule, so, in Nehemiah 8–10, we have the centrepiece of this part of the book – a national renewal of the covenant. At this point, Ezra reappears in the story. The national renewal of the covenant began as Ezra and his associates read the law (7:73b–8:12) and continued with an unforgettable celebration of the Feast of Tabernacles (7:13–18). This was followed by communal confession of sin (9:1–37), in which the nation's embarrassing record of covenant unfaithfulness was openly admitted. After this there was a corporate sealing of the covenant renewal document (10:1–39), in which the people committed themselves to obeying God's commands in specific areas of their lives..

Only after this were Jerusalem's newly-rebuilt walls dedicated with tumultuous joy and praise to God (12:47–43). By doing things in that order Ezra and Nehemiah were declaring that it is not the physical walls which will protect God's people who live in God's city. Nothing but the spiritual 'wall' that Ezra had put in place through his teaching of God's law will do this. Jerusalem's new inhabitants were not to make the same mistakes as previous inhabitants of Jerusalem when they put their trust in the strength of their walls and not in the strength of their God. The physical walls would protect them no more in 444 BC than they had in 587 BC They needed to rely exclusively on God's covenant promise to protect his people (*Gen.* 12:2–3).

The final chapter of Nehemiah underscores this point. When he returned to Jerusalem for a second term as governor, Nehemiah discovered that old abuses had reared their heads while he was away. Tobiah had been provided with accommodation in the Temple complex (13:4–5); the Levites' support had dried up, with a serious effect on God's worship (13:5, 10); trading was taking place on the Sabbath (13:15); and the old sin of marrying non-Jews had resurfaced (13:23–24). With typical vigour, Nehemiah corrected these abuses. He informs us that he threw Tobiah's stuff out on to the street and purified the rooms (13:7–9); he reinstated the payment of tithes (13:11–13); he enforced the Sabbath regulations with their trading restrictions (13:15–22); and he disciplined the disobedient (13:25–31). By these actions Nehemiah reinforced the need for God's people to have a lifestyle of covenant faithfulness. He was determined not only to reconstruct the physical infrastructure but also the religious and moral structures, so that God's rebuilt city might contain God's rebuilt society.

By any standards what Nehemiah achieved was remarkable. Lessons can be and have been drawn from Nehemiah about how to be a godly leader and how to do God's work, especially in the face of determined opposition. However, that is not why the book of Nehemiah is in the Bible. All of the Bible informs us about God's salvation and how we can experience it for ourselves through faith in Christ Jesus (*2 Tim.* 3:15), and Nehemiah does just that. One of the images the Bible uses to describe what it means to be saved is that of being a citizen of God's city (*Isa.* 26:1; *Heb.* 11:10; *Rev.* 21:2). That imagery is found in Nehemiah. Another theme of Nehemiah, as well as of Ezra, is that of separation. Nehemiah built a physical wall, which divided God's people from others, but Ezra too built a 'wall' to act as a boundary between God's people and all other nations – only his was spiritual, the law of God which he taught. The New Testament also describes salvation in terms of breaking down walls that divide. Through his death, Jesus tore down the wall that divided God from sinners so that we can approach God (*Mark* 15:37–38). Through his death, again, Jesus removed the barriers which separate Christians from each other and united believing Jews and Gentiles as one new society in him (*Eph.* 2:14–18). One day, the new united society, taken from every part of the earth and every period in history, all the citizens of the New Jerusalem, will gather in front of the throne to worship the triune God for all eternity (*Rev.* 7:9–12).

Nehemiah is in the Old Testament for the same reason that all the other books are there: to pave the way for the coming of the Messiah, the Christ. And it is the final chapter which prepares us for his coming. Nehemiah 12 finishes on a high note with the dedication of the city's walls. If only the book had stopped there! But Nehemiah 12 is followed by Nehemiah 13, and Nehemiah 13 is disappointing. After all Ezra and Nehemiah's hard labour in terms of teaching, motivating, prayer, and effort, the people were committing the same sins which a few chapters before they had given their word not to do. We should not be too harsh on them, because we too are very prone to drift away from God and fall back into the very sins we thought we had dealt with. While the way in which Nehemiah closes, not with a bang but with a whimper, should certainly remind us how superficial our devotion to God can be, the book's anti-climactic end is meant to get our minds turning towards Jesus. The failure of the Jews makes us look out towards one who cannot fail. Covenants are solemnly sworn, yet so easily broken. Where will we find a constantly faithful covenant-keeper, except in our Saviour?

Nehemiah belongs among the Bible's great and godly leaders. In his description of the way he went about leading God's people (5:14–19), Nehemiah seems to have been consciously modelling his leadership on Deuteronomy 17:14–20. But, while he can go a long way towards rebuilding the nation, Nehemiah 13 teaches us the painful lesson that he cannot really rescue the people from that to which the Exile pointed, namely God's judgment on sin. If a leader as competent as Nehemiah cannot do this, who can? There is only one answer: the Lord Jesus Christ can and has. Only he, our completely sufficient Saviour, can radically and effectively set us free from sin's control over our lives and rescue us from God's judgment. This is how Nehemiah's great but incomplete achievements pave the way for 'Jesus, the author and perfecter of our faith' (*Heb.* 12:2).

17

Esther

Some people love to be the same as everyone else while others love to be different. The book of Esther falls into the second category. Its reputation for being unconventional is built on several factors. For one thing, it is uncommon for a book of the Bible to be named after a woman. Again, its place in the running order of the Old Testament in the English Bible is a bit surprising and potentially confusing. Because it comes after Ezra and Nehemiah we might assume that its action took place long after all that happened in those books. However, Esther records events during the reign of Ahasuerus, or Xerxes, who ruled over the Persian Empire from 486 to 465 BC. This places Esther chronologically between Ezra 1–6 and Ezra 7–10. What raises Esther's unconventionality to a unique level is the well-known fact that the book does not mention God. In a book about God – which is what the Bible is – this is more than a little puzzling. As well as all that, the contents are not what we might expect. It is not that Esther's plot is hard to follow: it is a classic story of good versus evil – the saving of the Jews in the Persian Empire from extermination. But in telling the story it deals with the sexual exploitation of women, racism, attempted genocide, sinister political dealings, and violent bloodshed. We might well ask, how did the book find its way into the Bible?

But in the Bible it is, and therefore we must get to grips with the story and what it means. We therefore begin with ESTHER'S STORYLINE.

If Esther was a play, it would have four acts of unequal length. The first concerns *the scheme of evil anticipated* (1:1–2:23). As the curtain goes up, we are immediately introduced to Xerxes, the Persian king. Though the story does not tell us this, the main thing on his mind is revenge. In 490 BC a Greek army inflicted a humiliating defeat on

Darius I, Xerxes' father, at the Battle of Marathon. When he succeeded his father, Xerxes started to plan a punitive war against the Greeks to restore Persian honour and avenge the defeat. So, in 483 B.C. (1:3), Xerxes threw a lavish party for all the power brokers of his empire to ensure their support for his planned expedition. For six months (1:4), Xerxes tried to impress everyone with a display of his opulence. Proceedings concluded with one final banquet for the men, while Vashti, his queen, entertained the women (1:5, 9).

After seven straight days of drinking Xerxes did something that would have massive ramifications for our story: he ordered Vashti, who was very attractive, to appear before him and his guests, so that everyone would admire her beauty (1:10–11). But Vashti refused to be treated like a trophy wife, a mere object to be paraded before a crowd of drunken men (1:12). Xerxes exploded with rage. How was he going to persuade all these princes, nobles and leaders that he could bring the Greeks into line if he could not get his wife to do what she was told?

So Xerxes hurriedly asks his advisors to formulate a response to Vashti's conduct (1:13–15). They are worried that the queen's conduct might spread to every home in the empire and cause social upheaval (1:16–18). Their advice is that Vashti should be deposed as queen (1:19), and her position given to a woman who knows her place. So Vashti was stripped of her status , and a royal edict announcing the decision, was dispatched to every part of the Persian Empire (1:20–22).

Chapters 1 and 2 are separated by about four years. Xerxes' invasion of Greece in the meantime was an unmitigated disaster. Xerxes' navy was destroyed in the Battle of Salamis in 480 BC and his army defeated at the Battle of Plataea a year later. As Esther 2 opens he is back in Susa, missing Vashti and having second thoughts about how he had treated her (2:1). Those close to him raise again the earlier suggestion that he should get a new wife (1:19; 2:2–4). Their suggestion was that a sort of competition should be organized for women who were young, unmarried and beautiful. The winner would be the new queen. At this point the story's two main characters make their first appearance. Living in Susa was a Jew called Mordecai, and his cousin whom he had adopted as his daughter when her parents died. She was called Hadassah, but we know her better as Esther (2:5–7). Esther had all the qualifications for the competition, and she was soon caught up in the search for a new queen.

There is nothing glamorous or romantic about what is going on here. Esther and the other girls did not choose to 'run for queen', but were forcibly removed from their homes and conscripted into the king's harem. They might have had a year's pampering as they waited their turn to go to the king, but if not selected as queen the outlook was bleak. The losers did not return home but were shut away in the women's quarters for the rest of their lives. However, there would only be one winner, and that turned out to be Esther. She won Xerxes' favour, and he immediately announced that the search for a new queen was over (2:15–18).

It is important to look below the surface here. Esther 1–2 is not in the Bible just to fill us with rage at the crude exploitation of women which was taking place. We must see that God was behind the scenes, moving his players into position in order to deal with the threat he knew his people would face. Do not overlook Esther 2:19–23 either. Mordecai heard of a plot by two disgruntled royal officials to kill Xerxes, and, through Esther, he passed on the information to the king. The plot was nipped in the bud, the two conspirators were executed, and Mordecai was mentioned in the official records. Acts of loyalty were usually rewarded immediately and generously by Persian kings, but inexplicably Xerxes overlooked rewarding Mordecai. His oversight is going to play a significant role as the plot develops.

If Esther was a play in which audience participation was encouraged, as the second act opens there would be a lot of booing and hissing, because, at the start of Esther 3, we meet the villain of the story – Haman. Act Two of Esther has to do with *the scheme of evil hatched* (3:1–15), and Haman is in the thick of it. Xerxes appointed Haman, a proud and arrogant non-Persian, as his new Grand Vizier (3:1), and, when he was informed that Mordecai had refused to bow and scrape to him, Haman was incandescent with rage (3:2–5). His informers made a great deal about Mordecai's Jewishness, so Haman decided not simply to kill Mordecai for disrespecting him, but to slaughter every Jew within the Persian Empire (3:6). So confident was Haman that he could flatter and bribe the king into agreeing with his plan that he even threw dice to determine the day for the massacre before he raised the matter with Xerxes (3:7). The king was easily persuaded and gave the scheme royal sanction (3:8–14). The only thing which might have irritated Haman a little was the fact that he would have to wait for almost a year to carry out his plan since the dice had come up with a date eleven months in the future.

Haman's disproportionate response to what seems a personal slight shows that more is happening here than meets the eye. Haman's hatred of Mordecai went far beyond personal animosity, and Mordecai's refusal to bow to Haman had nothing to do with personal jealousy. Mordecai is introduced as an exiled Jew (2:5–6), who lived as if he was still in Judah, retaining his Jewish mindset and attitudes. Haman was an Agagite (3:1), a descendant of Agag the Amalekite. It would have been impossible for Mordecai to show respect to Haman the Amalekite because there was long-running hostility between the Jews and the Amalekites, stretching back to Exodus 17:8–16 when the Amalekites attacked the Israelites as they made their way from Egypt to Canaan. That was the first of many Amalekite attempts to eradicate the Jews, and Haman's scheme was just the latest. But this is not simply one racial grouping planning the destruction of another. It is part of an even longer-running feud going back to the aftermath of the Fall. It is simply another phase in Satan's ongoing war against God (*Gen.* 3:15). God's promised Saviour would be descended from Abraham (*Gen.* 12:3). In planning to annihilate the Jews, Haman was only one in a long line of Satan's pawns by whom he tried to thwart God's plan of salvation.

Act Three, which is the longest, describes *the scheme of evil thwarted* (4:1–9:17). When the imperial edict was spread throughout the Persian Empire, a shockwave of horror and disbelief passed through the Jewish community (4:1–3). The Persian government had a fairly relaxed attitude towards minorities, provided they behaved themselves. This may explain why most Jews did not return home when Cyrus gave them the opportunity to do so in 539 BC: they were too well off. But now the policy was suddenly reversed. Mordecai realized that there was one person who had influence with the king and so was in a position to do something about the extermination edict, and that was Esther. However, cocooned within the confines of the royal palace, Esther seems to have been oblivious to what was happening. Mordecai managed to gain her attention (4:1), and get news to her of the threat to the Jews. When he urged her to plead with the king for mercy (4:7–9), Esther initially hesitated, seeking to justify her caution by appealing to Persian court protocol (4:11).

Mordecai's reply was direct. He reminded Esther that she too was part of the Jewish community and her position as queen was no insurance policy against being massacred in Haman's 'Final Solution'. Besides, might the fact that she was queen at that particular moment not be part of the solution to the problem (4:12–14)? Mordecai's directness was the spur Esther needed. She told Mordecai to organize a three-day fast among the Jews in Susa. She would do the same, and then she would ignore court etiquette and approach the king uninvited, irrespective of the personal consequences (4:15–17). Esther needed to get Xerxes' attention, so she used her greatest asset – her head-turning beauty. Her plan worked (5:1–2). When Xerxes asked her what she wanted, instead of blurting out what was wrong, she played a longer game and invited the king and Haman to a dinner party (5:3–5). Surely she would reveal her Jewish identity and expose Haman at the dinner party? But no, she invited Xerxes and Haman back the next day for another meal, although she did say that at it she would tell the king what was on her mind (5:6–8).

As he left the first meal, Haman was on top of the world, until he saw Mordecai. Then his mood turned ugly (5:9). When he complained to his wife and friends about how Mordecai was still ruining his happiness, they suggested that he should build a huge gallows and, in the morning, get the king's approval to have Mordecai hanged on it. With that pleasing prospect before him, Haman slept soundly.

Meanwhile in the palace Xerxes could not sleep (6:1), so he called for the record of his reign to be brought in and read to him. The part that was read 'just happened' to be about how Mordecai had foiled the plot to assassinate the king (6:2). Xerxes was sufficiently awake to ask what had been done to honour Mordecai for his act of loyalty. When he heard of the unaccountable oversight in not rewarding Mordecai, the king was now wide awake (6:3) Something must be done to make amends, so he asked if there was anyone in the court who could advise him. Now, who should 'just happen' to walk into the court but Haman! When Xerxes asked him how someone who had shown the king exemplary loyalty should be rewarded, vain Haman thought the king was talking about him, so he made the most of the opportunity (6:7–9). One can only imagine his expression when Xerxes told him to arrange the things he had just suggested for Mordecai (6:10). We are not told how Mordecai felt as Haman paraded him around Susa, but we are told that Haman was totally humiliated (6:12). His day was turning into a nightmare; but things were about to get even worse.

Before Haman could regain his composure, it was time for Esther's second party. During the course of the meal, she not only revealed her nationality – which, on Mordecai's instructions, she had kept hidden for years (2:10, 20) – but she also exposed Haman's conspiracy to exterminate her and her fellow Jews (7:3–6). Xerxes stormed out of the room in a fury. Knowing the game was up, the terrified Haman grabbed hold of Esther to plead for his life. This only made matters worse, because, as he did so, Xerxes came back into the room and saw Haman apparently molesting his wife. Hearing about the gallows Haman had erected for Mordecai, Xerxes immediately ordered that Haman should be hung on it (7:9–10).

However, Haman's death and his replacement by Mordecai as Grand Vizier did not end the threat of annihilation against the Jews. Persian royal laws – and Haman's evil scheme fell into that category – could not be repealed. However, at Mordecai's suggestion, Xerxes issued a counter-edict that, on the day Haman's extermination edict was due to come into effect, the Jews could defend themselves against attack (8:8–12), and news of it was quickly rushed out to all parts of the sprawling Persian Empire (8:13–14). On the authority of the counter-edict, the Jews were able to deal with as many of their enemies as were foolish enough to attack them, and so they were saved from the threatened annihilation (9:1–17).

There is one final short act in Esther and it concerns *the defeat of evil celebrated* (9:18–10:3). In order to remember and celebrate their rescue from Haman's 'Final Solution', a new religious festival was established. It was called the Feast of Purim.

Happily the debate about whether or not Esther should be included in the Old Testament canon was settled in Esther's favour; otherwise we would have missed out on ESTHER'S LESSONS. To begin with, Esther reminds us that worship must be regulated by God. The main reason the Jews included Esther in the Old Testament canon may have been to explain the celebration of Purim. Purim was not inaugurated by Moses when God gave his law to Israel through him. However, because it was sanctioned by the book of Esther, it was legitimate to celebrate it. When we take this principle through into the New Testament, baptism and the Lord's Supper are the only sacraments which Christians can legitimately celebrate today, because they were the only ones established by Jesus (*Matt.* 28:18–19; *1 Cor.* 11:23–26).

The reason Esther was only slowly accepted into the Old Testament canon is that, although it came from God, it does not mention God. That very fact highlights important lessons for us. Although he seems to be absent, God is always at work behind the scenes. What seem to the causal observer to be coincidences, such as the events which took place during Xerxes' sleepless night, are the result of God's sovereign control. God works, not only in the miraculous and extraordinary, but in the natural and ordinary. Even when his own people, such as Mordecai and Esther, do things from doubtful motives or even from outright disobedience, God still overrules them for his glory and his people's blessing. Theologians label the truth that God governs all his creatures and all their actions through normal means and without the intervention of miracles the *doctrine of providence*. The reality of it jumps at us from every incident in Esther. However, the great paradox that when God appears to be most conspicuously absent, he is actually most omnipotently present, is seen supremely in Jesus, particularly in his death. As his Son hangs on the cross, God seems absent, but in reality he is there, bringing his plan of salvation to a powerful conclusion. Or consider the ascension. The Lord's last words were, 'I am with you always' (*Matt.* 28:20), and then he left! Nevertheless, through his Spirit's activity, Jesus is omnipotently present with us even though physically absent.

Yet God's providence is exercised in a specific way: to protect his covenant promises. If Haman had had his way, God's promises would have come to a premature end. But by rescuing the Jews from Haman's genocide, God kept his promises to Abraham and David intact. God's promise to send a Saviour who would be a descendant of Abraham and David was preserved through his protection of the Jews throughout the Persian Empire.

One of Esther's main themes is that God, in his grace, reverses his people's destinies. Through Esther's intervention, Jewish fortunes were reversed. Instead of being destroyed, the Jews were not only rescued but empowered as Mordecai replaced Haman. Because of our sin, we have nothing to look forward to except death and destruction. But our destiny has been reversed through Jesus' intervention. He took the death that should have been ours so that we might have the life that was his. His resurrection confirmed this great and gracious reversal, guaranteeing us a life that is imperishable and eternal (*1 Pet.* 1:3–4), and which no one can snatch away (*John* 10:28–29).

18

Job

As we make the transition from Esther to Job, it is not hard to work out that we have moved into a different Old Testament neighbourhood. Out goes the focus of the previous books on national and international matters and in comes a new interest in individual concerns. Although it is not totally absent, prose is largely replaced by poetry, and this is reflected in the change of format in modern translations of the Bible. Historical facts, lists, records, and family trees give way to word pictures, rhyme and rhythm that appeal directly to our emotions as well as to our minds. This is the world of Old Testament wisdom literature.

The Septuagint, the Greek translation of the Old Testament, downsized the Hebrew Bible's 'Writings' section by relocating many of its books elsewhere. Only five books were left in that section: Job, Psalms, Proverbs, Ecclesiastes and Song of Songs, which were grouped together in one unit. As the English Bible follows the Septuagint's running order, we have inherited this five-book section of the Old Testament which we classify as 'wisdom literature'.

Job, which is the English Bible's first wisdom book, is named after its main player, and is, apart from prose sections at the beginning and the end, a long poem. We have no idea who the writer was. There are hints that Job might be at least a contemporary of Abraham or may have lived even earlier. There is no mention of Israel, or of a centralized sacrificial system based within the nation of Israel, located at the Tabernacle or the Temple and served by priests descended from Aaron. Instead Job carries out the same religious rituals that we find Abraham doing: as the head of the extended family, he offers sacrifices and prays for others (1:5, *Gen.* 12:8; 13:18; 20:17). Genesis 10 indicates that, after the Flood, people did not live as long as before. From the fact that he already had a family of adult children before disaster hit him and lived a further one hundred and forty years after his troubles (42:16), it is reckoned that Job lived about two hundred years. This would place him around the time of Abraham, if not slightly earlier. Job lived in Uz (1:1), which was east of the Jordan (1:3), but exactly where is not known. However, the book's purpose is clear. It is grappling with the age-old yet very modern question of why bad things happen to good people. This issue of personal suffering is addressed in a three-act drama.

The drama's first act deals with JOB AND HIS OPPONENT (1–2), and in it we are introduced to Job for the first time. As well as being an extremely wealthy and devoutly religious family man (1:2–5), respected in the community for his integrity, wisdom and generosity (29:7–17, 21–25), Job is a truly godly man. This is something about which the writer and God himself are insistent from the start (1:1, 8), so that we do not jump to the wrong conclusion as to why he suffers so much. However, God's evaluation of Job is seized upon by Satan and used to question Job's motives. While he concedes that Job's spirituality is impressive, Satan insinuates that the only reason he is righteous is because of all the benefits that come his way (1:9). If he were stripped of his prosperity, Satan argues, Job would soon be singing a different tune (1:10–11). God gives Satan permission to take away all Job's wealth (1:12), which he does quickly and dramatically (1:13–19). While he feels his losses deeply and laments them, Job does not turn against God (1:20–22). But Satan comes back for another attack on Job. He suggests that if Job himself had to suffer, he would soon be raging against God (2:1–6). Once more God gives permission for Satan to afflict Job with an excruciatingly painful skin disease (2:7–8); yet, in spite of his wife's provocation, he still refuses to curse God (2:10).

In the opening act of the drama, we have been allowed to see behind the scenes and we know that Job's suffering has nothing to do with moral failure on his part. But Job does not have access to this information. All he knows is that disaster has struck on a grand scale: his property is all gone, his children have all been killed in a freak accident, his health has collapsed, and his wife's faith has disintegrated.

The second and longest act of this drama concentrates on JOB AND HIS FRIENDS (3–37). Three friends of Job get word of the tragedies that have befallen him and come to give him some support (2:11). Job is so badly disfigured by his disease that when Eliphaz, Bildad and Zophar turn up, they hardly recognize their friend. They are so shocked that for a week they sit in silence (2:12–13), which is probably their most helpful contribution because, when they open their mouths to give Job the benefit of their wisdom, they sound more like enemies than friends. After an opening lament from Job (3), in which he reveals the depths of his anguish and pain, his friends start to make a series of pretentious and tortuous theological reflections on his condition and predicament. The author sets out their pontificating in four rounds of dialogue. In the first and second rounds (4–14 and 15–21), Eliphaz, Bildad and Zophar speak in turn, and Job responds to each of them. The third round is slightly different: only Eliphaz and Bildad make a contribution, to which Job gives his reply. In the meantime, a fourth friend called Elihu has arrived, and in the fourth round of discussions (32–37), he makes his contribution.

As the friends give their take on his predicament, they all have the same simplistic answer: that Job is suffering as a result of some sin he has committed, and, as he is suffering a great deal, he must have sinned in a major way. Their advice is straightforward: Job must own up to his sins, even his hidden ones, turn away from them, and obtain restoration from God. In fairness to Elihu it must be said that he adds something else to the mix. While he makes the same point as Eliphaz, Bildad and Zophar, he also makes the point that there is a disciplinary element to suffering that needs to be considered. Their speeches may be well-constructed and expertly delivered but they all lack sympathy. We wince as we witness them kicking Job when he is down.

They arrive at the same wrong conclusion about Job's suffering from different directions. Eliphaz is a mystic who has seen visions and heard voices (4:12–16), and because he imagines he has a direct line to heaven, there is no arguing with him. Bildad is a traditionalist who appeals to the received wisdom of the past (8:8–10). Unsurprisingly, it backs up his conclusions. Zophar is a dogmatist who has his theology all sorted out and, as a result, has all the answers. Elihu is the original angry young man who, with the overconfidence of youth, really believes that his older colleagues have lost the plot and he is smarter and more insightful than they (32:1–14).

The various rounds of discussions become progressively shorter, probably because the friends are running out of different ways of making the same argument, and also because Job is becoming increasingly forceful in protesting his innocence. By the end of chapter 37 there is nothing more to say. The discussions have reached gridlock.

At this point we reach the third act in the drama. It centres on JOB AND HIS GOD (38–42). God speaks. He begins by telling Job to get ready to defend himself because he is going to be required to give some straight answers (38:3). We can imagine Job starting to squirm. It is not hard to imagine that what is about to happen will not be a pleasant experience. And that is exactly how it turns out, for God bombards Job with question after question after question.

It has been suggested that God's treatment of Job is somewhat harsh. Has he not been through enough without having to undergo such an aggressive cross-examination? Why does God assault him verbally and not give him an answer to his 'Why?' question? But God *is* giving Job answers, though perhaps not in the way we think he should. The form of argument is one often used in Scripture: the argument from the greater to the lesser. The main thrust of all these questions about creation is to impress upon Job that if God controls the intricacies of the universe, most of which Job cannot begin to understand, then he ought to be able to trust that God knows what he is doing in his life, even in those circumstances that he cannot fathom. Although there is much to admire in the way Job responds to his suffering, there are times when he comes very close to stepping over the mark. Occasionally he seems to say that if he could find God, he would have it out with him, almost viewing himself as God's equal, with a right to demand an explanation of everything (23:2–5). As he questions Job, God is essentially reminding him that he is God and as such he does things that human beings cannot understand. Job needs to trust, not to argue or demand explanations.

All this questioning seems to have the desired effect, because when Job responds to God, his tone is very humble (42:1–6). Confronted with God's awesome majesty, Job repents of speaking foolishly, saying things he – a creature – should never have said to his Creator. The drama ends with Job ceasing to debate with God (40:4–5) and reaffirming his trust in him (42:1–5). He confesses his sins (42:6) and forgives his friends, whom God has rebuked for all their foolish talk (42:7–9). The book travels full circle as God restores Job's health, family life and prosperity (42:10–17).

There are a number of LESSONS which this ancient yet modern poem is teaching us. The most obvious one is that *Christians are not immune from personal suffering*. A myth often urged on people in the contemporary church is that the norm for the person who follows Jesus is a life largely exempt from illness, financial difficulties and stress, so that if you are not experiencing health, wealth and happiness, there must be something seriously wrong with your relationship with Jesus. Surely Job's experience should bury that idea for good! His relationship with God was praised by God himself and grudgingly acknowledged by Satan too as exemplary, yet he suffered, and the reason he did so was because he was following the way of God wholeheartedly. The road that Jesus travelled was marked 'suffering', for it led straight to the cross, and he calls on those who follow him to walk where he walked (*Luke* 9:23). If we follow him, we should not be surprised that we suffer, and the more wholeheartedly we follow him, the more we will suffer. In fact, our suffering is an indication that we are following Jesus rather than a sign – as is often mistakenly assumed – that we have drifted away from him.

Another obvious lesson from Job is that there are *no simplistic answers to the question of personal suffering*. That was the mistake of the friends, who were reprimanded by God for their response to Job's suffering (42:7–9). Not only was their thinking one-dimensional and far too simplistic; it also led them to make a negative and false assessment of Job's spirituality and morality. Suffering can be explained in terms of punishment for sin, but that is only one possibility. It may also be an indicator of God's grace, not his anger as the friends were trying to make out. The ultimate place of suffering for our sin is hell, but, in his mercy toward us, God sends suffering into our lives as a forewarning of hell. By means of it he calls on us to turn away from our self-centred rebellion to the Saviour he has provided, so that we may escape the coming wrath (*Psa.* 119:67).

To see suffering only in terms of retribution is like having only one tool in a toolkit. There are other reasons for personal suffering. One of them is that it expands our understanding of who God is. When we think that we have everything sorted out and neatly packaged, God brings us into the maelstrom of suffering to make us realize that God is much greater than we ever imagined. In Mark 4:25–41, Jesus, seeing that his disciples are in danger of domesticating him, takes them out on the Sea of Galilee where they run into a fearsome storm. The upshot of this crisis is that his disciples see in a way they had not done before how great Jesus is, and yet they also realize that he cares for them more than they had ever dared imagine. God was doing exactly the same thing with Job. Job not only knew about God, he also knew God – a fact seen in the way he constantly talked to God as well as talking about him. Perhaps at times he prayed out of frustration with his friends, but he did so also because he knew to whom to turn in a time of crisis (7:7–21; 9:28–31; 10:2–22). Yet his suffering took Job to a deeper level in his knowledge of God (42:5). Could his relationship with God have progressed without the need to suffer? We cannot say, but suffering is one of the means God uses in his mysterious providence to bring his people closer to him (*Psa.* 119:71, *Heb.* 2:10).

Undoubtedly suffering deepens our trust in God. Tough circumstances may have the effect of causing us to question God's love for us, and, as we see in Job's case, Satan is always trying to muddy the waters by insinuating that God is being unfair and harsh. But God takes us to the cross, that permanent historical reminder that he loves us (*Rom.* 5:8). Then we are faced with a choice: what are we going to believe – God's Word or Satan's lie? Are we going to live by faith or by sight? Are we going to trust God (*Psa.* 31:14–15), or allow our circumstances to dictate to us? Perhaps a major reason God does not give Job a black and white answer to his 'Why?' question is that when we suffer, God wants us primarily to trust in him rather than to demand explanations from him.

Suffering causes Christians to long for heaven. It is part and parcel of the reality of living in sin-riddled bodies in a sin-riddled world. But one day all this will change when the Lord returns to bring into reality a new heaven and earth, free from the ravages of sin, and to give us new resurrection bodies perfectly suited to spending eternity with him in the perfect new creation (*Rom.* 8:18–21; *Phil.* 3:20–21). His suffering caused Job to long for all this, even though he only grasped it tentatively (19:25–27).

During the early centuries of the Christian church, part of the liturgy at services held in the run-up to Good Friday involved reading from Job, reminding us that the book can only be understood by looking at it through the lens of Jesus' death on the cross. The great lesson of Job is that *Jesus is the only completely innocent sufferer*. He was the only human being who was totally sinless, and yet he suffered. But, in contrast to Job, Jesus voluntarily submitted to suffering for the benefit of others. He suffered to assure us, as we experience personal pain, that he fully understands exactly what we are going through (*Heb.* 4:15). But above all he suffered so that he might bring salvation to his people (*John* 10:17–18; *Phil.* 2:8).

When we suffer, the desire for an explanation is very strong within us; but God's 'explanation' is to take us to the cross. There we see that in normal Christian living the way God deals with us is often hidden behind a mask of suffering. The awful fact of Jesus' brutal, horrible and agonizing death on a Roman cross was, despite all appearances, a revelation of God's supreme wisdom and breathtaking love. As we live as Christians in this fallen world, we cannot expect to decipher the reasons for suffering. Yet we can be assured through the display of God's love at the cross that death brings life, that Christ's blood produces justification, and that suffering generates endurance and ultimate joy.

19

Psalms

When polls are conducted among Christians asking them their favourite book of the Bible, the Book of Psalms consistently comes top. The New Testament writers clearly loved this book for when they draw quotations and allusions concerning Jesus from the Old Testament a very high proportion are taken from the Psalms. With one hundred and fifty chapters it is the longest book of the Bible and contains both the longest chapter, Psalm 119 and almost next to it the shortest chapter, Psalm 117. But the reason Christians are so fond of the Psalms is that no matter what our spiritual state, whether triumphant or defeated, excited or depressed, joyful or sad, grateful or contrite, full of wonder or angry, there is a Psalm which reflects how we feel. Again and again as we read the Psalms, we find that we ourselves are being read, so that we say, 'This man understands me and what I am going through.' Because we sense that the writers of the Psalms have taken the same route as we are travelling, we often use their words as prayers to verbalize our experiences and as songs to express our praise.

The most common way to describe the Psalms is as the hymnbook of the Old Testament, but that description is not totally accurate. Many were specifically written to be sung when God's people met together for worship, but many of them are not songs but prayers. In addition, some of the Psalms are so individual and personal that to use them in corporate worship would mean doing some violence to the context. But the most significant difference between the Psalms and a hymnbook, as we conceive of one, is its structure. While some are arranged alphabetically, most hymnbooks have a topical or liturgical arrangement, while the Psalms have, for the most part, no discernible order.

Having said that, the book, as it has come to us under the Holy Spirit's supervision, can be sub-divided into five 'books', probably collected separately before being compiled into one book. The five 'books' of the Psalms correspond to the five books of the Pentateuch, and this numerical connection reminds us that the Psalms are authoritative: as well as being songs and prayers to God from his people, they are words from God to his people.

There are also several mini-collections within the Psalms which form separate units. Psalms 93–100 celebrate God's kingship. Another unit is the 'Hallel' psalms (113–118), which were sung on Passover night (*Mark* 14:26). Another is the 'Songs of Ascent' (120–134). Three times a year pilgrims made the trip to Jerusalem for the annual religious festivals (*Deut.* 16:16) and as they did so, they undoubtedly sang. It may be that, over time, these songs were collected as the 'Songs of Ascent'. Psalms 146–150 all begin and end with 'Hallelujah'. It is reasonable to assume that they formed yet another originally-separate group of psalms.

Various people or groups of people wrote the Psalms. Solomon composed a thousand and five songs (*1 Kings* 4:32), and his name is associated with two of the Psalms (72; 127). Heman the Ezrahite, Ethan the Ezrahite and Moses contributed one each (88–90). The sons of Korah and Asaph wrote twelve Psalms each (42–49; 84–85; 87–88; 50; 73–83). But the most prolific composer of Psalms was David, who was a highly acclaimed singer-songwriter (*2 Sam.* 23:1). Seventy-three, nearly half the book, were written by him, and it can be argued that he is behind many more Psalms whose composition is attributed to no one in particular.

Many Psalms have a 'title' giving information about the composer, the tune the Psalm is to be sung to, or the Psalm's background (3; 7; 18; 30; 34; 51–52; 56–57; 59–60; 63). Occasionally we can work out when the Psalm was written from its content; for example, Psalm 137 belongs to the period of the Exile, and Psalm 126 seems to have been written after God's people returned to Judah. If we combine what we can deduce from the titles of various Psalms and from the text of others, we can see that the Psalms were written over a long period of time, from Moses (90) to the post-Exile period (126). It is assumed that some time after the return from exile the Psalms were compiled into the book we have today.

As we approach what the book is saying to us, we need to remember that it is poetry and approach it as such. Hebrew poetry is character-ized by compactness of expression, parallelism rather than rhyme, the use of rhythm and an intense use of imagery. In addition to all this, the various writers use such conventions as word play, alliteration and acrostics (see below). As poetry, the Psalms interact with us at an emotional level as well as an intellectual one, and one of the best ways to feel their impact is to read them aloud slowly.

Another factor is that there are various genres, or types, of Psalms. How many there are is a matter of opinion, but let me suggest the following categories. There are the *hymns*, in which the majestic splendour of God's character is celebrated with exuberant joy (24; 98; 145). There are *songs of thanksgiving*, similar to the hymns but differing in that they are expressions of thanksgiving to God for his response to a situation of national trouble or personal distress (3). There are *royal* Psalms: songs and prayers connected with the king. Psalm 2 is a coronation anthem; Psalm 45 announces itself as a song to be sung at a royal wedding; Psalm 21 is David's meditation on the privileges of kingship; Psalm 89 recalls God's promises to David and prays for their fulfilment; Psalm 101 reads like a coronation oath for David and his successors; and Psalm 110 reflects on the union of the functions of priest and king in the figure of Melchizedek. The discrepancy between what these royal Psalms promised and the reality in the lives of Israel's kings was so glaring that people realized that they pointed forward to the appearance of God's ideal king.

Then there are the so-called 'Imprecatory Psalms' in which God is asked to bring judgments on people, including breaking teeth or arms (3:7; 10:15; 58:6), causing sudden death (55:15), orphaning children, causing financial ruin, and blotting out enemies' posterity (109:9–15). But the imprecatory Psalm which people most love to hate is Psalm 137 with its grim conclusion that appears to incite infanticide. We come across Psalms of *lament*, songs of disorientation, in which feelings of discouragement, grief, disappointment and anger are expressed. Some are personal laments (77), while others are corporate (83). Laments in the Psalms have a distinctive pattern which ends up in some statement of praise to God (28; 69): the one exception is Psalm 88. Many Psalms are *songs of confidence* in God's care for and guidance of his people, and this genre of Psalm is characterised by striking metaphors for God (11; 16; 23; 27; 62; 91; 121; 125; 131). There are *wisdom* Psalms which offer instruction on how to live for God in the details of life as we struggle to live under God's rule in a fallen world (1; 37; 73). If we keep in mind the Psalm's genre, we will more easily grasp its purpose, and therefore its meaning.

The Psalms bring so much information before us that we need a filter which helps us sift through it all, and the one I am going to suggest is this: *What do the Psalms teach us about God?* The entire Bible is about him, but what specifically do the Psalms contribute to our understanding of who God is?

The God of the Psalms is *the God who deserves to be praised.* Not only do the Psalms underscore the fact that God is worthy to be praised (145:3), but they explain why this is so. Praising God is not an optional extra. What he has done in creating the world by the power of his word (33:9; 148:5) demands our praise. Yet above all else, God is to be praised for his work of redeeming his people. While many of the Psalms celebrate what God did in the events of the Exodus (105–106), some of them focus on how God brought his people home again from exile in a second Exodus (107). These twin themes of praise to God as Creator and Redeemer are fused together in the praise of Jesus in heaven (*Rev.* 4:11; 5:9–11).

He is also *the King who rules over all.* God's sovereign rule over all he has made is celebrated in many Psalms, and it is this theme which unites Psalms 93–100. Not only is there celebration of God's rule on a macro-level, over national and international affairs; many psalms also rejoice in God's reign at a micro-level, over the circumstances of an individual believer (84; 145). This theme of God as King reaches its apex in the Messiah, and two Psalms in particular are often used in Christian worship to celebrate Christ's triumphal return to heaven after his victory and his coronation to the supreme place in the universe (2; 24).

Yet great and splendid though this King is, he is also *the Saviour who hears our cries*, and it is the Psalms of lament that specifically point us in that direction. Sins are confessed and God is asked to forgive and restore. God hears and acts, bringing relief at a national level (85; 126) and a personal level (32; 51). This assurance of a God who responds to his people's cries reaches its fulfilment in Jesus who, because he shares our humanity and has triumphed over sin, death and all evil, hears our prayers and rescues us (*Heb.* 2:14–15; 4:15–16; 7:25).

Because God is King by virtue of being Creator (24:1), he is *the Lord who demands our obedience*. While it is true that God has revealed himself through his creation (19:1–6), he has supremely done so in his Word (19:7–14). He has given us his kingly Word, not to fill our minds with information but, as we live in obedience to his commands, to transform our lives. The great example of this way of thinking is Psalm 119, because, with very few exceptions, every verse in the Psalm refers explicitly to God's Word. Its emphasis is that believers should take delight in his Word and express that delight in wholehearted obedience to its teaching. Psalm 119 is not only the longest Psalm but the most elaborate. There are twenty-two letters in the Hebrew alphabet, and Psalm 119 is divided into twenty-two stanzas, allowing each Hebrew letter its turn to introduce eight successive verses on the subject of God's Word. There are other acrostic Psalms, as this type of Psalm is labelled (9–10; 25; 34; 37; 111; 112; 145), but none of them is as complex as Psalm 119.

Living in obedience to God's rule does not guarantee us an easy life, but in God we have *a Helper who rewards our trust* in him. It is not that God takes our difficulties away, but, as we trust him, we experience his help in the crucible of our troubles (23:4–5; 31; 34; 37; 73; 121; 123–125; 128).

While the imprecatory Psalms may sound at best strange and probably embarrassing to most Christians, these 'war psalms of the Prince of Peace' remind us that God is *the Judge who enforces his covenant*. The commonest way to deal with these thirty or so grim prayers is to try to grab the moral high ground and say that, after all, this is the Old Testament and Jesus offers us a better way. But that 'solution' is a non-starter, particularly in the light of the use the New Testament makes of some of these Psalms (for example *John* 15:25; *Acts* 1:20; *Rom.* 11:7–9). To arrive at a much more satisfactory answer, we need to set them in their covenantal framework. The sentiments expressed in the imprecatory Psalms are not those of personal revenge, but must be seen in the context of Satan's constant attempts to use people as pawns in his efforts to thwart God's carrying out of his covenant (*Rev.* 12:1–6, 13–17). When people try to stand in the way of God fulfilling his promises to Abraham and David, they are not to be given kid-glove treatment but ought to be treated with the utmost severity. It is the passion that the Psalmists had for God's glory – in terms of the carrying out of his plan – that caused them to pray as they did. Perhaps this is one reason why we are so uncomfortable with the imprecatory Psalms: they expose our lack of passion for God's glory. As part of his covenant with Abraham, God warned that if anyone went against his people he would deal with them (*Gen.* 12:3). So when people pray these imprecatory Psalms, they are simply asking God to do what he promised he would do, and that kind of praying is always applauded in the Bible – never condemned.

The clearest picture we have of God in the Psalms is of *the Messiah who is to come*. The New Testament writers cite the Psalms to support their inspired understanding of many issues: for example, Paul quotes from the Psalms in Romans 3:10–18 to reinforce his teaching that every human being has sinned and that sin has polluted every aspect of our humanity (14:1–3; 5:9; 140:3; 10:7; 36:1). However, it is when they set out to establish Jesus' identity as the promised Messiah and Son of God that the New Testament writers' use of the Psalms comes into its own. They had clearly understood Jesus' teaching about how the Psalms, along with the rest of the Old Testament, focused on who he is and what he achieved on the basis of his death and resurrection. (*Luke* 24:44). While some Psalms have a very sharp and clear witness to Jesus (2; 16; 22; 110), as the table below indicates, pointers to Jesus are found throughout the Psalms.

One specifically Christian way in which we can approach the Psalms is to see them as prayers of Jesus (*Heb.* 2:12) and as prayers to Jesus.

For example, what we called the hymns (24; 98; 145) are the songs of Jesus indicating his glorification and so are sung to glorify him. The laments point towards his humiliation – which is how the New Testament writers view them – and so they are prayed to him as expressions of the way in which we suffer as we seek to follow him.

SOME POINTERS TO JESUS IN THE PSALMS

Psalm	Fulfilment	Psalm	Fulfilment
2:7	Matt. 3:17	45:6	Heb. 8:1
8:6	Heb. 2:8	68:18	Mark 16:19
16:10	Mark 16:6–7	69:9	John 2:17
22:1	Matt. 27:46	69:21	Matt. 27:34
22:7–8	Luke 23:35	72:11	Matt. 2:11
22:16	John 20:25, 27	109:4	Luke 23:34
22:18	Matt. 27:35–36	109:8	Acts 1:20
34:10	John 19:32–36	110:1	Matt. 22:44
35:11	Mark 14:57	110:4	Heb. 5:6
35:19	John 15:25	118:22	Matt. 21:42
40:7–8	Heb. 10:7	118:26	Matt. 21:9
41:9	Luke 22:47		

20

Proverbs

As a small boy, I was intrigued by my granny's calendar. It not only told you the date, but it also had some advice for that day. It was from it that I learnt that 'an apple a day keeps the doctor away'. At first glance the book of Proverbs, with its bite-sized suggestions for living, seems to be like my granny's calendar. But is it? Let us take a closer look.

Although various people, such as a group simply known as 'the wise' (22:17; 24:23) and two men called Agur (30:1) and Lemuel (31:1), contributed to what we find in Proverbs, the book's main author is Solomon, king of Israel, who gained a region-wide reputation for being incredibly wise (1 *Kings* 4:29–31). Yet, in spite of various people being behind the composition of Proverbs, the book has a consistent STYLE. It is *paternalistic* but not patronising, and this is flagged up by the way the phrase 'my son' crops up twenty-three times, especially in the opening chapters. As a middle-aged man, Solomon is reflecting on his life in order to pass on to the next generation what he has learnt. He wants those following him to avoid making the mistakes he made and to go after wisdom, which will help them to live in a way that pleases God.

With the sharp eyes of a sociologist and the curious mind of a scientist (1 *Kings* 4:33), Solomon observes life, and writes down his reflections in the form of *proverbs*, rather than promises. These are not the same thing because a promise implies an obligation: if A is done, then B will follow; while a proverb has to do with a general principle of life that is usually true but to which there may be some exceptions: if A is done, then generally B will follow. Proverbs must be read as a book of proverbs and not promises, and we avoid big problems if we do this.

For example, many Christian parents take Proverbs 22:6 to be a promise. Then when their children go astray they suffer a massive crisis of faith, imagining that God has not kept his word. But Proverbs 22:6 is a proverb, setting out a general observation that if parents point their children in the right direction, they will generally not go too far astray, either when growing up or when they have grown up. Life tells us that things do not *always* work out that way, but normally they do.

We also need to take on board the fact that it is *poetry* and not prose. The main reason for this is that poetry is more easily remembered than prose, something that was vital in the oral culture of Solomon's time, compared with the written culture in which we live. For example, which is easier to remember: the statement, 'In advance of committing yourself to a course of action, you should carefully consider all the possible outcomes', or the proverb, 'Look before you leap'? Yet Hebrew poetry is not the same as English poetry. It is not based on rhyme but on rhythm, and not only rhythm of metre but mainly the rhythm of thought. A key element in this is what is called 'parallelism'. There is more than one kind of parallelism. There is *synonymous* parallelism, in which the thought of the first line is repeated in the second. An example of this is Proverbs 16:23. Not far away, in Proverbs 16:25, we bump into *antithetical* parallelism, where the thought of the second line stands in contrast to the first. The final type of parallelism is *synthetical* parallelism, in which the thought of the first line is advanced by the second, as in Proverbs 14:7. While parallelism is the main poetic device used in Proverbs, there are also acrostics, where each line begins with a new letter of the Hebrew alphabet (31:10–31), or number sequences (6:16–19; 30:7–9, 15–16, 18–19, 21–31).

Solomon wrote three thousand proverbs (*1 Kings* 4:32), so what we have in Proverbs is only a selection, perhaps an anthology of his best proverbs. The book as we have it was compiled later by an editor who was so supervised in his work by the Holy Spirit that Proverbs has a clear STRUCTURE. At its most basic level, it can be divided into two large sections. Proverbs 1–9 contains extended discourses, similar in many respects to the wisdom literature that was current in the region at that time. Then in Proverbs 10–31 we come across masses of short, pithy sayings, the kind we usually associate with the term 'proverb'. However, these two large sections can be further subdivided. Proverbs opens with a short but significant *preamble* (1:1–7), in which we are introduced to the book. Its purpose is set out: to point the impressionable in the direction of prudence, knowledge and discretion, and to give the already wise an even stronger grasp on true wisdom (1:2–5). How this will be done is explained in Proverbs 1:6, but the most crucial statement in the preamble is Proverbs 1:7. 'The fear of the LORD' is the key. All that we are instructed to do in Proverbs presupposes that we live under God's rule, taking delight in obeying him because we love him. This sets Proverbs apart from all man-made morality, including the advice on my granny's calendar, because here relationship with God precedes ethics.

After the preamble, we come across a series of extended *discourses on wisdom* (1:8–9:18). They take the form either of a teacher addressing his son – meaning probably his disciple, rather than his actual offspring (1:8–19), or of speeches in which wisdom is personified and speaks for herself (1:20–33).

Proverbs 10:1 flags up the fact that we are moving into a new subsection of the book. It comprises a series of *proverbs by Solomon* (10:1–22:16), in which he aims his instruction at everyone. About ninety percent of these proverbs are in the antithetical parallelism style, in which a truth is examined from opposite perspectives. So Solomon is setting out the alternatives in a wide variety of scenarios and inviting us to decide which of the two ways of behaving exhibits the fear of the Lord.

A small section of *proverbs attributed to the wise* (22:17–24:34) is inserted at this point, and this is followed by *another collection of proverbs composed by Solomon* (25:1–29:27), which were put together by some people at Hezekiah's court (25:1).

Proverbs concludes with three short independent collections of proverbs. These are *the sayings of Agur* (30), *the sayings of Lemuel* that he learnt from his mother about the proper way for kings to behave (31:1-9), and finally a powerful acrostic *poem in praise of the virtues of a good wife* (31:10–31). It is worth noting that in the Hebrew Bible

Proverbs 31:10–31 is followed by the books of Ruth and Song of Songs. All three texts present us with positive feminine characters, who are capable, wise and deserving of our respect. Perhaps the feminist idea that the Bible is intrinsically an anti-female book needs to be radically revised.

Proverbs can be challenging to read because, due to the compactness of its style, so much information about so many different topics is fired at us so rapidly. The best way to make sense of all that we are being taught is to keep the book's overall THEME in mind. In that way we can see where the individual proverbs fit into the big picture. It is not hard to work out that *wisdom* is the book's theme. The words 'wisdom' and 'wise' occur more than one hundred times. However, we need twenty-twenty vision about what the Old Testament means by wisdom or we will totally miss the point of Proverbs. Our culture has devalued wisdom to mean the same thing as knowledge, so that to be wise simply means to know facts, usually trivia, and to be able to access them instantly. In the Bible wisdom has to do with living, especially living in a way that pleases God. It is not acquired through education, whether formal or that arising from life's experiences, but it comes to us from God, by means of his revelation in the Bible. Wisdom is achieved only by submission to God's authority, expressed in obedience to his Word (9:10; 15:33).

Proverbs spells out how to live wisely, and it begins with *a proper relationship with God*. The wise person fears the Lord (1:7), trusts in the Lord (3:5–6), accepts the Lord's discipline (3:11–12), makes cultivating his relationship to God a top priority (4:23), and has a confidence that God is in control (16:1–3). This initial relationship with God will lead to *a good relationship with others* as the wise person speaks the truth (22:20–21), chooses good companions (22:24–25), and values family life (30:17; 31:28). On top of this, a wise person maintains *a healthy relationship to himself*. According to Proverbs, this is done primarily by exercising self-control in such areas as morality (2:16–19; 7:6–27), speech (18:7–8, 21), attitudes to people whom one could potentially exploit (22:22; 25:21–22), realistic self-knowledge (27:1–2; 29:23), wealth and possessions (28:2) and anger (29:22). By exercising self-control, the wise person will avoid such dangers as easy money – using corruption and fraud to exploit others – and sexual licence. Instead he will work hard for his money (10:4–5; 24:30–34) and he will love his wife faithfully (5:18–19).

When it comes to its contemporary RELEVANCE, many Christians misuse Proverbs, seeing it simply as a collection of motto texts to be dipped into at random. They take a 'my-granny's-calendar' approach to it because they detect little which is plainly Christian about Proverbs. The prophet, priest and king, the key players in the development of God's plan of salvation in the Old Testament, are either not mentioned or only get the occasional passing nod of the head. The themes of redemption, which are common in other parts of the Old Testament, appear to be absent from Proverbs. But we need to look more closely because Proverbs does contain a strong redemptive motif, particularly in the *movement from folly to wisdom*. Paul plugs into this motif in almost the last thing he wrote as he speaks about becoming a Christian in terms of being made wise for salvation (*2 Tim.* 3:15). We reject folly and embrace wisdom, as, by God's grace, we are enabled to shift from a life dominated by our self-centred, independent rebellion against God to a life of submission to his rule. When it refers to salvation, Proverbs focuses on what we have been saved for – a life of wisdom in which we delight to do what God has told us to do in his Word and with which God is pleased. So often we concentrate on what we have been saved from rather than what we have been saved for, and Proverbs gives us a timely corrective to this imbalance in our thinking. When we read Proverbs, especially in the statements which use antithetical parallelism, we are confronted with the question: 'Will we dine with Wisdom or with Folly? The Wisdom who beckons us is none other than Jesus Christ, while the folly that attempts to seduce us is any created thing that we put in the place of the Creator (*Rom.* 1:22–23).'[1] Embracing wisdom is compared to eating from the Tree of Life (3:18), that tree which first crops up in the Garden of Eden and makes its final biblical appearance in heaven (*Gen.* 2:9; *Rev.* 22:2) as a symbol of eternal life.

[1] Raymond B. Dillard and Tremper Longman III, *An Introduction to the Old Testament* (Leicester: Apollos, 1995), page 245.

We must not step over the contrast Proverbs is setting up here. Eve ate from the tree of the knowledge of good and evil because she wanted to be wise (*Gen.* 3:6). But her way of achieving wisdom was not along the route of the fear of the Lord: she deliberately opted to go along the slippery slope of self-assertive independence from God's clear command (*Gen.* 2:17). This rebellion resulted in her forfeiting access to eternal life (*Gen.* 3:22–24). In contrast we find in Proverbs another woman – for wisdom is always personified as female – instructing us as to where wisdom can be found. It can only be experienced through the fear of the Lord as we embrace his rule, submitting to his legitimate authority to tell us what to do and obeying his Word.

But Christ and his salvation are present in Proverbs in other ways. He is the one who provides mercy to the penitent (28:13). His name is the strong tower in which the righteous find refuge (18:10). He is the friend who loves at all times, and sticks closer than a brother (17:17, 18:24). Unfortunately, many Christians fail to see him there. Centuries after Solomon, Israel's wisest king (*1 Kings* 3:4–12), there appeared another king of Israel, who was wiser than Solomon, and that king was Jesus (*Matt.* 12:42). Again and again in his account of Jesus' life, Matthew highlights the links between Jesus and Solomon to reinforce Jesus' credentials as a greater person than Solomon. As he gives us Jesus' family tree, Matthew – in contrast to Luke – traces Jesus' descent from David through Solomon (*Matt.* 1:6). In the Sermon on the Mount Jesus not only refers to Solomon (*Matt.* 6:29), but uses Solomon's experience of asking for wisdom and being given more besides (*1 Kings* 3:12–13) as a template for how Christians should live (*Matt.* 6:33). When he taught Jesus utilized similar teaching methods to Solomon: parables drawn from his observations on life and creation, pithy sayings and parallelism. Even the theme of the Sermon on the Mount is the same as that of Proverbs: how to live under God's rule.

The New Testament writers draw connections between Jesus and the figure of Wisdom in Proverbs. So, when Paul refers to Jesus as 'the image of the invisible God, the firstborn over all creation' (*Col.* 1:15), his language reflects Proverbs 8. And when John describes Jesus as the 'ruler of God's creation' (*Rev.* 3:14), his words harmonize well with

Proverbs' picture of Wisdom's role in creation. Jesus himself made this connection because when his behaviour was challenged, he responded by saying, 'Wisdom is proved right by her actions' (*Matt.* 11:19).

However, this connection between Jesus and Wisdom needs to be approached with care, because Proverbs 8 is a poetic representation of God's characteristic of wisdom, not a literal description of the Son of God. If Proverbs 8 were taken too literally it might give rise to a heretical view of Jesus as having been created at a point in time by an already-existing God, although there is no real ground for this in the text. Having sounded that note of caution, the connection between Jesus and Wisdom is appropriate because Jesus embodies the wisdom of God (*1 Cor.* 1:30). He is the one 'in whom are hidden all the treasures of wisdom and knowledge' (*Col.* 2:3). What he said was continually labelled as being wise (*Luke* 2:41–50; *Mark* 1:22; 6:2). However, God's wisdom in Jesus is supremely displayed in the cross (*1 Cor.* 1:18–25). Only an infinitely wise God could have thought up and carried through such an audacious plan of salvation in which his justice was not compromised nor his love frustrated (*Rom.* 3:25–26). It is little wonder that when he reflects on God's salvation achieved on the basis of Jesus' death, Paul exults in praise of the wisdom of God (*Rom.* 11:33).

21
Ecclesiastes

A feature of modern life is the rise of the 'Public Inquiry'. Disasters are followed by demands for answers, usually from the opposition parties who hope that the public inquiry will embarrass the government. So some eminent person is duly appointed to chair a public inquiry which will hear the evidence, draw up a conclusion and make recommendations. This obsession for public inquiries reveals our in-built desire that life should make sense. The book of Ecclesiastes has the feel of a public inquiry, as a wise man attempts to work out what kind of life is worth living. He introduces himself to us as *Qohelet*, a Hebrew title which is translated as 'the Teacher' or 'Preacher' in Ecclesiastes 1:1, but as that designation is a broad one, it leaves the door open for speculation as to who he is. So he narrows things down by referring to himself as the 'son of David, king of Jerusalem' (1:1). The classical view is that it is Solomon who is conducting this inquiry because he has all the qualifications. He was the only successor of David who ruled in Jerusalem over the whole Israelite nation (1:12). He certainly had the resources, abilities, acumen and clout to engage in all the activities in which *Qohelet* claims to have been involved (1:12–2:23). Although some have thought the book was compiled by an anonymous writer using Solomon's name as a pseudonym, the classical view still has a great deal to be said for it, and I am going to stick with it.

From Ecclesiastes' STYLE it is clear that it fits neatly into the 'Wisdom Literature' section of the Bible because, like Proverbs, the book contains general observations on life which are expressed in a variety of ways: poetry (3:1–8), parables (4:13–16), pithy statements (11:1; 12:1) and prose passages (5:4–7). As he writes, Solomon uses all these different literary devices to inspire confidence in us that his inquiry into the kind of life that is worth living will be thorough, pre-empting any suspicions of a cover-up or a whitewash.

When some write about Ecclesiastes they use words like 'rambling' and 'random' to describe its STRUCTURE, but that is a little disingenuous as an analysis of the book reveals a framework that has been clearly thought through. As Proverbs shows, one of Solomon's favourite literary devices is the use of antithetical parallelism in which the thought of the second line of a proverb stands in contrast with the drift of the first line. In Ecclesiastes, Solomon uses antithetical parallelism on a grand scale as throughout the book he looks at life from two opposite perspectives: from the negative standpoint of unbelief, as God is left out of the picture and from the positive viewpoint of faith which keeps God at the centre. When reading the book, the clue as to which perspective Solomon is adopting is found by asking what clusters of words and phrases appear in that section. If he is examining life from the negative standpoint of unbelief, the phrase 'under the sun' recurs repeatedly, and if it is from the positive viewpoint of faith God's name crops up again and again. If Ecclesiastes is thought of as an example of large-scale antithetical parallelism as Solomon switches between these two opposite ways of looking at life, a clearly defined structure emerges. Rather than being rambling and random, the book has all the hallmarks of a carefully crafted document that leaves no stone unturned as it inquires into the characteristics of a life worth living.

Ecclesiastes starts with an *introduction* (1:1–11), which looks at life from the perspective of unbelief. Life is a waste of time, something pointless and purposeless (1:2). Everything just goes round and round and round on a treadmill of monotonous repetitiveness (1:2–9). Even when people imagine that they have come up with something novel, all they have done is rebranded and repackaged the old (1:10). What is the point of life when our best efforts and achievements are so quickly forgotten (1:11)? Life is totally absurd. Our actions have no significance.

Next we step into the core of the book, discovering that it is made up of *four sermons*, all of which are constructed in a pattern of antithetical parallelism. The first one runs from 1:12 to 3:15. Solomon explores various avenues which he thinks might lead to true and lasting satisfaction, pushing at the boundaries all the time. He discovers that education cannot take him where he wants to go (1:12–18) because life's anomalies cannot be easily sorted out or life's experiences reduced to a neat system. Neither can pleasure do so (2:1–11) because a hedonistic lifestyle based on laughter, alcohol, creative activity, power and self-indulgence cannot take him there. Living his life in line with traditional values is not much better (2:12–16), and neither is hard work (2:17–23), because we have to leave all that we have worked for to someone else. In his search for true and lasting satisfaction, Solomon still has not found what he is looking for. Then everything changes as God is brought into the picture (2:24–3:15). Everything is part of God's plan and so everything immediately has significance, which means that life is filled with purpose and direction.

In the second sermon (concluding at 5:20), Solomon gives us a double dose of the negative standpoint of unbelief but he counters it with two sections of the positive viewpoint of faith. He starts off by asking what the point of certain things is (3:16–4:16). What is the point of being good, as there is no justice in the world? What is the point in being creative and hardworking, as we will end up dead and all we get at present is stress and exhaustion? What is the point in being popular? It might make us feel good for a while as we think of how everyone loves us, but people are so fickle that popularity is a very shaky foundation upon which to build our lives and careers. Then, in Ecclesiastes 5:1–7, Solomon reminds us that there is a God who is to be worshipped and feared. This is the only stable basis for all true and satisfying living (*Prov.* 9:10). However, he slips back into negativity (5:8–17) and wants to know what the value of wealth is. Money cannot buy justice, much less satisfaction. No matter how much wealth we accumulate, we will have to leave it all behind when we die. Fortunately Solomon returns to looking at life from the viewpoint of faith (5:18–20), and when he does all the frustration disappears. Not only is everything seen as a gift from God, but for those who believe there is something greater than the gifts – the Giver. Having this perspective makes all the difference: we can not only enjoy God's gifts but we can also enjoy God himself.

In the third sermon (6:1–8:13), life is examined again, from the negative standpoint of unbelief and then from the positive viewpoint of faith. In 6:1–12 Solomon highlights three matters which are a total waste of space. We are living in fantasy land if we think that wealth will last or satisfy. We also need to wake up if we imagine that things will change or that we will leave the world a better place than we found it. But then Solomon reverses perspective again (7:1–8:13), concluding that some things are worth pursuing. It is better to go after honour than luxury, seriousness than frivolity, restraint than impulsiveness, wisdom than wealth, consent than rebellion, godliness than everything else, revelation than reason, discretion than inflexibility; and the fear of the Lord absolutely trumps evil.

The fourth sermon runs from 8:14 right through to 12:7, and for the final time Solomon takes us down the well-travelled route of looking at life under the sun (8:14–10:20) and then life under God's rule (11:1–12:7). When people step out of the sphere of God's rule and go off in their own self-centred rebellious independent way, they find life frustrating. They do not want to know God, so they do not even try to. All they know is that they will die, so they need to have fun now. Yet people are not totally unrestrained in their pursuit of pleasure. Instead of constantly steamrollering everyone to get what he wants, even the person who has no time for God is wise enough to realise that at times it is better to exercise a little common sense in what he says and does. However, the person living under God's rule looks at life from a completely different point of view. Instead of saying that, because death will soon be knocking at his door, he should live it up and enjoy himself while he can, he says that because he will not always have the opportunity to do good, he should serve God and others while he can (12:1–7).

Solomon ends with a positive *conclusion* (12:8–14). This acts as a counterbalance to the negative introduction since it looks at life from the viewpoint of faith. He restates the viewpoint of the person who rejects God's rule when all is said and done, life is a waste of time, something pointless and purposeless (12:8). Then he goes on to interact with and challenge that standpoint. He explains that there is no need for us to set out on a long and exhaustive search for the meaning of life by reading every book ever written: that would drive anyone to distraction (12:12b). Instead we should read his book because it is designed to show us the way of life (12:9–12a). If we listen to what God has to say to us through him, our quest will be over. In 12:13–14 Solomon summarizes the conclusion of his inquiry into the life worth living. If we fear God, living under his rule by obeying what he has to say in his Word, we will experience life. We are ultimately answerable to God, so if we live for anything or anyone else, life will be meaningless. But if we live for God and his glory, we will enjoy him and the eternal life he offers now and forever.

The findings of some public inquiries are judged by history as significant, resulting in vital changes in the area studied. The findings of others bring no change. When the media interest has moved on to something else, they gather dust. Ecclesiastes' RELEVANCE lies in the fact that Solomon's public inquiry falls into the first category. Strange as it may sound, Ecclesiastes' relevance comes out in its negative sections. After reading them, you might want to lie down in a dark room for half an hour to regain your composure. But listen carefully to them and you will realise that the parts describing life under the sun actually highlight the book's timeless relevance.

First, the negative sections show us the *idol-shattering* function of Ecclesiastes. They describe a world that has turned away from God and made the deliberate decision to live in independence from him, and in self-centred rebellion against his rule (*Psa.* 2:1–3). However, our human nature is such that, when God is rejected, we must replace him with a substitute. Our culture has made idols of the very things Solomon exposes as being meaningless and a chasing after the wind. Rather than worshipping the true and living God, we worship our careers, our physical appearance, our wealth, our popularity, our reputation, and our families. Solomon's critique brings to light the impotence of our idols, showing the bankruptcy of what they claim to offer. Those who reject God are doomed to a life of meaninglessness.

The negative sections also show us the *Messiah-foreshadowing* function of Ecclesiastes, and this is where Solomon's introduction of himself as the 'son of David, king of Jerusalem . . . king over Israel' (1:1, 12) comes in. During his reign it looked as if all of God's covenant promises to Abraham and David had reached their fulfilment. Was not Solomon the successor God had promised David (2 *Sam.* 7:12)? Were not the Genesis 12 promises of a people, protection, a place and a programme involving the nations being realized? The population had exploded (*Gen.* 22:17; 32:12; *1 Kings* 4:20) as the nation experienced peace (*1 Kings* 4:21). God was present among his people at the Temple in Jerusalem, the place he had designated as his dwelling. People from various nations came to Jerusalem to receive God's wisdom from Solomon (*1 Kings* 4:34; 10:1–13). But if people were getting excited about what was happening, Ecclesiastes completely stifled their enthusiasm. Things might be good, but life was still meaningless. Disorder still prowled around the world. Good as his reign might have been, a greater than Solomon was needed – a greater son of David who would rule over God's people. In him alone, and under his rule alone, all of God's covenant promises to Abraham and David would reach their ultimate conclusion. All of Solomon's negativity about life is designed to direct our attention away from him and his reign to 'the Lord's anointed, great David's greater Son'.

The negative sections are also significant because they show us the *salvation-anticipating* function of Ecclesiastes. The book's redemptive movement is from frustration to satisfaction. The frustration Solomon describes in the negative sections is the outworking of God's curse on the world (*Gen.* 3), and the salvation Ecclesiastes anticipates is the reversal of that curse so that we return to the environment of God's blessings in Genesis 2, only better.

While Ecclesiastes is never directly quoted in the New Testament, Paul has it in mind in Romans 8 when he mentions creation's frustration (*Rom.* 8:20). The Greek word for 'frustration' is used by the Septuagint, the Greek translation of the Old Testament, to translate 'meaninglessness', the motto-word of Ecclesiastes. In Romans 8, Paul is writing about what God has achieved through his Son, and by linking him to the theme of Ecclesiastes' negative side he is signalling that the curse-reversing salvation anticipated by Ecclesiastes has been accomplished by Jesus.

God's curse on human sin results in pain and frustration (*Gen.* 3:16–19), but Jesus has redeemed us from this curse in order to bring meaning and satisfaction to work, marriage and life (*Col.* 3:17–4:1). The negative sections of Ecclesiastes highlight the way in which death is the great enigma and absurdity to the unbeliever; but by his death Jesus has dealt radically and effectively with death (*Heb.* 2:14–15). Death is no longer the ultimate cause of meaninglessness and frustration, but for the Christian it is full of purpose as the entrance into God's presence forever. By his resurrection Jesus has filled us with hope that one day when he returns, the whole creation will finally be set free from the frustration and futility caused by sin (*Rom.* 8:18–20). This curse-reversing salvation anticipated by Ecclesiastes is achieved by Jesus. On the basis of his death and resurrection,

> He comes to make his blessings flow,
> Far as the curse is found.[1]

---

[1] Isaac Watts' hymn, 'Joy to the World'.

22

Song of Songs

At his best Solomon was very much an all-rounder: a wise king, a shrewd diplomat, a clever politician, an able administrator, a prudent economist, a fine scientist and an insightful writer. He even wrote one thousand and five songs (*1 Kings* 4:32). Of the three that survive, Psalm 72, Psalm 127 and Song of Songs, the last named must have been considered the best. That is why it is called, 'Solomon's Song of Songs' (1:1). This type of expression indicates the best of a kind: the Holy of Holies is the Temple's most sacred place and the King of kings is the supreme ruler.

It is obvious that the GENRE of the Song of Songs is poetry. The way it is formatted in modern English translations of the Bible illustrates this. Beyond that it has to be characterized as 'love poetry'. Another adjective I would apply is 'dramatic' because this poem tells a story, charting the course of a relationship between Solomon and an unnamed girl who is referred to as 'the Shulammite' (6:13). In the NIV, Solomon and the girl are given the titles 'Lover' and 'Beloved' respectively, so that we know who is saying what, though a footnote remarks that the divisions and their captions are debatable. The titles are not part of the Song's original text, first appearing in the margins of a fifth century AD copy of part of the Old Testament known as *Codex Sinaiticus*. Another group of people who turn up are the 'Friends', who act like a chorus, speaking up to encourage, help and learn from the couple. The appearance of these titles gives the feel of a drama to the poem.

There is no getting away from the fact that the poem contains intensely sensuous – though never lewd – imagery. Being a dramatic poem, Song of Songs has a STORYLINE, and it is fairly simple to follow in outline. Solomon had a vineyard in the hill country about fifty miles north of Jerusalem, which he let out to tenants. The tenants were a mother, her two sons and their younger sister, the Shulammite. She was the 'Cinderella' of the family; naturally beautiful but, because she worked so hard in the vineyard, she had no time to take care of her personal appearance. One day Solomon arrived *incognito* at the vineyard, and started to take an interest in her. She thought he was a shepherd and asked him questions about sheep, to which he gave an evasive answer. However, he did speak lovingly to her and won her heart. He left with the promise that he would return for her some day. Finally he did return, in all his kingly splendour, and took her to be his bride. The relationship, like all marriages had its ups and downs, but it emerged from these trials mature and settled.

While poetry usually defies exact analysis, there is a clear STRUCTURE. The first section describes *the courtship* (1:1–3:5). The main speaker is the Shulammite, who recalls the events that led to her wedding.

The central part of Song of Songs focuses on *the wedding* (3:6–5:1). We are not only spectators on the route as the bridal procession makes its way to Jerusalem, but we have the privilege of being guests at a royal wedding. The main speaker is Solomon, who lavishes praise on his bride. Some of his metaphors sound very unromantic and are not recommended for use in the West at the start of the twenty-first century AD! But they were obviously the sort of things that appealed to an Israelite.

The third section of the poem recalls *the marriage* (5:2–8:14), and it breaks down into three smaller units. With sadness in her voice, the Shulammite recalls a very emotionally difficult time when the marriage ran into some turbulence and there was a period of coldness on her part towards her husband (5:2–6:3). However, the next segment of the poem describes the renewal of their love as Solomon comes to reassure her of his love for her (6:4–8:4). After this there is the experience of settled devotion to each other (8:5–14), and in this final part of the poem, Solomon and the Shulammite speak equally, indicating that their marriage is the partnership God intended it to be.

While there is general agreement about the type of literature the book is, when we read Song of Songs we scratch our heads, some more nervously than others, concerning its MEANING. In order to understand the book's purpose we have to consider the various ways in which Song of Songs has been interpreted.

Song of Songs has been interpreted as *an allegory*. In this type of writing the story is really about something other than what is literally expressed. In an allegory, each person and image is designed to convey a spiritual truth deeper than that which lies on the surface of the text. So Song of Songs is only superficially the story of the relationship between Solomon and the Shulammite. It is about something deeper, namely the relationship between Jesus and the church, his bride. The Scriptures do contain many mystical and allegorical passages. God compares himself to a bridegroom and his people to a bride (*Isa.* 62:5), and he calls himself the husband of his people (*Isa.* 54:5, *Hos.* 2:16, 19, 20). The allegorical interpretation of Song of Songs has a long history in the church, and many of the finest interpreters have taken this view, while many have also come up with some very fanciful interpretations.

More recently Song of Songs has been regarded as mainly *a love poem*. Viewed in this way, it has been very helpful in enabling the church to deal with one of the major issues it faces today: that of human sexuality. At the start of the twenty-first century, human sexuality has been perverted in at least two ways. Secular Western culture makes an idol of sex. It aggressively promotes the idea that life without some kind of sexual activity, whether heterosexual or homosexual, within marriage or outside of it, is boring and meaningless. Technological advances have heightened this perversion of sexuality. Because the majority in the West have turned away from the true and living God they have to replace him with a substitute 'god' and, for many, this has been the idol of choice. But the church's attitude has not always been altogether wholesome either. It has demeaned human sexuality by giving the impression that, even within the context of marriage, it is a bit low and almost a necessary evil.

Song of Songs defeats both these perversions by celebrating the beauty of human sexuality within its God-approved context. The suggestion that physical love is allowable in any setting is not countenanced in Song of Songs. Old Testament Wisdom Literature, of which this love poem is a part, constantly affirms the doctrine of creation and its resulting creation ordinances, one of which is marriage (*Gen.* 2:18–25). So Song of Songs underscores the fact that monogamous heterosexual marriage is the only God-approved context for the physical expression of human sexuality: any other setting is out of bounds.

In that context, this love poem underscores the fact that sex is a good gift from God. The garden setting reminds us of the Garden of Eden. There we see that physical love within marriage is one of God's gifts for humanity to enjoy, and part of what God pronounced 'very good' (*Gen.* 1:31). In this way Song of Songs can be seen as a celebration of married love.

However, in the context of the whole of the Bible, Song of Songs is much more than a love poem. It has to be seen as *an analogy*, which suggests spiritual truths without there being such an exact equivalence as there is in an allegory. Throughout the Old and New Testaments, marriage is a metaphor for the personal and intimate relationship between God and his people. In the Old Testament the covenant is represented as a marriage, placing upon God's people a lifelong and exclusive commitment to him. When Israel falls into idolatry, this is condemned as spiritual adultery (*Hos.* 1–3). The metaphor is carried over into the New Testament, and is especially to be found in Ephesians 5:22–33, where Paul compares the relationship of Christ to Christians with that of husband and wife.

Viewing Song of Songs as an analogy we see in the relationship between Solomon and the Shulammite, parallels with our relationship to the Lord. We are staggered and thrilled by his grace in choosing us as his bride (1:5–6). We are refreshed by the constant reassurances of his love which he gives us (4:1–15; 6:4–9; 7:1–9). We are encouraged to lavish our praise on our Husband (2:3–13; 5:10–16). We are warned that sometimes our love for him can grow cold (5:2–8), but then we are comforted by the way in which he restores our love for him (6:4–9).

If Song of Songs were simply a love poem, it might help to instruct Christians in how to have happier marriages and how to be more loving spouses, but that would be to reduce it to the level of just another self-help marriage manual in an already overcrowded market place. But Song of Songs – like the entire Bible – is about the gospel; about the love of Christ for us, and about how he works resolutely in us to prepare us for the day when in heaven, as his stunningly beautiful bride, we will be with him forever (*Rev.* 21:2).

23

Isaiah

While the Hebrew Bible is normally subdivided into the Law, the Prophets and the Writings, or Psalms (*Luke* 24:44), the English Bible has adopted a different classification. While it retains the Law intact, the English Bible introduces a History section by bringing together material from the Prophets and Writings categories of the Hebrew Bible. Then it has a Wisdom Literature section, made up of part of the Writings. Finally the English Bible has a Prophets section, sometimes divided into the Major and Minor Prophets.

In Isaiah, Jeremiah and Ezekiel, we encounter the Major Prophets. Isaiah comes first for a number of reasons. First, Isaiah's ministry pre-dates those of Jeremiah and Ezekiel. His call to be a prophet came in 740 BC, in the year of Uzziah's death (6:1), and he was active in Judah for the next forty years, throughout the reigns of Jotham, Ahaz and Hezekiah (1:1). Jewish tradition has it that Isaiah was killed during Manasseh's reign (696–642 BC), something which may be alluded to in Hebrews 11:37. As far as God's patience with Judah's covenant unfaithfulness was concerned, the straw that broke the camel's back was the flood of paganism that engulfed the nation during Manasseh's reign (*2 Kings* 21:10-15). So Isaiah ministered as Judah stumbled and staggered towards the point of no return, while Jeremiah and Ezekiel were active after it.

Another reason why he precedes Jeremiah and Ezekiel is Isaiah's theological importance. He is directly quoted sixty-five times in the New Testament. As well as that, many of the New Testament's best known metaphors have their roots in Isaiah. For example, when, in Ephesians 6:10–20, Paul writes about the Armour of God, his jumping-off point is not primarily the Roman soldier who was guarding him but what God says about himself in Isaiah 59:15–17. When Jesus describes himself as 'the true vine' (*John* 15:1), he was deliberately alluding to a song Isaiah had composed in Isaiah 5:1–7. Neither Jeremiah nor Ezekiel shapes the New Testament's theological categories in the way Isaiah does. A final factor which contributes to its premier placing among the Major Prophets is Isaiah's quality as literature. Without demeaning Jeremiah's and Ezekiel's literary qualities, Isaiah is in a class of its own. Just read it aloud in an English translation and its richness will strike you immediately. Isaiah's vocabulary is much more extensive than the other Major Prophets, consisting of 2,186 different words compared with Jeremiah's 1,653 and Ezekiel's 1,535.

What do we know about Isaiah that will help us get to grips with his message? On a personal level, Isaiah lived in Jerusalem, capital of the southern kingdom. Sources outside the Bible suggest that he was part of the wider royal family, perhaps a cousin of Uzziah. His father was called Amoz (1:1). His wife, whose name we are not told, was a prophetess (8:3), and he had at least two sons by her (7:3; 8:3). On a national level, Isaiah ministered during times of crises as the dark shadow of Assyria began to fall upon Judah's political landscape. Frightened by the expansionist noises coming from Assyria, Syria and Israel, Judah's northern neighbours, tried to force her into an anti-Assyrian coalition. When Ahaz, Judah's king, refused, Syria and Israel invaded. Ahaz was panicking (7:2), but Isaiah told him to trust in God and his covenant promises because Syria and Israel were on the way out (7:4–9). However, Ahaz refused to do so and instead appealed to Assyria for help. From that point on Judah lost its political independence. What was worse, Ahaz introduced aspects of Assyrian worship into the Temple (2 *Kings* 16). Hezekiah, Ahaz's son and successor, longed to be free from outside political interference. In the turmoil that surrounded Sennacherib's accession to the Assyrian throne in 705 BC, egged on by promises of Egyptian backing, Hezekiah attempted to restore Judah's independence by rebelling against Assyria. Not long afterwards, Sennacherib besieged Jerusalem to punish Hezekiah for stepping out of line. When the promised Egyptian help did not materialize, Hezekiah, with Isaiah's encouragement, did what he should have done all along:

he trusted God. The result of his faith was Sennacherib's retreat when his army was destroyed by the angel of the Lord (36–37). But Hezekiah made a major blunder. On hearing of his recovery from a serious illness (38), Merodach-Baladan, a Babylonian prince, sent Hezekiah a congratulatory letter and present (39:1). However, Merodach-Baladan was not really interested in Hezekiah's health: he wanted to bring Hezekiah into another anti-Assyrian alliance. Hezekiah was totally taken in by the flattery and signed up to Merodach-Baladan's plan, which is what Isaiah 39:2 is all about. He had once more set off down the path of unbelief rather than sticking to the way of dependence on God. He was brought down to earth when Isaiah announced that God was going to use the Babylonians as his instruments of judgment on Judah's covenant unfaithfulness (39:5–7), just as he used Assyria to punish Israel. This political setting is crucial to understanding Isaiah's message. Everything he says is against the backdrop of the present Assyrian or the future Babylonian threat.

As far as Isaiah's STRUCTURE is concerned, its sixty-six chapters divide into two main sections: 1–39 and 40–66. The statistically-minded will immediately have spotted the numerical connection between Isaiah and the Bible as a whole. Isaiah's sixty-six chapters correspond to the sixty-six books of the Bible, while the thirty-nine chapters of the first main section parallel the thirty-nine books of the Old Testament, leaving twenty-seven chapters in the second section, which, of course, is the number of books in the New Testament. The basic theme of each of these two main sections is highlighted by the names of Isaiah's sons. God had told Isaiah what to call the boys because their names were going to symbolize the way he would deal with his people (8:18). One son was called Maher-Shalal-Hash-Baz (8:3), which meant, 'Quick to plunder and swift to spoil'. His name points to the way in which Isaiah 1–39 is primarily about God's judgment. The other boy's name would be Shear-Jashub (7:3), which meant, 'A remnant will return', indicating that Isaiah 40–66 would have to do with God's grace.

If we fill out this basic structure, we will discover that Isaiah 1–39 focuses on *the announcement of God's judgment*. Isaiah opens with prophecies of judgment on Judah (1:1–12:6). There follow prophecies of judgment on the surrounding nations (13:1–24:33). After this there are hymns and prophecies encouraging Judah to trust in God (25:1–35:10), and the first main section concludes with some history that illustrates how God delivers his people when they trust in him and judges them when they do not. Then there is a shift as Isaiah turns from addressing the contemporary situation to talking about the future: *the prediction of God's salvation* (40–66). He wants God's people, decades in the future, to read what he has written and be encouraged that God has not deserted them. So, in the second main section of his book, Isaiah talks about the coming deliverance (40:1–48:22), the coming Saviour (49:1–57:21), and the glorious future (58:1–66:24).

Differences between the two main sections of Isaiah in terms of style and focus have given rise to the idea that Isaiah was written by two different people. Just to muddy the waters further, differences in emphasis within the second main section have led others to speculate that there were, in fact, three authors at work in the writing of Isaiah. The case for the multiple authorship of Isaiah, which is taken as read by the majority of Old Testament specialists, even by those who should know better, is insubstantial. The argument from different styles does not hold much water, while the idea that Isaiah could not have predicted something decades in the future is foolish. Predicting the future was one of the functions of a prophet in the Bible, and, in Isaiah 40–66, Isaiah is just doing what he has been called to do. We must refuse to veer off the traditional route and, even though it may be unfashionable, continue to affirm that all sixty-six chapters were authored, under the inspiration of the Holy Spirit, by one man – Isaiah, the son of Amoz.

To understand Isaiah's MESSAGE, we need to go straight to Isaiah 6:1–13, where we have the record of Isaiah's call to be a prophet. In this passage he flags up the themes he is going to develop in the rest of the book. His call came in the form of a vision in which he 'saw the Lord' (6:1), or, more precisely, he saw Jesus (*John* 12:41). What immediately struck Isaiah was *God's kingship*, because he saw 'the Lord seated on a throne' (6:1). God is no constitutional monarch with very limited powers. He is the sovereign king who controls history, so that his purposes come to pass. This sovereign king is going to raise up

Assyria to punish Israel (10:5–6), then Babylon to do the same to Judah (39:6–7), and finally Cyrus to set in motion events that would pave the way for a return from exile (44:24–45:7). It was while he was in the Temple mourning Uzziah's death that Isaiah had his commissioning vision (6:1). Unlike human kings who come and go, God is the eternal king, whose rule continues uninterrupted. Nor is God a localized tribal deity with a limited sphere of influence: he is the universal king, whose glory fills the whole earth (6:3). Isaiah is connecting with God's covenant promise of a programme for the nations (*Gen.* 12:3), which is not simply to use the nations to realize his plans but to bless them with his salvation in Jesus the Messiah. The inclusion of the nations in God's saving purposes is such a major thread running through Isaiah (2:3; 24:14–16; 49:6; 55:5; 56:7–8; 60:3) that, when he wants to explain the Gentiles' incorporation into God's people, Paul turns to Isaiah (11:10 in *Rom.* 15:12; 65:1 in *Rom.* 10:20).

Isaiah was so overwhelmed by a sense of *God's holiness* that, throughout his book, his favourite designation for God is 'the Holy One of Israel'. He uses that title for God twenty-five times, too many to list here. You will have to use a concordance or the search facility in your Bible software to find the exact references. The great benefit of God's holiness is that everything associated with him is holy too. Israel is a holy people (62:12); Jerusalem is the holy city (48:2); the Temple is holy (64:11); and Zion is a holy mountain (11:9); even the road leading to it is labelled holy (35:8). But the drawback is that, in comparison with God, his people, including Isaiah himself, are 'unclean' and under God's judgment (6:5). Due to their spiritual blindness and insensitivity, they cannot grasp what God is saying to them (6:9–10) and end up deriding God's message (28:7–13). This is an indication that the nation is only going in one direction – towards the disaster of a future exile (6:11–12).

However, there is something else Isaiah experienced which impacted his whole ministry, and it was *God's grace*. So, the moment he confesses his personal sinfulness, God instantly, by means of a substitutionary sacrifice, removes the defilement caused by his uncleanness and makes atonement for his sin (6:6–7). Having personally experienced God's grace, Isaiah announces that, after punishing his people, God will be gracious towards them, because grace, not judgment, is his final word. God's grace will be seen in the way that, in spite of a widespread desertion of him, God will preserve a remnant who will remain true to him (6:13). When Paul wants to remind us that, despite Israel's wholesale unbelief, God will always have ethnic Jews who trust in Jesus, he uses Isaiah's theme of the remnant to back up his argument (1:9 in *Rom.* 9:29; 10:22–23 in *Rom.* 9:27–28). God's grace will be supremely seen in the restoration after the return from exile, the theme which dominates Isaiah 40–66. However, Isaiah's presentation of this restoration takes it far beyond the mere replacement of what was lost in 587 BC (11:6–9; 30:26; 65:17–18, 21, 25; 66:22–23). Isaiah is looking to a more distant horizon than 539 BC – to a time when God brings into existence a new order, with a renewed heavens and a new earth.

Isaiah's message of God's kingship and grace is personified in two figures who dominate each half of the book. Isaiah is negative in the way he alludes to how human kings rule, comparing their rule unfavourably with that of God. This gives rise to the hope that one day an *ideal king* will appear. He will be a descendant of David (9:7; 11:1), perfect in character (11:2–3), ruling with justice (9:7; 32:1–6). His reign will be characterized by security and harmony (11:6–16; 33:17–24). This was such a huge ask that only God himself could make it happen, so Isaiah began to talk about God himself coming in real humanity to make this hope of an ideal Davidic king a reality (7:14; 9:6–7). Then, tucked away in the second part of Isaiah are four poems known collectively as 'The Servant Songs' (42:1–8; 49:1–6; 50:4–9; 52:13–53:12). They tell of the activity of the *Servant of the Lord*. As he makes God's covenant promise of a programme to bless all peoples a reality by communicating God's truth to the Gentiles (42:6) and, as well as bringing Israel back to God, by taking God's salvation to all (49:6), we feel the loving heartbeat of God's grace. But the Servant of the Lord will pay a heavy price for his obedience to God's purposes for him (50:5): he will die under God's judgment as he is punished for the sins of God's people (53:4–9).

Then Isaiah does the totally unexpected by fusing these two figures together, highlighting connections between the ideal Davidic king and the Servant of the Lord which are striking. The Lord as king is 'high and lifted up' (6:1), but so is the Servant of the Lord (52:13). God has put his Spirit on each of them so that they can carry out their activities successfully (11:2; 42:1). The Servant of the Lord will establish justice (42:1, 3–4), which is exactly what the ideal Davidic king will do (9:7; 11:4–5). The Servant of the Lord will be the hope of all the earth (42:4), and, in the same way, the ideal Davidic king will lead the Gentiles out of darkness (9:1). These connections indicate that the ideal Davidic king and the Servant of the Lord are one and the same, for the humiliated, suffering one is the glorious, reigning one. Isaiah's message establishes the pattern of suffering and glory, humiliation and exaltation which is picked up in the New Testament and applied to Jesus.

This fusion is identical with Jesus' own understanding of his mission. When he outlines to his disciples why he has come to earth (*Mark* 8:31; *Mark* 9:31; *Mark* 10:33–34), Jesus consciously aligns himself with Isaiah's pattern of suffering and glory. He, the Son of Man, which is a royal title, would be – and notice the language of Isaiah 53 – rejected and killed, but he would be raised to life and to God's throne, totally vindicated. Paul uses Isaiah's fusion of the ideal Davidic king and the Servant of the Lord in Philippians 2:6–11, as he explains Jesus' saving work. What Paul says is directly shaped by Isaiah. He even applies the words of Isaiah 45:23 directly to Jesus in Philippians 2:10–11.

When Matthew, Mark, Luke and John reinforce their argument that in Jesus God has kept all his covenant promises, they often draw on Isaiah because his POINTERS TO JESUS are everywhere. When they speak of how John the Baptist prepared the way for Jesus' public ministry, they all refer to Isaiah 40:3 (*Matt.* 3:3; *Mark* 1:3; *Luke* 3:4–6; *John* 1:23). Matthew sees Jesus' virgin birth as the fulfilment of Isaiah 7:14 (*Matt.* 1:20–23). When news reached Jesus of John the Baptist's arrest, he withdrew to Galilee and began his public ministry there. In doing so, he was bringing about Isaiah's prediction of Isaiah 9:1–2 (*Matt.* 4:12–16). When Jesus preached in the synagogue in Nazareth, he appealed to Isaiah 61:1–3 (*Luke* 4:16–30). Isaiah 6:9–10, 29:13 and 53:1 are cited to explain why Jesus taught the crowds in parables and why his message was not accepted by his audiences (*Matt.* 13:13–15;

15:7–9; *Mark* 4:12; 7:6–7; *Luke* 8:10; *John* 12:37–40). When his disciples watched Jesus perform miracles such as restoring a deaf and dumb man's hearing and speech, feeding a hungry crowd and giving a blind man back his sight, they realised that, before their very eyes, they were watching something that Isaiah said would happen (35:5–6; 44:9–10, 13; 55:1–2). Jesus' policy of avoiding any heavy-handed tactics and notoriety was a clear fulfilment of what Isaiah said about the Servant of the Lord (42:2–3; 50:4).

However, it is in the way that the fourth Servant Song (52:13–53:12) provides the sub-text for the events surrounding Jesus' death and resurrection that Isaiah's prophecy comes into its own as a pointer to Jesus. The Servant of the Lord would be rejected (53:3), and Jesus' claim to be God's Son and God's king was firmly rejected by the Sanhedrin (*Mark* 14:61–64), by the mob on the street as they voted that Barabbas should benefit from the Passover Amnesty (*Mark* 15:6–11), by Pilate, the Roman Procurator of Judea, who passed the death sentence on him (*Mark* 15:12–15), and by the Roman soldiers deployed to execute him (*Mark* 15:16–20). Jesus' silence as he stood before Pilate was a fulfilment of Isaiah 53:7. Just as Isaiah had predicted, the violence carried out against Jesus was so brutal and savage that his physical appearance was mutilated beyond recognition and people looked away in horror (52:12; 53:3). The Servant of the Lord would die in the place of others, bearing their sins (53:5–6). Just so, in his death Jesus died as our substitute, dying the death we should have died, being punished for the very sins we were guilty of – blasphemy and rebellion (*Mark* 14:64; 15:26). His execution between two criminals was foreseen by Isaiah 53:12 (*Mark* 15:28). Jesus' burial in Joseph of Arimathea's tomb (*Mark* 15:42–47) was also foretold (53:9); and with his resurrection (*Mark* 16:1–8), the final piece of the Isaiah 53 portrayal fell into place (53:11–12).

With so many pointers to Jesus in Isaiah, it is little wonder that Christians have wholeheartedly approved of the description, apparently first given to Isaiah by Jerome – 'the evangelical prophet'.

24

Jeremiah

A friend of mine told me he was once described as 'a bit of a Jeremiah', meaning that he was a pessimist. The remark made me think: does Jeremiah deserve such a negative press? To find out, we have to read his book, the second of the Major Prophets. It is not an easy book to read. Its variety of material, ranging from sermons in poetry and prose to biography, historical narrative and personal lament, may perplex us, but in addition it is not straightforward chronologically.

Having said that, there is a STRUCTURE to Jeremiah. The book opens with Jeremiah's call (1:1–19) and ends with Jerusalem's fall (52:1–34). Between these, Jeremiah divides into four major sections. The first contains *the announcement of God's judgment on Judah and Jerusalem* (2:1–25:38). Jeremiah confronts the nation with its covenant unfaithfulness, spelling out their sins, and then states in no uncertain terms that it will be punished with exile for its rejection of God. Within this section is a segment in which Jeremiah records his interaction with God over how he feels about the negative contents of his message and the hostile reception it received (11:1–20:18). The next section (26:1–36:32) is *a collection of non-chronological narratives* that revisit some of the issues raised in the first section. For example, the content of the famous 'Temple Sermon' is recorded in Jeremiah 7:1–29, but the reaction to it only appears in Jeremiah 26; Jeremiah's policy of surrender to Babylon (21:8–10) becomes the focus of chapters 27–29; and the reasons for God's judgment (22–23) find historical expression in chapters 26–29 and 34–36. Tucked away in this section are chapters referred to as 'The Book of Consolation' (29:1–33:26), in which Jeremiah holds out hope of a return from exile, and much more. Then, just when we thought we had grasped the fact that narrative in Jeremiah is sometimes arranged thematically, we arrive at the third section of the book (37:1–45:5), which is arranged chronologically. It outlines *incidents surrounding the fall of Jerusalem*, an event which validates Jeremiah's prophecies in the first section. The final segment (46:1–51:64) contains announcements of *God's judgment on the nations* of Egypt, Philistia, Moab and Babylon as Jeremiah fulfils his calling to be a prophet to the nations (1:10).

Jeremiah did not operate in a vacuum, and understanding his LIFE AND TIMES will help us arrive at a better assessment of him. During his ministry five kings occupied Judah's throne, but only Josiah, Jehoiakim and Zedekiah are mentioned (1:2–3) because the other two – Jehoahaz and Jehoiachin – are only minor players. If we look at how Jeremiah got on during the reigns of Josiah, Jehoiakim and Zedekiah, it will help us get the measure of the man.

Jeremiah came from a priestly family in Anathoth (1:1), a village three miles north-east of Jerusalem, but, in 627 BC (1:2), God called him to be a prophet (1:4–19). It might have seemed a good time to be a prophet because, in the previous year, *Josiah*, Judah's last godly king, had started his reform movement by stamping out idolatry (2 *Chron.* 34:3). Impetus was given to Josiah's reforms by the unearthing of the Book of the Law during the restoration project (2 *Chron.* 34:14). All that was going on had a massive impact on Jeremiah. After a national renewal of the covenant based on the rediscovered law (2 *Chron.* 29–33), Jeremiah was sent on a preaching tour to bring home the challenge of the covenant to the nation (11:6). This brought him his first bitter taste of hostility, even from his own family and acquaintances in Anathoth (12:6), because not everyone was overjoyed at what Josiah was doing. As the very personal and sometimes even bitter protests which are scattered throughout chapters 11–20 indicate, Jeremiah was not slow to tell God how this rejection made him feel (11:19; 15:17–18; 20:7–8). But God reassures him of his presence and help (15:20), explaining that this baptism of fire is to prepare him for tougher times ahead (12:5). And so it proved, for Jeremiah emerged from these early skirmishes no longer a raw recruit but a battle-hardened veteran, able to stand his ground. During this time, Jeremiah began to realize that even the best of laws could only bring about external changes and not inward transformation. One of the pagan cults popular before Josiah's reforms was the worship of the Queen of Heaven (7:17–18). But the king's reforms had forced it underground. Later, when Josiah was no longer around, it re-emerged (44:15–19). If there was to be real spiritual transformation, Jeremiah grasped that there had to be a change of heart, and not just a change of laws. This is why there is so much emphasis in his preaching on the heart (4:4, 14; 9:26; 17:9–10; 24:7; 29:13; 31:33; 32:39).

In 609 BC, disaster struck: Josiah was killed in battle, having become embroiled in the crossfire of regional politics. For more than a century Assyria had controlled the area, but now Babylon was flexing its military and political muscles. In a frantic attempt to hold back its inevitable downfall, Assyria appealed to Egypt for help against the Babylonians. Neco, the Egyptian Pharaoh extracted a high price for his backing: control of Judah and the old kingdom of Israel would revert to Egypt. Assyria agreed, as desperate times called for desperate measures, and so Neco marched his army north through Judah in support of Assyria. This was the last thing Josiah wanted to see happening as the decline in Assyrian influence had given him the political breathing space to operate like an independent king and introduce all his reforms without outside interference. So, in 609 BC, Josiah's army intercepted Neco's army at Megiddo, and, in the ensuing battle, Josiah was fatally wounded and his army defeated. Jehoahaz, Josiah's son, was proclaimed as Judah's new king, but the Egyptians were having none of it. They deposed Jehoahaz and replaced him with their puppet king, *Jehoiakim*. With his accession, everything changed for Jeremiah.

Jehoiakim reintroduced paganism, and Jeremiah, incensed by the state-sponsored unfaithfulness engulfing Judah, denounced him. But he paid a high price for declaring God's judgment on all that was going on. He no longer enjoyed royal protection. Not only was what he said treated with contempt (36:21–24), but he was publicly flogged and humiliated (20:2), and later threatened with death (20:10–11). In 605 BC, the political centre of gravity in the area shifted dramatically when Nebuchadnezzar's Babylonian army thrashed the Egyptians at the Battle of Carchemish. Judah was now under Babylonian control and Jehoiakim had a new master. But, not content with being unfaithful to God, he decided to rebel against his Babylonian overlord, with predictable consequences. Jerusalem was besieged. At that point Jehoiakim died, leaving Jehoiachin, his son to face the situation. Jehoiachin wisely decided to surrender. His life was spared, but, along with the royal establishment and Judah's leading citizens and artisans, he was deported to Babylon in 597 BC.

Nebuchadnezzar placed another of Josiah's sons on the throne as puppet ruler and renamed him *Zedekiah*. His reign proved to be the most testing of Jeremiah's long ministry. Bullied by the hawks among his advisors and taken in by promises of support from the surrounding nations (27:3), Zedekiah rebelled against Babylon. There are no prizes for guessing how the Babylonians reacted: a rather large army arrived outside Jerusalem. Jewish nationalism, already at a high level, was cranked up even further by false prophets who preached a message of 'no surrender' and held out the hope of a Hezekiah-style deliverance (8:11; 28:1–17). But Jeremiah announced God's message: resistance was futile. The right course was surrender to the Babylonians (38:2–3). The Judean leadership was incensed, branding Jeremiah as a traitor for demoralizing the army (38:4). He was imprisoned (37:15–16) and then thrown into a cistern (38:1–6). But for the intervention of Ebed–Melech (38:7–13), Jeremiah would have died there.

After a long and grisly siege, Jerusalem was captured in 587 BC. Nebuchadnezzar's revenge was terrible. The city was systematically reduced to a pile of rubble, and those who were not executed were herded off into exile. Only the poorest of the poor were allowed to remain under the governorship of Gedaliah, the Babylonian appointee. Jeremiah was offered the choice of staying in Judah with Gedaliah, or going into comparatively comfortable 'retirement' in Babylon (40:4). He opted to stay, refuting any suggestion that he was not a patriot. But Gedaliah was assassinated by an Ammon-backed royal pretender called Ishmael (41:1–2). Fearing indiscriminate Babylonian reprisals for the killing of their governor, Judah's leaders panicked and suggested a mass migration to Egypt (41:17–18). Jeremiah told them that God wanted them to stay (42:1–22), but, true to form, they rejected God's Word and headed for Egypt, forcing Jeremiah and Baruch, his loyal secretary, to come with them to act, as they imagined, like some kind of magic charm against God's wrath (43:1–7). The last glimpse we have of Jeremiah is in the midst of a confrontation between him and those who forced him to go with them (44). Jeremiah declares that time will vindicate his words (44:28). He was proved right.

In the turbulent times in which he ministered, what was Jeremiah's MESSAGE to a nation in terminal decline and intent on self–destruction? In line with his mandate from God to uproot, tear down, destroy and overthrow (1:10), Jeremiah announced God's judgment on *the sins of the people*. Judah was committing spiritual adultery by deserting God and going after idols (3:6–14), blatantly breaking God's law (5:1–9). Judah's infatuation with idols was irrational (2:9–13). The idols were worthless and useless. Unlike the living God (10:1–16) who controls the nations (46:1–51:64), they were powerless to help. God's Word had been rejected, as Jehoiakim's burning of Jeremiah's prophecy indicated (36:1–24), and false prophets were being heeded (8:4–12). Their poison was having a deadly effect on the people: it filled them with a deceptive sense of hope and security. The people were being fed a diet of platitudes which informed them that, irrespective of how they lived, they would enjoy covenant blessings. They could sleep easily in their beds at night because God would never allow Jerusalem to be captured. After all, it contained the Temple, God's sanctuary. In his famous 'Temple Sermon' (7:1–15; 26:1–24), Jeremiah tackled these lies head on. The people were being deluded. They were constantly breaking God's law (7:4–10). Worship not linked to covenant faithfulness was worthless (7:21–26). All the talk of God not allowing the Temple to be destroyed was folly. Had they forgotten their history? God had permitted his sanctuary at Shiloh to be desecrated because of his people's unfaithfulness (7:12–15). What was to prevent him doing so again? While his indictment of the people for their sins pulls no punches, it is not all negative. He appeals to the people to return (3:22–23; 14:7–9, 19–22), but he is not hopeful they will do so (13:23). We should note that things were similar during Jesus' ministry. When he cleansed the Temple, he used words from Jeremiah's 'Temple Sermon' to rebuke his contemporaries (*Matt.* 21:13).

Jeremiah used *symbolic actions* to illustrate what he was saying. He hid a linen belt in a rock crevice to show how Judah would become ruined and useless (13:1–11). He appealed to the actions of a potter, who may alter his design and make something different from his original intention, to illustrate the freedom of God to change his actions in line with people's responses (18:1–12). In Romans 9:20–24, Paul used this illustration in speaking of God's sovereignty. Then Jeremiah bought a pot, took it to the Potsherd Gate, and shattered it (19:1–15) to show how God would break Jerusalem and its inhabitants. He made a yoke and wore it around his neck to drive home his message that God would bring the nations under Nebuchadnezzar's control (27:1–15). Later he had a scroll, upon which he had written God's judgment on Babylon, thrown into the Euphrates to show how Babylon would 'sink to rise no more' (51:59–64). In obeying God's command to him not to marry (16:2), Jeremiah was embodying the idea of the extinction of a line, as would happen with Judah.

What we have considered so far has done little to shake the negative perception which has become attached to Jeremiah, but there is another side to his message. As well as uprooting, tearing down, destroying and overthrowing, he was charged to build up and plant (1:10). In fulfilment of this Jeremiah spoke about *the salvation of God*. God's salvation would be seen in the restoration from exile (32:6–33:13). In a letter to those already in Babylon, Jeremiah informs them that in seventy years there will be a return home (29:1–14). To back up his confidence in God's promise, Jeremiah conducts some long-term investment by buying a field at Anathoth from his cousin, so that, when the Exile is over, it can be cultivated again (32:6–15). God's salvation would also be seen in the appearance of the Righteous Branch (33:14–18). He would be a descendant of David and be righteous in character and rule, bringing salvation and security to God's people. When, in 1 Corinthians 1:30, Paul refers to Jesus as 'our righteousness', he clearly has in mind what Jeremiah had said (*Jer*. 23:6; 33:16). However, the supreme display of God's salvation would be in the inauguration of the new covenant (31:31–34). The problem with the existing covenant was not the covenant itself but the people: their default mode was covenant unfaithfulness (31:32).

The new covenant would change all that by imparting a transformed inner nature. The law would be written on the mind and heart, resulting in obedience and the true knowledge of God (31:33–34). These blessings would be realized on the basis of a full and final work of forgiveness (31:34). Jeremiah does not specify how this will come about but, from our vantage point, we know. In Hebrews 8, while speaking of Jesus' superior priestly activity, the writer quotes the whole of Jeremiah 31:31–34 – the longest Old Testament quotation in the New Testament. The truth that it is the cross which inaugurated the new covenant is confirmed by Jesus himself. As he established the Lord's Supper, he told his disciples that the cup, which symbolized his blood shed in death, was 'the new covenant in [his] blood' (*Luke* 22:20). It was through Jesus' death that all the new covenant blessings came into effect. This emphasis in his preaching shows conclusively that Jeremiah is much more than a prophet of doom.

Our increasingly positive image of him is further reinforced when we realize that Jeremiah takes Moses as his ROLE MODEL. The book of Deuteronomy, rediscovered during the Temple renovations in Josiah's reign, shaped Jeremiah's preaching. Like Moses in Deuteronomy, Jeremiah sets out God's covenant demands, and, like Moses, he warns the people that if they disobey God, they will be punished. However, if they obey him they will live. For Jeremiah, the drama of Mount Ebal and Mount Gerizim and the blessings and curses of the covenant (*Deut.* 27–28) are as real as they were in Moses' time.

There are further links between these two men. Both had God's words put in their mouths (1:9; *Deut.* 18:18), and both initially complained about their inability to speak (1:6; *Exod.* 4:10). Both were intercessors for the nation (37:3; 42:2–4; *Num.* 14:13–19), although there came a point when Jeremiah was told not to pray for the nation any more (7:16). Moses led the nation out of Egypt, but, after Gedaliah's assassination, Jeremiah was forced to return there (43:1–7). Just as God treated Joshua and Caleb differently from their contemporaries because of their faithfulness to his covenant promises, so God would treat Ebed-Melech and Baruch differently from their contemporaries because of their faithfulness to him (39:16–18; 45:1–5).

However, what really settles the need to rehabilitate Jeremiah's reputation completely is the SIMILARITY between Jeremiah and Jesus. When Jesus was on earth, some people thought he was Jeremiah returned from the dead (*Matt.* 16:14), and it is not hard to see connections. Like Jeremiah, Jesus was rejected in his home town, hated by the religious establishment for what he preached, falsely accused of treason, beaten and imprisoned. Perhaps the most striking similarity lies in their reactions to Jerusalem's covenant unfaithfulness. Jeremiah is known traditionally as 'the weeping prophet' because of the tears he shed over Jerusalem's future judgment. Jesus too wept over Jerusalem because, instead of enjoying peace, it would experience a siege and destruction (*Luke* 19:41–44). In another place he laments that her house will be left to her desolate (*Matt.* 23:37–38; *Luke* 13:34–35). It seems clear that the underlying thought comes from Jeremiah 22:5.

When my friend was described as 'a bit of a Jeremiah' it was meant as a reproach. Maybe he should see it as a compliment, because he was being told that he resembled a man of unflinching loyalty to God, who stood for God's truth when everyone else was running away from it. Most of all, he should see it as the highest praise because being like Jeremiah means being like Jesus, and that is something to which every Christian aspires.

25

Lamentations

While our ignorance of Lamentations is to be lamented, it has to be admitted that there are reasons for our failure to get to know the book better. Though it is a book of poetry, closely related in style and theme to the Bible's Wisdom Literature, it is found among the Major Prophets, and easy to neglect among its larger neighbours. But the main reason we tend to neglect Lamentations is that – apart from some statements in chapter 3 – the sombreness of its tone is almost unrelieved.

It is located among the Major Prophets because it has traditionally been linked with Jeremiah. Arguments for and against his authorship are fairly evenly balanced, but I am going to follow the traditional route and say that it was Jeremiah. The book's CONTEXT is not in dispute. It was written as a response to Jerusalem's destruction in 587 BC by Nebuchadnezzar's army. For its author this was a disaster on many levels. It was *a military disaster* since the once mighty Israelite army, which, under David's command, had swept all challengers aside, had been crushed and utterly defeated. It was *a political disaster* because Judah's independence had vanished. It is true that for decades Judah had only been nominally independent, but now even that had gone. Never again, except during the time of the Maccabees and the Hasmonean dynasty (142–63 BC) – and since 1948 with the present state of Israel – would the Jews be in charge of their own affairs.

Most of all, it was *a spiritual disaster*. After stripping it of anything valuable and shipping it back to Babylon (2 *Kings* 25:13–17), Nebuchad-nezzar ordered that the Temple was to be levelled to the ground. Gone was the place to celebrate the great religious festivals. Gone were the priesthood and the sacrificial system. Gone was the Holy of Holies, in which God dwelt symbolically. Gone, so it seemed, were God's covenant promises to Abraham and David. All this made it *a personal disaster* for Jeremiah, because he was not a detached spectator. Jerusalem was his city, and the Temple, in spite of the problems associated with it, was where he worshipped. The king, despite royal hostility towards his preaching, was his king, and the defeated army was his army. Jeremiah was personally shattered by the events of 587 BC, and it is almost impossible for us to overestimate the intensity and depth of pain he felt when Jerusalem was destroyed. The worst that could have happened had happened.

The trauma Jeremiah experienced is reflected in the book's STYLE. As its name suggests, Lamentations is a lament, or a funeral dirge, because the book's dominant metaphor is that Jerusalem is like a widow (1:1). The language is also very funereal: gloomy, depressing, dressed in black. Even the metre in which Jeremiah writes takes us to a funeral. He utilizes what is known as *qinah* metre, which creates a falling-rising-falling rhythmic pattern, and this gives the impression that Lamentations is mimicking the start-stop movement of mourners walking behind the coffin in a funeral cortege.

Lamentations is dealing with deep emotions, and poetry, rather than prose, is the best vehicle for doing so. However, Lamentations is a special type of poem: an acrostic one, in which the letters of the Hebrew alphabet are used as the framework for each chapter. The Hebrew alphabet has twenty-two letters, so Lamentations 1, 2 and 4 each are twenty-two verses long. Lamentations 3 has sixty-six verses, a multiple of twenty-two, suggesting that Lamentations 3 is more complex than the other chapters. Lamentations 5 is not strictly an acrostic, but it has twenty-two verses, giving it an acrostic feel.

The book is made up of five distinct poems, and it is this that gives us a clue to Lamentations' STRUCTURE since each of them looks at Jerusalem's destruction from a different angle. Lamentations 1 shows us the extent of the *catastrophe*. Jerusalem is in ruins with its buildings destroyed, its streets deserted and its reputation in tatters. Those who are left after all the carnage are shell-shocked and destitute. The *cause* of all this devastation is given to us in Lamentations 2. When all the pundits have had their say, in the last analysis it is God himself who is primarily behind what happened to Jerusalem (2:8, 17). In this second poem, there are six references to God's anger against his people (2:1, 3, 6, 21, 22). Then, in Lamentations 3, we are informed of the *cure*. In the middle of all this darkness, a few rays of light begin to appear in the shape of the phrases 'the Lord's great love', 'his compassions' and his 'faithfulness' (3:21-26). These are all covenant terms, and it is because of God's commitment to his covenant that there is hope of a cure. It was their covenant unfaithfulness which provoked God's anger and brought his judgment upon them. But, in spite of their unfaithfulness, God is still faithful to his covenant, and so he will not totally abandon his people. It is the Lord's love, compassion and faithfulness which bring hope in the midst of all the gloom. In Lamentations 4, Jeremiah again reminds everyone that this disaster was the *consequence* of the people's sin. As to assigning blame, the first place people should look is in the mirror, for their sin is the reason for God's anger. In Lamentations 5, the people are encouraged to *cry* to God for help (5:1), and the book ends with an appeal to God, as the sovereign king, to restore his people (5:19-22).

What is Lamentations' MESSAGE? At the simplest level, Lamentations explains to us *how to deal with disaster* when it enters our lives. Disaster can hit us on a personal level, as in Job, or we can be involved in a national disaster, as in Lamentations. Either way, God does not immunize us against tragedy. Lamentations reminds us that the first thing we need to do is to use our minds. Pop psychology encourages us to start with our feelings and to get everything off our chests. Jeremiah does not accept that. Lamentations is a thoroughly thought through poem, which reminds us that Jeremiah started by thinking about what was going on, and his thinking was not driven by raw pain but by the light of the Bible's teaching about God. We need to think about things carefully and biblically, but we also need to pursue them to their conclusion. The A-to-Z acrostic nature of the poems points us to this. Jeremiah moved step by step from horrible loss and personal shame to restored hope and prayer for renewal. No matter how carefully and biblically we think matters through, we may well still have questions. Jeremiah is aware of this, which is why he makes his final chapter non-acrostic. Things are not always as neat and systematized as we would wish. No matter how careful and biblical our thinking is, unresolved or partially resolved issues may persist in swirling around in our minds and keeping us awake at night. We get a flavour of this in the final verses as Jeremiah's hope is dampened by some lingering questions (5:19–22). When this is the case with us, we need to continue to trust in God, reminding ourselves that he is in control and knows what he is doing (5:19).

One of the issues which the destruction of Jerusalem posed in a painful way was *God's faithfulness to his covenant promises*. Was God unable to do as he had said? Lamentations is a strong reminder that that is not true. As in his prophecy, the issue of blessings and curses (*Deut.* 11:26–29; 27:12) is central to Jeremiah's thinking. God had threatened that, if his people disobeyed him, he would punish them with exile (*Deut.* 29:22–28). God was now faithful to his covenant threats in sending them into exile. Jerusalem's destruction actually proved God's faithfulness, and this is the basis for hope in Lamentations (3:22–26). God had said that he would bring his people back from exile (*Deut.* 30:1–10), and that is exactly what he would do. God is not just well-intentioned; he is totally faithful and does exactly what he promises or threatens.

The paramount picture we have of God in Lamentations is that he is *a warrior*. While the Old Testament usually portrays God as fighting for his people, such as at the Red Sea (*Exod.* 14:14) and at Jericho (*Josh.* 6:16), he is also presented to us as the warrior who punishes his people when they disobey him, such as at Ai (*Josh.* 7:1–12). Lamentations pictures God as a warrior in this second sense: he is fighting against his people because of their covenant unfaithfulness. However, the prophets of the Exile and those after it look forward to the time when God would come and fight for his people again (*Dan.* 7; *Zech.* 14). The New Testament identifies Jesus as the divine warrior (*Isa.* 9:6), who defeated the forces of evil on the cross (*Col.* 2:13–15), a victory confirmed by his resurrection (*1 Cor.* 15:55–57). One day, Jesus will return to defeat and crush all God's enemies finally (*Rev.* 19:11–21).

26

Ezekiel

Ezekiel is the last of the three Major Prophets because chronologically he began and finished his ministry after Isaiah and Jeremiah. He was called to be a prophet in 592 BC (1:3) and the last date point we have in the book is 574 BC (40:1). Of all the prophets, only Haggai, Zechariah and Malachi, the three post-exilic prophets, are active after Ezekiel.

However, what is much more important than his dates in understanding his message is EZEKIEL'S LOCATION. In Ezekiel 1:1–2, which serves as an introduction to the book, he informs us that he ministered to the Jewish community that was living in Babylon along the Kebar (or Chebar) River, a huge irrigation canal in what is now Iraq. To understand this we need to go back about one hundred and seventy years. In 722 BC, the Assyrians absorbed Israel, the northern kingdom, into their empire by deporting the Israelites. Assyrian deportation policy involved splitting up a conquered nation into small groups, and resettling them in various places throughout their sprawling empire. The idea was to disorientate the conquered people so that they would not be able to mount an effective rebellion, and also to remove any sense of national identity. As a result, the northern tribes disappeared as a definable group and were absorbed into the Assyrian Empire. The Babylonian policy was different. Conquered nations were moved *en bloc* to Babylonia itself, where they were allowed to settle in large ethnic groups and encouraged to use their abilities and skills for the benefit of Babylon. This meant that deported peoples did not lose their distinctive identity. This is why Ezekiel found himself in Babylonia, surrounded by a sizeable Jewish community. Judah had experienced Babylonian – not Assyrian – deportation policy.

In fact, Judah had been on the receiving end of three separate deportations. The first was in 605 BC, when, after the Battle of Carchemish, Babylon took control of Judah. Jehoiakim, Judah's king, swore loyalty to Babylon, and, just to make sure he paid his tribute money in full and on time, hostages were taken to Babylon from among the Judean nobility. These included Daniel and his three friends (*Dan.* 1:1–6). However, Jehoiakim rebelled and soon a Babylonian army invaded Judah. But Jehoiakim died, leaving Jehoiachin, his son and successor, to face the consequences. Wisely he surrendered, but, although his life was spared, Jehoiachin, the nobility and the artisans were dragged off to Babylon in 597 BC. Among the deportees was Ezekiel. In 589 BC, Zedekiah, the new king, decided to rebel. It was a fateful decision as Nebuchadnezzar turned up at Jerusalem to teach Zedekiah and Judah one final, hard lesson. By 587 BC the rebellion was brutally crushed. Nebuchadnezzar then carried off the survivors into exile. So, after three Babylonian deportations, there were many Jewish communities, including Ezekiel's, located throughout Babylonia.

On the banks of the Kebar River in Babylonia, Ezekiel was called to prophesy. He had turned thirty in 592 BC (1:2). As the son of a priest (1:3), he would have been expecting to serve in the Temple at this point in his life (*Num.* 4:3). That had become impossible, but a different kind of spiritual service was required of him (1:3). The final vision of his book took place twenty years later (40:1). Ezekiel would then have been fifty, the age at which priests stepped down from active service (*Num.* 4:3). So his prophetic ministry coincided with what would have been his 'working life', had he been a priest in Jerusalem.

What did he have to say to this community in exile over a twenty-year period? To answer that we need to look at THE STRUCTURE OF EZEKIEL'S PROPHECY. In his ministry we find both judgment and hope. Ezekiel is the most chronologically structured of the Major Prophets. It revolves around the fall of Jerusalem, or, more accurately, the time when news of the city's capture reached the exile community in Babylon (33:21–22). The book opens with *Ezekiel's call* (1–3). By constantly calling him 'son of man', God impresses on Ezekiel that he cannot carry out the tough assignment he is being asked to perform in his own strength.

Nevertheless, God assures him of his help. Ezekiel will experience the reality of what his name means – 'God strengthens'.

The first main section is *the announcement of God's judgment on Judah and Jerusalem* (4–24). The popular preachers were saying that the city would never be taken, but Ezekiel demolishes this false hope. Jerusalem will be destroyed because of the people's covenant unfaithfulness. His prophecy deliberately uses offensive imagery and shocking language to convey the truth. Comparing Jerusalem to a prostitute (23:3) and labelling it worse than Sodom (16:46–48) shows that sin cannot be sanitized or prettified. It is ugly, gross, and deeply offensive to God.

The second main part is *the announcement of God's judgment on Judah's neighbours* (25–32). These sermons were primarily preached during the siege of Jerusalem. The neighbouring countries are warned not to gloat over or laugh at Jerusalem's fate because they too will feel the weight of God's anger (25:3, 6, 8, 12, 15; 26:2). This is not mere revenge, for God's judgment will show the world that he alone is the true God (25:7, 11, 17; 26:6; 28:22, 24, 26; 29:6, 16, 21; 30:8, 19, 25–26; 32:15). It will also pave the way for Judah's restoration. Ever since the era of the Judges, Israel's neighbours had posed a spiritual threat to them (*Judg.* 2:3), but, with God's judgment of the nations, that threat will be removed (28:24), allowing the people to return safely.

The news of Jerusalem's fall marks a significant shift from the negative to the positive, but there have already been hints that the fall of Jerusalem would not be the end of the story. Ezekiel had seen God's throne arched by a rainbow (1:28), the covenant sign that judgment will always be tempered with mercy (*Gen.* 9:13–15). Even God's judgment on the surrounding nations can be seen in a positive light. It is a reminder that God's covenant with Abraham has not failed because God's promise that 'whoever curses you I will curse' (*Gen.* 12:3) is still in force. But now the hints give way to clarity in Ezekiel's message of *hope and restoration* (33–48). This section focuses on a prediction of restoration (34–37), a conflict involving Gog and Magog (38–39), and a restored Temple (40–48).

We need to focus on THE METHOD OF EZEKIEL'S PROPHECY as he communicated the message God had given him. First, it involved *visions* given to him by God. By the Kebar River he saw a vision of the Lord himself (1:4–28), a scroll (2:9–3:3), a plain (3:22–23), a valley of dry bones coming to life (37:1–10), and an extended view of the new Temple (40:1–48:35). God transports him back to Jerusalem where he observes the horrible idolatry going on in the Temple (8:1–18), judgment on idolaters (9:1–11) and God's glory leaving the Temple (10:1–22). In condemning Judah's sins, Ezekiel made use of *parables*. He talked about a worthless vine (15:1–8), an unfaithful wife (16:1–63), a vine and two eagles (17:1–24), two lion cubs (19:1–9), an uprooted vine (19:10–14), two adulterous sisters (23:1–49), and a cooking pot (24:1–14).

Like Jeremiah, Ezekiel used *symbolic acts* to underscore his message. Four of them come together in Ezekiel 4–5: the sign of a besieged clay tablet (4:1–3), a prone prophet (4:4–8), a siege diet (4:9–17) and a shaved head (5:1–4). All these actions drive home what he has been saying about Jerusalem's siege. God is opposing his people, so they will suffer discomfort, deprivation and destruction, but there is a glimmer of hope. A remnant will be saved, just as Ezekiel tucked away a few hairs in the folds of his clothing. Then, in another symbolic act pointing to moving to another land, Ezekiel packs up his belongings and digs through the wall of his house (12:1–17, 17–20). God's use of Babylon to be the instrument of his fast-approaching judgment is signified by the signs of a sharpened sword (21:1–17) and Nebuchadnezzar's sword (21:18–23), and the sign of a smelting furnace (22:17–31) draws attention to the purifying effect of God's judgment. The most personally devastating sign was that of his wife's death (24:15–27), highlighting the blessings which would be forfeited when the crushing blow of Jerusalem's capture fell. The final sign was that of the two sticks (37:15–17). Unlike the others, this was a symbol of hope, pointing to the reunification of the nation.

As for EZEKIEL'S MESSAGE, its focus was on God's glory. There are three pivotal moments in Ezekiel, and each of them is linked with God's glory. The first is *the appearance of God's glory* to Ezekiel as part of his call to be a prophet (1:1–28). As a priest-in-preparation, Ezekiel would have been quite at home with the idea of God's glory in the Temple, but what he saw went far beyond this. He saw God's glory beside the

Kebar River, far away from Jerusalem. And God's glory was radiating, not from a temple, but from a throne mounted on a war chariot whose wheels within wheels gave it incredible speed, power and manoeuvrability (1:15–21). Assyrian and Babylonian designers had developed war chariots which had allowed their armies to dominate Middle Eastern battlefields for as long as anyone could remember. But compared to God's war chariot, they were pathetic and clumsy. This vision of God riding in majestic glory removed all Ezekiel's preconceptions. He saw that God's sphere of influence was not restricted to one location. He was the all-powerful God, in total control of everything that was going on everywhere. Nebuchadnezzar was not determining events; God was, and everything he did was designed to show exactly who he was. 'They will know that I am the LORD' (6:7, 10, 13, 14 – and another fifty-six times throughout the book).

The second pivotal moment in Ezekiel is *the departure of God's glory* from the Temple (8:1–11:25). In this vision, Ezekiel is transported to Jerusalem and sees God's glory at the Temple, which, for him, was its proper location. But just when he thinks everything is as it should be he sees that God's glory is *leaving* the Temple. For four centuries, God's glory – the symbol of his presence with his people – was located at the Temple, but all this is coming to an end. Because of his people's sins, which Ezekiel is shown in graphic detail, he is deliberately abandoning Jerusalem. He moves slowly, as if sorrowing over the scene. After leaving the Temple, God's glory stops above the Mount of Olives to the east. Jerusalem is now unprotected because God has left, and, from his vantage point on the Mount of Olives, God is now in position to witness its destruction by the invading hordes. It is not coincidental that, centuries later, Jesus sat on the same Mount of Olives, looking over the same city, while he predicted its imminent destruction by another invading army (*Matt.* 24:3; *Luke* 21:20–24).

And where did God's glory relocate itself? With the exiles (11:16). This reminds us that, just as God's glory left Jerusalem and went into exile to be with his people away from the clean land, so Jesus left his Father's glory to identify with sinful humanity, suffering 'outside the camp' on behalf of his people (*Heb.* 13:12–13). As someone from a priestly background, the departure of God's glory must have been the saddest moment of Ezekiel's life. Yet it was not without hope, because Ezekiel 11:16 declares loudly that God does not live in human-constructed buildings but with his people, and any location on earth can afford him a place to meet with them. About six hundred years later Jesus developed this line of thought as he spoke with the Samaritan woman beside the well at Sychar. Not in any specific holy site – such as Jerusalem or Mount Gerizim – is God to be found, but wherever he is worshipped in spirit and in truth. There God will be present in all his glory (*John* 4:21–24).

The third pivotal moment comes at the end of the last section, which deals with restoration after the exile (34:1–48:35). It involves *the return of God's glory*. The book ends with the triumphant affirmation that God is among his people once more (48:35). The restoration is defined in several ways. In the first place it involves the appearance of the Shepherd-King (34). The nation's shepherds had failed miserably to carry out their responsibilities (43:1–10), so God himself would take on the task of shepherding the people (34:11, 13, 16). At the same time, this shepherding responsibility would fall on the shoulders of someone who could trace his family tree back to David (34:23–24). The idea of God himself and a descendant of David serving simultaneously as Shepherd-King reaches its fulfilment in Jesus, the Good Shepherd (*John* 10:11). Restoration results in the fulfilment of the covenant (36:24–28; 37:24–28). Ezekiel uses categories taken from God's covenant with Abraham, Moses and David, and from Jeremiah's announcement of the new covenant. The restored people will live in the promised land of blessing (36:28; 37:25), an allusion to God's covenant with Abraham. They will follow God's laws (36:27; 37:24), in fulfilment of God's covenant with Moses; and, fulfilling God's covenant with David, a Davidic king will rule over them (37:24–25). In harmony with the new covenant, they will be given a new heart and a new spirit, so enjoying covenantal blessing (36:26; 37:26). While Ezekiel describes the restoration in Old Testament terms, the realities to which it points can only be understood in New Testament categories. Abraham was not looking for earthly territory at the eastern end of the Mediterranean but for a heavenly city (*Heb.* 11:9–10, 16). Moses grasped that the law was preparing us for salvation by faith in Christ alone (*Gal.* 3:24). David tasted death, but Jesus, David's ultimate descendant, defeated death by his resurrection (*Psa.* 16:10–11; *Acts* 2:24–33). Whatever their ethnic roots, all Christians celebrate their restoration to God every time they eat the bread and drink the cup of the new covenant, sealed by Jesus' blood (*Matt.* 26:27–29; *Luke* 22:20).

Restoration is seen in terms of a valley full of dry bones coming to life again (37:1–14). This giving of new life to the dead goes far beyond a mere return from exile. It anticipates the regenerating activity of the Holy Spirit who gives spiritual life to the spiritually dead. When Jesus speaks of regeneration to Nicodemus in John 3, he expects him to be familiar with the concept through understanding Old Testament passages such as Ezekiel 37:1–14 and Ezekiel 36:24–28. Chapter 37 also points to the hope of a bodily resurrection, seen as a return to the land in its fullest sense. As Ezekiel's last symbolic act highlights, restoration also brings about the reunification of God's people (37:15–28). How can reunification happen when the northern kingdom has been absorbed into the Gentile world and obliterated as a separate entity? Paul sees its realization in the calling of the Gentiles, by the grace of God, into union with his favoured people (*Rom.* 9:23–28). Restoration will see the final victory of God's purposes (38:1–39:29). The Bible itself cautions us not to take what Ezekiel is saying in a literal way. Since the names of the nations attacking God's people crop up in the 'Table of Nations' in Genesis 10, this struggle mirrors the broader conflict between the descendants of Japheth and Ham and the descendants of Shem, which goes back to the ancient battle between the woman's seed and Satan (*Gen.* 3:15). The powers of darkness will never ultimately defeat God's people or thwart God's purposes (*Matt.* 16:18).

The final element of the restoration is the building of a new Temple, to which God's glory would return (40:1–48:35). What Ezekiel describes cannot be literally or physically realized. How then can the vision be fulfilled? Like everything in God's purposes, it is fulfilled in Jesus Christ. In him we see God's glory (*John* 1:14). Jesus identified himself as the temple that would be destroyed but restored in greater glory

(*John* 2:19–22). Ezekiel saw a river emerging from under the temple, flowing eastward, whose waters were so potently life-giving that, when they met the Dead Sea, the salty water instantly became fresh. In John 7:38–39, Jesus made it clear that he is the source of living water.

There are at least sixty-five direct or indirect references to Ezekiel in the New Testament, forty-eight of them in Revelation alone. Nowhere is Ezekiel's impact on Revelation felt more than in John's vision of the New Jerusalem. It has no temple because all the temple symbolism has been fulfilled in Jesus (*Rev.* 21:22). However, in the New Jerusalem, as in Ezekiel 47:1–12, there is a river of life on whose banks are trees that produce fruit each month (*Rev.* 22:1–2). Worshipping in the New Jerusalem there will be, not only a full complement of ethnic Jews, but also a vast crowd, too huge to count, from every nation, tribe, race and language group (*Rev.* 7:7–9). Ezekiel's final vision may have been enormous in its proportions, but its realization was far more enormous than he could have imagined. It turns out that even his wildest dreams were not wild enough! This is why Ezekiel thoroughly deserves his place among those favoured men who 'predicted the sufferings of Christ and the glories that would follow' (*1 Pet.* 1:11).

27
Daniel

D aniel is a book of contrasts. On the one hand, it contains stories so simple that generations of children have listened to them with wide-eyed fascination, and yet, on the other hand, Daniel includes material so complex that it makes veteran Bible interpreters unsure whether they have really understood it. Parts of it are written in Hebrew (1:1–2:4a; 8:1–12:13), but in contrast the middle section (2:4b–7:28) is written in Aramaic. Daniel contains two distinct types of writing: in the first part narrative, or more precisely what is referred to as 'court narrative', but then in the second part a type of writing known as 'apocalyptic literature' takes over, requiring us to alter our strategy for reading and interpreting it when we move from one to the other.

At first sight, Daniel seems similar to the prophetic books, which is why the English Bible places it between the Major and Minor Prophets. Sections of Daniel predict the future, so in Daniel 11 we come across an outline of many events which took place centuries later. In common with the Major and Minor Prophets, Daniel wrote down what God had shown him, and God's covenant underpins the message of the book. But as we zoom in closer, we see that the presence of the apocalyptic style of writing distinguishes Daniel from the other prophetic books. For example, its use of strange imagery, such as the four hybrid sea beasts of chapter 7, make its predictions stand apart. Again, God often spoke to Daniel, not directly, but through the mediation of an angel, and when he received what God wanted him to know, Daniel was sometimes told to keep the information secret (12:4–13). In the other prophets, what God had said in Deuteronomy and his promise to David usually loomed largest in the background, but in Daniel it is God's promises to Abraham of his presence, his protection, a place of blessing and a programme for all nations that lie in the background. It is probably for reasons like these that the Hebrew Bible placed Daniel among the Writings, rather than with the Prophets.

The MAIN CHARACTER, of course, is Daniel himself. After his army had routed their Egyptian counterparts at the Battle of Carchemish, Nebuchadnezzar took control of Judah. He ordered one of his high-ranking palace staff to single out some younger members of the Judean royal family and nobility and bring them to Babylon, where they would be subjected to a three-year indoctrination programme to turn them into good Babylonians (1:3–5). One of those selected was Daniel (1:6). So, in 605 BC, as a young man, probably in his mid-teens, Daniel found himself in Babylon, and never returned home. However, as his daily prayer routine (6:10) and the prayer recorded in Daniel 9:1–19 highlight, Jerusalem was never far from his thoughts. The last date we have in Daniel is in 10:1 and it is 535 BC. This would mean that he was in his eighties, simply too old to make the hard journey home. When the Jews were allowed to return to Jerusalem, Daniel's spirit may have been willing but his flesh was too weak.

In his long life, Daniel rose up the ranks of the Babylonian and Persian civil service (2:48; 6:1–3). Kings came and went, but for seventy years he remained at the heart of affairs. He retained his position because of his character. He was a man of uncompromising faith in God, a faith which was tested throughout his life, but which always triumphed because it was rooted in the Scriptures (9:2) and toughened by disciplined private prayer (6:10). Though recognized as talented (1:19–20; 6:1–3), Daniel did not let his reputation go to his head, but was quick to give all the credit for his ability to God (2:27–28). In the cut-throat world of Babylonian and Persian court life, Daniel stood head and shoulders over the rest as a man of massive personal integrity, as even his jealous political enemies had to admit (6:4–5). We should avoid a purely moralistic approach to Daniel, in which we reduce its message to a bland 'Dare to be a Daniel', but the book does have great ethical value (1 Cor. 10:6; Heb. 12:1), showing us how we can stand firm for the Lord in the midst of a hostile and oppressive culture, but also make an impact there for his kingdom.

As for Daniel's STRUCTURE, the book is usually divided into two halves. The first (1–6) is clearly biographical, telling the story of Daniel's witness in the Babylonian and Persian courts. This section records how Daniel and his three friends faced the challenge of Nebuchadnezzar's indoctrination programme (1:1–21); how Daniel interpreted Nebuchadnezzar's first dream (2:1–49); how Shadrach, Meshach and Abednego were rescued from Nebuchadnezzar's fiery furnace (3:1–30); and how Daniel explained the meaning of Nebuchadnezzar's dream concerning a tree (4:1–37). The narrative part of Daniel finishes off with the book's two best-known stories: Belshazzar's drunken banquet and the writing on the wall (5:1–31), and Daniel being thrown into the lions' den (6:1–28). The second half (7–12) contains four visions: that of four hybrid sea beasts, which moves into another about the Son of Man and the Ancient of Days (7:1–28); a vision of a ram, a goat and a horn (8:1–27); a vision about the seventy weeks (9:20–27); and a final vision (10–12) in which Daniel sees an outline of the history of the final two centuries before the coming of Christ, as it impacts God's people and land. Among the visions we have Daniel's prayer for God to forgive his people and have mercy on Jerusalem (9:1–19).

But the structure is a little more complex than that because Daniel 2–7 was written in Aramaic and it seems right to treat it as a unit. This does not fit neatly with the normal division of the book. But if we divide the book on the basis of its contrasting languages we discover that it has a three-section structure, and that this more complex structure reveals Daniel's THEMES much better that the usual division, since each of the three sections highlights the message that God *rules, rescues* and *reveals*. Chapter 1, written in Hebrew, forms the introduction to the book. It is like an overture to a piece of music and flags up the main themes by the repetition of the verb 'to give' in 1:2, 9 and 17. Everyone in Babylon may have been singing Nebuchadnezzar's praises after his victory over Judah, but Daniel 1:2 silences this adulation. The reason he triumphed was that the God who rules *gave* him victory. Cynics might attribute it to luck that the official running Nebuchadnezzar's re-education programme accepted Daniel's vegetarian suggestion, but 1:9 shows that he agreed because the God who rescues his people *gave* him favour with the official, and the same God who rescues ensured that the vegetarians looked considerably healthier than the carnivores (1:15–16). No doubt Daniel and his three friends studied hard, but 1:17 stresses that they succeeded (1:18–20) because the God who reveals secrets *gave* them knowledge and understanding.

These three themes, introduced in chapter 1, are spelt out in chapters 2–7, the Aramaic part of the book. These chapters, which form the centrepiece of the book, belong in three sub-sections of two chapters each, 2 and 7, 3 and 6, and 4 and 5, with each pairing highlighting one of Daniel's main themes. With obvious similarities between the two chapters, the theme of *the God who reveals* is dealt with in chapters 2 and 7. Chapter 2 contains the vision of a huge statue made up of gold, silver, bronze, and a mixture of iron and clay, representing the Babylonian Empire, the Persian Empire, the Greek Empire of Alexander the Great, and the Roman Empire respectively. But the key part of the vision was the appearance of the rock, which shattered the colossus and then expanded to fill the whole earth. The New Testament identifies Jesus as the living stone or rock (*1 Pet.* 2:4–8), something affirmed by Jesus himself (*Mark* 12:10), and, although he used different imagery, he spoke of how his kingdom would be a worldwide phenomenon (*Mark* 4:30–32). Although Daniel 7 initially seems to be a vision of four hybrid sea beasts, first impressions are misleading because, once more, the crucial point is at the end where Daniel sees the Son of Man before the Ancient of Days (7:9–14). Just as the four beasts correspond to the various parts of the colossus, Babylon, Persia, Greece and Rome, so the Son of Man parallels the rock. Jesus constantly referred to himself as the Son of Man, even when he knew it would lead to certain death (*Mark* 14:61–62). In doing so, he emphasized that his kingdom would be an eternal one. In these two complementary visions God reveals that all history is moving towards the coming of the Messiah to set up his kingdom by means of his death, resurrection, ascension, gift of the Holy Spirit to empower the church for mission (*Acts* 1:6–8), and return.

In the parallel stories recorded in Daniel 3 and 6 of Shadrach, Meshach and Abednego being thrown into Nebuchadnezzar's furnace and of Daniel being thrown into Darius' den of lions, the theme of *the*

God who rescues stares us in the face. In both incidents we find a king with an over-inflated ego being persuaded by minions who were out to destroy God's people into demanding an act of loyalty with which no-one loyal to the true God could comply (3:1–12; 6:1–9). Firmly but graciously all four refused to toe the line (3:13–18; 6:10–11). For them the choice lay between being loyal to God and being loyal to a human being, irrespective of how powerful he was. For their uncompromising faithfulness all four were sentenced to a very unpleasant death (3:19–23; 6:12–16). But all four were miraculously rescued from death (3:24–29; 6:17–23). Both incidents end with Shadrach, Meshach, Abednego and Daniel being promoted instead of destroyed (3:30; 6:28).

The theme of *the God who rules* makes its appearance in Daniel 4 and 5. Although there are points of convergence between the stories of Nebuchadnezzar's madness and Belshazzar's feast, watch out for the significant place in which they diverge. Both revolve around a king who is so intoxicated with pride that he has forgotten that he is where he is because the God who rules has given him his position of power. Both kings were warned beforehand to recognize that God rules and that his judgment falls on all who do not acknowledge this fact. Nebuchadnezzar received his warning by means of a dream of an impressive tree whose branches were cut off while its stump and roots were left intact (4:4–27). What happened to Nebuchadnezzar should have served as a cautionary tale to Belshazzar concerning his pride and refusal to acknowledge God's rule (5:18–21). However, neither man heeded God's warning and each continued to be full of a sense of his own importance (4:28–30; 5:1–4), until God's judgment fell (4:31–33; 5:5, 22–28). But here is where the stories diverge: Nebuchadnezzar and Belshazzar responded differently to God's judgment. Nebuchadnezzar turned from his self-absorbed pride, recognized that he was not in control but that God ruled (4:34–35), and, as a result, had his kingdom restored to him (4:36) and was transformed (4:37). Belshazzar, on the other hand, refused to turn from his pride, continued to act as if he was the master of his fate (5:29) and, as a consequence of his refusal to change, had his kingdom taken from him by Darius, just as the God who rules had said (5:28; 30–31).

At the start of chapter 8, the book switches back to Hebrew, and we find a fusing together of the three themes. Each of the visions that make up the final section of the book concern ways in which God *reveals, rules* and *rescues*. These chapters inform us of the future rise of the Persian Empire, the two-horned ram of 8:3–4; its crushing defeat by Alexander the Great, the billy goat of 8:5–7; and the partitioning of his empire into four by his generals after his premature death, the four horns of 8:8. In chapter 11, we have a prophecy of how the Seleucid kings of Syria, the kings of the north (as Syria is located north of Israel), and the Ptolemaic kings of Egypt, the kings of the south, constantly crossed swords to see who would control Israel, 'the Beautiful Land' (11:16, 41). Instead of dismissing all that is recorded here as historical record masquerading as predictive prophecy, we need to see that behind these visions lies the God who is so in control of history that he can say what will happen centuries before it does. They declare loudly that God is the sovereign king, ruling over his world, so that history is *his* story. What stability this truth brings to God's people! It reminds us that, in spite of all the turbulence of global history and our own personal history, God is in control of everything that happens, working out his eternal purpose for his glory and our spiritual good.

Yet, through the grotesque imagery of these visions, God reveals that, although he rules, there are still beasts on the rampage, making life hard for his people. The epitome of this hostility towards God's people is a figure who is symbolically represented as a horn (8:9–13) and a king who has an overweening opinion of himself (11:36–45). His antagonism towards God's people reaches its height when he sets up what is referred to an 'abomination that causes desolation' (9:27; 11:31; 12:11). This imagery has in view Antiochus Epiphanes, a second century BC king of Syria, who set about eradicating all expressions of Jewishness. His antagonism towards God's people reached an all-time low when, in 167 BC, he set up a statue of Zeus in the Temple and sacrificed a pig upon the altar. However, Antiochus Epiphanes does not exhaust the meaning of what Daniel saw. Biblical prophecy operates on many levels, which means that one prophetic statement can have many fulfilments. So, although he is aware that the abomination had been erected by Antiochus Epiphanes, when Jesus talks about it (*Mark* 13:4) he is thinking of a future event: the time when, after Titus' legions had captured Jerusalem in 70 AD, the Roman commander ordered his army's eagle standards, which the Jews regarded as idols, to be raised in the Temple. In 2 Thessalonians 2:1–12 when he writes about the Man of Lawlessness, Paul sees him as the ultimate expression of this anti-God principle that has been operating throughout history, for his terminology answers directly to Daniel's imagery.

While all this might seem full of gloom, there is an insertion of hope, since, running alongside all that Daniel saw, there is the reality of a God who rescues. Just when it looked as if the arrogant Antiochus Epiphanes was going to succeed in his devilish plan to stamp out God's people, they are rescued when God destroys him (8:25). The same is true of the Man of Lawlessness, the definitive rebel of whom Antiochus Epiphanes is but a pale reflection. He seems to be the focus of Daniel 11:26–45, because what is said about his self-absorption, single-minded hatred of God, and ruthless exercise of power goes beyond anything that was true of Antiochus Epiphanes. But, once again, just as it looks as if he is going to get his own way, he is destroyed (11:45).

However, Daniel's prayer (9:1–19) draws attention to a more fundamental human need than physical deliverance: we need to be rescued from our sin and its consequences. This is why Daniel's confession of sin and plea for mercy is followed by a vision of seventy sevens (9:20–27), in which God shows him what we can see with hindsight to be our rescue from sin through Jesus Christ. The seventy sevens, or seventy weeks, are divided in two: sixty-nine weeks and one final week. Then there is a further sub-division with the sixty-nine weeks split into seven sevens and sixty-two sevens, and the seventh week broken by a pivotal episode within it, though not necessarily at its midpoint. As for the timetable of the seventy weeks, the seven sevens runs from Cyrus' edict to allow the rebuilding of the Temple and city to Nehemiah; the sixty-two sevens stretch from Nehemiah to Jesus' baptism (9:25); and the final week takes in Jesus' mission. The pivotal episode within the final seven is Jesus' death (9:26a), and this will be followed by an end event, which is the destruction of Jerusalem in AD

70 (9:26b). But what the vision concentrates on is what Jesus achieves by his death: our rebellion against God is overcome and replaced by peace between him and us; righteousness is obtained for us; all God's purposes of salvation reach their fulfilment; God's presence among us becomes a reality; and the sacrificial system is made redundant (9:24, 27). Here is a God who tackles the real issue and rescues his people in the most thoroughgoing way possible.

We can now see that Daniel's PURPOSE is not to stir up controversy among Bible interpreters, or to confuse Christians, but to bring us comfort. It does this by reminding us that God's *presence* will remain with us all the way because he is faithful to his promises. In particular, it is God's faithfulness to his promises to Abraham in Genesis 12 that is strongly reinforced in Daniel. God made a promise to Abraham of a people who would be special to him, but in Daniel's time God's people looked anything but special. They were a small minority who always seemed to be in trouble. But when they experienced the worst trials, God's promise to be with them came into effect. So Jesus walks with Shadrach, Meshach and Abednego in the middle of Nebuchadnezzar's fiery furnace (3:24–25).

God's people always seemed to be about to be destroyed altogether. This would have caused God's promise of a Saviour – which was tied up with their continuing existence – to come to nothing. But God's promise to Abraham of *protection* took effect, allowing God's plan of salvation to keep on moving forward. This is why Shadrach, Meshach and Abednego were rescued from the fiery furnace and Daniel from the lions' den. This is why, just when it looks as if Antiochus Epiphanes is going to have his way, and the Man of Lawlessness is poised to wipe out the church, God steps in to protect his people. Even if God does not physically save us, we are reminded that death will not be the end. We will rise to eternal life, for in Daniel 12:2–3 we have one of the Old Testament clearest pointers to resurrection on the basis of Jesus' victory over death (*John* 11:24–25).

We might laugh at medieval cartographers who placed the Holy Land at the centre of their maps of the world, but Daniel had the same perspective because the outline of history contained in the book is focused on how it impacts the Beautiful Land. As he looks at history through that lens, Daniel is reminding us of God's promise to Abraham of a *place of blessing*, in which he would make his presence known in a momentous way (*John* 1:14). Having said that, the kingdom of God Daniel envisages is not a restored state of Israel: it is a worldwide kingdom that is global in its reach, because the colossus-smashing rock will fill the whole earth (2:35) and the Son of Man's rule is universal in its scope (7:14).

This is totally in line with God's promise to Abraham of a *programme* which would embrace all nations, since all peoples on earth are blessed through Jesus, the son of Abraham. The main actor in Daniel is our covenant Lord, who has promised to rescue us from our sins through Jesus' death and not to release his hold on us, particularly when the going is hard, until he has brought us safely home to heaven. This is why Daniel is such a comforting book.

28

Hosea

With our arrival at Hosea, we have come to the final section of the Old Testament, the Minor Prophets. The fact that they are labelled 'minor' does not mean they are unimportant. They are called 'minor' only because, compared with Isaiah, Jeremiah and Ezekiel, these twelve books are very short. They are so short that they fit on to one scroll, so, in the Hebrew Bible, they make up one book, 'The Book of the Twelve'. They might be short, but they are powerful.

The time-honoured way of categorizing the Minor Prophets is to divide them into those who carried out their ministries *before* the Exile – Hosea, Joel, Amos, Obadiah, Jonah, Micah, Nahum, Habakkuk and Zephaniah – and those who prophesied *after* it – Haggai, Zechariah and Malachi. We can go further and sub-divide the pre-exilic prophets into those who preached in Israel, the northern kingdom – Hosea, Amos and Jonah – and the rest who operated in Judah, the southern kingdom – Joel, Obadiah, Micah, Nahum, Habakkuk and Zephaniah.

Before we look at Hosea, I want to step back and consider some issues that relate to the Minor Prophets as a whole. The authoritative way in which they spoke stemmed from their consciousness that *God had sent them*. Amos speaks for all of them in Amos 7:15. After being told to go home, prophesy there, and stop upsetting the cosy religious *status quo*, Amos tells Amaziah, the priest of Bethel, that he would have been nowhere near Bethel if God had not sent him. Their authoritative preaching also arises from their consciousness that *they were speaking God's words*, and not their own ideas (*Hos.* 4:1; *Amos* 7:16). This consciousness can be seen in the number of times the phrases 'the word of the LORD that came . . .', and, 'This is what the LORD says' occur in the Minor Prophets. There are too many to list, so you will have to look them up for yourself. In all this, the Minor Prophets pave the way for Jesus, God's final prophet. The authoritative way in which he spoke, which often left people astonished, flowed from the same consciousness. Jesus was aware that he had been sent by God. Thirty-three times in John he speaks of God the Father as the one who 'sent me'. He was also aware that the words he spoke were not his own but what his Father had told him to say (*John* 7:16; 8:28; 12:49; 14:10, 24).

At the same time we should not think that prophecy was unprepared utterance which bypassed the minds of the prophets. Part of their preparation to speak God's words was the gift of a special ability to understand his law and apply it to their own situation. They were primarily preachers who took the law, especially Deuteronomy – and in particular, Deuteronomy 28, the blessings and curses section within that book – and related it to what was happening all around them. In their role as enforcers of the terms of the covenant, we can see the legacy of Elijah and Elisha. They seem to have gathered groups of men around them, referred to as 'the sons of the prophets' (*1 Kings* 20:35) or 'the company of prophets' (*2 Kings* 2:3, 5, 7, 15; 4:1, 38; 5:22; 6:1; 9:1), and taught them the principles of biblical prophecy.

Let us look specifically at Hosea, the first of the Minor Prophets. The only biographical information he gives us is his father's name (1:1). Some have suggested from hints in the book that he was a baker. Others conclude from his use of agricultural imagery (4:16; 6:4; 10:12–13a) that he was from a farming background. The truth is that the Holy Spirit has left us without such details so that we may focus on his message.

We do know that his preaching was primarily aimed at Israel, the northern kingdom, and we also know the approximate time frame within which he ministered (1:1). The 'Jeroboam' Hosea mentions is Jeroboam, son of Jehoash, or Jeroboam II, and he and Uzziah began to reign at around the same time, 791 BC and 793 BC respectively. Hezekiah died in 687 BC. Hosea obviously did not preach all that time, and we can assume that he started to prophesy late in Jeroboam's reign and completed his work early in Hezekiah's, which means he was active between roughly 750 and 715 BC. Israel was coming to the end of its Indian Summer. Jeroboam's reign was a time of political expansion and economic success, but for the last time. After Jeroboam's death, instability engulfed the nation, with six kings in thirty years as coup followed coup. With the rise of Assyria, Israel, as an independent state, was rapidly on the way out. The end came in 722 BC when, after a bloody siege, Samaria was captured and its inhabitants deported into exile in Assyria. Hosea was to Israel what Jeremiah was going to be to Judah – God's spokesman to a dying and soon-to-be-conquered nation. It was as if, through Hosea, God was reaching out to his people and giving them one final opportunity to repent. This would account for the urgency in Hosea's preaching, and also for the passion with which he spoke. He was not a spectator, emotionally detached from all that was going on. This was his country, and he was watching it hurtling towards God's judgment, and oblivion.

Hosea divides into two unequal sections, and the first one has to do with HOSEA'S MARRIAGE (1–3). Through his marriage to Gomer, Hosea is going to *become* the word he will preach. It reminds us that centuries later, another 'Hosea' – for the name *Jesus* is a variant of 'Hosea' – was to come who, as God's final Prophet, was himself the Word (*John* 1:14). For Hosea, love was not blind. When, at God's command, he married Gomer he knew exactly where everything was heading. Yet, in spite of this, their marriage had a promising start and soon little Jezreel was born (1:3). God was making a statement through his unconventional name (1:4–5). But then a coldness set into their relationship. Gomer became increasingly distant from her husband, and, when Lo-Ruhamah and Lo-Ammi were born (1:6, 8–9), the implication is that Hosea was not their father. Gomer soon dropped all pretences and left Hosea. But everything in her life turned sour (2:5b–7a). At the beginning of Hosea 3, we find that her life has imploded. She is at rock-bottom, in abject poverty, deserted by her lovers, and having to sell herself as a slave to make ends meet. As Gomer stood in the market that day, about to be sold to the highest bidder, the phrase on most lips would be, 'It serves her right', and this was true. But then the story takes an unexpected turn which stunned everyone. Hosea had never stopped loving his unfaithful wife, so, when God told him to redeem Gomer, he obeyed at once, buying her back and rescuing her from the mess into which her unfaithfulness had plunged her (3:1–2). This was startling – even shocking – grace, but it was not cheap grace (3:2).

This story of extraordinary love and surprising grace on Hosea's part towards Gomer, while real, was also symbolic. Gomer's unfaithfulness paralleled Israel's religious promiscuity and covenant unfaithfulness (1:2), and Hosea's love for Gomer illustrated God's love for Israel (3:1). God entered into a covenant relationship with Israel – taking them to be his wife and committing himself to them to be their husband – with his eyes wide open, knowing exactly what they were like. There were times when the relationship was a happy one. One thinks of the periods when Joshua and David led Israel, or the reigns of Solomon, Hezekiah and Josiah. But Israel's unfaithfulness began to dominate the relationship, as what happened when the Israelites worshipped the Golden Calf (*Exod.* 32:1–20) became the template for Israel's behaviour. God then punished Israel for their covenant unfaithfulness. Sometimes he left them to reap the bitter harvest of their spiritual betrayal, but ultimately he punished them by giving them into the hands of the Assyrians. Just as the names of Hosea's children indicate, God judges his people, for Jezreel was a place synonymous with God's judgment (1:3b–5). He did what he said he would do in Deuteronomy 28 and put his covenant into reverse. Instead of loving his people, God would punish them without pity (1:6), and, instead of regarding them as his people and blessing them, God would treat Israel as if they were not his people and curse them (1:9). It looks as if God has torn up the covenant, but appearances do not reflect reality. God *will* judge his people and his judgment will be humiliating and devastating, but he still loves them and judgment will not be his last word. He will graciously restore them, bringing them back to himself so that he can love them again and they can love him again (1:10–2:1; 2:14-23; 3:4–5). God's love will not let his people go.

God's grace initially leaves us stunned, but then it makes us fall down to worship God, because we realize that Israel's story is our story. The Lord graciously brought us into a relationship with him fully aware how prone to wander we were. Like Israel, our lives have been characterized by unfaithfulness to God as we have been seduced into worshipping the idols of our culture. God responds in chastisement against us. Often his discipline is to give us what we stupidly think will bring us freedom and satisfaction, only for us to make the painful discovery that our idols cannot deliver the goods. But in his amazing grace, God does not leave us floundering in our own folly or exposed to his just anger, because he sent his Son into the marketplace of sin to redeem us at the cost of his own blood, securing our freedom from sin's control and bringing us under his gracious rule (*1 Pet.* 1:18–19; 2:24; 3:18).

After the story of his turbulent marriage, we are given, in Hosea 4–14, Hosea's application of God's Word to the contemporary situation. Although it is difficult to see a clear structure in HOSEA'S MESSAGE, the same three themes which crop up in the story of his marriage are found here: *sin, punishment,* and *restoration.* From 4:1 to 9:9, Hosea takes Israel into God's courtroom where the charges against them are outlined. They have been unfaithful to him, violating the covenant (4:1). The image of spiritual prostitution, or going after other gods, recurs frequently (4:18; 5:3–4, 7; 7:4; 8:9; 9:1). The people's covenant unfaithfulness is seen in their lifestyle (4:2–3); the character of the religious leaders (4:4–9); the way in which worship has been contaminated (4:10–19; 8:11–14); and the corrupt behaviour of the nation's political hierarchy (7:1–16; 8:8–10). Hosea points out that God's judgment is inexorably approaching (5:1–5). Sometimes the judgment will involve keeping his people at a distance and letting them suffer for their sins (4:17; 5:6; 8:7); but more often it will involve using the Assyrians to bring destruction and devastation upon Israel (5:14–15; 8:9–10, 14). Hosea warns Israel that God will not be fooled by superficial repentance (6:1–11).

Then, in Hosea 9:10–12:14, Hosea takes Israel back to school and gives them a painful history lesson. His topic is, 'A history of betrayal'. The prophet hammers home the point that unfaithfulness to God is no new development. It happened at Baal Peor (9:10–14) where Israel fell into shameful immorality. In the past Israel had forgotten all that God had done for them in rescuing them from slavery in Egypt (11:1–11). This forgetfulness had resulted in disloyalty to God. They acted just like Jacob in some of his worst moments, practising deceit and dishonesty (11:12–12:14).

The final two chapters see Hosea setting the issues before Israel with passion and clarity. He tells them, in no uncertain terms, that rebellion will lead to death (13:1–16). No king will be able to save Israel: their only hope is God (13:4–13). The consequences of refusing to recognize this are horrible (13:14–16). Hosea appeals to Israel to turn to God because repentance leads to life (14:1–9). With moving tenderness, he appeals to wayward and unfaithful Israel to return to God, assuring them that, if they do, God will graciously forgive and restore them (14:4–9).

There are several significant quotations from and allusions to Hosea in the New Testament which confirm that his prophecy POINTS TO JESUS. When, as her kinsman-redeemer, Hosea buys Gomer back out of slavery (3:1–3), we see the work of Christ our Redeemer. At the price of his blood, he sets us free from sin's control and brings us under the gracious discipline of his rule. Matthew quotes Hosea 11:1 in Matthew 2:15 as a prediction of Jesus' return from his time as a refugee in Egypt. As he celebrates Jesus' victory over death, in 1 Corinthians 15:55, Paul cites Hosea 13:14. Death, seen as a menacing warrior, has been defeated, and death, seen as a deadly scorpion, has had its sting pulled. In Romans 9:25 Paul quotes from Hosea 2:23 and, in 1 Peter 2:10, Peter also alludes to this passage to show that Hosea's vision of restoration had a much longer reach than the return from exile. It ultimately reaches its destination with the inclusion of the Gentiles among God's people alongside and on equal terms with ethnic Jews. This influx fulfils the covenant promise to Abraham of blessing to all peoples on earth (*Gen.* 12:3). There also can be little doubt that Paul had Hosea in mind when, in Ephesians 5:22–33, he compares Christian marriage to the relationship between Jesus and the church.

Running throughout Hosea is the underlying tension between God's justice and God's love for his people. This tension reaches its heart-wrenching climax in Hosea 11. The image is still domestic but it is not that of a husband coming to terms with his wife's adultery but that of a father dealing with a delinquent son. God has done everything to give Israel, his son, a good upbringing (11:1–4), but Israel has thrown all God's care, instruction and love back in his face (11:7). God is justifiably angry at Israel's ingratitude and rebellion, yet, at the same time, he still loves his wayward son, and the thought of punishing him to the point of extinction breaks his heart (11:8–9). How can this tension be resolved, so that God does not condone sin in an unprincipled way and, at the same time, does not condemn the obviously guilty without mercy? The tension between God's justice and God's love was only fully resolved centuries later at the place called Calvary, the hill of a skull, where Jesus died in the place of sinners. There, on the cross, God's holy justice was satisfied and yet at the same time his gracious love was displayed (*Rom.* 3:26).

29

Joel

A part from telling us who his father was (1:1), Joel gives no biographical information about himself. His references to the Temple and its worship (1:9, 13–14) may suggest that he was from a priestly family and lived near Jerusalem, but we just do not know. Rather than speculating about him we should listen to what God has to say through him, and God's message is clear: the land is going to suffer a devastating judgment as a result of a plague of locusts (1:2–2:12). The land in question is Judah, for Joel constantly mentions Jerusalem (2:32; 3:1, 6, 16, 17, 20), or Zion (2:1, 15, 23, 32; 3:16, 17, 21), indicating that his ministry was primarily directed towards the southern kingdom.

Joel does not make it easy for us to say when he prophesied because he does not say which kings were reigning during his ministry. However, there are indicators which make it feasible to suggest that Joel was active during the ninth century BC. Assyria and Babylon are two noticeable absentees from the list of nations God summons to be judged by him in the Valley of Jehoshaphat (3:1–21). These two superpowers dominated the military and political landscape of the region from the mid-eighth to the mid-sixth centuries. Does the fact that Joel does not mention them imply that he was exercising his ministry before the Assyrians and the Babylonians became the main tormentors of God's people? As for the nations God will judge – Egypt, Edom, Tyre, Sidon, Philistia, Greece and the Sabeans of Arabia (3:4, 6, 8, 19), a number of them made life religiously, politically and militarily difficult for Judah, especially during the ninth century BC (*2 Chron.* 21; *2 Kings* 8:16–24). Another possible indicator of an early date for Joel is its place in the running order of the Minor Prophets. This is not chronological, but the fact that Joel is placed second after Hosea should not be dismissed, since it reflects the long-held view that he was one of the earliest pre-exilic Minor Prophets.

If personal details about him are minimal and if the historical context is a matter of debate, there is nothing unclear about JOEL'S THEME. In this short book we come across the first appearance in the Minor Prophets of the term 'the Day of the LORD'. That phrase occurs twelve times in the Minor Prophets, and five of them are in Joel (1:15; 2:1, 11, 31; 3:14). For that reason Joel has been dubbed 'The Prophet of the Day of the Lord'. There are two aspects to this theme: God would come as the sovereign King to *judge*, punishing those who had not submitted to his rule and been loyal to his covenant, and to *save*, honouring those who had handed control of their lives over to him and shown faithfulness to his covenant.

These twin aspects are reflected in JOEL'S STRUCTURE. The book has two main sections. The first deals with *God's judgment* (1:2–2:17). A culture's language can flag up its concerns; so when we discover that Hebrew has nine words for 'locust', four of which are used in Joel 1:4, we can be pretty confident that one of the worst nightmares in this agricultural society was to have a swarm of locusts descend and strip the fields bare. As Joel preached, this was not a nightmare that disappeared when people woke up: it was an awful reality.

What Joel is making clear is that this plague of locusts was not some ecological imbalance, but God's judgment on the land (2:11a). Because God was behind all the devastation, what was happening was to afford instruction (1:2–3). Lessons should be learnt from it and instilled in the minds of future generations. It was indiscriminate (1:4–13), and had huge effects on all facets of the nation's life. No one's status, religious piety, or economic position exempted them from God's judgment. Because it was God's judgment, it was just (1:14–20), and here we come to the reason for the appearance of these destructive locust swarms: Joel is taking us back to Deuteronomy 28 where God had warned his people that, if they were unfaithful to their covenant obligations, he would curse them instead of blessing them. One of those curses would be that the countryside would be devoured by locusts (*Deut.* 28:38–39, 42). God warned his people that disobedience would result in their experiencing the plagues that he had brought upon the Egyptians (*Deut.* 28:58–60), and what Joel describes sounds very much like a repeat of the eighth plague on Egypt – a plague of locusts (*Exod.* 10:1–20). Joel is spelling out the reason for all this destruction: covenant unfaithfulness. Another frightening aspect of God's judgment is that it is inescapable (2:1–11). The destruction locusts cause is horrendous (2:3) and nothing can stop them laying the countryside to waste. Their appearance cannot be prevented (2:1–2) and their advance cannot be halted (2:4–11). The sense of awful inevitability in these verses overwhelms us.

But then, when everything seems lost, there is a glimmer of hope. There is a way to escape (2:12–17). God's judgment is not meant to leave us paralysed by fear, but is intended to drive us to repentance. So Joel urges the people to change their ways and turn to God, holding out the prospect that, if they do, he will reverse his judgment. Repentance, however, is never easy: it involves inward transformation and not an outward cosmetic change (2:13a). Joel therefore gives the people incentives to return to God. He reminds them that any decision on God's part to rescind his judgment ultimately rests not upon how sincere his people's repentance may or may not be, but upon God's initiative (2:12), his gracious nature (2:13) and the fact that his reputation is at stake in the whole affair (2:17). When they turn to him in repentance, God's people will find him more than willing to bless them, rather than continuing to curse them.

Judgment is only one side of the Day of the LORD. The other is *God's salvation*, and this is what the second part of Joel (2:18–3:21) is about. It seems that when they heard God's call to repentance in the form of the locust hordes, Judah did wake up. They turned back to God, and, as they did, God showered them with promises. God takes pity on his people's desperate plight (2:18) and provides food for them (2:19) by annihilating the locust swarms (2:20). Restored productivity is promised (2:21–27). It will not be a matter of just enough to get by, but, in keeping with God's generous nature and the way in which he delights to bless, food production will be at far higher levels than it was before the descent of the locusts.

Then God promises his people spiritual renewal (2:28–32). To the casual onlooker it might seem that Judah's biggest problem was economic; but the real problem was spiritual. God's judgment had fallen, not because of agrarian mismanagement, but because of covenant unfaithfulness. What Judah needed most was not an economic rescue package but spiritual renewal, so that the spiritual decline in the nation, which precipitated the crisis, might be dealt with. In Joel's key passage, therefore, God promises spiritual renewal, which will enable the people to be faithful to their covenant obligations and so reverse God's curse. Judah had been an object of scorn to the surrounding nations (2:19b, 27b). Her neighbours exploited the nation's dire straits for their own ends as people resorted to desperate measures to survive the economic collapse (3:2b–3). But God promises that he will bring relief to Judah by judging their tormentors (3:1–17) and by lavishing his blessings on his people (3:18–21).

When we review what Joel said, we quickly realise that we are being taken far beyond the immediate historical setting of his prophecy. There is a universality about it which shows that Joel is talking about a salvation which is not just for that time and place. When we arrive in the New Testament and take note of the way Joel's key passage (2:28–32) and his central theme, the Day of the Lord, are used, we discover that Joel does indeed give us clear POINTERS TO JESUS and the salvation with which he will bless his people. On the Day of Pentecost, as he explains what is really going on, Peter quotes Joel 2:28–32 (*Acts* 2:14–21). Peter is unequivocal in declaring that the coming of the Holy Spirit is the fulfilment of Joel's key passage. More than that, Peter sees the coming of the Holy Spirit as directing us to the ascended, exalted Jesus – the gift of the Spirit is part of his saving activity (*Acts* 2:33). Also the supreme blessing of the new age – inaugurated by Jesus' first coming – was the coming of the Holy Spirit. This definitively displayed the superiority of the new administration of the covenant made with Jesus, of which he is the Mediator. Under the old administration of the covenant, the gift of the Spirit had been restricted to certain groups of people, but now it will be more broadly based. In ancient Israel, older males had many privileges, but now the gift of the Spirit would not be for men alone, but also for women; not for the old alone, but also for the young; and not for the free alone, but also for the enslaved. When the Spirit comes, the divisions that separate people and the barriers that stop them experiencing salvation are removed out of the way. Paul perhaps had Joel 2:28 in mind when he made the same point in Galatians 3:28: 'There is neither Jew nor Greek, slave nor free, male nor female, for you are all one in Christ Jesus.'

Joel chapter 2 is also crucial for Paul as he argues, in Romans 10, that Jews and Gentiles are saved in exactly the same way. He is adamant that, because God has always had only one plan of salvation – not one way of saving the Jews and another completely separate way of saving the Gentiles – there has always been only one way of salvation. Salvation is only ever on the basis of what Jesus has done, and only ever received by faith in him. To clinch his argument in Romans 10:12–13, therefore, Paul cites Joel 2:32.

The New Testament writers – especially Paul – also apply Joel's central theme concerning the Day of the Lord to Jesus' return. They make it clear that, although there are many partial fulfilments throughout history, these are only pointers to the future Day of the Lord when the Lord will return in power and glory to wind up history. Although Peter also refers to the time when Jesus will come back as 'the Day of the Lord', Paul is particularly keen to apply that designation (*1 Cor.* 5:5; *2 Cor.* 1:14; *1 Thess.* 5:2; *2 Thess.* 2:2). Echoing Joel 3:1–2a and 3:12–15, Paul stresses that when Jesus returns he will summon all to appear before him (*2 Cor.* 5:10). As in Joel's prophecy, this will mean the judgment of the wicked, who have not believed the gospel (*2 Thess.* 1:7–9), and the salvation of the righteous, who have called on the name of the Lord (*2 Thess.* 1:10). It is easy to see that Paul's teaching about Jesus' return has its roots in the Old Testament portrayal of the Day of the Lord, a theme which first appears in the prophecy of Joel.

30

Amos

All my Christian life, I have been specially fond of Amos. One of the first Christian books I bought was a commentary on Amos, and it still has pride of place in my library. At the first Christian Union conference I attended as a student, the Bible readings were based on Amos. Another reason I like this Minor Prophet is that he gives us a great deal of information about himself and the times in which he prophesied.

Amos was a southerner from Tekoa (1:1), an area among the Judean Hills roughly twelve miles south of Jerusalem. Tekoa lies in the rain shadow of higher hills to the west, making it too dry for crops but with just enough rainfall to support scrubby vegetation upon which sheep and goats could graze. Although Amos' main job was shepherding (1:1), he also harvested the crop of the sycamore fig (7:14), which was very low grade fruit. It has been suggested that he did this, either to supplement his meagre income by selling them, or to exchange them for grazing rights for his sheep and goats.

He was not a professional prophet, in the sense that he was not from one of the schools of the prophets which Elijah and Elisha had been instrumental in setting up (7:14), but, as he was going about his work, God called him to be a prophet, who would bring his word to Israel, the northern kingdom (7:15). The way Amaziah, the priest of Bethel, attacked him, accusing him of rabble-rousing and plotting subversion (7:10–13), is evidence that Amos preached in Bethel, one of the shrines Jeroboam, son of Nebat (Jeroboam I) had set up (*1 Kings* 12:26-33). He did not harangue Israel from a safe distance but engaged in hand-to-hand combat with the country's spiritual, moral and social corruption. This was a tough assignment. It would take a tough man with mental and spiritual toughness to see it through to the end, and Amos was such a man.

We have a rough idea when Amos ministered. He tells us that it was when Uzziah reigned in Judah and Jeroboam, son of Jehoash (Jeroboam II) ruled in Israel (1:1). Those historical markers leave us plenty of scope, however, because both men had long reigns, fifty-one years (791–740 BC) in Uzziah's case and forty years (793–753 BC) in Jeroboam's. Amos does define the time of his ministry by saying that it was 'two years before the earthquake' (1:1). Belvoir, the area of south Belfast in which I work, was devastated by a huge bomb in 1992. But people who lived through this traumatic event do not talk about 1992; instead they refer to it as 'the year of the bomb'. Perhaps something similar is going on here. In any event, we cannot date Amos' prophecy more precisely than to say that it belongs to the first half of the eighth century BC.

To understand the thrust of his message we need to consider AMOS' SETTING. He was active during the reign of Jeroboam II, when Israel experienced its last hurrah. In less than thirty years after Jeroboam's death, the northern kingdom would cease to exist. In its two-hundred-and-nine-year existence, Israel had nineteen kings, making the average reign eleven years. But Jeroboam II reigned for forty years and brought solidity and continuity to the country. He was an energetic and talented man. During his reign the power of Syria, which had been a nuisance to Israel for years, was checked, and the frontiers restored to where they had been before the kingdom split (2 *Kings* 14:25).

Amos' prophecy hints at the prosperity of the time. Money was lavished on second homes (3:15), expensive and showy furniture, interior decorations (3:15; 6:4), and self-indulgent pleasures (4:1; 6:4–5). Religion, too, appeared to be flourishing (5:21), sacrifices were meticulously offered (4:4; 5:22), and music was cultivated (5:23; 8:3). But affluence had bred smugness, complacency, and social heartlessness. Getting rich, having a good time, and exploiting the poor (8:5) were rife, rich women were decadent (4:1), and leaders pursued the trivial instead of the important (6:1–6). All of this stank in the nostrils of God. It required to be challenged. The challenge came in the shape of his prophet Amos.

We should pause briefly to consider AMOS' STRUCTURE. He may not have been a professional prophet (7:14–15), but he wrote in a clear and well-structured way. The book begins with a series of *sermons* (1:2–6:14). These can be sub-divided into two groups. The first is made up of *eight roars of judgment* (1:2–2:16). The key phrase is 'for three sins of . . . , even for four, I will not turn back my wrath' (1:3, 6, 9, 11, 13; 2:1, 4, 6). Amos announces God's judgment on Damascus (1:3–5), Gaza (1:6–8), Tyre (1:9–10), Edom (1:11–12), Ammon (1:13–15), Moab (2:1–3), Judah (2:4–5) and finally Israel (2:6–16). We can imagine Amos reprimanding the pagan nations, to the warm approval of his audience. But as he set his sights on Edom, Ammon and Moab some will have realized that he was moving closer to home. And as he denounced Judah, everyone would see who was to be next. And they were not wrong, because Amos finally turned his fire on Israel.

These eight roars of judgment are carefully thought out and based upon solid theological convictions about God. He is the God of all the world, the only Lord of heaven and earth, and this is why he will hold these pagan nations accountable for their sins. They have sinned in many other ways – the 'three sins' – but there is a 'fourth sin' to which God will not turn a blind eye. For Damascus and Gaza, the 'fourth sin' is inhumane cruelty, whether in war or in commerce; for Tyre and Edom, it is the betrayal of their brothers; and for Ammon and Moab, it is gross disrespect for the unborn, the dead and the helpless, all of whom deserved protection. The 'fourth sins' of these pagan nations were crimes against humanity; but Judah and Israel's 'fourth sin' was different: they had committed crimes against God. Judah had spurned God's teaching, rejected his commands, and preferred human lies. Israel was no better, as she had embraced corrupt religion (2:8); put pressure on people who wished to be committed to God to slacken off in their commitment (2:12; *Num.* 6:1–8); silenced God's voice through the prophets (2:12); and refused to live as God's people should (2:9–10).

The second sub-division of Amos' sermons consists of *three pleas to hear* (3:1–6:14). The key phrase is 'hear this word' (3:1; 4:1; 5:1). Amos pleads with the people to listen to what God is saying to them and to obey it. The first plea is the most important because it sets out why

God is going to punish Israel: he will do so because of their special status and relationship to him (3:1–2). This would have brought gasps of disbelief from his audience. It ran counter to everything they thought. They assumed that because they were God's people, chosen by him and redeemed by him, God would only bless them. But Amos turns that idea on its head. It is because Israel was special, having received God's covenant promises and experienced his salvation, that God was going to punish them. They should have used their spiritual privileges as a springboard to loyalty to God and obedience to his Word, but instead they were disloyal to God and disobedient to their covenant obligations. God's judgment would come upon Israel because they had experienced his favour. 'Because of the covenant they came to possess the land, and because of the covenant they will be exiled from the land.'[1]

Following hard on the heels of Amos' sermons are a series of *visions* he saw (7:1–9:10). The key phrase is, 'This is what the Sovereign LORD showed me' (7:1, 4, 7; 8:1). Again, Amos' visions can be sub-divided into, first of all, *visions of judgments God refused to use* (7:1–6). As a result of Amos' prayers, God would not send a plague of locusts and uncontrollable fire to decimate Israel. Devastation by locusts was among the Deuteronomy 28 curses for covenant unfaithfulness (*Deut.* 28:38,42), and destruction by fire was one of the features of God's judgment upon the Israelites for their constant grumbling as they travelled through the desert (*Num.* 11:1–3; 16:35). The refusal of God to judge in this way was an indication of his grace, not giving Israel what they deserve. However, the second sub-division records *visions of judgments God would use* (7:7–9:10). These visions – about a plumb line (7:7–9), a basket of ripe summer fruit (8:1–14), and pillars which are about to topple (9:1–10) all focus on the fairness and inevitability of God's judgment. After the vision of the plumb line, there is some narrative mixed with prediction as we come across Amos' showdown with Amaziah, the priest of Bethel (7:10–17).

It would be wrong to write Amos off as only a prophet of doom, with the uncertain-sounding 'perhaps the LORD God Almighty will

[1] O. Palmer Robertson, *The Christ of the Prophets* (Phillipsburg, New Jersey: P & R Publishing, 2004), pp 208–9.

have mercy on the remnant of Joseph' (5:15) being the best he can offer in terms of hope. Amos finishes with a series of *promises* (9:11–15). There was to be a restoration – because judgment is never God's final word to his people – and this restoration would take place under the leadership of one of David's descendants. So God's promise to David would remain intact and on course for fulfilment.

What was AMOS' MESSAGE? The picture of God with which Amos opens is that he is a lion (1:2). Looking at the book through the lens of that image, we see that *the lion roars*. God, the divine lion, roars through his prophets (1:2; 3:7–8). The sound is one of judgment. God's people had been unfaithful to their covenant obligations, and Amos, as a prophet and covenant enforcer, was to roar out God's anger. Two sins are highlighted in particular. The first is *idolatry*. Although 'religion' was thriving, it was not the worship of God but the counterfeit religion set up by Jeroboam I as a state-sponsored alternative to God's worship in Jerusalem. This cult was nothing more than an exercise in self-congratulation (4:5) and disgusted God (5:21–23). The classic product of this idolatry was Amaziah. He was all for the establishment and the *status quo* (7:10), careful to maintain all ecclesiastical niceties (7:13), but supremely against any word from God (7:12, 16). One upshot of this corrupt religion was that moral standards had slumped. Amos could speak against sexual immorality (2:7) and how justice was perverted through the widespread use of bribes (5:12), without being contradicted. The other particular sin about which the roar of God's judgment could be heard was *social injustice*. Only a small minority of Israel's society, the already-wealthy upper class, had benefited from the nation's economic boom. They had made their money at the expense of the poor, who sank deeper and deeper into poverty. Their affluence came on the back of dubious deals (2:6–7), legal sharp practice (5:10, 12) and shady business transactions (8:5). When people failed to generate any more wealth for the already rich, they were tossed to one side. When Jesus was asked to summarize the main thrust of God's law, he replied that we were to love God with all our being and to love our neighbour in the same way as we love ourselves (*Mark* 12:28–31). On both counts, Israel had failed miserably. No wonder the lion's roar was heard.

But God will do more, because Amos speaks of how *the lion will pounce*. Because Israel had violated the covenant, they were going to reap the consequences. God had warned them (4:6–11). The warnings had come in the form of some of the covenant curses of Deuteronomy 28, but Israel did not recognize them as such. Their religion, with its emphasis on ritual, had desensitized them to God's voice. Amos pleaded with the people not to live in a fantasy world (5:18–20). They thought that the Day of the Lord would be a time of vindication when God, the divine warrior, would fight on their side against their enemies. But Amos throws that view into reverse as he points out, in no uncertain terms, that it would a time of national judgment for Israel. God, the divine warrior, would fight against them. Because of their sin, Israel was included with the pagan nations and would fare no better than they would on the Day of the Lord. When the lion pounced in judgment, it would be terrible. Fathers and sons who had slept with the same cult prostitute (2:7) would see their wives and mothers turned into prostitutes and their children killed (7:17). Those who crushed the poor (2:7), would be crushed themselves (2:13). The land would be devastated and its inhabitants deported into exile (5:5, 27; 7:11, 17). But an even worse judgment would befall the people: the disappearance of words from God (8:11–12). When the lion pounced in judgment, there would be no escape (9:2–4).

Yet there was hope because *the lion would heal*. Those brought up on C. S. Lewis' stories about Aslan, the great lion-king of Narnia, will not find this so surprising. Amos lays considerable stress on the location from which God, the divine lion, roared: 'from Zion . . . from Jerusalem' (1:2). That is not a geographical reference, but a theological one. Mount Zion in Jerusalem, where the Temple was situated, was the place God had chosen for the offering of sacrifices, sacrifices that pointed to the great sacrifice that would finally deal with sin. So the book opens with a note of hope for, in spite of all the sin that is going to be exposed and condemned, there is a clear reminder that God forgives sin. The book also ends on a note of hope because, in Amos 9:11–15, the prophet shows how God will restore his people. The ultimate fulfilment of this promise did not lie in the return from exile, though the initial one did.

It is in this promise with which Amos ends that we see a clear POINTER TO JESUS. Just as he had predicted (*Acts* 1:8), the good news about Jesus spilled over the frontiers of Judea and many Gentiles had become his followers. This sounded alarm bells for some who were more Jewish than Christian, and they started to urge that these new non-Jewish Christians needed to become Jews by means of the rite of circumcision as well as being Christians by faith in Christ. A church gathering was held in Jerusalem to thrash out the issue once and for all (*Acts* 15:35). This was a crossroads moment in the short existence of the early church. Would the church become a mere backwater sect of Judaism through embracing circumcision, or would it reject this and burst out of its Jewish limitations (*Mark* 2:21–22) to become a world-wide and universal phenomenon? The Council of Jerusalem, as this gathering is known, rejected the idea that Gentiles needed to be circumcised. They were saved on the same basis as Jews – by believing in the Lord Jesus alone (*Acts* 15:11). The clinching speech was made by James, who cited Amos 9:11–12 to reinforce his point. He argued that the ultimate fulfilment of Amos' promise was not the return from exile but the inclusion of Gentiles among God's people.

When explaining to us how Jesus would have his followers live, the apostles often refer to Amos. For example, when Paul instructs us to 'hate what is evil' and 'cling to what is good' (*Rom.* 12:9), he has at least one eye on Amos 5:15. Amos' concern about social justice and our attitude towards the poor is taken up by the New Testament writers. Jesus' followers are to treat the poor in exactly the same way as they do the rich (*1 Cor.* 11:22; *James* 2:1–10). True religion involves caring for those in need, and not exploiting them (*James* 1:27). This is not a 'social gospel' but a by-product of the true and only gospel.

31

Obadiah

Obadiah is certainly the most 'minor' of all the Minor Prophets, as well as being the shortest book in the Old Testament. Some, like Jerome, the translator of the Bible into Latin, have thought the book just as difficult as it is brief. Obadiah himself gives us no information about himself or when he wrote, so we have to look for clues in what he said.

After the briefest of introductions – 'The vision of Obadiah', two words in Hebrew – Obadiah informs us that his God-given message is directed against Edom (1), because of her violence against her 'brother Jacob' (10–14). There were several occasions when Edom's hostility spilled over into aggressive action. In the ninth century, Edom joined forces with Moab and Ammon to attack Jehoshaphat, but their vast army was routed in the Valley of Beracah (2 *Chron.* 20:1–26). A few years later Edom successfully rebelled against Jehoram, shaking off outside interference in her affairs for about forty years (2 *Chron.* 21:8–10). In the early eighth century Amaziah defeated Edom in the Valley of Salt, pulling it into line once again (2 *Kings* 14:7), but this was short-lived, because by the middle of the eighth century Edom was launching raids against Ahaz and causing trouble for him (2 *Chron.* 28:17). The final instance of Edom's antagonism towards Judah was her collusion with the Babylonians when they captured Jerusalem in 587 BC (*Psa.* 137:7). It seems probable that it was the last of these occasions which provided the historical context of Obadiah's message. This makes him one of the last prophets before the Exile.

Obadiah's STRUCTURE is shaped by the fact that he is, like Joel and Amos, a prophet of the Day of the Lord (15). This grouping together of the 'Day of the Lord' prophets gives one explanation why Obadiah, a seventh-century prophet, is out of his proper chronological order, placed as he is, next to the eighth-century prophets Joel and Amos. However, Obadiah uses the idea of the Day of the Lord differently from Amos, his nearest neighbour. In Amos the Day of the Lord acts as a warning to God's people (*Amos* 5:18–20). In Obadiah it is used to bring hope.

The first of the twin themes associated with the Day of the Lord is that *God's enemies will be destroyed*, and this is reflected in Obadiah 2–16. The first cause of God's anger against Edom is her pride (3). This was partly based on her apparently impregnable defences (3). If you look up the facts about Petra, or if you have seen the film *Indiana Jones and the Last Crusade*, you will realize that Petra is a defender's dream. It is approached by a steep, narrow gorge, and some military experts think that the city could be defended by about twenty well-armed men. Edom had a reputation throughout the region for wisdom and sharp diplomacy (8), and she put these to good use in making alliances with her more powerful neighbours. She was confident that if she was under threat, her allies would come to her aid. But God was also angry with Edom because of her mistreatment of God's people (10–14). Judah and Edom were blood relatives, descended from Jacob and Esau respectively. But, as far as Edom was concerned, blood was not thicker than water, so when the Babylonians captured Jerusalem Edom stood aloof, only gloating over Judah's trauma. In particular, she had done nothing while foreigners cast lots for Jerusalem (11).

God's judgment will be total (5–6). If a thief burgles a house, he will at least leave something. Harvesters do not strip a vineyard of every single grape. But when God does what he is about to do, Edom will be defenceless (4); her allies will betray her (7); and her wisdom will prove useless (8). As a result of God's judgment, Edom will be obliterated (9, 18). Any cultural legacy will disappear (8). For Edom there will be nowhere to run, and nowhere to hide.

The second of the twin themes associated with the Day of the Lord is that *God's people will be delivered*, and this is brought out in verses 17–21. Obadiah sets up a contrast between Mount Zion (17, 21) and Mount Esau (8, 9, 21). For Mount Esau, the Day of the Lord will bring destruction, while for Mount Zion it will result in deliverance, as God intervenes and reverses his people's fortunes. The historical events which give rise to Obadiah seemed to have destroyed God's promise in Genesis 12 of a place of blessing, but as Obadiah scans the horizon (19–20), south-west to Philistia, north-west to Sidon, south to the Negev, north to Ephraim and Samaria, south-east to Edom and north-east to Gilead, he forecasts that the promise will be reinstated. This will not happen as a result of military might or shrewd alliances but by the mighty working of God himself (21), so that all the glory will be his.

What MESSAGE is Obadiah presenting? First, he is warning us that *God takes sin seriously*. Some get nervous about the severity of God's judgment. Is his reaction disproportionate? To understand God's response to Edom's pride and mistreatment of others we have to see what Edom represents in the flow of biblical thought. Jacob and Esau stand for opposing principles. Jacob – and his descendants, Judah – embody the principle of God's undeserved and unearned grace. Esau – and his descendants, Edom – represent humanity in rebellion against God. While Edom's arrogance (3–4) certainly echoes the boasts of Babylon (*Isa.* 14:13), behind the pride of both lies the haughty conceit of Satan – showing from whom both nations are taking their spiritual cue. Edom had rejected God's truth in favour of her own wisdom, imagining that she knew better than he did. Throughout the Old Testament trusting in God and seeking the help of foreign powers always stand at odds with each other. Edom's fixation with setting up alliances with other nations speaks of a deep-seated refusal to trust in God. Edom's sin of doing nothing as foreigners gambled for Jerusalem (11) is far worse than it seems because it goes back to humanity's ultimate rejection of God. When Jesus was crucified, all he owned were the clothes that were stripped off him before he was nailed to the cross. The Roman soldiers ripped most of his clothing into quarters, a part for each of them, but they gambled to see who would get his seamless undergarment (*John* 19:23–24).

Edom's pride and mistreatment of others was not something trivial: it was a calculated rejection of God. This was so much part of Edom's spiritual DNA that when, in the person of Jesus, God himself came to earth in a real humanity, Herod the Great, who was half-Idumean, or half-Edomite, tried to kill him (*Matt.* 2:13–18). While our egotistical and self-absorbed culture may not think of Edom's sins as being particularly serious, God has a totally different view of them. He sees in them a deliberate rejection of himself and his rule. Because he takes sin – rebellion against him in any shape of form – seriously, he comes down hard on Edom, and all who reject him.

However, Obadiah also reminds us that *God brings the hope of salvation*. The focus of Obadiah 19–20 on God's promise of a place of blessing might appear to indicate that there is only hope for the Jews, and that non-Jews like Edom will be permanently left out. But Obadiah ends with verse 21 which refers to deliverers [saviours (KJV/ESV)] going up on Mount Zion to judge Mount Esau. This final statement inserts hope for Edom into the situation. The language of Obadiah 21 is a reference to the role of the Judges, which was not primarily judicial but designed to bring people into an experience of God's undeserved salvation. Obadiah 21 indicates that, as a result of God's gracious activity, Edom will be given a window of opportunity to experience God's deliverance. What we are seeing here is another of God's promises in Genesis 12 – the promise of a programme to bring blessing to all nations. Despite all its past antagonism towards God, Edom can benefit from God's salvation and grace. When God acts in his Son to bring his covenant promises to fulfilment, non-Jews, like the people of Edom, can be brought in.

The hope of salvation for all nations points to another reason why Obadiah is out of its proper chronological order: Obadiah is going to pick up something Amos has said. In Amos 9:11–12, God explains that he will repair David's fallen tent, 'so that they may possess the remnant of Edom'. When James quotes that statement in Acts 15:16–18 to prove that salvation is experienced through faith alone in Christ alone, he expands the concept of 'Edom' to mean all Gentile outsiders. In the Spirit-inspired New Testament interpretation of the Old Testament, Edom has shifted from representing humanity in rebellion against God and under his judgment to representing humanity trusting in Christ and receiving God's salvation. Obadiah is placed after Amos so that the book might take further what Amos merely hinted at – that God's salvation in Jesus Christ is for all nations. Like Edom, we reject God's legitimate claim over our lives, but the salvation of God can change all that. Through faith alone in Christ alone we are brought under his rule, embraced by his salvation, and made to experience the blessings which abound where Jesus reigns.

32

Jonah

Writing about Jonah makes me blush, because, as a young minister, the first series of sermons I preached was based on this book. I am embarrassed to recall the patience with which my congregation listened – not only was my series much too long but my grasp of what Jonah is about was very superficial. I hope that, almost thirty years on, I have a little more understanding of what God is saying through what is probably the best known of all the Minor Prophets. We know a little bit about Jonah himself, not just from the book named after him, but also from a reference to him in 2 Kings 14:25. His father was called Amittai and he came from Gath Hepher, a village northeast of Nazareth. He was active in Israel, the northern kingdom, sometime between 786 and 746 BC, during the reign of Jeroboam II.

The book of Jonah has some PECULIARITIES which distinguish it from the other Minor Prophets. Some of the others contain some storyline and many sermons, but Jonah is nearly all storyline and a tiny amount of sermon. However, it does belong among the prophets. All the prophets had a message from God to communicate. Most of them conveyed it by what they said, but Jonah does so mainly in a non-verbal way, through what happened to him. Another peculiarity of the book is that God wanted Jonah to take his message outside the borders of the land of promise to the pagan inhabitants of Nineveh, the capital of Assyria (1:2).

We must also think about the book's GENRE. Is it a historical narrative or a fictional narrative? This issue is settled by Jesus' understanding of the book. He informs us that what happened to Jonah is a pointer to his own death and resurrection (*Matt.* 12:40), and he tells us that on Judgment Day the people of Nineveh will point a condemning finger at his contemporaries for not repenting (*Matt.* 12:41). If the story is fictional then Jesus' resurrection and Judgment Day may be non-historical too, and this is something the New Testament denies in the strongest terms. Jesus clearly views the book as historical narrative, telling us about incidents that really happened in time and space.

If we turn to Jonah's STORYLINE, it can be unlocked by asking a question about each chapter. Jonah 1 is opened up by asking this: *Where are you going, Jonah?* God told Jonah clearly what he wanted him to do: he was to go to Nineveh and announce God's judgment against it (1:2). But instead of heading east to Nineveh, Jonah makes straight for Joppa, a port on Israel's Mediterranean seaboard, and buys a ticket on a ship sailing due west to Tarshish, in what is now Spain. This has nothing to with poor map reading skills: he is deliberately disobeying God (1:3). Jonah even tells us why he did what he did, but we must wait until Jonah 4 to find out.

Jonah soon discovers that running away from God is impossible. The ship runs into a tremendous storm, sent by God to stop his disobedient prophet in his tracks (1:4). The pagan sailors are terrified by the storm, and cast lots to find out whose fault it was. No surprise here: the lot falls on Jonah. He admits that he is responsible for putting their lives in danger because he is trying to escape from God (1:8–10). He tells them that the only way to calm the raging sea is to throw him overboard (1:11–12). To their credit the sailors refuse; but, when their attempts to row back to land prove futile, they reluctantly do what Jonah says. To their astonishment, the storm subsides (1:13-15). The sailors probably thought that that was the end of Jonah, but God had arranged for a huge fish to swallow him (1:17). He should have been going to Nineveh and, although he wanted to go to Tarshish, he is now going to the bottom of the Mediterranean inside a fish.

The question that unlocks Jonah 2 is: *What are you doing, Jonah?* Being swallowed by the fish was the shock Jonah needed. In its dark belly he prayed as he had never prayed before. Drawing on the Scriptures, especially the Psalms, Jonah repented of his disobedience and asked God to forgive him (2:1–9). God heard his prayer and ordered the fish to deposit Jonah back on dry land (2:10).

We can think of Jonah 3 in terms of the question: *What are you saying, Jonah?* God took his grace towards Jonah to a new level by renewing his commission (3:1–2). This time he set off for Nineveh. We must not imagine that Nineveh was one group of buildings surrounded by a wall. Like other ancient cities it was made up of many smaller settlements built around a central citadel, which is why it was so expansive (3:3b). Jonah went into this sprawling metropolis and announced God's judgment on it (3:4). His preaching was incredibly successful, affecting every part of Nineveh's society (3:5). As huge numbers turned to God, the king proclaimed a fast throughout the city, calling on people to plead with God to withhold his judgment (3:6–9). God hears them, and, in response to their repentance, he graciously lifts the threat of judgment and shows mercy to Nineveh (3:10).

But the book does not finish there. In chapter 4 the story takes some strange turns, which would have left those hearing it for the first time amazed. The question we might ask is: *What are you up to now, Jonah?* Incredibly, in the light of all God's grace towards him, Jonah is furious at what has happened (4:1). As he complains bitterly, the reason he fled in the first place comes to light. It all has to do with the reality that God is extraordinarily gracious (4:2).

Jonah was aware of the threat Assyria posed to Israel and thought that if Assyria was destroyed his country would be safe. He wanted God to wipe out Nineveh, not have mercy on it. But Jonah was also very aware that God was gracious, compassionate, and slow to anger. He had already seen this in his own ministry (2 *Kings* 14:25). Jeroboam II had done nothing to discourage the false religion established by his namesake, Israel's first king (2 *Kings* 14:24). But God still blessed Israel outwardly, extending her boundaries so that she experienced prosperity. God had not treated Israel as she deserved, and Jonah had a gut feeling he might do the same to Nineveh. His suspicions were heightened by his message. It might be a message of judgment (1:2; 3:4), but 'a prophetic announcement of doom left open the possibility of mercy in the event of repentance.'[1] Based on past

---

[1] O. Palmer Robertson, *Jonah: A Study in Compassion* (Edinburgh: Banner of Truth, 1990), page 11.

history and God's character, Jonah knew it was likely that God would graciously show Nineveh mercy, and he did not want to be part of it.

Jonah is not the hero of the book: he is more like the anti-hero, angry with God. He wants God to destroy Nineveh. He does not want God to be himself – generous and forgiving – preferring a God who is full of wrath and vengeance. How strange to see a prophet having such a massive problem with God's grace! Yet God's grace in forgiving and accepting obviously bad people has always posed a problem for religious people. It certainly did for the Pharisees when, to their horror, they saw Jesus mixing with sinners, those who were, in their estimation, beyond the pale. They condemned him as 'the friend of sinners' (*Luke* 7:34) and muttered constantly about how he welcomed them (*Luke* 15:2). Religious people, by and large, find it scandalous that God, in his grace, forgives sinners. They are even more offended when they realize that God accepts sinners not because they have earned his forgiveness but because Jesus came from heaven not just to mix with sinners but to seek and save them by means of his death on the cross as their substitute.

God now begins to deal with Jonah. As he sat watching to see what would happen (4:5), God caused a quick-growing, big-leafed plant to provide him with some shelter from the sun, and for the first time in ages Jonah smiled (4:6). But the next day, God sent a worm which attacked the plant and caused it to wither (3:7). With no shelter from the sun and the hot wind, Jonah became faint (4:7–8). Once more he complained and wished to die (4:9). Then God asked him a question – an argument from the lesser to the greater – that went straight for Jonah's self-pitying state. If it was right for Jonah to feel sorry for the plant, was it not right for God to have pity on the people of Nineveh, entrapped in sinful habits from which they did not know how to escape? Are not people more important than plants? (4:10–11)

We are not told how Jonah responded. The book ends abruptly. But the absence of a neat conclusion is deliberate, because God wants each of us to answer the question for ourselves. Jonah grieved over a repentant city that had been spared, but Jesus grieved over an unrepentant city that had to be judged (*Luke* 19:41–44). Jonah's ending leaves us with the choice: Are we like Jonah or Jesus? The untidy conclusion leaves us uncomfortable because there is far too much of Jonah in us, and far too little of Jesus. We would like to think we are like Jesus, but we suspect that we are like Jonah, preferring to see evil people punished rather than forgiven and accepted by God. Like Jonah, we struggle not with God's anger and judgment but with his mercy and grace.

There is more to the story than first meets the eye, and it is the same with Jonah's MESSAGE. There are obvious lessons on the surface about obeying God, prayer and God's sovereign rule over the whole of his creation, but we have to look more closely to see what its main lessons are. Embedded in the story are two lessons. The first is that Jonah's experience is *a sign of good things to come* in relation to *Jesus' death and resurrection*. God acted in judgment against Jonah, punishing him for his sin. In the fish, he experienced 'death' (2:2b) as he was penalized by being banished from God's presence (2:4a). But then he experienced God's grace as he was rescued from his watery grave and given back his life (2:6b). In Matthew 12:38–41, Jesus indicated that Jonah's experience was a pointer to what would happen to him. God judged Jesus, punishing him, not because he himself had sinned, but because he was acting as his people's representative. As he took responsibility for our sins, Jesus actually tasted the bitter reality of death (*Heb.* 2:9), for death is the penalty for sin (*Ezek.* 18:20; *Rom.* 6:23), and he was banished from God's presence (*Mark* 15:34). Then, on the third day, God raised him from the dead (*1 Cor.* 15:4) and brought him back to life again. Through the real death and physical resurrection of the one who is 'greater than Jonah' (*Matt.* 12:41), the salvation of the Lord comes to us (2:9).

The second lesson embedded in the story also has to do with God's salvation. It is *a sign of more good things to come* because it highlights how *Gentiles are included in God's saving purposes*. Freshly 'resurrected from the dead' Jonah takes God's message to Nineveh and those hardhearted Gentiles repent and experience God's grace. One reason why this offended Jonah so much was that he had forgotten that God had always intended non-Jews to receive his blessings. One of the definitive promises in Genesis 12 is that God has a programme to bring his salvation to all peoples through Jesus, Abraham's descendant *par excellence*. Here, with the conversion of the people of Nineveh, God's covenant promise moves forward with increasing speed. Until now a few individuals have been incorporated into God's people, but here a whole city is brought into God's saving purpose. This is a preview of the good things to come when the actually-resurrected Jesus stands in front of his disciples and sends them to all nations with the message of his salvation (*Matt.* 28:19; *Luke* 24:46–47). The result of Jesus sending his church out is that God's promise of a programme broadens out to all nations, to us. Our sins have been judged in Jesus, and through faith in him alone we have been raised to new life. We have been brought to experience God's covenant blessings, as he becomes our God and we become his people.

Jonah is a great story, not because of the great fish, but because it is the story of Jesus, the 'greater than Jonah', and how God's salvation on the basis of his death and resurrection has a long and wide reach. It is a story for everyone, irrespective of ethnicity, gender, spirituality or morality.

33
Micah

The last of the eighth-century-BC prophets is Micah. He came from Moresheth. The precise location of this village is uncertain but it was probably about twenty-five miles south-west of Jerusalem, on the edge of the rolling hills known as the Shephelah, not far from the modern-day Gaza Strip. While the three Judean kings listed in Micah 1:1 provide us with the time framework within which Micah was active, it is a rather wide one because Jotham, Ahaz and Hezekiah reigned from 750 right through to 686 BC. However, there are a number of indications which narrow down the time when Micah ministered. In Micah 1:6 he announces God's judgment on Samaria, the northern kingdom's capital, and because it was captured by the Assyrians in 722 BC, we can work out that he was active prior to that date. Micah 3:12 is quoted in Jeremiah 26:18, where it is hinted that Hezekiah's reformation of 715 BC was sparked by Micah's preaching. The lament of Micah 1:8–16 may be dated to around 701 BC, as the cities mentioned in it trace the route taken by Sennacharib's invading army. These three time markers indicate that Micah was preaching from before 722 to at least 701 BC.

If these dates are correct, they indicate that Micah was a contemporary of Isaiah, so he ministered in a time of political upheaval and spiritual decline. The relative glory days of Uzziah's reign were in the past and on the political horizon loomed a resurgent Assyria. By Ahaz's disastrous reign, although not officially part of the expanding Assyrian Empire, Judah was firmly under the heel of Assyria. It not only cast its dark shadow over Judah's political landscape but Assyrian influence was also felt in Judah's religious life as Ahaz introduced many Assyrian religious rituals into worship in order to keep his Assyrian overlords happy. All the tell-tale signs of spiritual decline were present, and Micah pulls no punches in dealing with them. He condemns the religious spokesmen for not speaking God's truth but telling people whatever they wanted to hear for the payment of a bribe (2:11; 3:11). The pagan practices are condemned in 5:12–14. With spiritual decline came moral decay, and Judean society was becoming unstable and violent (2:2, 8). Justice was perverted (3:9), business life was riddled with sharp practices (6:10–12), and normal family values were disintegrating (7:5–6). In these turbulent times God called Micah to be his spokesman to Judah and – until it was overthrown – Israel too (1:1).

Like every preacher, each of the Minor Prophets had his own distinctive STYLE, and Micah is no exception. One of his strategies is to engage his audience by using rhetorical questions (1:5; 2:7; 4:9; 6:3, 7, 10–11; 7:18). He also uses clever word plays and – although it is lost in translation from Hebrew to English – almost every place mentioned in the Assyrian advance on Jerusalem (1:8–16) becomes the vehicle for one of these. As he reaches the climax of his book (7:18–20), Micah combines these two elements of his preaching style as he asks the question, 'Who is a God like you?' This rhetorical quesion involves a wordplay because his name literally means, 'Who is like the LORD?'

Micah's prophecy should be viewed as a collection of his most significant sermons. If we think about it in that way, we can detect a clear STRUCTURE to it. The book contains three major sermons, each one moving from judgment to hope, a well-travelled route taken by the prophets. Each sermon begins with 'Listen' (1:2; 3:1; 6:1). That word takes us straight into the courtroom, indicating the legal setting of the book. While judgment is the dominant note in Micah, hope has not departed, because judgment is never God's last word to his people. So each sermon ends positively as Micah speaks about God's salvation for a remnant (2:12–13; 5:1–15; 7:18–20).

In the first sermon, *the capital cities are brought before the Lord's court* (1:2–2:13). Both Jerusalem and Samaria have failed to keep their covenant obligations, and as a result both will be destroyed (1:6; 3:12). However, beyond the Exile, there will be restoration as a remnant returns (2:12–13). The numbers will not be as large as those who were deported, but there will be a people coming home. The second sermon sees *the leaders brought before the Lord's court* (3:1–5:15). The civil leaders and the religious establishment, the prophets and priests, have rejected God's rule as expressed in his law (3:1–3, 5, 11), and they will experience the terrible consequences of their attitude and actions as God's judgment comes down upon them (3:4, 6–7, 12). However, amidst the gloom, there is a chink of light because God will raise up a ruler who will be everything that the nation's present leaders are not (5:1–15). The same pattern of judgment and hope is detected in Micah's third sermon as *the whole nation is brought before the Lord* (6:1–7:20). When he has gone over the history of all that God has done for the nation, he accuses them of failing to respond appropriately (6:4–5). In Jewish tradition, Micah 6:8 is taken to be a summary of the law. In other words, it is how the people should have responded to God's grace, but they had not: instead of consistent covenant faithfulness there had been abject covenant unfaithfulness. God was angry with them, but this state of affairs would not go on indefinitely, for he would forgive them (7:8–9, 18–20).

Many congregations have had their minds stretched, their emotions stirred, their hearts warmed, their attitudes transformed and their wills moved to obedience by sermons taken from places such as Micah 5:2, 6:8 and 7:18–19. Even the greatest preacher ever to address an audience quoted Micah in his preaching, for when Jesus wanted to stress the divisions that would be caused by his challenge to put our relationship with him above every other relationship, he quoted Micah 7:6 (*Matt.* 10:34–39). However, while it may be a source of great preaching texts, it is Micah's THEMES that show what he was really saying. The actual term does not appear in his book, but the foundation theme of Micah's message is *covenant*, particularly the way this is handled in Deuteronomy. In echoes of Moses, Micah stressed how God had blessed his people (6:4–5), but they had failed to live up to their covenant obligations (6:6–8). Consequently God was bringing a lawsuit against his people and, in language derived from Deuteronomy, the whole world is called to be witnesses against God's people for their covenant unfaithfulness (compare 1:2; 6:1–2 with *Deut.* 4:26; 30:19; 31:28; 32:1.) In the light of their failure to carry out their covenant obligations, Micah announces that Judah will be deported to Babylon (4:10). Deuteronomy's covenantal structure and its message of covenant unfaithfulness leading to covenant cursing feeds into Micah. He is driving home the point that God is always true to his word. He promised life if people obeyed him, but judgment if they disobeyed.

However, embedded within the structure of Deuteronomy, there is hope of a return from exile (*Deut.* 30:1–10), and this hope appears in Micah in the shape of *the remnant*. What he has to say about the remnant is perhaps Micah's most significant contribution to the Old Testament's teaching on hope. The whole nation will not come back, but a remnant will (2:12; 4:7; 5:7–8; 7:18). Moreover, the remnant will not be a diverse group who skulk home beaten and discouraged; they will be a force to be reckoned with and will ultimately conquer (4:11–13). The reason is that from the remnant will come Jesus, God's universal king (*Matt.* 1:12–13), who will conquer by his death and resurrection.

Because they are contemporaries, there are similarities between Micah and Isaiah, and one of the areas of overlap is imagery concerning *the mountain of the* Lord. You do not need a degree in literature to realize that Micah 4:1–5 and Isaiah 2:1–5 are the same. In the 'which-came-first' discussions which academics love, Micah is usually accused of plagiarism. But that is a little disingenuous, since a simpler explanation is that both were inspired by the same Holy Spirit to express a similar idea in similar words. In the Old Testament, 'the mountain of the Lord' is often used as a symbol for God's kingdom (*Dan.* 2:35, 45). As he draws on God's covenant promise in Genesis 12 of a programme to bring blessing to all nations, Micah points out how God's rule will spread to all peoples (4:1). God's Word will give direction to all nations (4:2), and obedience to the king's standards and values will bring peace (4:3) and prosperity (4:4). Micah may have expressed it differently, but in the imagery of 'the mountain of the Lord' he is drawing on Deuteronomy's main theme: obey the king's covenant obligations and there will be life.

The final and best-known theme in Micah is that of *God's king*. One of the Old Testament passages that fuelled the expectation of the appearance of God's ultimate king was Micah 5:1–5a. It was fulfilled in

Jesus' coming, since it signalled the place of his birth (*Matt.* 2:3–6). Yet this segment of Micah highlights a great deal more than where Jesus would be born. It informs us that Jesus, God's ultimate king, would be no ordinary human being but God himself in real humanity (5:2b). The 'for me' of Micah 5:2 shows that Jesus, God's ultimate king, would come primarily to be God's servant.

We can so easily slip into self-centredness when we think about Jesus' mission. While it is gloriously true that he came to save his people from their sins (*Matt.* 1:21), first and foremost he came to obey his Father and to carry out his will (*Heb.* 10:5–7). Jesus, God's ultimate king, comes to rule as God (5:2), and when he does, we are spiritually revitalised (5:3), all our needs are met (5:4a; *Psa.* 23:1), we have security from every fear that can paralyse us, especially the fear of death (5:4b; *Heb.* 2:14-15), and we experience peace in every situation in life (5:5a; *John* 14:27; 16:33).

34
Nahum

With Nahum we enter the seventh century BC. The only thing the prophet tells us about himself is that he is from Elkosh, but we have no idea where that was. We do know, however, that he was active sometime between 664 and 612 BC. There is a reference to the Egyptian city of Thebes in Nahum 3:8, and sources outside of the Bible inform us that it was captured by Ashurbanipal, the Assyrian king, in 664 BC, making that the earliest possible date for the book. In Nahum the fall of Nineveh lies in the future. It occurred in 612 BC, making that the book's latest possible date. It follows that he prophesied in Judah, because by that time Israel, the northern kingdom, had been absorbed into the Assyrian Empire.

Nahum is exclusively occupied with the fate of the Assyrian capital, Nineveh. He reminds us of the Roman statesman Cato the Elder who was convinced that Rome would not be safe till its rival in the Mediterranean region, Carthage, was destroyed. Whenever he made a speech, and whatever subject he was speaking on, he always finished with the slogan, '*Carthago delenda est!* Carthage must be destroyed!' Nahum's MESSAGE has a similar feel to it, except that his target is Nineveh, and he is certain it will be destroyed because God is going to do it.

In delivering his MESSAGE, Nahum blends together *mockery* directed at Nineveh (1:15; 2:1, 9–10; 3:5–6, 12–17) with a *song of celebration*, and what sounds like a *funeral dirge*. Nahum is not mocking Nineveh for something that has happened but concerning something that will happen in the future. He is even mocking Nineveh when the Assyrian Empire is at the height of its power. Yet he is so confident of Nineveh's downfall that he sings his taunting song years before the event takes place. His *song of celebration* and of praise to God is in the opening stanzas of the book (1:2-8). He wants the reader to be so impressed by God's majesty that he will be completely convinced of his ability to deliver his judgment on evil. The third style he employs is that of a *funeral dirge* (3:1–3). God has dug Nineveh's grave (1:14) and is going to bury the city. Yet no mourners will attend the funeral (3:7). Rather than shedding tears, those who have been the victims of Assyrian oppression and brutality will be rejoicing (3:19).

The book's STRUCTURE reflects Nahum's unrelenting denunciation of Nineveh and his pronouncement of God's judgment upon it. It opens with a section that concentrates on *the source of Nineveh's downfall* (1:1–8). We cannot avoid comparing Nahum and Jonah. Both have to do with God's attitude towards Nineveh, but the difference between them is vast. In Jonah, God had mercy on the Ninevites and withdrew his judgment, but in the hundred years or so which have elapsed since then, Nineveh has slipped back into her habits of violence and cruelty. She has crossed an invisible line. Now God's mercy is withdrawn and all that is left for Nineveh is his wrath. Although there are references to God's mercy (1:3a, 7b), the overwhelming emphasis here is on his anger. Nahum portrays God as an imposing warrior, heavily armed, striding purposefully out to engage Nineveh in battle.

In consequence the book's second section focuses on *the certainty of Nineveh's downfall* (1:9–15). Five times Nahum stresses that God will utterly destroy Nineveh (1:9, 13, 14, 15). The great Warrior bears down menacingly on his enemy (2:13; 3:5), so that Nineveh has no chance of surviving. The destruction of Nineveh will be as effortless as a man tossing dry twigs on to a bonfire (1:10) or cutting grass (1:12). God will need to wield no second blow (1:9).

Why is this judgment falling now? One reason is Nineveh's oppression and brutality. Assyria had a chilling reputation for gratuitous violence, barbarity, cruel exploitation, treachery and terror, and this is reflected in some of the things said about Nineveh in the book (1:11; 2:11–13; 3:1, 4, 10, 16, 19). God is the universal king. He is not some minor, impotent tribal deity. When he sees a nation abusing its power and crushing human beings without a trace of pity, he acts against it. Assyria's behaviour had gone too far and God is going to judge it. But the main reason God is going to destroy Nineveh lies in his covenant promise to his people that he will protect them: 'Whoever curses you I will curse' (*Gen.* 12:3). Assyria had made the mistake of tyrannizing over God's people (1:12–13, 15; 2:2). She will pay dearly for it.

The longest section of the book deals with *the horror of Nineveh's downfall* (2:1–3:7). It is a remarkable example of predictive prophecy. Years before it actually happened, Nahum describes how Nineveh will be captured by a coalition spearheaded by the Babylonians and Medes. He taunts Nineveh because, no matter how many precautions she takes, and no matter how much she braces herself for the contest, it will be a waste of time (2:1). As he describes the battle for Nineveh, Nahum shows all his flair as a poet. The attacking troops with their copper-overlaid shields and red uniforms gather outside the city in preparation for the final assault on the citadel at the heart of the Assyrian capital. As the phalanxes of infantry march forward with their spears erect, it seems as if a great forest is moving in on Nineveh (2:3). The coalition's chariots charge through Nineveh's suburbs, flattening any opposition (2:4), and their special forces rush forward at a stumbling run towards the citadel's fortifications (2:5).

But how would they enter Fortress Nineveh? It was guarded on all sides by formidable water barriers, the River Tigris to the west and man-made defensive moats to the north, east and south. It was protected by massive walls which were about thirty metres high and wide enough for three chariots to ride side-by-side. But Nahum tells us that they will use the Tigris itself against Nineveh (2:6), a fact confirmed by Diodorus, a first-century-BC Greek historian. He wrote of the way in which Nineveh's attackers cleverly diverted the Tigris and unleashed all its destructive power upon the city walls so that two and a half miles of them were washed away. Coalition forces poured in through the breach. In Nahum 3:2–3, we are right on the frontline, in the thick of the action witnessing the sights and sounds of the slaughter. Nineveh's vast wealth is looted (2:9–10), the survivors humiliated (3:5–6), and the once-proud city razed to the ground (2:11–13). While we watch the drama unfolding in front of us, we have to remember that none of this has happened; it all lies in the future. Yet everything Nahum predicted took place.

So certain is Nahum of Nineveh's downfall that he returns to a topic he has already mentioned: *the inevitability of Nineveh's downfall* (3:8–19). If his hearers believed that Nineveh's defences could not be breached, they should remember the fate of Thebes (3:8–10). Thebes, the capital of Upper Egypt, was regarded as unconquerable. It had constructed an impressive water-based defensive system around its strategic location on the Upper Nile. But it fell, captured by the Assyrians. Just so would Nineveh fall. God would shake Nineveh and it would collapse spectacularly, like ripe figs falling from a tree when it is shaken (3:12).

It has been suggested that because its message is so specific and so violent, Nahum has little to say to Christians today. But we need to think again. The book has important LESSONS to teach us. It reminds us that *mercy triumphs over judgment.* In his celebration song Nahum seems to be sending us mixed messages about what God is like. On the one hand he is angry concerning sin and judges with ferocious justice those who commit it (1:2, 6), and yet he is also patient and loving (1:3a, 7). We can only make sense of this apparent contradiction at the cross. In Jesus' death God demonstrates that he is just and at the same time loving. The cross is the simultaneous display of God's justice and love (*Rom.* 3:26; 5:8). He refuses to condone sin in an unprincipled way, while also refusing to condemn sinners without mercy.

Another important lesson which surfaces in Nahum is that *judgment is part of the good news.* Nahum presents himself as a messenger delivering good news (1:15), and the good news focuses on God's destruction of Nineveh. Isaiah uses identical language to signal how God is going to rescue his people and bring them home (*Isa.* 52:17), but how could Nahum's negative message of judgment be thought of as good news, on a par with Isaiah's positive message of salvation? Only in this way: for the positive to take place, something negative had to happen first. For God's people to return from exile (Isaiah's message) their enemies had to be destroyed (Nahum's message). Judgment was necessary before there could be salvation, which is why it is part of the good news. Our Christian experience backs up the reality of what Nahum is saying. If we are to be saved from the control of Satan, sin and death, they must be dealt with decisively, and that happened at the cross (*Col.* 2:14–15). Because Satan, sin and death have been judged (the gospel negatives) we can experience freedom, forgiveness, life and hope (the gospel positives).

The dominant lesson of Nahum is that God is a *Warrior* (1:2–8), who comes and fights against his enemies, taking the battle to them. In the New Testament this idea is applied to Jesus, but with a significant shift. In the Old Testament God fought against flesh-and-blood enemies like Assyria, and even disobedient Israel (*Lam.* 2:4–6). In the New Testament, however, Jesus fights against spiritual enemies. So he goes out into the Judean Desert and takes on Satan (*Mark* 1:12–13). His exorcisms and clashes with the Jewish religious establishment are further skirmishes in his war against the forces of darkness. But the final showdown took place on the Hill of the Skull, and the New Testament presents Jesus' death and resurrection as his great and decisive victory over his enemies (*Eph.* 4:7–11; *Heb.* 2:14–15; *Rev.* 1:17–18). The victory march of Jesus the Warrior reaches its triumphant climax when he brings evil to an end (*Rev.* 19:11–21). Although Nineveh no longer exists, the significance of Nahum lies in the way he points us in the direction of Jesus the Warrior who has defeated Satan, sin and death, and who will, when he returns, finally eradicate every enemy.

35

Habakkuk

Personal details about Habakkuk are sparse. He does not tell us who his father was, nor where he came from. There are hints that he had musical flair. The wonderful psalm which makes up the last chapter is not only an inspiring poem but was meant to be sung, because Habakkuk sprinkles musical terms and instructions within it (3:1, 3, 9, 13, 19). Perhaps he had a role in the musical side of the Temple worship. We can deduce when he was active from a number of clues. He speaks of the rise of Babylon to a position of political and military supremacy as being in the future (1:6), so the book must have been written before 605 BC. In that year Babylon rose to become the region's undisputed superpower. The tone of 1:2–4 seems to suggest that the reforms put in place by Josiah were overthrown, so we are dealing with post-Josiah Judah. Josiah was fatally wounded at the Battle of Megiddo in 609 BC, so Habakkuk was probably written between 609 and 605 BC, during the early years of Jehoiakim. This would mean that Habakkuk was a pre-exilic prophet to Judah and a contemporary of Jeremiah, Nahum and Zephaniah.

The Minor Prophets all have their individual distinctives and Habakkuk's PECULIARITY lies in the fact that, rather than speak for God to the people, Habakkuk speaks to God about the people. We can view Habakkuk as a diary the prophet kept of a spiritual journey he made 'from fear to faith.'[1]

It opens with Habakkuk firing a volley of questions towards God concerning his supposed inaction (1:2–4), but by the end the questioning tone has vanished and Habakkuk is content with what God is doing (3:16–19). As we read his book we notice that he 'grows out

---

[1] See Martyn Lloyd-Jones, *From Fear to Faith* (London: IVP, 1953).

of an attitude of rigorous complaint against God into a spirit of total submission.'[1]

It is his spiritual journey from fear to faith which determines the SHAPE of the book. After the briefest of introductions (1:1), Habakkuk fires off his *first complaint* (1:2–4). The Judah of Habakkuk's time was a dangerous place. Gratuitous violence and anti-social behaviour were the order of the day. The law was unable to tackle society's woes. The authorities ignored crime, and even if they made an arrest there were long delays in getting the case to court. When the offender was brought before a judge it was a waste of time, as the judiciary was more interested in legal wrangling and backhanders than in dispensing justice impartially. The fabric of society was unravelling and what made matters worse was that it was God's people who were breaking the law. The moral dimension of God's covenant was shelved. Yet if we look more closely at Habakkuk's complaint, we see that it was not primarily the disintegration of society but God's apparent inactivity which troubled him. Why was God doing nothing about what was happening?

God's *first reply* (1:5–11) was not long in coming, and it completely cut the ground from under Habakkuk's feet. Far from being inactive, God is doing something about his people's covenant unfaithfulness. He is raising up Babylon to be his rod to punish his people, and to do to Judah what Assyria had done to Israel.

Perhaps Habakkuk was expecting another batch of reforms like Josiah's to sort out the nation's moral and spiritual mess, but punishment at the hands of the Babylonians was certainly not his desired solution. Had he forgotten that God's ways are not our ways (*Isa.* 55:8), though they are always in line with his Word (*Deut.* 28:49–52; *Mic.* 4:10)? But Habakkuk is a combative character, so when he has recovered from the shock of the first reply, he launches a *second complaint* (1:12–2:1). What God had told him had raised more questions than it answered, and once more Habakkuk's problem is not with people but with God. God is holy and cannot tolerate or do anything wrong (1:12–13a). How then can he use the Babylonians to punish Judah? God's people are bad – he is not denying that for a moment – but when it comes to badness

---

[1] O. Palmer Robertson, *The Christ of the Prophets*, p. 260.

they are not in the same league as the Babylonians. As if God did not already know, Habakkuk goes over, in graphic detail, the Babylonians' ruthless brutality, callous savagery and unquenchable lust for cruelty (1:14–17). Habakkuk is having a major struggle with the being and nature of God. He thought he had everything worked out, but now he is beginning to see that God will not submit to the limits he had tried to place on him.

When he realizes that God is going to use a very unrighteous nation to punish what he thinks is only a mildly unrighteous nation, Habakkuk is about to say more (2:1).[1] But before he can do so, God speaks to give his *second reply* (2:2-20), and it catches Habakkuk completely off guard. What he has to say has such far-reaching implications that, like the Ten Commandments, it should be chiselled in stone for posterity (2:2). But it is also very simple: trust in the God who controls what is going on, and live by that faith (2:4). God tells Habakkuk that he will punish his people, but when the period of discipline is over, he will restore them. On the basis of the principle, 'whoever curses you I will curse', in Genesis 12:3, God will turn his attention to the Babylonians themselves. They will be punished for their inhumane treatment of his people (2:5–10): the plunderer will be plundered (2:6–8), the conqueror conquered (2:9–11), the builder demolished (2:12–14), the shameless shamed (2:15–18) and the idolater silenced (2:19–20). While the Babylonians are causing carnage, Habakkuk is to live by faith, trusting in the fact that God is in control and will not allow evil to have the last word. Wickedness will not triumph because the earth will be filled with the knowledge of God's glory (2:14) and stand in awe-struck silence before him (2:20). God will vindicate himself, and even though his people may not fully understand all that he is doing, they will trust him.

At this point in the book Habakkuk stops arguing and starts to praise, and so he concludes his prophecy with a *psalm of submission* (3:1–19). It is a victory song, celebrating the triumphs of God the Warrior (3:2–15). As he rehearses all of God's past victories, especially at the time of the Exodus and the Conquest, he is building up his faith, because these

---

[1] The NIV is too meek and mild here. Habakkuk is fuming with irritation at God and wants to say much more.

displays of God's invincible power remind Habakkuk that God is in complete control over everything and that no one can stand against him. In the light of his renewed confidence in who God is, Habakkuk submits to him (3:16–19). All the complaining is gone leaving only trust in God. The transition from fear to faith is complete.

Part of the MESSAGE Habakkuk is sending us is *an important lesson for living*. Like Psalm 37 and Psalm 73, Habakkuk teaches us that when evil prospers and life becomes increasingly tough for the righteous, we are to live by faith and trust in God (2:4). In spite of all appearances and no matter what our emotions are telling us, we are to continue to believe that God is in control of everything, working out his plan for his glory and our spiritual good (*Rom.* 8:28). Fundamentally we are to look to the Lord Jesus, the ultimate Righteous One who lived by faith. As he hung on the cross, he was taunted by his enemies over God's apparent inactivity (*Matt.* 27:41–43). Because God did not, at that very moment, step in to rescue him, it seemed that evil had triumphed. But Jesus trusted in God, and was vindicated when he was raised from the dead. Jesus' resurrection forms the solid foundation upon which we build our confidence in God. It shows that he is not remote and distant when evil is rampant but active, so that evil will not have the last word. When evil is on the rampage and we need hope and stability, we should certainly go to places like Habakkuk, Psalm 37 and Psalm 73. But ultimately we should head straight for the empty tomb.

The main message Habakkuk is sending us concerns *the most important lesson for living*. As it is quoted three times in the New Testament, a case can be made for Habakkuk 2:4 being the Old Testament's most crucial statement. Paul refers to it in Romans 1:17 as he explains how we enter a right relationship with God. In Romans, Paul's focus is on the expression 'the just', as he shows that we are justified on the basis of Jesus' death and resurrection. In his perfect obedience Jesus kept God's law for us, coming as the last Adam to succeed where the first Adam so tragically failed. By his obedience in going to the cross for us, Jesus accepted full responsibility for our sin and was punished in our place. The outcome of his obedience is that our justification has been secured.

The Christians in Galatia were in danger of being engulfed by a dangerous error which said in effect that faith in Christ was fine as far as it went, but to be justified one had to be circumcised and keep the law. To combat this error of adding to the perfect work of Christ, Paul wrote to the Galatians to show them that we enter a right relationship with God by faith alone. To back up what he is saying he quotes Habakkuk 2:4 (*Gal.* 3:11), but this time he is stressing the expression 'by faith'. We are justified, not by earning credit with God through our religious activity, or by a mixture of our own efforts and God's grace, but by faith alone in Christ alone. There can be no additives here. It is a matter of trusting in Jesus, and nothing else.

The writer of Hebrews turns to Habakkuk 2:4 in Hebrews 10:37–38 to outline how one who is in a right relationship with God should live. He underlines the phrase 'shall live' to instruct us that we should go through life trusting in God's control over everything that happens. If we can trust God with the most important matter of all, namely our eternal destiny, surely we can trust him with the lesser affairs of our lives?

36

Zephaniah

Zephaniah is probably a complete stranger to most Christians, so it is helpful that he tells us something about himself in the opening verse. In the longest genealogy found in the Minor Prophets he traces his family tree back four generations to Hezekiah, his great-great grandfather, who was one of Judah's best kings. Today Zephaniah might be described as a 'minor royal'. He also locates his ministry in the reign of Josiah, Judah's last good king, who reigned from 640 to 609 BC. From what he says it is possible to narrow down the time frame. A reference to Assyria (2:13–15) indicates that he was active before 612 BC, which was the year in which Nineveh, the Assyrian capital, was destroyed. We can narrow down the date even further to around 622 BC. In that year, during repair work in the Temple, Deuteronomy was unearthed among the rubble. Its discovery led Josiah to try to bring about a major reformation in the nation. It seems that Zephaniah was preached and then written down to add support to the radical reforms Josiah was instigating.

It is worth taking a look at Zephaniah's STYLE because it gives us a clue as to why it was written. Critics accuse him of copying from others. They draw attention to how his call for silence before God (1:7) sounds like Habakkuk 2:20, and his main theme of 'The Day of the Lord' is one that Amos and Joel had already developed over a century before. They point out that the language he uses to describe God's judgment in 1:2–3 appears to be taken straight from the Genesis account of the Flood (*Gen.* 6:7), and that the imagery of 1:15–16 is very reminiscent of the description of how God appeared to the Israelites at Mount Sinai (*Exod.* 19:16–19). But, according to the critics, Zephaniah's lack of originality is seen most clearly in his over-reliance on Deuteronomy.

The parallels between the two books are striking, not just in terms of single words but in the way longer phrases from Deuteronomy recur in Zephaniah (1:13, *Deut.* 28:30; 1:13, *Deut.* 28:39; 1:15, *Deut.* 28:53; 1:15, *Deut.* 4:11; 1:17, *Deut.* 28:29; 1:18, *Deut.* 32:21-22; 3:5, *Deut.* 32:4; 3:17, *Deut.* 28:63; 3:19-20, *Deut.* 26:19). Zephaniah would be the first to admit that he borrows from others, and especially from Deuteronomy. But this should be seen as a plus, not a minus, because it points to what his preaching and writing were intended to do.

Judah had been steeped in the raw paganism of Manasseh and Amon for two generations, so when Josiah launched his spiritual offensive on his father's and grandfather's idolatry, not everyone was elated. Anyone who has tried to bring about change, especially rapid and radical change, will know that there will always be those who will dig in their heels. Josiah would need strong support, and it came in the shape of Zephaniah. By deliberately incorporating into his message the very phrases and ideas found in the recently-discovered book of Deuteronomy, Zephaniah was confirming that Josiah's reformation had God's Word behind it. This would encourage the king to press on with his reforms in spite of resistance.

Another reason for Zephaniah's references to others is that his book is a summary of the Minor Prophets who preceded him or were his contemporaries. This is why the Old Testament places Zephaniah last of the nine Minor Prophets who were active before the Exile of 587 BC. He is at the end of the line, not for a chronological reason, since he ministered in Judah before Habakkuk and Obadiah, but for a theological reason: he is bringing together all the main themes of the pre-exilic Minor Prophets.

It will come as no surprise that Zephaniah's MESSAGE was the familiar one of judgment and salvation found in the other Minor Prophets. He links these themes together under the heading of 'The Day of the LORD'. This idea had been current for a long time. Everyone knew that on the Day of the Lord, God would destroy his enemies and save his people. But it is here that Zephaniah shows that he does not lack originality. He asks the questions: Who are God's enemies? Who are his people? His answer was totally unexpected. God's enemies were not just other nations. They included Judah. God is not on Judah's side because of her covenant unfaithfulness, particularly her idolatry (1:4–6). This is why Judah is included in the list of God's enemies who will be exposed to his judgment (2:1–3:8). If that was not shock enough, Zephaniah is about to go even further. It is not the whole nation, irrespective of how they behave, who constitute God's people, but a remnant who carry out their covenant obligations and worship God alone (3:9–13).

His message, centred on 'The Day of the LORD', is reflected in Zephaniah's STRUCTURE. He begins by writing about *a day of God's judgment* (1:2–3:8). God announces his judgment (1:2–3), and his use of language similar to the announcement of judgment at the time of the Flood indicates that he is going to act in a cataclysmic way. Care needs to be taken not to read these words over-literally. At the same time, Zephaniah's language, perhaps foreshadowing the final judgment, highlights the seriousness of the situation. His words show that when God moves in judgment it is not a minor matter. This judgment is totally justified (1:4–9) because of Judah's unfaithfulness. Idols like Baal and Molech are being worshipped (1:4–5), pagan ideas have been incorporated into worship (1:5, 9), and the relationship between God and his people has turned cold (1:6). The covenant has been broken and God has been forsaken by Judah. His reaction is not surprising.

God's judgment will be terrible (1:10–13), and the language of this section echoes Deuteronomy 28 where God spells out in graphic and frightening detail the curses he will bring upon his people if they are unfaithful to him. Instead of receiving God's blessings, God turns the covenant on its head and sends his curses upon his people. Because it is God acting against Judah, his judgment is inevitable (1:14–18). The Day of the Lord is coming in all its awfulness, and humanly speaking there can be no escape.

Zephaniah goes on to point out that those subject to God's anger can have no complaints. His judgment is deserved. This is why he lists the names and sins of the nations God is going to judge (2:1–3:8). No one will be able to accuse him of injustice. This carefully constructed passage opens with a three-verse summons to repent (2:1–3). Then in nine lines Philistia's doom is stated (2:4–7), and after that in another nine lines Moab and Ammon's fate is disclosed (2:8–11). This is followed by a one-line declaration of Cush's destruction (2:12), another nine line proclamation of Assyria's ruin (2:13–15), and in nine more lines Judah's downfall is announced (3:1–5). As a result of her covenant unfaithfulness, God includes Judah with the other nations. The passage's symmetry is rounded off by a three-verse statement of these nations' refusal to repent (3:6–8).

Zephaniah's supposed lack of originality is deliberate. He carefully aligns what he is saying with God's covenant with his people, especially the ratification of it on Mount Sinai. He is reminding Judah that God will display his sovereign lordship by enforcing all the sworn curses of the covenant.

Zephaniah then turns to the positive aspect of the Day of the Lord, reminding us that it is *a day of God's joy* (3:9–20). After the Exile, God would act again in a decisive way to save his people by bringing a remnant home. Once more Zephaniah draws upon Deuteronomy when he states that the purified remnant will live securely, humbly and righteously (3:9–13). These are the blessings Deuteronomy 28 says God will send to his people as they keep the covenant. With the return from exile, the curse has been reversed. God now takes delight in and rejoices over his people (3:14–17). 'One of the most awesome descriptions of the wrath of God in judgment found anywhere in Scripture appears in the opening verses of Zephaniah. . . . One of the most moving descriptions of the love of God for his people found anywhere in Scripture appears in the closing verses of Zephaniah.'[1] It catches us totally unawares. Normally we expect God's people to be singing about him, but now God is singing about his people! Again in terms of Deuteronomy, Zephaniah described the restoration of the remnant and the honour with which they will be showered (3:18–20).

Although Zephaniah might seem a stranger to many, there are LESSONS to be learnt from the way many of his motifs are picked up and developed by the New Testament writers. 'The Day of the Lord' is applied to the return of Christ. What will happen to Christians when

[1] O. Palmer Robertson, *The Books of Nahum, Habakkuk and Zephaniah* (Grand Rapids: Eerdmans, 1990), p. 334.

Jesus comes back is described in Zephaniah-like terms: we will be purified, freed from shame, granted security and given honour (*Phil.* 1:6; 2 *Thess.* 1:10; 1 *John* 3:1–3; *Rev.* 7:15–17). Along with other prophets, Zephaniah looks forward to a time when all nations worship God (3:9–10), and in the church, the new Israel, made up of both Jews and Gentiles (*Gal.* 3:8–9, 14, 26–29; 6:16), this is now a present reality. Zephaniah holds out the hope that God will turn the covenant curses into covenant blessings. How can this happen? How can God no longer be angry with his people but instead take delight in them and rejoice over them with singing? Ultimately the curse turns to blessing because of Jesus' saving activity. Jesus fulfilled the covenant by being faithful where we were unfaithful as he lived the life we should have lived, and by being punished for our covenant unfaithfulness as he died the death we should have died (*Gal.* 3:13–14). The true restoration which reverses the covenant curses is not the return from exile but God's salvation in Christ (*Eph.* 2:13).

37
Haggai

We know little about Haggai other than that he is called 'the prophet' (1:1), which may indicate that he was very well known to his contemporaries. However, we do know exactly when he was active because he dates the sermons he preached, and they were all delivered within a four month period from 29 August to 18 December 520 BC. When he had carried out his mission, Haggai stepped aside, making way for Zechariah.

His sermons were preached in 'the second year of King Darius' (1:1, 15; 2:10), so the HISTORICAL SETTING for Haggai is the events recorded in the opening chapters of Ezra. When they came to power, the Persians reversed the policy of the previous regimes towards defeated nations from deportation to repatriation, which is why Cyrus, the first Persian king, issued an edict giving permission for the Jews to return home (*Ezra* 1:2–4). However, only about fifty thousand made the journey (*Ezra* 2:64–65). They soon faced huge challenges. Most of the buildings were in ruins and the land had been largely uncultivated for seventy years. The poorest class had not been deported, so during the Exile they claimed squatters' rights on the land owned by the people taken off to Babylon. Complex legal negotiations had to take place to restore the land to its rightful owners and to compensate those who had been looking after it for the past seventy years, creating tensions in the Jewish community that hung around for many years. On top of this, their neighbours saw the returned exiles as a huge threat and began to harass and intimidate them.

Work started on building a new temple to replace the one destroyed in 587 BC. However, after an initial surge of enthusiasm, everything began to slow down as the scale of the task, the legal wrangling about land, and the external opposition all began to take their toll. Sadly building came to a halt. Nothing happened for almost sixteen years until August 520 BC when Haggai began to challenge the people to begin again. Haggai is therefore the first of the three post-exilic prophets.

Haggai came to a discouraged people with five messages from God, and it is the record of what he said which gives the book its STRUCTURE. His first sermon was preached on 29 August 520 BC, and it was *a word of challenge* (1:1–11). Haggai used a New Moon festival as an opportunity to challenge the Jews to restart the construction of the Temple. The reason God's people were on earth was to worship him, which is why he had redeemed them from Egypt at the time of the Exodus (*Exod.* 4:22–23) and why he had restored them after the Exile in a second Exodus (*Ezra* 1:2–4). Central to God's worship was the Temple which symbolized God's presence with his people. Haggai challenged God's people to fulfil their *raison d'être,* to worship God and to show their renewed commitment by getting back to work on the Temple (1:8). As we listen we realize that God's people were suffering from a centuries-old complaint – idolatry. While there were no images of Baal or his like in Jerusalem, the Jews were worshipping a much more sinister idol – themselves. While the Temple was still a ruin, people were building houses for themselves with the latest in interior design (1:4). They were worshipping themselves, spending all their time, energy, money and creativity on their own houses while neglecting God's house.

Haggai warns the people that God is displeased with them. This comes across in the way he refers to them: they are 'these people' (1:2) instead of the covenantal term 'my people'. It also comes across in what is happening to them (1:6). They dream of wealth, but struggle to make ends meet. They work hard to maintain the food supply, but all they experience is shortages, as drought and disease blight their crops. They crave comfort, but all they know is hardship. After challenging them to ask why all this was happening to them (1:5), Haggai gives them an answer they do not want to hear. Their difficulties come from covenant unfaithfulness (*Deut.* 28:38–40). God had brought all these difficulties into their lives (1:10–11) because he was displeased with their idolatrous self-absorption. The way out was simple: they were to put God and his worship first by restarting construction work on the Temple (1:7–8). Many years later, Jesus would say much the same thing to another group of God's people who had become sidetracked from their calling: 'Repent and do the things you did at first' (*Rev.* 2:5).

The people obeyed and, as God worked within them, recommenced the rebuilding of the Temple (1:12, 14; *Phil.* 2:12–13). Into this context of repentance and renewed commitment, Haggai came with another message, and it was *a word of encouragement* (1:12–15). We should not miss what Haggai is saying just because it is short, since the words, 'I am with you', are bursting with covenant significance. Up to that point God had not been with his people, due to their idolatrous self-absorption. But now everything had changed dramatically. No longer would they experience curses, but rather blessings as God helped them to carry out their covenant obligations. They were still faced with a massive reconstruction project. They would still run into fierce opposition from enemies who hated them. They would still have to cope with discouragements and setbacks. But God assures them of his presence and this is a huge encouragement. The overarching obligation Jesus places upon us is to take the good news of his victory over sin, death and Satan to all nations (*Matt.* 28:18–20a). What a huge task! It is massive in its scope; we will encounter determined opposition, and often we will not be motivated enough to carry it out. How can we fulfil our calling? Jesus' promise is this: 'I am with you always' (*Matt.* 28:20b).

After less than a month, the reconstruction work was in danger of faltering. It was the end of the Feast of Tabernacles. The dedication of the old Temple, which Solomon had built, had taken place in connection with the Feast of Tabernacles (2 *Chron.* 7:8–10), but now something demoralizing was going on. The seniors among the returned exiles who remembered Solomon's Temple were making unfavourable comparisons between it and the new one, so God sent Haggai with a third message, and it was *a word of reassurance* (2:1–9). While some of the seniors might be quite negative about what was being constructed, God was not. He was very positive about the project, and in a huge boost to morale, he reassures the builders that he is one hundred per cent with them (2:4–5).

Then, in Haggai 2:6–9, God takes his word of reassurance much higher by informing them that the glory of the new Temple would far exceed that of Solomon's Temple because the new one would witness what the old one never did – the fulfilment of God's promises to Abraham in Genesis 12 concerning his presence, his protection (which would result in peace), and his programme to bring the blessings of his salvation to all nations. In Hebrews 12:25–28 the writer backs up his assertion that Jesus is the true Temple, fulfilling all that the physical one symbolized, by quoting Haggai 2:6. God's glory would fill the new Temple when Jesus, 'the radiance of God's glory' (*Heb.* 1:3), came to it. When he did, God's glory would be seen (*John* 1:14). God himself would be present with his people truly, not just symbolically. The universal reach of God's covenant promises would become a reality when people from all nations – not just Jews – would worship Jesus, the fulfilment of the new Temple (2:7). In Matthew 2:1–12, when the Gentile Wise Men presented their gifts to Jesus, the true Temple, what Haggai 2:8 is getting at happened. As for God's promised peace, when Jesus died, the curtain separating the Holy of Holies from the rest of the Temple, which symbolized humanity's alienation from God, split in two (*Mark* 15:38). By his death Jesus has secured our peace with God (*2 Cor.* 5:19–21). What a boost to a small group of beleaguered builders! God reassures them that what they are engaged in is right at the heart of his purposes for the world because, in the Temple they are building, he is going to fulfil all his covenant promises.

The dates of Haggai's messages are significant, and that is also true of the fourth, preached on 18 December 520 BC. It was the growing season and the builders were wondering whether they should go back to their farms in order to prepare for harvest. The temptation to have time out from the reconstruction work was strong, so Haggai comes to them with *a word of motivation* (2:10–19). The priests are consulted about the Old Testament's laws in relation to clean and unclean (*Lev.* 10:10). Their ruling is straightforward. Cleanness is not communicable because if something holy touches something ordinary, the ordinary does not become holy (2:12). However, uncleanness is contagious because if something defiled touches something ordinary, the ordinary is contaminated (2:13). Haggai then calls on the people to sit down and apply the priests' ruling to their situation (2:15, 18). Four months ago life was grim, filled with disappointments and crushed dreams (2:15–16). God was cursing their efforts (2:17) because they had not rebuilt the Temple. Their defilement had led to a contamination across the whole spectrum of their lives. Haggai is asking them, 'Do you want to go back to that?' Clearly they do not, but that is the direction the temptation to down tools and go back to their farms is taking them: away from God's blessing and back to his curses. Haggai now assures them positively that if they continue working, God will provide a good harvest (2:18–20). Obedience to covenant obligations always results in God's blessing. Centuries later Jesus would spell out the same principle when he said, 'Seek first his kingdom and his righteousness, and all these things will be given to you as well' (*Matt.* 6:33).

Haggai also preaches a second message on the same day. It is *a word of promise* for Zerubbabel, Judah's governor (2:20–23). Enormous pressures rested on his shoulders, not only in seeing to the Temple's reconstruction, but also in leading the nation to serve and honour God. Would they be able to do this in such a volatile and dangerous world? God reassures Zerubbabel not only that he is in control of history and will protect his people (2:21–22), but that he is also with him personally and will help him to carry out his leadership responsibilities (2:23).

But Haggai's final message has a much longer reach. It concerns the future, because what he says to Zerubbabel is full of connections to God's covenant with David. Zerubbabel is the grandson of Jehoiachin, Judah's last-but-one king, and therefore represents the continuation of David's line. But the flow of Haggai's prophecies also reinforces the connection with David because it is shaped by 2 Samuel 7. David proposed to build God a house (*2 Sam.* 7:1–3), but in place of this there is put God's plan to build David a house (*2 Sam.* 7:8–11). In the same way Haggai moves from God's call to Zerubbabel to build God's house (1:1–3) to God's commitment to Zerubbabel to build David's house (2:20–23). The description of Zerubbabel in Haggai 2:23 greatly increases his Davidic credentials for he is God's chosen servant, just as David was (*Psa.* 78:70), and he is God's signet ring. Jehoiachin, Zerubbabel's grandfather, was also described as God's signet ring, but one which God would pull off and throw away, and when that happened with his deportation to Babylon, it looked as if God's promise to David had come to nothing (*Jer.* 22:24–25). But now God would reverse everything and, through Zerubbabel – God's signet ring – the covenant with David would be reinstated. Even though the monarchy was never re-established, what Haggai says to Zerubbabel is charged with significance. It anticipated the appearance of a future descendant of David who would bring God's promises to a climax. By listing Zerubbabel's name in Jesus' family tree (*Matt.* 1:12), Matthew makes it clear that Haggai's word of promise was fulfilled in Jesus.

A new era had been inaugurated with Cyrus' decree allowing the Jews to return home, the rebuilding of the temple and the governorship of Zerubbabel, the Davidic leader. But these events were only a sign of things to come. Jesus would appear as the true Temple to rule over God's people by his Spirit through his Word, and to lead us home from the exile of our sin by means of the cross. But even these things are just a step towards the final consummation of all things, when everything will be made new, and the dwelling of God will be with men in a city rich beyond description where every tear will be wiped from every eye (*Rev.* 21).

38
Zechariah

No one could accuse the fifty thousand exiles who returned to Judah of doing so for gain. Economically they would have been better off in the Persian Empire. They returned for spiritual reasons: to re-establish God's worship in the place of promised blessing, and – as a central part of this – to build a new temple (*Gen.* 12:7; *Ezra* 1:2–3). This is why a high proportion of them were from priestly families. Among them was a man called Iddo and his grandson Zechariah (*Neh.* 12:16). When, after sixteen years, building work had come to a halt, God raised up two prophets to challenge and encourage the people to begin again: Haggai and Zechariah (*Ezra* 5:1). Although he began his ministry two months after Haggai (*Hag.* 1:1; *Zech.* 1:1), and although he was active longer, Zechariah was engaging with the same audience about the same issues. At least in the first part of the book, therefore, Zechariah's overall thrust is similar to Haggai's: to ensure that construction work is begun again, and continued until it is completed.

We need to consider Zechariah's STYLE. Two features strike us. The first is his use of *visions*. Others of the Minor Prophets, particularly Amos, saw visions, but Zechariah sees far more than any other. In his eight visions, which he possibly saw in one memorable night, we find horsemen, a man with a measuring line surveying Jerusalem, a lamp-stand fed by two olive trees, a flying scroll and a woman in a basket. If we jump forward to Revelation, we come across similar images (*Rev.* 1:12–13; 5:1–10; 6:1–8; 11:4; 17:1–11; 21:15–16), leading to this observation: 'Apart from Ezekiel, this book has exerted more influence than any other on the author of Revelation.'[1]

---

[1] Raymond B. Dillard and Tremper Longman III, *An Introduction to the Old Testament* (Leicester: Apollos, 1995), page 427.

The other feature of Zechariah's style is the careful arrangement of the material. For example, the night visions in Zechariah 1–6 have all the hallmarks of thought and organization. We can imagine the eight visions as a target with a centre, an inner ring and an outer ring. The first and eighth visions, with horses of various colours, are the outer ring. The inner ring consists of two pairs of visions, Visions Two and Three and Visions Six and Seven. They all have to do with obstacles to the rebuilding of the Temple. Visions Two and Three concentrate on external barriers, while Visions Six and Seven focus on internal ones. Visions Four and Five are the target's centre. They deal with Joshua the High Priest and Zerubbabel's critical leadership in the rebuilding of the Temple and of community life.

If we examine Zechariah's STRUCTURE, we see that it falls into two definite parts. Chapters 1–8 deal with the present. Zechariah tackles issues of immediate concern to the returned exiles. They need answers to questions about retribution against the nations who have oppressed them, about the construction and completion of the Temple, about whether or not to fast, and about the problem of sin in a supposedly purified remnant. Zechariah also addresses the matter of Jerusalem's security, because this is pre-Nehemiah Judah; the city walls have not yet been rebuilt. What protection was there for an apparently defence-less people? There is a distinct shift of emphasis when we arrive at Zechariah 9–14. These chapters focus on events and issues that are further into the future.

Further sub-dividing the book, we have a short *introduction* (1:1–6), in which Zechariah warns against the kind of behaviour which previously led to spiritual disaster. The people are to remember that they are bound to God, not just by the Exodus, but also by their personal involvement in the return from exile. God expects them to carry out his will. If they return to God and his purposes for them, in terms of rebuilding the Temple, he will bless them (1:3).

There follow Zechariah's *eight night visions* (1:7–6:15). The first concerns horsemen who have gone out on a reconnaissance to see what is happening on earth (1:7–17). They report back that all is quiet and at rest; but God's people are not to rest; they are to rebuild the Temple, because God is returning to Jerusalem. The second vision concentrates on the destruction of four horns (1:18–21). The horns symbolize the raw secular power of the nations which, in their pride, have mercilessly scattered God's people. But their power will be shattered, and those responsible for the exile of Israel and Judah, Assyria and Babylon, will never oppress them again. Vision Three features a man with a measuring line surveying Jerusalem (2:1–13). God's people will re-inhabit the city and God himself will come to live among them in the rebuilt Temple. His presence will not only bring prosperity but – in keeping with his promise (*Gen.* 12) – God will protect his people, making them secure. The imagery of Zechariah 2:5 refers back to God protecting his people from the Egyptian army, so that they could make their escape through the Red Sea (*Exod.* 14:5–20). The enemies might be formidable but God would be with his people, protecting them and empowering them to carry out his purposes.

Vision Four, about the reinstatement of Joshua the High Priest (3:1–10), is the first of the two central visions. Once the Temple was rebuilt, the main leader in worship would be the High Priest, because he alone could enter the Holy of Holies on the Day of Atonement to secure cleansing for the people and the land. So Joshua the High Priest is cleansed, put right with God (3:3–5), and re-commissioned for God's service (3:6–7). The second of the two central visions – Vision Five – concerning a lampstand and two olive trees (4:1–14) is designed to encourage Zerubbabel, the Davidic prince, to grasp that God can bring about what human effort and ingenuity cannot (4:6). This vision also reaffirms his and Joshua's joint leadership of God's people as, in tandem, they direct the Temple's reconstruction (4:11–14).

The sixth vision is that of a flying scroll (5:1–4), and states that the evil which persists in Judah will be banished. Vision Seven, about a woman in a basket (5:5–11), says something similar. She represents wickedness and, in an ironic twist which would not have been lost on the exiles, she is sent off into exile in Babylon, banished from God's presence permanently. With the eighth vision of four chariots (6:1–15), we have come full circle. A new reconnaissance patrol goes out and finds no political upheavals taking place. This would encourage the returned exiles to get to work on the Temple, since everything is now in place.

In the second section of the book Zechariah tackles the issue of *fasting* (7:1–8:23). During the Exile a fast had been started to remember Jerusalem's fall, and some were anxious to know if this fast should continue now that God's people had come home (7:1–3). Before he gives an answer, Zechariah sets the scene by reminding everyone that God is against fasting if it is just a matter of an outward religious ritual, not accompanied by obedience to covenant obligations (7:4–14). In chapter 8 Zechariah appears to go off at a tangent by giving a picture of a restored Jerusalem that is designed to inspire those rebuilding the Temple (8:1–8), and he follows this up with an encouragement to keep going (8:9–13). After that Zechariah comes back to the issue of fasting by explaining how true fasting expresses itself in the practices of mercy and justice (8:14–17). Finally he returns to the original question in 8:18–23, showing that his apparent digressions were not digressions at all. The fast should not continue as a sad, doleful occasion but should be turned into a joyful celebration of what God is going to do in the restored Jerusalem and its temple.

In the third section of the book Zechariah turns away from the present situation to give some *oracles about the future* (9:1–14:21). The first is about Zion's king and the glorious future of God's people (9:1–11:17). What begins as an announcement of God's judgment on the surrounding nations (9:1–8) turns into a promise of a restored Davidic king (9:9–17) and of a united people (10:1, 3b–12). Enclosed within this first oracle is a scathing criticism of false shepherds (10:2–3a; 11:1–6, 14–17) and a declaration about God's shepherd who will be rejected by the people (11:7–13). The second oracle focuses on the smiting and final triumph of God's king (12:1–14:21). The king, God's shepherd, is killed (12:10–13:7), but in the end God's glorious kingdom emerges (12:3b–9; 14:3–21).

What LESSONS is Zechariah teaching us? First, we find *encouragement in our Christian service*. God's plan was to build a temple in which his Son would appear, reveal God's glory, and fulfil all his covenant promises to Abraham and David. But the Jews had few resources, faced a huge task, and had to deal with constant opposition. So God assured them that he would be with them, protecting them and giving them the strength to carry out his purposes by his Spirit (4:6). The same Holy Spirit is promised to us as we carry out God's purpose of building a temple made up of people from all nations (*Eph.* 2:11–22) and take the gospel to the whole world (*Acts* 1:8). We also glimpse *Jesus in his offices towards us*. The priests emerge here as the leaders of the people (6:11). God's people had been led by *prophets* from Moses to Samuel, by *kings* and princes from Saul to Zerubbabel, and finally by *priests* from Joshua to Jesus' time. But each kind of leadership had failed. Even their best leaders were flawed. What was really needed was one perfect leader to combine all three roles in himself, and that is exactly what we find in Jesus, our Prophet, Priest and King.

Zechariah also gives us *a realistic view about Christian living*. The fact that chapters 1–8 and 9–14 are so different in their perspective, with one section focusing on the present and the other on the future has led some to speculate that the book was written by two distinct authors. The difference can be seen in terms of a development in Zechariah's style, but there is a more substantial reason. The Holy Spirit inspired Zechariah to write his book in these two distinct sections with different perspectives to remind us what life in God's kingdom is like. Christian living has an 'already, but not yet' shape to it. Our Saviour has come, lived, died, risen, and ascended, so certain aspects of our salvation are *already* a present reality in our experience. However, the kingdom has *not yet* been consummated. We are still waiting for Jesus' return, so the experience of other aspects of our salvation lies in the future, in the *not yet*.

An idea widely held in the contemporary church is that, as Christians, we should always be upbeat, positive, on top of things, allowing nothing to get us down; and, if this is not our experience every day, there is something seriously wrong in our relationship with God. The 'already, but not yet' perspective to which Zechariah's structure points us should get rid of this idea. Our location on the timeline of God's plan of salvation is between the two comings of Christ, and the main feature of life in this location is tension, because, although we have *already* experienced the power of Jesus' death and resurrection in our lives, we have *not yet* arrived in heaven. The tension shows itself in all sorts of ways: we have been forgiven, but we still sin; we have been set free from sin's control, but we are often defeated by it; we have been rescued from Satan's grip, but we still give in to his temptations; we are more than conquerors, but we still suffer and struggle; we are God's children, but we are not recognized as such and are often marginalized; we have hope, yet at times we are full of fear. We scratch our heads, puzzled by what is going on in our lives and wonder if we are really following Jesus at all. But Zechariah's 'already, but not yet' structure should remind us that there is nothing wrong with us. In fact, our experience is normal for those living in God's kingdom, under his rule, between the first and second comings of Christ.

Zechariah's final lesson has to do with its *clear pointers to Jesus*. In their accounts of the week leading up to Jesus' death, the section of the Old Testament to which Matthew, Mark, Luke and John frequently refer is Zechariah 9–14. Jesus is the *humble* king (9:9–10; *Matt.* 21:5, *John* 12:15). He is the *betrayed* king (11:12–13; *Matt.* 26:15; 27:9–10, *Acts* 1:18–19). He is the *smitten* shepherd-king (13:7–9; *Matt.* 26:31, *Mark* 14:27); but, as a result of the violence carried out against him, he will secure his people's cleansing from sin (13:1; *John* 19:34) and their justification (3:1–5), as our unrighteousness is taken away and his righteousness transferred to us. Jesus is the king who will subdue all nations (12:8–9) by establishing his kingdom and bringing people under his rule (14:3–9).

In his clear pointers to him, Zechariah is telling us that Jesus will fulfil God's covenant. He will reign over God's people, in line with the promise to David, but his rule will be inaugurated as a result of great personal suffering, just as Genesis 3:15 had predicted. Yet Jesus' kingdom will be worldwide, bringing God's programme to bless all nations (*Gen.* 12:3) to a climax.

39

Malachi

In both Hebrew and Christian Bibles, Malachi is the last of the Minor Prophets, but the book does not come at the end of the Hebrew Bible, since the Writings are placed after the Prophets. However, it is helpful to place the book there because Malachi provides a theological gateway through which we can move from the Old Testament into the New. It also makes chronological sense, since it was written against the background of some of the closing events described in the historical books. The evidence that Malachi was written after the exile is strong. The word for 'governor' in Malachi 1:8 is a Persian term for an official in charge of an administrative region. Frequent references to the Temple indicate that it had been completed, which took place in 516 BC. Malachi's failure to mention Ezra or Nehemiah may indicate that Malachi predates them, but probably not by much because many of the issues Malachi addresses were also tackled by them: marriages to pagan women (2:11–15; *Ezra* 9–10; *Neh.* 13:23–22); a failure to tithe (3:8–10; *Neh.* 13:10–14); disrespect for the Sabbath (2:8–9; *Neh.* 13:15–22); a corrupt priesthood (1:6–2:9; *Neh.* 13:7–9); and social injustice (3:5; *Neh.* 5:1–13). The general opinion is that the book was written between 475 and 450 BC.

Several decades after Haggai and Zechariah, Malachi took prophetic centre stage. Because his name means 'my messenger', some have speculated that it was not a real name but a title adopted by Ezra, or by some unknown person. Yet none of the arguments against regarding it as the name of an actual person have much weight.

The Judah to which God spoke through Malachi was not a happy place. Disillusionment had entered all levels of society. The high hopes of the returning exiles had long since evaporated and, even though the

Temple worship was again taking place, life was humdrum and dull. The pagan culture which surrounded them was beginning to exert a negative influence on people's lives. Worst of all, complaints against God were being voiced in increasingly strident tones. Staggering promises had been made to Zerubbabel, the Davidic prince, by God (*Hag.* 2:20–23), but there was no sign of them being fulfilled. The royal line of David had not risen to any position of authority and Judah remained an insignificant backwater of the Persian Empire. What was God doing? Was he doing *anything*? Into this atmosphere of cynicism, Malachi brought God's message, challenging the people to live as those who are in a right relationship with God should.

The urgency of the situation is reflected in Malachi's STYLE, which is aggressive and confrontational. There is no time to waste, so he engages in heated debate with his contemporaries. The six debates – which he records – have a similar pattern. There is an introductory statement in which God raises the issue to be discussed (1:2; 1:6; 2:10–11; 2:17; 3:6–7; 3:13). This is followed by a question from the people as they dispute what God says (1:2; 1:6; 2:14; 2:17; 3:7; 3:13). Then God responds by spelling out in no uncertain terms the truth of the situation (1:2–5; 1:7–2:9; 2:14–16; 2:17–3:5; 3:8–12; 3:14–4:3). These six debates are designed to awaken God's people to the need to change their ways.

The STRUCTURE of the book is shaped by these six debates. It does not take long for sparks to fly because, after the briefest of introductions, (1:1), Malachi goes on the offensive. The first issue debated is *God's love* (1:2–5). God assures his people that he loves them, but such is their disillusionment that they doubt even this (1:2). God's reply highlights two facts that make it clear how much he loves them. As the firstborn, Esau should have inherited all God's blessings, but God chose Jacob, their forefather, to receive them (1:2). God's choice of Jacob had nothing to do with performance as it was made before Isaac and Rebekah's twins were born (*Gen.* 25:21–23), so what motivated God to do what he did was grace. The historical fact that Judah, not Edom, were God's people points to God's love for them. It is also seen in the way he overthrew their enemies when they tried to oppress his people once more (1:3–5). When we are tempted by circumstances and our feelings to doubt

God's love, we must fix our eyes on our *election* – for the reason God chose us to be his children is his love (*Eph.* 1:4–5) – and *the cross* where Jesus defeated all his and our enemies (*Col.* 2:15). Christ's death is the supreme demonstration in history that God loves us (*Rom* 5:8).

Then, in the longest of the six debates, Malachi and the people discuss the matter of *worship* (1:6–2:9). When God accuses them of showing contempt for him, they question what he means (1:6). God's reply focuses on what is going on at the rebuilt Temple. It is called 'worship', but God says that it is nothing of the sort because it breaks the Law's regulations about sacrifice (1:7–8; *Lev.* 11:17–25). They would never offer the Persian governor a flawed, sub-standard gift (1:7–8), and yet they think they can do so in God's worship; then they wonder why he seems so far away (1:9). God startles them by saying that he would rather have no worship at all than what passes for worship at the Temple. Malachi issues a stern warning to the priests to act as they were supposed to act in the worship of God (2:1–9). They were to recall what Levi, the prototype priest, did, and copy his example (2:5–7).

In what he says about worship Malachi speaks clearly to the church in the twenty-first century. Not all that labels itself 'worship' pleases God. Sincerity is not the criterion for determining what should happen when God's people come together to worship him. God has set out his standards in the Bible, and he expects them to be followed. The idea that worship is acceptable as long as it is done genuinely and enthusiastically is not necessarily a sign of spiritual health. It could be, as in Malachi's time, an indicator that God's people have drifted away from him. There is worship that God finds totally unacceptable because its focus is not on Jesus and his salvation. God would rather have no worship at all than that which obscures his glory and downgrades what he has done.

The next topic is *marriage and divorce* (2:10–16). When the prophet speaks of the way some Jewish men were divorcing their Jewish wives in order to marry local pagan women, the people do not immediately answer him back. Their silence is a guilty one. Their reasons for doing what they did cut no ice with God. The problem is not people from different ethnic backgrounds marrying. It is God's people marrying those from outside the faith, because this introduces toxic spiritual influences into the community of his people. Had they forgotten how Solomon's relationship with God had gone disastrously wrong when he married many pagan wives (*1 Kings* 11:1–6)? Marriage is a picture of the covenant relationship between God and his people (*Eph.* 5:22–33). This is why God is so much against divorce (2:16). By breaking the covenant of marriage, the people were showing contempt for their covenant with God (2:10). Is it any wonder that God did not listen to their prayers or accept their worship (2:13–14)?

The next debate concerns *God's justice* (2:17–3:5). When God tells his people that they have wearied him, they want to know how they have done this. God tells them that he is tired of the way they are constantly questioning his justice. They are complaining that God does not really care about them because he treats those who do evil in the same way as those who do good. God's response is to reaffirm that he will come as a refining fire, and the result of his appearance will be that justice will be dispensed, all forms of injustice judged, and all wrongs righted.

In the fifth debate a challenge is issued in connection with *returning to God* (3:6–12). The people are in such spiritual confusion that they do not know how to return (3:7). God tells them that the road back to himself begins in their wallets. They are neglecting to pay their tithes (3:10). The tithes were meant to free the priests to perform their ministry at the Temple. If they had to become farmers to feed themselves and their families because no tithes were coming in, God's worship suffered. For this reason non-payment was bringing down God's covenant curses on his people (3:9, 11): they were robbing God of his worship because they were engaging in idolatry as they spent their money on themselves, not on God (3:8–9). If they made God's worship their top priority by paying tithes, they would break out of this downward spiral of covenant curses and experience God's covenant generosity.

We must be careful not to misread what is being said here: Malachi is not promoting the idea that, if Christians tithe, they will be protected from all business failure and financial stress. Like the rest of the Old Testament, Malachi uses physical and material concepts to express the blessing God will lavish upon us when we put him first in our lives; but if we view the Old Testament through a New Testament lens, we see that the inheritance God has in store for us is something money cannot buy and which goes infinitely beyond the physical and the material: it is himself.

The final showdown between God and his people came about because they were *speaking against God* (3:13–4:3). When God accuses them of saying harsh things against him, the people ask, in effect, 'Who? Us?' (3:13). But God is having none of their feigned shock. He gives the evidence for his accusation. They reckon that serving God is futile (3:14), and that people who ignore God have an easy time (3:15), while those who try to obey him have a hard life. God reminds them that a day is coming in which he will act in judgment (4:1), making a clear distinction between those who serve him and those who do not (3:18). The wicked will be punished (4:1,3) but the righteous will be blessed (4:2). Luther once suggested that there were only two days that ultimately mattered to the Christian: today and *that* Day. He counselled us to look in two directions, acknowledging that God has given us today (*Psa.* 118:24), and remembering that there is a Judgment Day coming (*2 Cor.* 5:10). When life is hard in the present, and we want to complain about God's apparently unfair treatment of us, we must remind ourselves of the day when Jesus will return and all wrongs will be righted. Malachi's contemporaries had forgotten to look at their situation in this way. The outcome was their accusations against God.

Malachi ends with what could be viewed as a double appendix (4:4–6). In the light of the distinction God is going to make between the righteous and the wicked, and their different ultimate destinations (3:18–4:3), Malachi calls on God's people not just to recall the teaching God had given them down through the years, but to put it into practice (4:4). However, it is in the announcement of the new Elijah (4:5–6) that we see how Malachi forms a bridge linking the Old Testament to the New. God's response to the people's disappointment at his apparent failure to fulfil his promises made through Haggai and Zechariah immediately was to focus on the arrival of 'the messenger of the covenant', who, although sent by God, will be God himself (3:1b). Before he bursts on to the scene, however, a herald is going to pave the way for his appearance (3:1a), and in 4:5–6 this herald is further identified as a new Elijah. We must not think in terms of a reincarnation of the old Elijah, but of someone who will come with a similar style of ministry. The New Testament identifies the new Elijah as John the Baptist.

Mark opens his account of Jesus' life with a composite quotation from the Old Testament which includes Malachi 3:1, and then immediately moves on to speak about John the Baptist (*Mark* 1:2, 4). When the angel Gabriel describes John the Baptist's future ministry to his father, Zechariah, his description is couched in terms similar to Malachi 4:6 (*Luke* 1:17). After the birth and naming of John the Baptist, when Zechariah is given back his speech, he praises God using language taken from Malachi 4:2 (*Luke* 1:78). When John begins his ministry, his dress is clearly modelled on Elijah's (2 *Kings* 1:8; *Mark* 1:6), and like Elijah's, his message is one of stern judgment (compare *Mal.* 3:1–5 with *Luke* 3:7–20). As well all this, Jesus clearly identifies John the Baptist as the new Elijah (*Matt.* 11:14).

The Old Testament closes with the prospect of a new Elijah coming, and the New Testament opens by informing us that the new Elijah has come, in the person of John the Baptist. With the herald's appearance, it will not be long before the one heralded arrives, and so John the Baptist's ministry opens the way for Jesus, the 'sun of righteousness', who brings 'healing in his wings' (4:2; *Mark* 2:17).

Between the Testaments

In most Bibles, the gap between the Old Testament and the New Testament consists of two or three blank pages, but as a matter of fact there was a period of approximately four centuries between the end of the Old Testament and the coming of Jesus Christ described in the New. During these years a great many important events took place and several formative trends emerged.

POLITICAL COMINGS AND GOINGS

Greek Influence

As the Old Testament closed, the land of Judah was part of the Persian Empire. But between 334 and 331 BC the Greeks seized control, following the spectacular victories of Alexander the Great at Granicus, Issus, and Gaugamela (*Dan.* 8:5–7a, 20–21). However, Alexander died suddenly (*Dan.* 8:8a) and his empire was divided between his four leading generals (*Dan.* 8:8b, 22). The two that concerned Judah most were Seleucus, whose power base was in Syria, and Ptolemy, whose power base was in Egypt. Judah was caught between these two rival kingdoms, which constantly fought each other over who should control the territory in the middle, including Judah (*Dan.* 11). Both the Egyptian Ptolemies and the Syrian Seleucids were Greek through and through, so, no matter who was in control, Judah was exposed to Greek influence.

Greek influence had its pluses and minuses. A big plus was that Greek, and especially a version of Greek called 'Koine', became the common language of the eastern Mediterranean area. Even when Rome became the main political player and Latin the official language, especially in the law courts, Greek was still the shared language. Most people could speak Greek, although some spoke it better than others because the further west you travelled, the less well it was spoken.

On the minus side, the Greek idea that matter was evil and only the spirit was good had a heavy influence on religion and philosophy. Although it was in the second century AD that this notion came to prominence in a heresy known as 'Gnosticism', there are hints of Gnostic-type ideas having to be countered in the New Testament. We see this Greek idea (that matter is evil and only the spirit is good) rearing its head in 1 Corinthians, Colossians, and 1 John.

Independence

In 175 BC, Antiochus IV 'Epiphanes' came to power in Syria and embarked on an aggressive policy of ridding Judah of all traces of Jewish religion and making it a thoroughly Greek place. He banned the Jews from keeping God's law, observing the Sabbath and other religious festivals, offering sacrifices, and circumcising their sons. Copies of the Old Testament were destroyed. Altars to the Greek gods and goddesses, especially Zeus, were erected, and Jews were ordered to make sacrifices on them. Jews were forced to eat pork. His greatest act of provocation was to enter the Holy of Holies in the Jerusalem temple, and there offer a sacrifice to Zeus (*Dan.* 8:9–12).

All this was too much for some Jews to stomach. In 166 BC in Modein, a village twenty miles from Jerusalem, Mattathias Hashmon and his five sons refused to offer a sacrifice to Zeus and killed the Seleucid officials who wanted them to do so: thus began the Maccabean Revolt. Under the leadership of Judas Maccabeus, the Jews conducted successful guerrilla warfare against the Seleucids, and their struggle eventually led to Jewish independence. The temple was cleansed and Jewish religion restored, an event still celebrated by the Jews in a festival called 'Hanukkah'. Self-rule was to last until 63 BC, when Judah was swallowed up by the Romans.

The successful Maccabean Revolt and the independence that followed it is significant in that it set the pattern for Jewish expectations about the Messiah in the first century AD. By the time Jesus was born, Judah was under Roman control, but, in the Jewish subconscious, there existed the memory of a time when a 'messiah' defeated the foreigners and restored Judah's independence. By the time of the New Testament, and especially in Galilee, the expectation that another Maccabean-type messiah would appear and drive the Romans out of the country had reached fever-pitch. It was against this background that Jesus set out his claim to be the Messiah. He *was* the Messiah, but not the type of Messiah the Jews were expecting. It was God's agenda, as set out in the Old Testament Scriptures, that would determine what kind of work Jesus the Messiah would do, not the popular nationalistic expectations of the Jewish people.

Enter the Romans

Throughout the second century BC, Rome had been gradually expanding its influence. From its power base in central Italy, Rome began to spread out, conquering more and more peoples around the Mediterranean Sea. In 63 BC, the Roman general, Pompey, defeated the Seleucids, and, as part of the spoils of war, Judah was absorbed into the Roman Empire. Towards the end of the first century BC, Rome was embroiled in great internal turmoil, with strong military and political figures such as Julius Caesar, Pompey, Mark Anthony, and Octavian (Augustus), all competing to become the master of Rome. When the dust finally settled, after much political intrigue, various battles, and many assassinations, Octavian emerged as the first Roman Emperor, and it was during his reign as Caesar Augustus that Jesus was born (*Luke* 2:1–7).

The Roman occupation of Judah was very significant. For a start, it fuelled the false and unbiblical messianic expectation we have already mentioned. The biggest bone of contention between the Jews and their occupiers was the level of taxation. It was reckoned that the average Jewish man paid out 40% of his income in taxes. As well as the Jewish tax for the upkeep of the temple and the tithe to keep the priests and Levites fed and clothed, the Romans imposed three levels of taxes: a poll tax paid by everyone in the Roman Empire except Roman citizens; a land tax levied on all landowners; and indirect taxes such as custom duties and sales taxes. Perhaps not surprisingly, the occupation fed the hope of a new messiah who would rid the people of the Romans and their oppressive tax burden.

The Roman taxation system spawned the group of tax-collectors that we meet on the pages of the Gospels. Instead of using their own civil servants to collect the taxes, the Romans contracted the job out to these freelance tax collectors, who made a one-off payment to Rome for the tax due in their area, and then collected that amount plus a bit extra. Those who secured the franchise for collecting taxes became very rich indeed. But they were hated by the people because they were seen as collaborators who worked for the Romans; they had a similar social standing to paedophiles and serial killers today. When Matthew, a tax-collector by profession, was converted and held an evangelistic dinner party to introduce all his friends to Jesus (*Matt.* 9:9–10), the guest list must have read like a who's who of the Galilean underworld.

The way the Romans administered their empire gave rise to the rule of Herod the Great. Wherever possible, the Romans liked to rule through local rulers. Herod exploited this, using his connections with Mark Anthony and Augustus to become the puppet king of Judah. The half-Edomite Herod was never popular with the majority of the Jews; moreover he was politically ruthless and, in order to keep a tight hold on power, he 'eliminated' the opposition, including what members were left of the Judah's last ruling family, the descendants of the Maccabeans, some within his own family, and every boy aged two years and under in the vicinity of Bethlehem (*Matt.* 2:16). And, not least, Herod was unpopular with many Jews simply because he was too friendly with Rome. Nevertheless, he tried hard to win the affection of the Jews by building a magnificent temple in Jerusalem. This was the temple that Jesus visited on many occasions. Parts of it are still standing today.

Like the curate's egg, Roman rule did have good parts to it, and one of them was the provision of good communication links that facilitated the spread of the gospel. The gospel moved quickly throughout the Roman Empire because the Romans had brought peace to the Mediterranean area, clearing the seas of pirates and the roads of bandits. The Romans did not suppress Koine Greek as the universal language. This meant that when the first Christian missionaries were taking the good news about Jesus from place to place throughout the Roman Empire, they were able to communicate the message with ease because there was no language barrier. The Romans famously developed a fine system of roads along which soldiers, goods and the gospel could travel quickly from place to place. The Roman road system was what the worldwide web and mobile phones are to us today: they greatly reduced the 'distance' between people and places and helped to spread news and ideas quickly.

Religious Trends

The Septuagint

The Septuagint is a translation of the Hebrew Old Testament into Greek. Legend has it that one of the Ptolemaic kings of Egypt asked the High Priest at Jerusalem to send bilingual theologians to Alexandria in order to translate the Old Testament into Greek for the Greek-speaking Jewish community who lived there. Seventy-two people, six from each tribe, were sent and, over the course of seventy-two days, they completed the translation. Based on the number of translators, it was called 'The Septuagint', which comes from the Latin word for seventy. The name of the translation is abbreviated as LXX, the Roman numerals for seventy. While that story of its origins cannot be taken as fact, what is true is that during the second century BC, a Greek translation of the Hebrew Old Testament did emerge and was widely used among the Greek-speaking Jews. When the New Testament writers quote the Old Testament, they most often cite the Septuagint.

The Pharisees

The Pharisees first emerged about 200 years before Jesus' birth. They were appalled at the inroads Greek culture and thought had made into Jewish beliefs and behaviour and called the people to return to the teaching of God's law and to be faithful to it. However, as Phariseeism developed, it went to seed, and, in spite of recent attempts by some scholars to rehabilitate it – telling us that it was really quite a good movement and we have done it a great disservice by misunderstanding it – by Jesus' time it was riddled with problems. It had fallen back to the human default position, that people can get right with God by their own efforts (see *Phil.* 3:4-11). The Pharisees appeared to be very spiritual, but their spirituality was skin-deep and did not transform the heart (*Mark* 7:5-6). Alongside the teaching of God's law, the Pharisees developed their own human rules, regulations, and traditions. Over time, due to the sinfulness of the human heart, these rules became more important than the teaching of God's law, and could even be used to justify side-stepping the plain duties required in the commandments of God (*Mark* 7:7-9).

Jesus frequently attacked the Pharisees' shallow spirituality and superficial teaching (*Matt.* 5:21-48), and they, in turn, constantly sniped at him, embarrassed by the amazing grace he showed towards sinners. As Galatians indicates, even after Jesus' ascension, Phariseeism still continued to hound the early church, constantly trying to drag down the grace of God into the spiritually toxic swamp of legalism.

The Sadducees

The Sadducees were the wealthy, aristocratic class that controlled the priesthood and the Jewish religious establishment. One of their members chaired the Sanhedrin, the supreme Jewish religious and civil court. Caiaphas and Annas the High Priests were Sadducees. The members of this party were the rationalists of their day. They did not believe in the supernatural in religion (*Mark* 12:18-27). While bitter opponents of the Pharisees, they were united with them in their implacable hostility towards Jesus (*Mark* 3:6).

The Remnant

In Judah and Galilee there were still a few brave souls who did not buy into the popular aspirations for a military and political messiah. They were waiting for a spiritual Saviour. Neither did they hold to the legalism that permeated the Judaism of that time. They believed that salvation could not be earned, but was a free gift from God. While they were numerically few and not very influential, they remained faithful to God. The remnant included believers like Zechariah and

Elizabeth (*Luke* 1:5), Joseph (*Matt.* 1:19), Mary (*Luke* 1:46–55), Simeon (*Luke* 2:25–35) and Anna (*Luke* 2:26–38). It was within this group of individuals that God worked. This is the way God always operates, so that all the glory goes to him (*1 Cor.* 1:26–29).

Emperor Worship

By the end of the New Testament period, the Roman Empire stretched from Spain in the west to Syria in the east, and from Britain and the Rhine in the north to Egypt, Tunisia and Libya in the south. How could the Romans control such a sprawling empire, populated by different ethnic groups, extremely heavily taxed and exploited unmercifully? The most obvious way was to use brute force, something for which the Romans had a special flair. Throughout the empire, but especially on its fringes, Roman legions were garrisoned, ready to stamp out any hint of unrest ruthlessly. However, oppression has its limits. Something positive was needed to unite the empire, and this is where worship of the emperor came in. From the time of Augustus, the imperial cult, as it was known, developed, especially in the eastern half of the Roman Empire. Those who promoted it hoped that it would provide some cohesion to the empire.

Participation in the imperial cult was simple. You were still allowed to worship whatever other gods or goddesses you desired, so long as you offered up some incense to the emperor from time to time. In return you would get a certificate verifying that you were a good Roman subject. Although they tried hard to be loyal Roman subjects (*Rom.* 13:1–7; *1 Tim.* 2:1–4; *1 Pet.* 2:13–14), Christian involvement in emperor worship was out of the question: only Jesus was to be worshipped and given divine honours. Matters were also compounded by the fact that the Roman emperor was starting to call himself 'Saviour' and 'Lord', titles Christians reserved exclusively for Jesus.

Worship of the emperor was seen and presented as a test of loyalty, and many Christians suffered terribly, not because they were disloyal Roman subjects, but because they found it impossible to express their loyalty to the emperor in this way. Refusal to take part in the imperial cult may be among the reasons why John was incarcerated on the prison-island of Patmos (*Rev.* 1:9). Some of the letters written to the seven churches in Asia (*Rev.* 2–3) are set against the backdrop of persecution experienced by these Christians on account of their non-participation in emperor worship.

Gods and Goddesses

The first century world was awash with gods and goddesses of all shapes and sizes: a sumptuous assortment of beliefs and ideas. There was traditional religion, centring on the gods and goddesses of classical Greece and Rome; but traditional religion was very formal, even dull. If it was religious excitement you were looking for, the plethora of mystery cults, which had sprung up all over the empire, was where the action was to be found. These mystery religions offered spirituality through sensuality. Ritual sexual acts promised direct access, without the inconvenience of a mediator, to the deity and his – or more likely, her – power. This combination of spiritual ecstatic excitement with immorality (not to mention few restrictions on one's behaviour) proved seductive to many professing Christians, leading to all sorts of horrible behaviour within various churches. A great deal of what Paul wrote in 1 Corinthians has to be set against this background.

Conclusion

These events and trends shaped the world in which Jesus was born, lived, died, and rose again, and into which his people took the good news about their Saviour and Lord. A better understanding of this background information can help us in our prayerful and studious reading of the New Testament Scriptures.

40

Matthew

For Levi, son of Alphaeus, better known to us as Matthew, the downside of having secured the franchise to collect taxes for the Romans in the Capernaum area was being treated like a social pariah. However, this was more than offset by the huge profits he must have gained from tax collecting. But Matthew gave up his lucrative business to follow Jesus (*Matt.* 9:9–13), and became one of his closest associates, called apostles (10:2–4). Years later, perhaps sometime in the 70s or 80s, he wrote an account of Jesus' life which we call 'The Gospel According to Matthew'.

Matthew does not come first in the New Testament because it was the first New Testament book to be written: Galatians probably was. Indeed, all of Paul's letters were probably in circulation before Matthew wrote his Gospel. Nor is it because Matthew was the first Gospel to be written: that honour belongs to Mark. Matthew comes first because of its theme, which is that of *fulfilment*. In Jesus, all that the Old Testament promised has now been fulfilled (13:16–17). Eleven times Matthew writes about how the Old Testament Scriptures were fulfilled in something Jesus did or said, or in something that happened to him (1:22; 2:15; 2:17, 23; 4:14; 8:17; 12:17; 13:35; 21:4; 26:56; 27:9). The opening genealogy (1:1–17) deliberately and directly ties Matthew to the Old Testament.

MATTHEW'S STYLE

Matthew is very Jewish in his style. He begins with a genealogy (1:1–17), which, although it might not appear very important to us, was something first-century Jews considered highly significant. He quotes a great deal from the Old Testament, not only because he wants us to see

Jesus as the fulfilment of the Old Testament, but also because he wants us to realize that Jesus can only be properly understood in the light of the Old Testament. Matthew gives much attention to the teaching of Jesus as a Jewish rabbi. He constantly highlights Jesus' attitude to the Old Testament law – one of the clearest examples being 5:17–48, where Jesus states that he did not come to abolish the Old Testament but to fulfil it and to establish its true meaning. Matthew uses the phrase 'the kingdom of heaven' instead of 'the kingdom of God', because, with the Jews of his day, he shared a reverence that was reluctant to take the name of God upon its lips.

Along with Luke, Matthew incorporates large sections of Mark's Gospel in his own Gospel. Because of the material common to Matthew, Mark, and Luke, they are collectively known as 'The Synoptic Gospels' because they look at Jesus from a similar perspective – the term 'synoptic' comes from two Greek words meaning 'together' and 'to see'. However, Matthew also includes things he heard Jesus say and saw him do which are unique to his own eyewitness account. In doing so, he makes his own specific contribution to our understanding of who Jesus is.

MATTHEW'S STRUCTURE

In the *introduction* (1-4), Matthew sets the scene. He writes about Jesus' birth (1:18–2:23), telling the story from Joseph's point of view; the ministry of John the Baptist (3:1–12); Jesus' baptism and the Baptist's misgivings about Jesus, which serve to highlight the theme of fulfilment (3:13–17); and Jesus' temptation (4:1–11).

In the *central section* of the Gospel (5-25), Matthew alternates between what Jesus said and what he did. He records Jesus' words in five distinct blocks of teaching, but the common theme is God's kingdom, and each block focuses on a different aspect of it. The first block of teaching is what is known as 'The Sermon on the Mount' (5-7). In this Jesus teaches about the lifestyle of the kingdom. Then after recording some deeds of Jesus (8-9), Matthew goes on to give more of his teaching (10), this time concerning the mission of the kingdom. More of what Jesus did follows (11-12). Then Matthew records five parables which

Jesus taught the crowds (13), in which he explained the growth of the kingdom. More action (14–17) is followed by more teaching (18), in which Jesus outlines the character of relationships within his kingdom. After one more section primarily recounting things Jesus did (19–23), there is a final block of teaching (24–25), which focuses on the future of the kingdom. Millions of computer keys have been pressed in analysing the meaning of the kingdom of God in Jesus' teaching, but it is already clear that, for him, the kingdom has absolutely nothing to do with geography, territory, or politics. Instead it has to do with his government as the king of his people's lives. The question with which Jesus' teaching confronts us is not, 'What is your address?' but, 'What is your relationship to Jesus? Is he King of your life?'

From the overwhelming amount of attention given to it, Jesus' death is clearly the *climax* of Matthew's Gospel (26–28), and, in line with the theme of fulfilment, this event is described using strong Old Testament imagery. Throughout the Old Testament, as God unfolded the meaning of his covenant, he made it clear that the staggering blessings he had promised could not be experienced by his people without the shedding of innocent blood (*Gen.* 3:15; *Exod.* 24:4–8; *Heb.* 9:22). As Jesus celebrated a Passover meal and focused his disciples' minds on his imminent death through the institution of the Lord's Supper, he explained that his death would bring God's covenant blessings into effect (26:28). After the meal, Jesus went to the Garden of Gethsemane, where he prayed (26:36–46). As he did so, he was given an awful foretaste of the spiritual horror of his imminent death. He would drink from a cup that God would soon place in his hands (26:39, 42). From various Old Testament passages, Jesus knew that it was the cup of God's wrath against sin (*Jer.* 25:15–16; *Psa.* 75:8). As he died, he would absorb in his own innocent person the full fury of God's anger against sin. Only when he had drunk every last bitter drop from this cup would the salvation of his people be assured. This is exactly what happened when Jesus died. In an act, not, as some have said, of 'cosmic child abuse', but rather of breathtaking grace, the Father punished his only Son, whom he loved, in our place, turning his face away from him. As Jesus cried out in anguish (27:46), God's justice was satisfied.

When Jesus died, the whole land was enveloped in darkness (27:45). This darkness was not caused by an approaching storm, a volcanic eruption, or a solar eclipse. It was a supernatural darkness, a reference back to the period of the Exodus when, to demonstrate that he alone was God, and to encourage the Egyptian Pharaoh to release the Israelites from slavery, God unleashed plagues of judgment upon Egypt. The ninth plague was a supernatural darkness that shrouded Egypt and was a sign that God was against them. The darkness enclosing Jesus as he hung on the cross symbolized God's judgment upon him, just as it had done so many centuries earlier in the case of the Egyptians. But a tenth plague followed upon the darkness, the death of the firstborn. It was only after this final and most devastating act of God's judgment upon Egypt that the Israelites were set free from slavery (*Exod.* 12:29–36). When the darkness was lifted from Golgotha, Jesus, God's firstborn Son, was dead (27:50). The Exodus motif had been fulfilled in Jesus' death, and, since God's justice was satisfied, his people were set free from the dominion of sin.

In line with the theme of fulfilment, Matthew points out that Jesus' death brought the Old Testament era to completion. When he died, the huge curtain in the Jerusalem Temple was torn in two from top to bottom (27:51). That curtain separated the Holy of Holies, where God, in his awesome holiness, was understood to dwell, from the rest of the Temple courts. It symbolized the separation that existed between an absolutely holy God and thoroughly sinful human beings. It kept God away from sinners, preserving their very existence, because if they had come into contact with this God of absolute holiness they would have been instantly destroyed. The curtain blocked off the way to God. The only way through it was by means of a sacrifice offered by the High Priest on the Day of Atonement (*Lev.* 16). By tearing the curtain in two, and thereby opening up the way into his presence, God is showing that sinners can approach him only through the death of his Son. Through his death, the Old Testament sacrificial system has been fulfilled and has passed away.

In *the conclusion* to his Gospel, Matthew gives his own eyewitness account of Jesus' resurrection. He outlines the classic pointers to Jesus' physical and bodily resurrection: that when the women went to Jesus' tomb the stone had been rolled away (28:1–4), that Jesus' body was gone (28:5–6), and that Jesus later appeared to his followers (28:7–10); but he also informs us of the explanation the Jewish religious leaders gave of the startling events of that first Easter in an endeavour to explain away the great fact that the body of Jesus was no longer in the tomb (28:11–15). They attempted to cover up the truth with a story of a security lapse, in which Jesus' disciples came and stole his body.

The Gospel ends with the risen Lord, after the defeat of all his enemies, commanding his disciples to take the good news of his victory to the whole world (28:16–20). We immediately recognize that 'The Great Commission' – as this command is known – is given in rich Old Testament language. The church's mission is to 'all nations', in order that God's covenant purposes might be carried out (*Gen.* 12:3), and Jesus assures his disciples of his help in just the same way that God assured Joshua of his help at the time of another period of conquest (*Josh.* 1:5, 9).

Matthew's Themes

This Gospel's central theme of fulfilment means that Matthew acts as a wonderful bridge between the Old and New Testaments. He develops this theme along four different tracks, each of which is flagged up in the opening genealogy (1:1–17).

Jesus Is Abraham's Seed

Jesus is a direct descendant of Abraham (1:1–2), with whom God had entered into covenant (*Gen.* 12:3). This makes Jesus the promised Saviour, for Genesis 12:3 brings into sharp focus the promise of Genesis 3:15. It points out that the promised Saviour will not only be a human being (the seed of the woman), but a human being of Hebrew descent (the seed of Abraham). Jesus is the promised Saviour who, at great personal cost, would undo all Satan's work in the Garden of Eden. This is why Matthew's Gospel reaches its climax with Jesus' death.

Jesus is also the promised Saviour for all nations. The focus of the Genesis 12:3 promise is 'all peoples'. Matthew, the most Jewish of all the Gospels has nevertheless a truly global perspective. Rahab and Ruth, two Gentile women, are included in Jesus' family tree (1:5). The non-Jewish Magi (Wise Men) come to worship Jesus (2:1–12) and in so doing fulfil Psalm 72:11 and point forward to the ultimate fulfilment in Revelation 7:9–10. Though the kingdom will have humble beginnings it will expand until it spreads through all the earth (13:31–32), so that heaven will be populated by people from every part of the earth (8:11). The last note the Gospel sounds is the great commission which drives forward the fulfilment of God's covenant promise to Abraham (28:18–20). Matthew is keen to point out that Abraham's true descendants are not ethnic Jews who are physically related to him but multiethnic Christians, who are spiritually related to him by faith in Christ (3:7–10; 12:46–50). Matthew traces Jesus' rejection by the Jews, Abraham's physical descendants, culminating in their rejection of him during his trial before Pilate (27:22–25). Running parallel to this is the teaching that the kingdom will be given to Gentiles who trust in Jesus (8:5–11; 21:43).

Jesus Is Moses' Successor

Although Moses is not specifically mentioned in 1:1–17, his shadow falls upon the passage. The first genealogies in the Bible were written by Moses. We can think in particular of the great censuses of the Israelites which took place under Moses and which are described in the book of Numbers, authored by Moses. Matthew picks up this theme concerning Moses and develops it in his Gospel. Jesus is the new Moses promised in Deuteronomy 18:15, to whom the people must pay careful attention and render obedience (17:5). Jesus taught with authority (7:28–29), just as Moses had done. Matthew arranges Jesus' teaching in five blocks which recall the five books of Moses.

Matthew also draws several parallels between Jesus and Moses. Herod tried to kill Jesus (2:13–18), just as Pharaoh had tried to kill Moses. Jesus fled to Egypt and emerged from Egypt to begin his public ministry, so fulfilling the pattern of the Exodus. Jesus went up a mountain to preach the Sermon on the Mount (5:1), just as Moses went up Sinai to receive the law from God.

However, there were two significant differences between Jesus and Moses. Jesus was more radical than Moses. People found the law hard to obey, so they tried to make it more manageable by saying that it only applied to outward actions and words. Jesus rejected this downgrading of God's law, and taught that the law applies to our thoughts and motives as well as our actions (5:21–26). But Jesus was also more gentle than Moses. Jesus gives rest to the labouring and heavy-laden conscience, and the yoke of this gentle and lowly Master is easy and light (11:28-30).

Jesus Is David's Son

The Jews were looking for a Messiah, a descendant of David, who would rule over God's people, and Matthew presents Jesus as the promised and long-awaited Messiah. Jesus is descended from David through Joseph, his foster-father (1:6), whose genealogy is that of Israel's royal line. Jesus was born in Bethlehem, David's city. In this Gospel Jesus is referred to as 'the Son of David' nine times (1:1; 9:27; 12:23; 15:22; 20:30, 31; 21:9; 21:15; 22:42); more than the three other Gospels put together. David, the greatest of Israel's kings, was the prototype of the great king who was to come. Matthew says that, with the coming of Jesus, that great king has come and God's promise of 2 Samuel 7:13–18 has been fulfilled. With Jesus' arrival, the kingdom has arrived (4:17). His casting out of demons is a clear sign of that (12:28). His parables are parables of the kingdom (13). He speaks about how he will return as the king who will judge (24–25). He is crucified as the king of the Jews (27:37). His death and resurrection are his kingly victories (28:18).

Jesus Suffers Our Exile

In 1:11–12 the Exile – the period in Israel's history when the Jews were deported to Babylon – is referred to. If David's reign stirred up memories of past greatness, the Exile conjured up memories of past shame. As the final and most terrible judgment upon their covenant-breaking, the Jews had been deported into a distant country (2 *Kings* 17:7–23). After seventy years of exile God intervened to end this period of suffering and to bring his people home. We too have broken God's covenant because, like Adam, we – who were made by God and for God – have rebelliously turned away from God and set about going our own way. As a result, we are in a state of spiritual exile, far away from God. But God, in his mercy and grace, has brought our exile to an end through the death and resurrection of Jesus (*Eph.* 2:13; *1 Pet.* 3:18). In our place Jesus suffered exile from God's presence on the cross (27:46); he was *abandoned* and *forsaken* – words associated with the Exile – in our place and for our sakes.

The genealogy of Matthew 1 is not, as family trees often are, a record of human fertility and biological productivity. Rather it is written evidence that God always keeps his word. Jesus' family tree includes Tamar (1:3) and Bathsheba, Uriah's wife (1:6). Their inclusion is not intended as a painful reminder of two low points in Israel's history – ancestral skeletons in Jesus' genealogical cupboard – but rather as a powerful reassurance that even the ugliest human sin cannot stop God from doing what he promised to do. The Old Testament is all about God making promises, and, here, right at the start of the New Testament, Matthew is teaching us that God has indeed kept his Old Testament promises, fulfilling them all in Jesus. That is why it is particularly appropriate that this Gospel should come first in the running order of the New Testament.

41

Mark

What would you say Margaret Thatcher, Neil Armstrong, Roger Bannister and John Mark have in common? They are all 'firsts': the first woman Prime Minister of the U.K.; the first man to set foot on the Moon; the first man to run a mile in under four minutes; and, we believe, the first person to write an account of Jesus' life. The story and sayings of Jesus had been passed on by word of mouth for about thirty years, but John Mark, Barnabas' cousin (*Col.* 4:10), put pen to paper and, around AD 65, the book that bears his name first began to circulate among the Christian communities of the Roman Empire.

Around 140, Papias, bishop of the church at Hierapolis in what is now Turkey, wrote down something he had heard from an older bishop – that Mark was 'the interpreter of Peter', and this gave rise to the idea that Mark is passing on Peter's recollections. This may well be true. Parts of Mark breathe the air of an eyewitness account. One example is 6:39, where, in his account of the miracle known as 'the feeding of the five thousand', Mark tells us that the crowd sat down, not on the ground, but 'on the green grass'. Only someone who was actually there, would have known that detail. It gives us a time reference for when the miracle took place, because, in Israel, grass is only green at certain times of the year. Another link to Peter is the pace of Mark's narrative, which travels along at breakneck speed, and which might reflect Peter's impetuous personality. There are also parallels between the structure of Mark and the structure of Peter's sermon in Cornelius' house (*Acts* 10:36–43). Both begin with Jesus' baptism by John the Baptist, after which he was anointed with the Holy Spirit. Then both move on to describe Jesus' ministry that started off in Galilee and ended up in Jerusalem. The climax of both is Jesus' death and resurrection.

MARK'S STYLE

Mark's account of Jesus is *compact*. In the original Luke has about 1,150 verses, Matthew 1,070 but Mark only six hundred and seventy. One reason Mark is more compact than the others is that he concentrates on what Jesus did rather than on what he said, omitting parts of Jesus' teaching that the other two include. Also there are incidents which Matthew and Luke describe in detail that Mark deals with very briefly. One example is Jesus' temptation. Mark tells us about it in two verses (1:12–13), but Matthew takes eleven (*Matt.* 4:1–11) and Luke thirteen (*Luke* 4:1–13), and Matthew and Luke give many details of what went on when Satan tempted Jesus, while Mark only mentions it.

Mark also tells a *fast moving* story, and he uses several literary techniques to do so. One of Mark's most used words is 'and', with almost every new sentence and paragraph starting with it. We almost run out of breath as Mark informs us that Jesus did this, and Jesus did that, and Jesus said something else. Many English translations do not translate the Greek word 'and' because it occurs so many times and because the translators felt that to translate it every single time Mark used it would make the account clumsy. Mark also injects pace into his story by using the historical present tense, which means he uses a present tense when recalling something that happened in the past, giving the impression that it is happening now. Mark uses the historical present tense one hundred and fifty-one times in six hundred and sixty-one verses because he wants to remind us that Jesus is not someone long ago and far away, but someone who is with us here and now.

A final way in which Mark keeps his story moving is that he records the huge distances Jesus travelled in just a few words. In 1:9–39, Mark takes only thirty-one verses to inform us that Jesus travelled from Nazareth in the north to the Jordan River in the south, then from the Jordan River further south to the Judean Desert, then back up to Galilee, then over to Capernaum on the northern shore of the Sea of Galilee, and finally throughout Galilee. Trace that journey using an atlas, or using *Google Earth* if you are a bit more high-tech, and you will be shocked at how far Jesus travelled, on foot, and at the fact that Mark covers it all in so few verses.

MARK'S STRUCTURE

The Old Testament had indicated that, one day, God was going to send a great leader, 'The Messiah', who would combine in himself the three great Old Testament roles of prophet, priest and king, even hinting in some places that God himself would be the Messiah. In the *introduction* to his gospel (1:1–8), Mark indicates that his aim in writing is to present Jesus as God himself, coming in human flesh, to be the Messiah promised in the Old Testament. These introductory verses are crammed with messianic and Old Testament connections. Jesus is described as the 'Christ' (1:1), which is the Greek word for 'Messiah', and as 'the Son of God' (1:1), which, as well as showing that Jesus was God, is a messianic title (*Psa.* 2:7). Mark begins, not with the story of Jesus' birth, but with a quotation from the Old Testament (1:2–3). Then he writes about the activity of John the Baptist (1:4–8), who, though we only read of him in the New Testament, is really the last of the Old Testament prophets. All these connections anchor Jesus firmly in the Old Testament's messianic promises and show him to be God himself, coming in our human nature to be the Messiah.

In the *main part* of his gospel, which runs from 1:9 through to 15:39, Mark shows us that Jesus is God's Son, the Messiah. Twice Mark records events involving a tearing apart immediately followed by a statement about Jesus being the Son of God. The first is when the sky is torn open at Jesus' baptism (1:10). The Father then speaks from heaven confirming Jesus' identity as his Son (1:11). The second is when the Temple curtain is torn in two at the moment of Jesus' death (15:38). Immediately the centurion in charge of the Roman soldiers carrying out Jesus' execution confesses his belief that Jesus is God's Son (15:39). Placed as they are at the very beginning and very end of the main part of Mark, they act as bookends, reinforcing the theme that Jesus is God the Son, coming in human flesh as the Messiah.

Mark's account of Jesus hinges on three incidents, each linked with a critical moment in Jesus' life and taking place in a specific geographical location. The first is Jesus' baptism in the Jordan (1:9–11). When a new leader of some kind is to be introduced to the public a press conference is called to inform the waiting media. In some ways Jesus' baptism had a similar function in revealing him as God's Son, the Messiah. The second critical incident was Peter's confession of Jesus near Caesarea Philippi (8:27–30). It confirmed that the disciples had recognized him to be the Christ. The third event is Jesus' death on the Hill of the Skull outside Jerusalem (15:21–39). Between the first two incidents, the question to be answered is: Is Jesus the Messiah? When this is confirmed (8:29), the question becomes: What kind of Messiah is Jesus? Everything recorded from 1:9 to 8:26 is designed to answer the first question, and everything from 8:31 to 15:39 the second.

In many English Bibles there seems to be doubt about the *conclusion* of Mark's gospel. In some a line is drawn after 16:8, and verses 9–20 are set apart from the rest or placed in brackets. This is because two of the oldest copies omit the last twelve verses, though the vast majority include them. We cannot settle this question here, but it is worth noting that, even if we stop at 16:8, all the classic New Testament arguments for Jesus' resurrection are still there: Jesus' burial, confirming the reality of his death (15:42–47); the stone being rolled away from the entrance to his tomb (16:2–4); the body being absent (16:5–6); and the report of his physical resurrection from the dead (16:6–7).

Mark's Themes

If we want to grasp Mark's message, we need to understand 8:27–9:1 because this passage contains all Mark's main themes. The first involves *who Jesus is*. Peter's confession (8:29) was a moment of astonishing significance. Peter, an orthodox Jew, brought up in the belief that God is one (*Deut.* 6:4), is acknowledging that Jesus is God himself, and the Messiah. He had not grasped this instantaneously, but, like the dawning of the day, the realization had come.

As he saw Jesus at odds with the Pharisees in the five conflict stories recorded in 2:1–3:6, Peter must have begun to wonder if there was more to him than he had first thought. The controversy with the Pharisees revolved around Jesus applying Old Testament imagery concerning God to himself, so making an indirect claim to be God. Peter's understanding of Jesus was strengthened when he saw him calm a fierce storm on the Sea of Galilee, cast a huge number of demons out of a man from Gadara, heal a woman who had been haemorrhaging for twelve years, and bring back to life Jairus' twelve-year-old daughter (4:35–5:43). Through the window of these miracles, Peter began to see Jesus as the Lord, to whom creation, evil, disease and death were subject.

His developing convictions were further strengthened by other miracles Jesus did, all of which had strong Old Testament connections. The feeding of the five thousand (6:30–44), as well as being laden with images from Exodus, answered to the promise that God himself would come and shepherd his people (*Ezek.* 35:15–16). When Jesus walked on the Sea of Galilee during the night (6:45–52), the miracle also brought Exodus to mind. The background to the healing of the deaf and dumb man (7:31–37) was Isaiah 35:4-6. When Jesus fed another crowd, this time of four thousand people (8:1–10), he deliberately enacted the imagery of the second part of Isaiah, especially Isaiah 49:1–13.

As Peter saw how Jesus' actions and words matched what the Old Testament predicted the Messiah would do and say, he was driven inescapably to the conclusion that Jesus was the Christ.

In this hinge passage, Mark also informs us about *what Jesus came to do*. Once his disciples had come to some understanding of his identity, Jesus began to teach them about his mission. Three times, in 8:31, 9:31 and 10:33–34, Jesus spelt out what messiahship meant by fusing together two seemingly conflicting Old Testament images. One was the 'Son of Man' imagery from Daniel 7:13–14 – an image of glory. The Son of Man came on 'the clouds of heaven', an Old Testament symbol of God's presence (*Exod.* 19:9; *1 Kings* 8:10–11), and received authority, worship, everlasting rule and an unshakeable kingdom, all pointers to his glory. By applying this title to himself, Jesus was indicating that his mission would be triumphant, successful and victorious. The second Old Testament idea which Jesus applied to himself seemed to go completely against the first. Jesus had also come to be the 'Servant of the Lord', and this was an image of shame. In the second half of Isaiah are four poems called the 'Servant Songs', the most famous of which is the fourth, Isaiah 52:12–53:12. The Servant of the Lord would suffer terribly as he was humiliated, mutilated, tortured and killed. By applying this image to himself, Jesus was indicating that his mission would involve shame, rejection and death. Fusing these two seemingly conflicting ideas together, Jesus was telling his disciples that he would be triumphant, but only after being rejected; he would be victorious, but only after suffering an apparent defeat; and he would receive glory, but only after being humiliated. He was explaining that he had come to die but that his death was the way to victory, and that he would only be exalted as the glorious Son of Man if he was first the suffering Servant of the Lord.

As the story moves on from Caesarea Philippi, we find the hostility towards Jesus mounting, until it reaches its crescendo in the days after his triumphal entry into Jerusalem riding on a donkey (11:1–11). Jesus was betrayed by Judas and arrested in the Garden of Gethsemane (14:32–52). He was tried before the Jewish Sanhedrin (14:53–65) and sentenced to death on the charge of blasphemy. He was then put on trial before Pilate, the Roman Procurator of Judea (15:1–20), and condemned to die for the crime of rebellion. Finally Jesus was executed by crucifixion on the Hill of the Skull (15:21–39). Everything Jesus said would happen in his three predictions of his death did happen.

Each time Jesus explained his mission to his disciples, they completely failed to see what he was talking about (8:32–33, 9:32–33 and 10:35–41). Because their ideas were driven by nationalistic prejudices and political expectations, they quite liked the idea of Jesus being the all-conquering, glorious Son of Man. But his being the suffering Servant of the Lord did not make sense to them. It would take the cross and the resurrection to clear up their misunderstandings and give them a complete insight into what Jesus had come to do.

The third theme that emerges from this watershed moment in Mark's account of Jesus has to do with *what Jesus expects from his followers*. If he is the Messiah, each of his followers must take up his cross (8:34). We are to make Jesus the pattern for our lives (*Phil.* 2:5–8) by firmly saying 'No!' to ourselves and our desires, ambitions and plans and consciously saying 'Yes!' to God's will as seen in the Scriptures. But Jesus also reminds us that it is only when we lose ourselves that we actually find ourselves, and it is only when we die that we experience life (8:35–37). In this sense, Jesus turns the old proverb on its head, so that, for his followers, it becomes a case of finders becoming weepers and losers becoming keepers.

If Jesus is the Messiah, his followers must not be ashamed of him (8:38). This would have been sharply relevant for Mark's original readers, who were experiencing the trauma of persecution. These were killing times in Rome as the Emperor Nero made Christians the scapegoats for his failed social and economic policies. Peter and Paul, two of the church's most prominent leaders, had already been executed, and many ordinary Christians had died horrible deaths. Mark was urging his readers to stand firm. If Jesus is the Messiah his followers must also be humble (9:33–37). Not personal prestige but humility is the characteristic of Jesus' followers. His disciples are recognized, not by ingratiating themselves with 'important' people, but by humbly interacting with 'little' people, who have no real status or importance in society.

If Jesus is the Messiah, his followers must be models of self-sacrificial love to others (10:43–44). True greatness is not seen in how far and how quickly we climb up the ladder, but in how low we stoop in order to benefit others. It is only when we self-sacrificially serve others that we show ourselves to be genuine followers of Jesus who stooped from the infinite heights of his throne to the infinite depths of the cross to bring the benefits of his salvation to us.

If you want a statement that captures Mark's picture of Jesus, you need look no further than 10:45. Jesus is the glorious Messiah, 'the Son of Man', but his mission was to die in such a way as to 'give his life as a ransom for many'. He calls on those who want to follow him truly, as opposed to merely toying with following him, to shape their lives by his example of coming 'not to be served, but to serve'.

42

Luke

I have always had a special fondness for Luke's Gospel. It was the first book of the Bible I began to study seriously. To my shame, for the first two years of my Christian life I failed to realize that, if I was going to make progress spiritually, I had to study the Bible seriously and not just skim-read it. A friend bought me an excellent study aid which encouraged me to begin serious study with Luke.

Luke was one of Paul's travelling companions, frequently accompanying him on parts of his journeys. He was a doctor by profession (*Col.* 4:14), and a non-Jew, because, in Colossians 4:7–14, Paul mentions first his Jewish fellow-workers, and then his Gentile associates. Luke's name crops up in the Gentile list. This makes him the only Gentile contributor to the New Testament.

Luke's Gospel is the first part of a two-volume work. The other part is Acts. Both were written to someone called Theophilus (1:1–4; *Acts* 1:1–2). Theophilus means 'lover of God', and some have questioned whether Theophilus was an actual person. Perhaps the name was just a literary device Luke used to show that he was addressing his gospel to anyone with a serious interest in learning more about God. Or perhaps Theophilus was a real person who contributed money to sponsor Luke's writing project and underwrote the cost of publishing Luke and Acts. I favour the idea that he was a real person.

Luke was certainly an excellent historian. When I read Ancient History at Queen's University, Belfast, in the early 1970s, my class was encouraged to read Acts because of the high regard in which Luke was held, even by secular historians. Luke often sets Jesus' story in the context of what was happening on the larger political stage of the Roman Empire (2:1–2; 3:1–2).

Luke's Style

When the Holy Spirit inspired the Bible writers, he did not obliterate their individual personalities. Each writer was so carefully superintended that he wrote down God's words without error, but each man wrote in his own unique style. As a doctor and a well-educated man of culture, Luke wrote in a polished Greek style. As a historian, his Gospel was very well-researched (1:1–4). Like any good historian, he dealt in primary sources. Around AD 57, Luke was in Jerusalem (*Acts* 21:17). During the following two years, while Paul was in prison in Caesarea (*Acts* 24:27), Luke was free to go about his business. Perhaps he spent that time researching his Gospel, visiting the places associated with Jesus and talking to eyewitnesses, and, in particular, to Mary, Jesus' mother, who, by this time, must have been an old woman. His careful research led Luke to write the longest of the three Synoptic Gospels, and to go into the details of many of the incidents he records.

Luke's Structure

Luke was well-travelled. While Matthew, Mark and John all refer to the 'Sea of Galilee', Luke calls it a lake (5:1; 8:22–23; 8:26; 8:33). Perhaps in comparison with the great Mediterranean Sea, on which he had sailed many times, the Sea of Galilee seemed only a lake to him. One way of looking at his Gospel is to use the theme of a journey. After the introduction (1:1–4), Luke tells the story of *Jesus' journey to earth* (1:5–2:52). Telling the story from Mary's point of view, Luke records the announcement to her by Gabriel that, as a result of the Holy Spirit's creative work, she is going to bear a child who will be God himself, coming in our human nature to save his people (1:26–38). Luke follows this with an account of Jesus' actual birth in Bethlehem (2:1–20). Interwoven with the story of Jesus' coming is the preparation for John the Baptist's birth (1:5–25), and the birth itself (1:57–66).

After recording the prelude to Jesus' ministry (3:1–4:13) – the appearance of John the Baptist, and Jesus' baptism and temptation – Luke recounts *Jesus' journey throughout Galilee* (4:14–9:50). Although there are references to Jesus' teaching in this section (6:1–11, 20–49), the focus is on his actions as he heals the sick, casts out demons and raises the dead. The pivotal statement here is 9:51. From this point, Luke tells about *Jesus' journey to Jerusalem* (9:51–19:27). Here the focus shifts from Jesus' actions to his teaching. After this, Luke describes *Jesus' journey to the cross*, recalling the events of the final week of his earthly ministry (19:28–23:56). The week begins with Jesus' triumphal entry into Jerusalem (19:28–39), and ends with his death and burial (23:26–56). Luke describes the night before Jesus' death in detail, covering the Last Supper (22:1–38), Jesus' prayer in the Garden of Gethsemane (22:39–46), Judas' betrayal (22:47–53), Peter's denials (22:54–62) and Jesus' trials (22:66–23:25). The final section of Luke deals with *Jesus' journey back to heaven* (24:1–53). Like Matthew and Mark, Luke highlights the fact that Jesus' body was no longer in the tomb. However, he approaches the resurrection from his own angle, telling us of Jesus' journey with the two disciples to Emmaus (24:13–35). In particular he shows how, on that journey, Jesus provided the key to understanding the Bible (24:27). Luke finishes with an account of an appearance of the risen Jesus to his disciples (24:36–49) and his ascension back into heaven (24:50–53).

Luke's Unique Features
Like Matthew, Luke draws from Mark, but there are some things which he alone writes about. A number of Jesus' parables are only found in Luke. The parables of 'The Two Debtors' (7:40–43), 'The Good Samaritan' (10:25–37), 'The Lost Sheep' (15:3–7), 'The Lost Coin' (15:8–10), 'The Prodigal Son' (15:11–32), 'The Shrewd Manager' (16:1–15), 'The Rich Man and Lazarus' (16:19–31), 'The Persistent Widow' (18:1–8) and 'The Pharisee and the Tax Collector' (16:9–14) are all unique to Luke. Only Luke tells us about Jesus' journey to Jerusalem with his parents when he was twelve years old (2:41–52), the miraculous catch of fish associated with Peter's call to follow Jesus (5:1–11), and the mission of the Seventy (10:1–24).

As we would expect from a doctor, Luke was interested in the people Jesus met. There are some well-known encounters that only he records. He tells us about the woman who gatecrashed a dinner in Simon the Pharisee's house to anoint Jesus' feet (7:36–50), Jesus' visit to Mary and

Martha's house (10:38–42), the healing of the ten lepers (17:11–19), Jesus and Zacchaeus (19:1–10), the widow who put two copper coins into the offering (21:1–4), the dying thief (23:39–43) and Jesus' encounter with the two disciples on the road to Emmaus (24:13–35). Only Luke records four songs that were sung during the events leading up to and surrounding Jesus' birth – the 'Magnificat' (1:46–55), the 'Benedictus' (1:68-79), the 'Gloria in Excelsis' (2:14) and the 'Nunc Dimittis' (2:29-32). Three of the seven utterances of Jesus as he hung on the cross are found only in Luke (23:34, 43, 46).

Luke's Themes

Luke's themes are summed up in four succinct statements that appear near the start of his gospel (2:10–11, 30–32; 3:6; 4:18–19). He informs us, first, that the Christian message is *good news about Jesus*. As a cosmopolitan Gentile, Luke was used to the Roman Emperor making announcements about some achievement of his, usually a victory in battle, that had saved the empire from some dire threat to its security. These announcements were officially packaged as 'Good News'. Luke applies this to Jesus. Jesus has come to save his people from a real threat to their spiritual and eternal security posed by sin, death, and Satan. The way he does so is through his death and resurrection. This is why Luke devotes so much space to the final week of Jesus' life on earth.

Luke also highlights the fact that the Christian message is good news about *salvation through Jesus*. 'Salvation' is a key theme in Luke. The words for *save* and *salvation* crop up seventeen times. This concept is made up of two components: the forgiveness of sins, and the gift of the Holy Spirit. Matthew, Mark and Luke all record that Jesus announced forgiveness to the paralysed man whose friends let him down through a hole in the roof (5:17–26), but only Luke records his forgiving a sinful woman in the house of Simon the Pharisee (7:36–50). And, as we have seen, only Luke tells the parable of the 'Prodigal Son', in which the father, in spite of the shame his younger son had brought on the family, forgave him when he repented and returned home (15:11–32). Only Luke records Jesus' commission to his disciples just before he returned to heaven in terms of the forgiveness of sins (24:47). As well as forgiveness, salvation involves the gift of the Holy Spirit. Luke shows great interest in the work of the Spirit. The Spirit is responsible for Jesus' conception (1:35). At his baptism he is anointed by the Spirit (3:22), and he exercises his ministry in the Spirit's power (4:1, 14, 18). Jesus connects prayer and the gift of the Spirit (11:13). Luke reminds us that God has not only dealt with the guilt and shame of our past in forgiving our sins, but transforms our present and fills us with hope for the future through the gift of his Spirit.

But there is more, and this brings us to the heart of Luke's Gospel: the Christian message is good news about salvation through Jesus *for the whole world*. Luke portrays Jesus as the Saviour of the world in tracing his family tree back to Adam (3:23–38). He records Jesus' deep interest in the poor, the oppressed and the marginalized, showing his gracious dealings with those who would normally have been socially and religiously excluded. Luke tells of Jesus' interaction with women (7:11–17; 13:10–17), children (18:15–17), tax collectors (19:1–10), sinners (7:34), Samaritans (17:11–19) and Gentiles (7:1–10). It is Luke who records that it was shepherds who were the first witnesses of his birth (2:8–20), and women who were the first witnesses of the resurrection (24:1–11). This reinforces his theme that Jesus is for all sorts of people. God bypassed the religious and the respectable, giving the privilege of bearing witness to two of the most significant events in all history to shepherds and women, people with a low social standing in Jewish society and no legal standing under Jewish law. He wanted to emphasize that Jesus is the Saviour, not just of religious and respectable people, but of the world, and of all kinds of people.

This Christian message – which is good news about salvation through Jesus for the whole world – *results in joy*. Luke begins with the angel's announcement to the shepherds of 'good news of great joy' (2:10) and ends with the statement that the apostles 'returned to Jerusalem with great joy' (24:52). Throughout Luke's Gospel salvation and joy are linked. He is the evangelist who informs that there is rejoicing in heaven over the salvation of even one sinner who repents (15:7, 10).

43

John

Around AD 90 the Holy Spirit inspired John, the son of Zebedee and brother of James, to write the fourth and final account of Jesus. John was a man at home in two worlds. He came from the rural north where he worked in his father's fishing business on the Sea of Galilee (*Mark* 1:19–20), but he was also at home in the urban setting of Jerusalem in the south, where he seemed to be well connected (18:15–16). Zebedee had done so well out of fishing that he was able to employ others to help with the work (*Mark* 1:20), and perhaps John was responsible for marketing fish in Jerusalem. John was also part of Jesus' inner circle. From all who followed him, Jesus chose twelve to be apostles. But among the apostles, John, along with Peter and James, belonged to a smaller group who were close to Jesus (*Mark* 9:2–8). A case can be made for saying that, of these three, John was closest to Jesus (13:23). John was the last surviving apostle, dying in the last decade of the first century, and this may imply that he was the youngest of the disciples.

JOHN'S STYLE

When we read John, we are in a different world stylistically from Matthew, Mark and Luke. John uses different Greek words from the others. In the account of the feeding of the five thousand, the only miracle recorded in all four gospels, Matthew, Mark and Luke have fifty-three words in common with each other, but just eight in common with John. John even uses a different word for 'fish' from the other three writers. One of my friends is a keen angler. If asked about his catch, he will not say that he caught some fish but that he landed three rainbow trout. For Matthew, Mark and Luke a fish was a fish, but for John, who was in the fishing business, Jesus did not use just fish to feed the huge crowd but a specific type of fish.

As you read John, you will realize that, while Matthew, Mark and Luke focus on Jesus' actions, John focuses on his teaching. Like any preacher, Jesus presented his material in different ways in different contexts. Matthew, Mark and Luke record the teaching that Jesus gave in short pithy statements and gripping parables, but John records Jesus' long carefully-argued discourses, informing us of things that Jesus said which Matthew, Mark and Luke do not.

John's Purpose

John tells us that when the Holy Spirit moved him to write he had a huge amount of source material from which he could draw (20:30 and 21:25). But out of all that Jesus did and said, John selected what he did for a reason, which he spells out in 20:31. On the one hand, John wrote to inform the reader. He wants us to understand that Jesus is the Messiah, God's Son. But he also wrote to transform the reader. In 20:31, John uses the verb 'to believe' with two possible meanings: to believe for the first time, or to go on believing. Because of this double purpose, John is an excellent place for all sorts of people to start reading the Bible. Those not yet Christians but interested in finding out more should read John. And those who have been Christians for years but want to grow in their Christian lives should read John.

This Gospel has often been compared to a pool in which a child may wade, and yet an elephant may swim. 'It is both simple and profound. It is for the . . . beginner in the faith and for the mature Christian . . . The humblest believer can read it and understand it and profit by it . . . But that is not the whole story . . . There are unplumbed depths.'[1] No matter where you are spiritually, read John, and the same Holy Spirit, who moved John to write this account of Jesus' life will exert his power on you so that your mind will be informed and your heart transformed, enabling you to put your faith in Jesus and continue to trust him all your life.

[1] Leon Morris, *The Gospel according to John* (Grand Rapids, Michigan: Wm. B. Eerdmans Publishing Company, 1971), p. 7.

JOHN'S STRUCTURE

John begins with a section known as *the Prologue* (1:1–18) which has become familiar to many by being read every Christmas in churches throughout the world. Of all the themes introduced in the Prologue – themes such as creation and new creation, grace and truth, light and darkness, and receiving and rejecting Jesus – the overriding theme is that of Jesus' real deity and real humanity. He is the Word who 'was God' (1:1) and who 'became flesh' (1:14). The Prologue can be seen as John directing his fire at the emerging threat of what was later to be called Gnosticism. According to the Gnostics, matter was evil and its creation was the work of some lesser being, not the supreme God. Because matter was evil, the idea that God might come in flesh, in a real human nature, was unacceptable. When John stated in no uncertain terms that Jesus, as God, created matter (1:3) and that he took upon himself a real and full humanity (1:14), the legitimacy of Gnostic ideas was forever ruled out.

Then John moves on to record *Jesus' public ministry* (1:19–12:50). Jesus showed who he was to ever-widening circles – to John the Baptist (1:19–34), to his disciples (1:35–2:12), to Jerusalem (2:13–3:21), to Judea (3:22–36), to Samaria (4:1–45) and to Galilee (4:46–54). Initially he was well received, but his actions and teaching brought him to the attention of the Jewish religious establishment, and they were outraged at what he was saying about himself (8:56–59), and at the conclusions people were drawing from his actions and teaching (7:40–47). So Jesus began to encounter fierce opposition in Jerusalem (5:1–47; 7:1–11:57) and in Galilee (6:1–71).

In the second half of his gospel, John tells us of *Jesus' private ministry* to his disciples in the final hours before his execution (13:1–17:26). He acted out the meaning of his life by the symbolic action of washing his disciples' feet (13:2–12). He comforted them (14:1–4, 27) in their fears that, with all his talk of leaving them and going away, something frightening and dramatic was going to happen quite soon. He promised them the Holy Spirit, and explained his ministry in their lives and in the lives of unbelievers (14:18, 26; 15:26; 16:5–16). He prayed for himself (17:1–5), for his disciples at that time (17:6–19) and for all who would, down the centuries, trust in him as a result of the apostolic witness to his person and work (17:20–26).

Like Matthew, Mark and Luke, John describes the events surrounding *Jesus' death and resurrection* (18:1–20:29), but he includes more details about certain events, such as Jesus' trial before the Sanhedrin and before Pilate; the visit of Peter and John to the empty tomb (20:1–9); and Jesus' resurrection appearances to Mary and to his disciples, with and without Thomas (20:10–29). John then rounds off his gospel with an *epilogue* (20:30–21:25), describing the way in which Jesus restored and reinstated Peter beside the Sea of Galilee.

JOHN'S THEMES

Because John wrote from Ephesus, a major Greek city, and used terms like the Word, light, and darkness, which were common in the Greek philosophy of the time, it is often assumed that John is the most non-Jewish of the gospels and does not rely as heavily on the Old Testament as the other three do. But that idea turns out to be mistaken. John's Gospel is rooted firmly in the Old Testament. We can see this particularly in the way in which John presents Jesus as the great fulfilment of the Exodus.

John develops this theme in a variety of ways. He does so by recording *Jesus' signs*. The miracles of Jesus were not displays of raw power designed to impress the masses but *signs* that directed people to the truth of who he was. John records seven signs that Jesus performed: He changed water into wine at a wedding in Cana (2:1–11), healed an official's son (4:46–54), cured a paralysed man at the Pool of Bethesda (5:1–15), fed a crowd of at least 5,000 people (6:1–14), walked on water (6:15–21), healed a blind man (9:1–41) and raised Lazarus from the dead (11:1–45). The signs led people to believe in Jesus (2:11, 23). However, in spite of having exactly the same evidence, the Jewish religious establishment refused to believe in Jesus (9:16).

The seven signs in John are meant to parallel the ten plagues in Exodus. We call them 'plagues', but God does not. In Exodus, he calls them 'signs': Moses' signs which show him to be God's deliverer (*Exod.* 4:1–9). When Moses performed the signs, the people believed him

(*Exod.* 4:29–31). But in spite of seeing all that God did through Moses, Pharaoh refused to believe and instead hardened his heart (*Exod.* 8:15, 32). The difference between Jesus' signs and Moses' signs is that Jesus' signs were signs of hope while those of Moses were signs of judgment. In Exodus, the first sign is the turning of water into blood, while in John the first sign is the turning of water into wine. In Exodus the final sign is the death of the firstborn, while in John the final sign is the raising of Lazarus from the dead.

John also portrays Jesus as the greater Exodus in his emphasis on the *Old Testament feasts*. This emphasis is much greater in John than in Matthew, Mark or Luke. He focuses on the Passover, the Feast of Weeks and the Feast of Tabernacles, all of which celebrate aspects of the rescue of the Israelites from Egypt. In particular, John highlights the Passover. When Jesus appeared at the River Jordan to be baptized, John the Baptist introduced him as the Lamb of God (1:29), the fulfilment of the Passover Lamb. By giving us a time reference (13:1), John points out that Jesus died at Passover, and that his death paralleled that of the Passover Lamb (*Exod.* 12:46; 19:36).

John presents him as the greater Exodus by recording *Jesus' 'I am'* *statements*. There are seven: Jesus says he is the Bread of Life (6:35, 48), the Light of the world (8:12), the Door (10:7), the Good Shepherd (10:11), the Resurrection and the Life (11:25), the Way, the Truth and the Life (14:6), and the True Vine (15:1). When Moses, in his futile attempt to evade what God wanted him to do, asked God what his name was, the reply came back, 'I AM' (*Exod.* 3:14). So, in all the 'I am' statements we have a direct reference to the period of the Exodus. Some of them have even stronger Exodus connections. When Jesus said, 'I am the Bread of Life', he was taking his audience back to the time when God fed his people with manna as they travelled from Egypt to the Promised Land. When he said, 'I am the Light of the World', he was claiming to be the fulfilment of the pillar of cloud and fire which guided God's people through the desert. When he said, 'I am the Good Shepherd', he was referring to the time when God led his people through the desert as a shepherd leads his sheep (*Psa.* 80:1). Even his statement, 'I am the True Vine', has the Exodus period as its backdrop (*Psa.* 80:8).

This theme also appears at a more detailed level. The Exodus story is the background for John 6. The miracle took place at the time of the Passover (6:4). Jesus tested Philip's faith (6:5-6), a fact that only John mentions, while one of the recurring notes of the Exodus story is that the Israelites constantly put God to the test. Jesus fed the people, just as God had fed the Israelites in the desert. Jesus' walking through the sea (6:16-21), with a strong wind blowing (6:18), parallels Moses' passing through the waters of the Red Sea (*Exod.* 14:21). As we have seen, Jesus' statement that he is the Bread of Life (6:35) reminds us of the Israelites' passage through the desert, and this parallel becomes explicit when Jesus says that he is the true manna (6:48-51). Just as the people grumbled in the wilderness, so many grumbled at Jesus' teaching (6:61), and the turning away of many from following Jesus (6:66) has echoes of the desert wanderings when the Israelites wished to return to Egypt (*Num.* 14:2-4).

The prominence John gives to Jesus' signs, the Old Testament feasts, and the 'I am' statements shows Jesus to be the great fulfilment of the Exodus, but the fulfilment is so much greater and better than the type. The Exodus brought freedom from physical slavery, but Jesus' death brings freedom from spiritual slavery to sin. The Exodus offered new life and hope to slaves, but Jesus' death and resurrection bring eternal life and hope of heaven to all believers (6:40; 3:14-16; 14:2-3).

Not only does the Exodus theme provide a way of looking at who Jesus is and what he accomplished as the Son of God, the promised Messiah, it also issues a searching challenge. John knew very well that only two of the Israelites who witnessed the signs in Egypt actually entered the Promised Land – Joshua and Caleb (*Num.* 14:30). Hence the vital importance of continuing to believe in Jesus Christ, the Son of God, to the very end (20:31), and finally receiving the crown of life in the land beyond the river – the glory that is to come.

44
Acts

The Acts of the Apostles is the companion volume to Luke's Gospel. Both books were addressed to Theophilus (*Luke* 1:3 and 1:1). Some would like to rename the book, 'The Acts of the Holy Spirit', because, as they point out, the Holy Spirit is mentioned sixty-one times. But this might give the impression that, when we come to Acts, Jesus' work is over and he ceases to be central. Rather, Acts tells how the ascended Jesus continued to work through his Spirit-empowered apostles and people. The traditional title reminds us that this is how the Lord Jesus advances his kingdom: through his people following the apostolic pattern and taking the apostolic message in the power of the Spirit to the ends of the earth.

Although Luke and Acts form two parts of the same story, they are separated in the order of New Testament books for a good reason. Just as Matthew served as a bridge between the Old Testament and the New, and so was placed first in the New Testament running order despite not being the first Gospel written, so Acts serves as a bridge between the Gospels and the New Testament letters, and so is split from Luke and placed by itself after John. The majority of the New Testament letters were written by Paul, and it is in Acts that we first meet him. Many of the congregations mentioned in the New Testament were planted by Paul, and Acts records his first three missionary journeys and how these congregations came into existence.

THE STYLE OF ACTS

What we said about Luke's style when we were discussing his Gospel is also true of Acts, but we should also notice his careful attention to detail. For example, Luke gave the civic leaders in each of the places

Paul visited their proper titles, and not simply some generic name. So the civic authorities in Philippi are referred to as *strategoi* (16:20), while a few miles down the road in Thessalonica the city officials are called *politarches* (17:6). Roman officials are also given their proper titles. Roman provinces were divided into imperial provinces and senatorial provinces, and the premier official in each had his own title. Luke takes note of this. The top Roman official in senatorial provinces was called the 'proconsul' (13:6 and 18:12), but in imperial provinces he was the 'governor' (24:1).

Another stylistic feature to notice is the 'They' passages and the 'We' passages. In the second part of Acts, when recording Paul's missionary travels, Luke sometimes writes in the third person plural and sometimes in the first person plural. In the 'We' passages Luke is travelling along with Paul, and in the 'They' passages he is not. A classic example of this is 16:6–10, where 'they' at the start of the section switches to 'we' as Luke joins up with Paul in Troas.

UNIQUE OR NORMATIVE?

A classic problem in the interpretation of Acts is: to what extent does what Luke records still apply everywhere today? If we do not discern between what is descriptive and what is regulative, we can run into trouble. While we might resolve this question by reading Acts in the light of the New Testament letters, the book itself enables us to work out the answer. In the text, Luke lays down certain markers which show which events are unique and which are normative. One marker is the use of *repetition*. Certain issues come up again and again: the need for evangelism, for example, and prayer as a means of receiving God's power to fulfil his commands. Opposition and persecution recur throughout Acts. By repeating these themes, Luke is telling us that these things are constant, not unique to the time.

Old Testament quotations are another marker. Should every Christian experience a baptism in the Spirit and speak in tongues subsequent to conversion? Christians with a pentecostal or charismatic leaning affirm that they should and point to 2:1–4 to support their view. However, this opening section of Acts is full of Old Testament quotations, which is Luke's indication that the event described is unique. The Day of Pentecost is seen as a unique fulfilment of Old Testament prophecy (compare *Mark* 1:8, with 2:1–4 and *Joel* 2:28–32 with 2:16–21), not a normative event. Using the events of the Day of Pentecost to support the theory of a distinct 'Baptism in the Spirit' fails to take account of the clues found in the text of Acts itself.

The apparent repetition of the events of Pentecost in Samaria (8:15–17), in Cornelius' house (10:44–46), and at Ephesus (19:1–7) has been used to prove that what happened then should happen to every Christian. But these events are not identical. At Samaria the people were already Christians and had been baptized before they received the Holy Spirit; moreover, they did not speak in tongues. In Cornelius' house the people received the Holy Spirit as they became Christians. They then spoke in tongues and were baptized. Events at Ephesus were very similar to those in Samaria, except that the men did speak in tongues. The Day of Pentecost, Samaria, Cornelius' house and Ephesus were all unique events. Besides, the theory that 'Baptism in the Spirit' follows conversion drives a wedge between Jesus' work and the Spirit's work, while in Acts 2:33 Peter makes it clear that the pouring out of the Spirit is an integral part of Christ's saving activity, not something separate from it.

The Purpose of Acts

One of the essential questions we must ask in order to understand the Bible's meaning is: What was the author's intention in writing this? Many Christians today prefer to ask, 'What do you think about that statement?', or, 'How do you feel about that statement?', or, worst of all, 'If you could change anything about this passage, what would it be?' If we ask these misleading questions, we will end up with a very skewed understanding of the Bible. What was Luke's intention when he wrote Acts? We do not have to guess. In the first place, he wrote Acts in order to give us certainty about what the Christian message is. That is why he wrote Luke (*Luke* 1:1–4), and, as Acts follows on from Luke, we should expect it to function in the same way. Acts will reinforce all that Luke said in his Gospel about the Christian message as the good news about salvation through Jesus' death for the whole world, resulting in great joy.

Another reason Luke put pen to paper was to chart the spread of the Christian message (see 1:8 and *Luke* 24:47, which looks forward to Acts). In Luke the stress is on how God's grace reaches down to everyone. The same note is sounded in Acts, but here the great emphasis is on how, as the church obeyed Jesus' words in 1:8, the gospel spread from Jerusalem to the ends of the earth.

THE STRUCTURE OF ACTS

The structure is determined by the pattern of 1:8. Before he tells how the gospel spread, Luke recalls how the church received power for its mission (1–2). Just as John the Baptist had predicted and just as he himself had promised, Jesus, from his position of supreme authority, poured the Holy Spirit upon the church (2:33). Luke goes on to record how the Spirit-empowered church witnessed in *Jerusalem* (3–7). As Peter preached about Jesus, thousands were converted (2–3). However, Satan contested this advance of God's kingdom, and so opposition, both external and internal, reared its head (4–5). Luke explains how the church, with such an explosion in numbers, organized itself (2:42–46; 6:1–7). This section ends with an account of Stephen's short but influential ministry, and his death (6:8–8:1a).

Ordinary Christians were forced out of Jerusalem by the persecution that arose after Stephen's death (8:1b), but they took the gospel with them, and so the church began to witness in the hinterland of *Judea and Samaria* (8–9). These chapters report Philip's evangelistic efforts in Samaria and in the south (8) and Peter's ministry in the Joppa area (9:32–43). But the most significant event in this section is Paul's conversion as he travelled to Damascus in his frenetic efforts to destroy the church (9:1-31).

The bulk of Acts is concerned with how the gospel came to *the ends of the earth* (10–28). Peter had been God's instrument in opening up the gospel to the Jews (2–3), the Samaritans (8:14–17), and now – as he preaches in Cornelius' house – the Gentiles (10). In this, Jesus' statement about him in Matthew 16:19 was fulfilled. But then, the church in Antioch was established (11:19–30), shifting the centre of gravity away from Jerusalem. Antioch was the base from which Paul set out on his three great missionary journeys: to Cyprus and southern Turkey (13–14); to Europe (16–18:23a); and to Turkey and Greece and back to Jerusalem (18:23b–20:19).

The conversion of non-Jews led to a great controversy in the church: Did Gentile converts have to submit to circumcision before they could become Christians? The matter was settled at the Council of Jerusalem (15). Peter, Barnabas and Paul all spoke of their experiences. James, the chairman of the gathering, quoted from Amos 9:11–12 and declared that Gentiles did not have to become Jews before they could become Christians. Thus Christianity was rescued from becoming a mere sect of Judaism. Acts finishes with Paul's arrival in Rome, the capital of the Roman Empire and the great world centre. In a sense, the gospel has reached 'the ends of the earth', and the paradigm of 1:8 is complete.

Through the paradigm of 1:8, we see that Acts' structure is theological, not just geographical. Jerusalem is where David reigned, and it is the place from which Jesus, great David's greater son, reigned through his death and resurrection. Judea and Samaria are not two randomly-chosen areas. They are the two halves of Solomon's kingdom, ripped apart by civil war after his death. The two are reunited in the kingdom of Jesus, the Prince of Peace, the one greater than Solomon. The fact of the gospel going to 'the ends of the earth' fulfilled Old Testament promises about the salvation of the Gentiles (*Gen.* 12:3; *Psa.* 98:3).

The Challenge of Acts

In another sense, the paradigm of 1:8 is not yet complete. Rome is not, for us, 'the ends of the earth'. There are still people who have not heard the gospel of salvation. This challenges us to pick up the baton from the apostles and the first Christians and run with it.

Acts reminds us of the *context* of mission. The first Christians were involved in mission to a world happy to worship many different gods (17:18), and there are huge parallels between the religious atmosphere in the first century and our own. We are not the first Christians to face the challenge of pluralism.

What is the *message* that we take to our world? It is the same as the first Christians took to theirs. It is focused on Jesus' death and resurrection, and on Jesus as the only way to God (4:12). In our pluralistic society, religious inclusion is the big thing, and the mantra, 'All religions lead to God', is heard all the time. Our message about Jesus' exclusive claims will be hated. In our relativistic society, where we are constantly told that there are no absolutes, our message about the reality and dire consequences of sin will be loathed. Nevertheless, we are to call on sinners to turn from their sins and trust in Jesus alone (2:38; 3:19; 17:30). Then their sins will be graciously forgiven by God (2:38; 3:19; 5:31; 10:43; 13:38).

Acts is also clear about the *methods* we are to use. There is a huge emphasis in Acts on Christians taking the gospel to others by speaking God's Word to them. Sometimes the apostles, and especially Peter and Paul, preached the Bible formally. Sometimes Paul used Bible-based discussions (17:17; 19:9–10) or debates with others (17:22–31). Sometimes ordinary Christians simply spoke to their friends about Jesus (11:19–21). Whatever the method, the first Christians were concerned to make the gospel known. Even in the Old Testament God wanted his people to be witnesses to him and his glory (*Psa.* 96:1–4). But how this was achieved was that God put his people in the midst of the nations to be a kind of mission station, shining in the darkness. The Israelites were to be a living embodiment of God's grace and rule, and to show what God is like. But in Acts this changes. The church is to be active in taking the message about Jesus to others. Acts challenges us as to whether we will conduct our mission in the Old Testament way or the New Testament way. Do we want people to come to us to hear the message about Jesus, or do we go to them?

The *result* of their methodology was the setting up of many churches throughout the Roman Empire (14:21–23). These congregations, most of them very small compared with today's megachurches, became in turn the launch pad for mission to their own communities. In the contemporary church, we have been seduced into thinking that the way to increase the gospel's impact on our society is to build large churches, centres of excellence to which people will be drawn in order to hear the gospel and see what it looks like. But that is Old Testament methodology. If we adopt the New Testament methodology of the first Christians, then, under God, many congregations will be set up, often in very unlikely and unpromising settings, which God will use to reach their communities with the gospel and transform them for his glory and their blessing.

Often the first Christians were reluctant to risk taking the gospel into other people's territory, and God had to use various means to get them out of their comfort zone (8:1; 11:19). Nevertheless, they went out with the gospel, often in the teeth of fierce opposition. What motivated them, and what should motivate us? The *motivation* for mission in Acts is twofold. Most obviously, there is the desire to obey Jesus (1:8). He had told them to go, and not to go would amount to gross rebellion. 'A dumb Christian is a disobedient Christian' (John Stott).

But the greatest motivation is a passion for Jesus' glory, which Paul displayed when he walked around Athens, saw the place submerged in idolatry, then reasoned in the synagogue and the market place (17:16–17). 'God has promoted [Jesus] to the supreme place of honour, in order that every knee and tongue should acknowledge his lordship. Whenever he is denied his rightful place in people's lives, we should feel inwardly wounded and jealous for his name.'[1]

The *power* for mission is not human strength or ingenuity; rather it is the Holy Spirit's power (1:8). References to the Holy Spirit are not scattered evenly throughout Acts; they occur in clusters, and, apart from the first cluster, each has to do with evangelism (4:31). This highlights the fact that the primary work of the Holy Spirit in Acts is to move the church outwards in new missionary activity. We tend to think that God has given us the Holy Spirit for our own personal benefit – to fill us with joy and peace; to give us wonderful experiences; or to help us exercise our gifts and feel fulfilled. Acts reminds us that God has given us the Holy Spirit primarily for the glory of Jesus (*John* 16:14): to empower us to take the gospel to others, so that they may be converted and bring glory to the Saviour.

[1] John R. W. Stott, *The Message of Acts* (Leicester: Inter-Varsity Press, 1990), p. 279.

The first Christians had no great influence and proclaimed an extremely unpopular gospel, but they turned the world upside down with that despised message (17:6). Today the church looks for influence and, in order to get it, files away the sharp edges of the message. We may imagine we have influence, but it certainly cannot be said – of the western church, at least – that we are turning our world upside down! May the gracious and sovereign Lord of the church 'in wrath remember mercy' (*Hab.* 3:2), 'restore us again' and 'revive us again' (*Psa.* 85:4, 6).

45

Romans

If you imagine the Bible as a mountain range, one of its most majestic peaks is Paul's letter to the Christians in Rome. In fact, a strong case could be made for saying that Romans is the Mount Everest of the Bible. If we are looking for a compact summary of the Christian message, we do not have to look any further than Romans, which is why it comes first among the apostolic letters of the New Testament. It was probably written in early AD 57 from Corinth, just before Paul left for Jerusalem with money he had collected to support the churches in Judea (15:25–26). Romans was not the first New Testament letter to be written: some think James was the earliest, others Galatians or 1 Thessalonians. But Romans is first because of its contents. It is the letter which deals with all the fundamental truths of Christianity.

People who have written books on Romans almost compete with each other to sing its praises. Martin Luther called it 'the clearest gospel of all', while John Calvin said, 'If a man understands it, he has a sure road opened for him to the understanding of the whole Scripture.' William Tyndale – the first man to translate the New Testament into English from the original Greek – described Romans as 'the most excellent part of the New Testament', adding that in his opinion every Christian should learn it by heart! More recently, Martyn Lloyd-Jones said that Romans has possibly played a more crucial and important part in the history of the church than any other single book in the entire Bible, and John Stott has called Romans 'the fullest, plainest and grandest statement of the gospel to be found anywhere in the New Testament'.[1]

---

[1] John R. W. Stott, *The Message of Romans* (Leicester: Inter-Varsity Press, 1994), p. 19.

The Influence of Romans

This praise is not excessive if we think of the remarkable way God has used Romans, down through the years, to transform people's lives. In spite of his godly mother's example and prayers, Augustine lived a wild life, until, in the summer of 386, he was converted as a result of reading Romans 13:13–14. What the church owes this great Christian thinker is beyond human calculation. In November 1515, Martin Luther began to lecture on Romans at Wittenberg University in eastern Germany. As he prepared his lectures, he came to see that sinners were put right with God, not by doing their best and making themselves righteous, but by faith in Christ. The consequences of this new understanding of Romans on the part of Luther led to the Protestant Reformation, which changed the political, cultural, economic but, most of all, spiritual landscape of Europe. On the evening of 24 May 1738, after listening to someone read the preface to Luther's lectures on Romans at a meeting in Aldersgate Street, London, a disillusioned missionary was converted. His name was John Wesley, and along with George Whitefield and many other preachers, he was to be used in a great revival which swept through Britain, Ireland and America in the eighteenth century.

The Purpose of Romans

Although Acts records three missionary journeys made by Paul, his letters hint at other evangelistic travels that he undertook or planned to undertake. One of those was a trip to Spain (15:24). Rome was about halfway between Jerusalem, where Paul was heading when he wrote Romans, and Spain. He planned to call in on the Christians in Rome on his way to Spain and enlist their help. Since he had never personally been to Rome and since the Christians in Rome had only heard about him, Paul wrote Romans in order to introduce himself and his message to the church there. This is why Romans is the nearest thing we have in the Bible to a systematic setting out of the Christian message.

The Style of Romans

In Romans the imagery of the law court is never far from Paul's mind. He argues carefully and logically, with each phase of his argument building on what has come before. He uses many connecting words and phrases, such as 'for', 'therefore', 'since' and 'in the light of this, what shall we say?' Some modern translations, such as the NIV, leave out connecting words (for example at 1:18). This can make it harder to follow Paul's argument in these translations.

Paul's style in Romans also follows a covenantal pattern. A classic example of this approach in the Old Testament is the Ten Command-ments (*Exod* 20:1-17), where God tells his people what he has done for them (*Exod* 20:2) before telling them what he wants them to do for him (*Exod* 20:3-17). In Romans, chapters 1–11 outline God's activity on his people's behalf, then chapters 12–16 explain how God wants us to live. This covenantal pattern rescues Christian living from being just the following of a moral code. God's grace comes first.

THE THEME OF ROMANS

This is found in 1:16-17. It is the theme of God's righteousness, which is summarized in the quotation from Habakkuk 2:4 – 'The just [or righteous] by faith will live.' In many ways, Romans is an unpacking of that significant Old Testament statement.

THE STRUCTURE OF ROMANS

After a longer-than-normal greeting, some introductory remarks to people he had not yet met personally and a summary of the letter's theme (1:1–17), Paul launches into his explanation of God's righteous-ness by establishing that *everyone needs righteousness* (1:18–3:20). In terms of a law court, Paul puts three types of people into the dock and demonstrates beyond doubt that all three are unrighteous. The three types are the immoral materialist (1:18–32), the outwardly moral and good-living person (2:1–16), and the religious person, as represented by the Jews (2:17–3:8). In echoes of Genesis 3, Paul shows that all of them, in different ways, knew God, and what his legitimate claims on them were (1:18–20; 2:14–15; 3:2), but they all rejected him. They preferred to believe error rather than truth (1:21–22, 25), and rebelliously made a bid for independence from God. The way they now live makes them subject to his judgment (1:24–32; 2:1–3, 21–24). In a series of quotations from the Old Testament, Paul proves his case (3:9–20). Every aspect of the lives and personalities of men and women has been totally polluted by sin. Everyone needs God's righteousness, because everyone is unrighteous. There are no exceptions (3:10).

Up to this point the picture is dark. But the turning point comes at 3:21 with the words, 'But now'. Here we see that God has shone the light of his gospel into the blackness of human guilt. From 3:21 through to 4:25, therefore, Paul announces that *God's righteousness has been revealed* in the death of his Son. In 3:21–31, he explains this by drawing on imagery from the courthouse, the slave market, and the temple. First he tells us that God has justified us (3:24). Because the death of Christ satisfied his justice, God can remain just and, at the same time, pardon the obviously guilty (3:25–26). Next, drawing upon the Old Testament figure of the Kinsman-Redeemer and the dramatic events of Hosea 3, as well as the buying and selling of slaves in the slave market, Paul explains that God has redeemed us (3:24). Our unrighteousness brought us under sin's tyranny, but the Son of God has paid the price to secure our redemption. Finally, Paul tells us that God's wrath against us has been propitiated (3:25), so that friendship between God and us can be restored.

Then in 4:1–15, Paul shows that God's righteousness is received by faith, not earned by keeping the law or by being religious. He is aware that this goes against the whole direction of Jewish religious thought, so he cites Abraham and David, both great heroes in the eyes of all Jews, to show that God's righteousness is not earned by living an upright life (4:4–8), or obtained through religious rituals (4:9–12), or by keeping God's law (4:13–15), but received by faith alone. In 4:16–25, Paul uses the example of Abraham to show what saving faith is like. It takes God at his word and believes his promises.

All this might seem too good to be true, but Paul confirms the truth of it in 5:1–21 and 8:1–39 where he deals with *assurance of salvation*. As a result of our justification, even now we enjoy peace with God, access to him and a hope which not even suffering can take away (5:1–5). God's love assures us that we will be saved (5:6–11), not because we are naturally lovable, but because God has shown his love for weak, ungodly sinners while they were still his enemies (5:6, 8, 10). The argument is further reinforced by what Paul says about our union with Christ in 5:12–21. In Adam, as a result of his disobedience, we were under sin, guilt, and death. Now in Christ, as a result of his obedience, we are under the reign of grace, freedom and life. Where sin abounded, grace abounds even more (5:20).

After a digression in 6–7, Paul returns in 8:1 to his theme of assurance. Another reason why our ultimate salvation is secure is because we have the Holy Spirit (8:1–17). He liberates us, indwells us, gives us life, controls us, witnesses with our spirits that we are God's children, and helps us when we are weak. But even so, we still live in a fallen world, in which we experience disappointments, frustrations and difficulties. In 8:18–27, Paul reminds us to focus on the glory that awaits us in heaven. This certainty about the future will help us to live in the present with eager yet patient expectation of our glorious final redemption.

In the last twelve verses of this section, Paul takes everything to a new level. He assures us that, in everything that happens to us, God is at work, bringing about our final salvation (8:28). Then he outlines the five stages of God's salvation, tracing it from eternity past through time and history into eternity future (8:29–30). Through faith in Christ we are locked into God's invincible purpose, and Paul is so confident that we will be saved that he uses a past tense to describe our future glorification, as if it has already happened. His words reach a majestic crescendo when, in 8:31–35, he flings out five defiant questions, to which nothing that would rob us of our assurance has any answer. He ends with the assurance that absolutely nothing can separate us from God's love in Christ Jesus our Lord (8:38–39).

In 6–7 and 9–11, Paul digresses to deal with objections to and misunderstandings of his teaching about God's righteousness. In 6, he refutes the suggestion that, because people are justified by faith alone without any reference to works, they can sin as much as they like. Those who think like that have not even begun to understand what happens when a person is converted. United to Christ in his death and resurrection, we are 'dead to sin but alive to God' (6:11). How then can we continue living in what we have died to? Similarly, having offered ourselves to

God as his slaves, the thought of lapsing back into doing what sin – our old master – wants is abhorrent (6:22). 'Far from encouraging sin, grace prohibits it.'[1] Paul's critics are also concerned that his teaching appears to sideline God's law, so, in chapter 7, he clarifies his position. Christians are released from the law, not to live as they like, but to serve God in the new way of the Spirit (7:1–6). Paul vindicates the law as 'holy, righteous and good'. Even though it reveals, stirs up, and condemns sin, it is not in any way responsible for sin.

Paul has mentioned that God's plan of salvation cannot be hindered (8:28–30). But does the fact that the Jews had, for the most part, rejected their Messiah place a question mark over this plan? Doesn't the inclusion of the Gentiles imply a Plan B, after Plan A had failed? Paul tackles these issues in 9–11. God's plan has not failed because his promises were never made to ethnic Israel as a whole but to spiritual Israel, an elect remnant within the nation (9). Israel's unbelief is due to her pride, ignorance and stubbornness (10). Then, in chapter 11, Paul looks to the future. Israel's sin is neither total – there will always be a believing remnant of Jews – nor final – since there will yet be a great ingathering of ethnic Jews before the Lord Jesus returns.

Paul then returns to his main theme and gives instructions about *working out God's righteousness* (12–15). Through the renewal of our minds (12:1–2), we are to commit ourselves to God and to his will for us. We are also to commit ourselves to our fellow-Christians and, in terms of church fellowship, we are to have a sober evaluation of our gifts, so that we neither think too highly of ourselves nor demean ourselves (12:3–8). We are to commit ourselves to other people, as we love them and express that love in the practical outworking of the qualities of sincerity, affection, honour, patience, hospitality, sympathy, harmony and humility (12:9–21; 13:8–14). We are to recognise the state's God-given authority and functions (13:1–7); and we are to respect the weaker Christian, whose over-scrupulous conscience is not to be trampled on (14:1–13). Paul concludes with some personal information about his travel plans and by sending greetings to people he knows and from people the Romans know (15:14–16:27).

[1] *Ibid.,* p. 38.

Let me conclude this brief attempt to scale the Bible's Mount Everest by mentioning again the influence Romans has had. Between October 1955 and March 1968, Dr Martyn Lloyd-Jones, the minister of Westminster Chapel in London, preached through Romans on Friday evenings. These sermons were later published,[1] and, if you will forgive a personal reference, they helped to sort out a very confused and floundering young Christian. They shaped my convictions, stretched my mind, warmed my heart and transformed my life as God spoke through the truths of this great book. 'There is no telling what may happen when people begin to study Romans.'[2] Church history has shown how true that is.

---

[1] D. M. Lloyd-Jones, *Romans* (14 volumes) (London and Edinburgh: Banner of Truth, 1970–2003).

[2] F. F. Bruce, *The Letter of Paul to the Romans* (Leicester: Inter-Varsity Press, 1963), p. 58.

46

1 Corinthians

In the course of Paul's second missionary journey (*Acts* 18:1–18), a church was formed in the major Greek city of Corinth. From a reference outside the Bible to Gallio, who is mentioned in Acts 18:12 as being the Roman proconsul during the eighteen months Paul spent in Corinth, we can date the founding of the church to either 51 or 52. The personal remarks Paul makes at the end of this letter hint that he could have written 1 Corinthians while he was in Ephesus (16:8), possibly sometime around 53 or 54.

It helps us to understand both 1 and 2 Corinthians if we understand something about Corinth. It was a wealthy city in a prime location. It was situated on the southern side of the Isthmus of Corinth, and all the north-south and east-west trade routes passed through it. The city was wealthy enough to stage the prestigious Isthmian Games – one of the four Pan-Hellenic Games – every two years. The status of Corinth was also heightened by the fact that, from 29 BC, it was the capital of the Roman senatorial province of Achaia. From here the proconsul controlled the legal, political and administrative affairs of the southern sector of Greece. The self-confidence and self-importance these things gave Corinth seem to have crept into the church and given Paul a good deal of anxiety. People from all over the Roman Empire and beyond came to Corinth hoping to make money. They brought with them their own religions and ideas, making Corinth a very cosmopolitan and pluralistic place. It was devoted to entertainment, self-indulgence and immorality. Status, money and success were valued, while the poor were despised or ignored. Again some of these values and attitudes found their way into the church. Corinth was also a haven for all the wandering philosophers of the day. They all had their own emphases, but most shared the Greek idea that matter is inherently evil, with all the bad consequences for behaviour that flowed from that idea. However, in the midst of all this, people were converted, and seeking to live their lives to the glory of their Lord and Saviour.

THE STYLE OF 1 CORINTHIANS

This letter has been described as 'the most difficult of the New Testament letters to summarize.'[1] This could be partly due to its position in the New Testament. Coming immediately after Romans, which is logical and tightly argued, perhaps the nearest we get to a systematic theology in the Bible, we can unconsciously assume that 1 Corinthians will be similar. But it is not. It is more like a classic letter than Romans – full of passionate instruction, depth of feeling and a great deal of irony. Its structure is more fluid than Romans. Although it deals with theological issues, we must remember that it is a pastoral letter, not a handbook of systematic theology.

THE PURPOSE OF 1 CORINTHIANS

Paul wrote 1 Corinthians to tackle some issues of behaviour and belief that had arisen in the Corinthian church. Some of them were extremely serious. From time to time I have been told by well-meaning Christians that it would be wonderful if we could reproduce in churches today something of what was going on in the New Testament churches. In the case of the Corinthian Church this would be a disaster. Rather than perfect and wonderful, it was a mess. Paul was trying to help the Corinthians to change the situation.

Paul's information about the Corinthian Church came from servants of a Christian lady called Chloe (1:11). She was probably from Ephesus, where Paul was staying at that time. Some of her servants had been to Corinth and were so disturbed about what was happening that they told Paul. This was not gossip behind people's backs. What they said was out in the open, and so was their identity. The fact that they were prepared to put their names to this report suggested to Paul that their motives were good. But Paul had also become aware of the

---

[1] Gordon Fee and Douglas Stuart, *How to Read the Bible Book by Book* (Grand Rapids, Michigan: Zondervan, 2002), p. 324.

situation from the Corinthians themselves. He had already written to the Corinthian Church (5:9), but the Holy Spirit, in his sovereign supervision of the Scriptures, did not wish this letter included in the New Testament canon. The Corinthians had responded to this first letter, raising some additional issues. So Paul wrote them a second letter – our '1 Corinthians'.

The Structure of 1 Corinthians

The letter begins with a greeting and a prayer (1:1–9). Although he is going to do some straight talking, Paul still prays for the Corinthians, thanking God for his grace in their lives. Though they are badly behaved Christians, they are still Christians.

The first main section of the letter, which runs from 1:10 through to 6:20, tackles THE PROBLEMS WHICH HAD ARISEN IN THE CORINTHIAN CHURCH. The first was that it was *a divided church* (1:10–4:21). The church had fragmented into four factions, each of them centred on an individual – Paul, Apollos, Peter, and Christ (1:12). This fourth grouping appeared to be more spiritual than the others, and no doubt they let the rest know that they were more spiritual because they followed the Lord himself and not a human preacher. But they were as bad as the others, for they were claiming that Christ belonged to them exclusively. Paul reminds them that, through the foolish preaching of a shameful message of a crucified Saviour, it was God, and not eloquent and clever humans, who had saved them (1:18–2:16). Notice Paul's emphasis on the activity of the Trinity in our salvation. It was God the Father who planned salvation and chose those who would receive it. It was God the Son who achieved salvation through his death on the cross. It was God the Spirit who applied salvation, so that what once seemed foolish and shameful became the wisest and most glorious thing in the world. To get their focus away from human beings and back to God, Paul points out that preachers are merely human agents that God uses in the building of his church and in the reaping of his harvest. God himself is the main Agent (3:1–23). Then Paul outlines what a real preacher is like (4:1–21).Real preachers are condemned men (4:9), fools (4:10), the scum of the earth (4:13), and the refuse of the world (4:13). They are not really the kind of men people boast about. 'While he did not want the Corinthians to stop prizing ministers of the gospel, he did want them to stop exalting preachers in undue measure.'[1]

A second major problem in the Corinthian Church is that it was *a worldly church* (5:1–6:20). It is sometimes rightly said that the church's relationship with the world should be like a boat's relationship with the ocean. The church should be in the world, just as a boat sails in the ocean. The church should be in the world, just as a boat sails in the ocean. Problems arise when the world gets into the church, or the ocean gets into the boat. A great deal of Corinth's culture had oozed into the church, so that tragically it had become hard to tell where the boundary between the two lay.

In particular, there were three moral issues which disturbed Paul. One of them was a matter of incest (5:1-13). A church member was living in an incestuous relationship with his stepmother. This went beyond the norms even of Corinth's relaxed code of morality, and set pagan tongues wagging. But, instead of disciplining the man for violating the Bible's teaching (*Lev.* 18:8), as Paul had told them to do, the church appeared to condone his actions. Another moral issue facing Paul was that of litigation (6:1–11). Church members were taking each other to court in order to settle the most trivial of disputes. That might have been acceptable to unbelievers in Corinth, but it was not something Christians should pursue. A final matter which Paul had to tackle was that of immorality (6:12–20). Some in the church found it hard to break away from their old immoral way of living. Greek philosophical ideas taught the separation of spirit and body and said that they did not influence each other. This concept was popular in Corinth. Members behaving badly would try to justify their behaviour by saying that what they did with their own bodies was their own business and did not really affect them spiritually. But Paul reminds them that their bodies are not their own. Believers have been bought body and soul by the Lord (6:19b–20a), and their bodies are actually the vehicles through which they glorify God (6:20b). He uses the cross to help these Christians stay pure.

[1] Roger Ellsworth, *The Bible Book by Book*, (Darlington, England: Evangelical Press, 2002), p. 305.

The second main section of the letter, which runs from 7:1 through to 16:4, deals with THE QUESTIONS WHICH HAD BEEN RAISED BY THE CORINTHIAN CHURCH. The first one was about *marriage* (7). How were Christians to behave in a sexually-obsessed society? Those already married were to continue to enjoy full marital relations (7:1–7). Widows and possibly widowers were to stay as they were (7:8–9). Those married to Christians were not to divorce their spouses (7:10–11), nor were Christians who were married to unbelievers. But if the unbeliever pulled out of the marriage, that was a completely different matter (7:12–16). In addressing the unmarried, Paul gives some reasons why someone might choose to remain single (7:25–35), but marriage is also good (7:28a, 38a).

The Corinthians also had questions about *Christian freedom* (8:1–11:1). The issue revolved around eating meat. The meat on sale in Corinthian butchers' shops had most likely first been involved in pagan rites. Some Christians felt that this contaminated it and so they refused to eat it. Others thought that it was fine to eat it because the idols were not really gods. These Christians were tempted to look down their noses at the other group, whom they regarded as less spiritually enlightened. Paul's instruction is not to flaunt Christian freedom but to look out for other Christians. Someone might feel free to eat meat, but if there is another Christian present who has problems with eating it, he should choose the vegetarian option. Christians can easily use freedom to draw attention to themselves and to show how spiritual and enlightened they are. If the way we use our freedom causes other Christians to stumble in their faith, we are abusing and misusing it.

Paul then goes on to tackle something which is still contentious today, the question of *worship* (11:2–13). He gives instructions about the place of women in worship and about how to celebrate the Lord's Supper, to try to bring some order into the worship of the Corinthian Church.

Paul next confronts another very up-to-date issue when he answers questions that the Corinthians had about *spiritual gifts* (12–14). These gifts are attributed to the activity of God the Holy Spirit, hence the adjective 'spiritual' (12:1–11). The use of that label implies that the Holy Spirit takes both the abilities we had from God in common grace before we were converted and the abilities he has developed in us since we became Christians, and uses them all for the glory of Christ. Paul points out that no one has all the gifts or the same gifts (12:7–11, 21–30). Therefore to say, as some do, that everyone can and should speak in tongues contradicts what the Bible states. Some seek to justify the gift of tongues by maintaining that God gives it for use in private prayer. But that is not what Paul says here. Gifts are given, not for our own private use and enjoyment, nor for self-promotion, but for use in public to help others and to build up the whole church (12:12–30). Paul repeats this principle that the gifts are given to build up others (14:1–25). It follows that when people exercise the more public gifts, there should be order (14:26–40), since this reflects God's character (14:33).

In chapter 13, Paul cautions against the obsession the Corinthians had with the more spectacular spiritual gifts. He reminds them that it is Christlikeness that counts with God rather than the exercise of gifts (13:1–7), and that, unlike love (13:8a, 13), these gifts are temporary (13:8b–12). When the canon of Scripture is finalized, there will be no more need for prophecy, tongues and knowledge, since the incomplete revelation of these revelatory gifts will be superseded by the complete revelation of Scripture. We are therefore to concentrate on the permanent and the more important.

Another question the Corinthians had concerned *the resurrection* (chapter 15). Because they had adopted the error of Greek philosophy that matter was evil, many Corinthians could not accept the idea of a physical, bodily resurrection, preferring to spiritualize it. Paul outlines the evidence for Jesus' physical resurrection (15:1–11). Then he examines the unthinkable and asks what the horrible consequences would have been if Jesus had not been raised bodily from the dead (15:12–19). Finally he states the glorious implications of Jesus' resurrection (15:20–57), in terms of his lordship and the hope of our resurrection, concluding with a call to perseverance in our Christian service (15:58).

The final question raised by the Corinthian Church had to do with *finances* (16:1–4). Paul gives instructions concerning the gathering of money for his project to take aid to the churches in Judea, which were facing hardship and famine.

The letter concludes with information on Paul's affairs and some closing greetings (16:5–24).

The Challenge of 1 Corinthians

1 Corinthians raises the important issue of what it means to be spiritual. The Corinthian Church seems to have thought that a truly spiritual person possessed many spiritual gifts – the more spectacular the better. He could display wisdom and knowledge, and communicate them impressively, even if these things were influenced more by secular thinking than the Word of God. His way of life was free and liberated, even if this led to licence or was exercised at the expense of others. Experience took priority over truth, performance over Christlikeness, and self-expression over obedience and consideration of the feelings of others. As a result Christians were not very different from non-Christians. The worrying thing is that this Corinthian spirituality sounds all too similar to what is being promoted in the contemporary church – especially in the newer, emerging congregations – and adopted by many young Christians.

Paul's view of spirituality is very different. For Paul, the truly spiritual person is becoming more and more like Jesus. He has a clear set of beliefs, based on the teaching of Scripture, and is sensitive to others. Holiness, truth, and love are the keynotes of this spirituality. The result is that Christians are radically different from non-Christians and visibly illustrate the transforming and life-changing power of the gospel.

This letter challenges us as to which vision of spirituality we will pursue – the world's, as represented by the Corinthian Church, or God's, as presented by Paul.

47

2 Corinthians

Reading 2 Corinthians can seem like beginning to read a story in the middle. Action and dialogue are going on, but we are not sure who some people are, or why certain things are being said. Few of the issues raised in 1 Corinthians come up again in 2 Corinthians, an exception being the collection that Paul is taking to help the Judean churches (*1 Cor.* 16:1–4; *2 Cor.* 8–9). What unites these two letters is the ongoing tension in the relationship between Paul and the Corinthians.

One reconstruction of the course of events is as follows, though there is some debate about it. At the end of 1 Corinthians, Paul spoke of Timothy visiting Corinth (*1 Cor.* 16:10). The visit took place, and Timothy brought back news of opposition to Paul in Corinth. Paul then went to Corinth himself. This visit is not mentioned in Acts, but can be deduced from some of the things Paul wrote in 2 Corinthians (2:1; 12:14; 13:1–2). It is known as 'the painful visit' (2:1) because an incident appears to have taken place in which Paul was verbally assaulted by a member of the church while other members said nothing. After returning to Ephesus, Paul wrote a difficult letter to the Corinthian church, calling on them to discipline the man who opposed him (2:4), and sent Titus to Corinth with it. We do not have this letter. Paul was so keen to hear how Titus got on at Corinth that he left Ephesus and went first to Troas (2:12), and then on to Macedonia to meet him (7:6 and 13). Paul heard from Titus that, although the relationship between him and the Corinthians was still not perfect, the man who opposed him had been disciplined and had repented. So Paul wrote another letter from Macedonia, probably in 56, and sent it to Corinth with Titus and another brother (12:18). We call this letter '2 Corinthians', although it may, in fact, be the fourth piece of correspondence from Paul to the Corinthians.

The Purpose of 2 Corinthians

Paul wrote 2 Corinthians to express his delight at the Corinthians' repentance; to ask them not to be too severe towards the man who was disciplined; to gain their support for the collection he was gathering; and to clear up any remaining doubts about his apostleship.

The Style of 2 Corinthians

Paul's relationship with the Corinthians was rather like the relationship a mother might have with a badly-behaved teenage son: affection, mingled with intense annoyance! This is reflected in his style of writing, which is very personal, unrestrained, and at times sarcastic. This means that 2 Corinthians does not have the logical flow we expect in Paul's writings. It is almost circular in its outline, which is not typical of Paul. After writing about his relationship with the Corinthians (1–7), Paul goes on to the collection he is gathering (8–9), but then he comes back to his relationship with the Corinthians (10–13). The unexpected shape of 2 Corinthians can be partly attributed to the emotion he felt. When our feelings are engaged, we are not always as logical as we would wish to be.

The Structure of 2 Corinthians

In the *introduction* to his letter (1:1–11), knowing that he would return to the issue later, Paul identifies himself as an apostle (1:1). He then thanks God for hearing his prayers and the prayers of the Corinthians, so that he experienced God's comfort in the very difficult circumstances he faced, and from which he was eventually rescued (1:3–11).

Then, from 1:12 to 7:16, the first main section of the letter, *Paul explains his ministry*. He had originally planned to visit Corinth on his way to and from Macedonia (1:15–17), but developments in the church caused him to send a letter instead (2:4, 9). This change of plan left him open to the accusation that he was unreliable (1:17), so he responds by saying that he changed his plans, not because he was not to be trusted, but in order not to inject more pain into an already raw situation (1:23; 2:1–2). It was love for them, not unpredictability and inconsistency, which led him to act as he did.

The questions which the misunderstanding over his change of plans raised gave Paul the opportunity to underline the genuineness of his ministry. This could be proved in many ways. To begin with, there was the transforming effect his ministry had on people, not least the Corinthians (3:1–3). They had to look no further than themselves for proof. Paul then goes on to show that he is a genuine minister because he preaches an unadulterated gospel in a straightforward way, rejecting the use of all underhand methods (3:4–4:7).

His willingness to suffer enhances Paul's qualifications as a genuine minister (4:8–5:8). He gives us three insights into what he was prepared to endure physically, emotionally and spiritually to make Christ known (4:8–9; 6:4–10; 11:23–29). His willingness to persevere despite frequent suffering, and not to escape to some safer, more comfortable form of Christian service, proves that he was a genuine minister (*John* 10:12–13). Considering the frequency and severity of his suffering, we are still left wondering how Paul kept going. In 4:16–5:8, Paul explains why he did not abandon apostolic ministry. His suffering made him focus on the really important things, which were inward renewal and eternal glory. In comparison with what lay in store for him in heaven – being with the Lord and receiving a new resurrection body (5:1–8) – what he was experiencing then was minor and almost inconsequential.

The genuine nature of Paul's ministry is also proved by what he tells us of his motives (5:9–21). He was driven by an overpowering longing to please the Lord (5:9). He was aware of his ultimate accountability to him (5:10–11), and, on the Day of Judgment, he wanted to hear him say, 'Well done, good and faithful servant' (*Matt.* 25:21). Paul felt the pressure of Jesus' love at the core of his being (5:14), squeezing out any thoughts of self-promotion and instead sending him out in his service with renewed passion for the salvation of his hearers (5:15–17). His sense of gratitude for being called to proclaim such an amazing salvation is almost tangible (5:17–21).

The second main section runs from 8:1 through to 9:15, and in it *Paul appeals for generous giving*. The collection to relieve the hardship of the churches in Judea was not just a matter of Christian philanthropy and compassion for those less well-off. For Paul it was also symbolic, representing the unity of Jewish and Gentile Christians. This is the message that God had given to him, as he shows in Ephesians 3:2–6, and he wanted to demonstrate it visibly, as well as preach it.

As he seeks to enlist the Corinthians' help in this project, Paul outlines nine features of Christian giving. It is an expression of God's grace (8:1–6), and can be a spiritual gift (8:7) for while all Christians are called to be generous, some are given the particular 'gift of giving'. It is inspired by Jesus' self-giving on the cross (8:8–9), which is why it should be generous. It is to be proportionate giving (8:10–12), for what counts, as far as God is concerned, is not the *amount* of their income Christians give but the *proportion* of their income Christians give (*Mark* 12:41–44). It contributes to equality (8:13–15) with the better-off helping the less well-off. It must be carefully supervised (8:16–24). It can be stimulated by a little friendly competition (9:1–5). It contributes to a spiritual harvest (9:6–11a), and it results in thanksgiving to God (9:11b–15).

As we move into the third main section of 2 Corinthians, *Paul defends his apostleship* (10:1–12:13). There is an abrupt change in Paul's tone. Until now, he has been fairly conciliatory as he tries to heal bruised relationships, but now he becomes very combative. This striking shift has led some to think that 2 Corinthians is actually made up of two letters Paul wrote to the Corinthians: the first being 1–9 and the second, 10–13. They suggest that the letters were joined together for safe keeping. This idea just bristles with problems. The reason for the dramatic swing is that, although the relationship between Paul and the Corinthians was improving, it had not totally healed. Titus had reported the presence in Corinth of supposedly 'super-apostles' (11:5), who were questioning Paul's apostolic credentials. The healing process was being hampered by their constant sniping at Paul. We can infer that Paul was being accused of being unreliable (1:15–17, 23), of not having the right connections (3:1), of being pushy (4:5), of being untrustworthy with money (8:20–21), of behaving in an unspiritual way (10:2), of being arrogant (10:8), of not being one of the Twelve (11:5) and of lacking dignity (11:7). Of course, by undermining Paul's credentials, these men were trying to establish their own. Reluctantly Paul stands up for himself, but stand up for himself he does. Robustly, vigorously and forcefully, he faces down his accusers, aiming his blows at them, not the Corinthians. This targeting of the 'super-apostles' would account for the movement from the conciliatory to the combative.

As he takes on the 'false apostles' (11:13) Paul speaks 'as a fool' (11:21). There may be an allusion here to Greek theatre where the fool, far from being contemptible, was a figure of importance. He was a character who let the writer of the play speak frankly with the audience and get away with it, and was often the only person who saw things as they really were. One of the best known examples of a fool who is no fool is the little boy in Hans Christian Andersen's story, *The Emperor's New Clothes*. It takes someone humble and insignificant, not blinded by conceit, to point out what should be obvious.

In his defence of his apostleship, Paul reminds the Corinthians that he too has had amazing spiritual experiences (12:1–4). But he is not trying to excel the false apostles by saying that his experiences were more exciting than theirs. He almost plays down his own experience, speaking of himself in the third person (12:2–4), because he sees the snare of spiritual pride (12:7a). To prevent this God gave him a 'thorn in the flesh' and refused to remove it (12:7b–9).

Paul also boasts about his weaknesses (11:21b–33; 12:10). While the 'super-apostles' boasted incessantly about their achievements, Paul actually boasts about his non-achievements. One was his escape from Damascus in a basket lowered down the wall. In the Roman army, the highest military honour, the Roman equivalent of the Victoria Cross, was given to the first person to scale a city wall in a siege. Paul's 'achievement' is at the other end of the bravery spectrum! But Paul's ministry is patterned on the cross where, in seeming weakness, God's power was actually greatest. Paul concludes the defence of his apostleship by mentioning the signs he has performed (12:11–13). The exercise of these miraculous and extraordinary gifts was to validate his apostleship and to authenticate the message the Lord had given him. This has always been the function of this type of gift (*1 Kings* 17:24; *Acts* 2:22; *Heb.* 2:4). Since there are no longer any apostles, there is no longer a need for this type of gift.

In the closing verses, *Paul announces his plans, and concludes* (12:14–13:14). He tells them that he is planning to visit Corinth again (12:14–19) and warns them against behaviour which would make the visit painful to them and to him (13:2–4).

THE MESSAGE OF 2 CORINTHIANS

Throughout 2 Corinthians a question is constantly implied: how will we recognize a true minister? Two completely different answers are on offer. The Corinthians had very clear ideas about what a minister should be like, and they all revolved around the idea of image, which for them was everything. The 'super-apostles' whom they idolized were what a minister should be. They had presence, with their smart clothes and confident smiles. They were articulate, with a commanding use of language and memorable turn of phrase. They had charisma, attracting people by their charm. They were well-connected, constantly name dropping – just happening to mention the important people who had contacted them for their advice. Their sermons were full of stories about their wonderful spiritual experiences, because that is what people wanted to hear, rather than an explanation of the Scriptures.

Paul's answer was very different. The true minister is focused on Christ. His preaching is full of the Lord and his achievements. It is never a self-promoting litany of his own spiritual experiences and exploits (4:5). Yet so much preaching today is a rambling series of stories about the preacher's own experiences and other miscellaneous anecdotes, rather than a simple, straightforward explanation of the Christ-centred Scriptures. That seems to be what the contemporary church wants, and what preachers provide. Is it any wonder, then, that the church is dying from spiritual malnutrition? The true minister is motivated by a passion for Jesus' glory, not by a craving to advance his own cause (5:14). In 5:14, is Paul speaking about Christ's love for him, or his love for Christ? I think it is the latter, because at the hub of everything he did was his zeal to see Jesus Christ glorified, not his own personal advancement. The true minister patterns his ministry on the Lord and his cross where power was displayed in weakness (12:9–10). Yet the contemporary church wants preachers who ooze self-confidence and convey the impression that they have everything under control. However, God wants ministers who, when they look at the commission they have been given, cry out to him in their weakness, 'Who is equal to such a task?' (2:16). When they do that, they will experience an inflowing of his power because 'weakness [is] the matrix in which God displays his strength'[1] (12:9–10).

That is what a true minister looks like, and we need to pray that God will raise up ministers like that and congregations who see their ministers in that way. Pray, too, for your own minister, because he is under constant pressure to be a Corinthian-type minister instead of a minister after the pattern of the Scriptures.

---

[1] D. A. Carson and Douglas J. Moo, *Introduction to the New Testament: Second Ed.* (Leicester: Apollos, 2005), p. 451.

48
Galatians

G alatians is widely regarded as the first New Testament letter Paul wrote, probably in the period AD 47–49. It deals with events occurring between the end of Acts 14 and the beginning of Acts 15, since it presupposes the forming of churches in southern Galatia (now south-east Turkey) as recorded in Acts 13–14, but does not mention the watershed Council of Jerusalem, described in Acts 15. This was a very crucial time for the Early Church. Thousands of non-Jews were converted and brought into the church. Up to this point, the church had been predominantly Jewish. Questions were now being raised about how these two sections of the church should relate to each other. One option would be for the two sections to develop separately. In effect there would be two churches: a Jewish church and a Gentile church – a system of ecclesiastical *apartheid*. A second option would be for the Gentiles to become Jews by obeying the Jewish ceremonial laws, with men submitting to the rite of circumcision. The third option was to forge both Jews and Gentiles into one church in which cultural, political, educational and social background – and especially ethnicity – did not matter, and faith in the Lord Jesus Christ was all that really counted.

THE REASON FOR GALATIANS
During his first missionary journey, Paul planted churches in the southern Galatian towns of Pisidian Antioch, Iconium, Lystra and Derbe (*Acts* 13:13–14:23). Then he returned to Antioch in Syria, his home base (*Acts* 14:24–28). Not long after Paul's departure, teachers who belonged to an extreme right-wing faction of the Jewish church, and were more Jewish than Christian, arrived in Galatia and started to teach something very different. Paul had taught that to become a

Christian a person had to place his trust exclusively in Jesus Christ. Salvation was in Christ alone, and received by grace alone, through faith alone. The false teachers, usually referred to as 'Judaizers', viewed salvation as a combination of faith and works. To become a Christian a person had to place his trust in Christ but must also keep the rites and rituals of the Jewish ceremonial law. For the Judaizers, sinners were justified by faith in Christ AND observing the law. Paul was aware that what they were teaching was a million miles away from the gospel he had received. He saw it as attacking the very core of the Christian message. He wrote Galatians to counter the false teaching and to warn the Galatian Christians that they must not be taken in by it.

THE STYLE OF GALATIANS

Galatians is direct. Paul does not waste time. There is no polite opening greeting: he goes straight into attack mode. 'In a display of bare-knuckle writing, [Paul] takes the gloves off and sallies in for the knockout. No punches are pulled.' Some of his language is blunt (3:1), and some is shocking, or even crude (5:12). But Galatians is well-argued: Paul deals with all the issues at stake logically, tackling them one by one. Because he wishes to take on the Judaizers on their home turf, he argues in a very Jewish way, making many references to Abraham, the law, observing the law, God's promise, and the promised seed. He even uses an allegory (4:21–31). The very Jewishness of Paul's argument can pose problems for twenty-first century non-Jews.

But, while it is well-argued, Galatians is not cold, objective or detached, for Paul writes with passion. In fact his very passion for the gospel (1:8–9) makes many Christians today uneasy. They represent him as an extreme religious fundamentalist, a kind of Christian jihadist. But surely the problem lies with us. Is it not because we are less than passionate about the glory of Christ that we fail to see the kind of error being promoted by the Judaizers and their contemporary disciples as a downgrading of Christ and his saving activity? This says much more about us than it does about Paul.

---

[1] Jay Adams, *The Christian Counsellor's Commentary – Galatians, Ephesians, Colossians, Philemon*, (Hackettstown, New Jersey: Timeless Texts, 1994), p. 1.

Paul is also moved by love for the Galatian Christians, his spiritual children (4:12–20). This false teaching puts them in grave danger, and with true pastoral concern he seeks to protect them from it.

THE STRUCTURE OF GALATIANS

After an introduction (1:1–5) in which the main issues he will tackle in the rest of the letter are flagged up, Paul launches into a fierce rebuke of all unfaithfulness to the gospel (1:6–10). This is not a bad-tempered outburst from a grumpy old man or the ranting of a bigot. Rather it is a noble protest, in the style of the Old Testament prophets, in defence of the one saving gospel. Paul is going to make it clear that the gospel of justification by faith alone, in Christ alone, through grace alone, is the true fulfilment of the Old Testament – not the false teachers' corruption of that gospel.

Paul begins his attack *by defending his apostleship* (1:11-2:21). Working on the old political method of discrediting the message by discrediting the messenger, the Judaizers were saying that Paul was not a real apostle. When Paul uses the term 'apostle' of himself, he is not saying that he is a gospel missionary. He is saying that he is a member of that unique group of men commissioned by the risen Jesus to teach the gospel authoritatively (*John* 14:26; 16:12–13). 'The authority of the person commissioned is that of the person who commissions him. So, when Paul speaks . . . as an apostle of Christ, he does so with Christ's authority.'[1] If the Judaizers can discredit Paul's apostleship, they can also discredit what he taught. This is why Paul defends his apostleship so robustly and vigorously. It is the gospel, not his personal credit, which is at stake.

Paul underlines the fact that he was appointed an apostle directly by Jesus Christ (1:11–24). No man contributed in any way to his becoming an apostle and no man gave him his apostolic teaching. He was completely independent of the church in Jerusalem, though what he preached was in total agreement with them and had their blessing (2:1-10). The only difference between Paul and the Jerusalem apostles, such

---

[1] F. F. Bruce, *The Epistle to the Galatians* (Exeter, England: Paternoster Press, 1982), p. 72.

as Peter, was their spheres of service. They would concentrate mainly on evangelizing the Jews, while he would focus predominantly on the Gentiles. When there was a disagreement between Paul and the Jerusalem apostles, represented by Peter, it was the Jerusalem apostles who had wandered from the gospel, not Paul (2:11–21). Until some Judaizers arrived from Jerusalem, Peter was more than happy to have fellowship with non-Jewish believers. But then his old weakness pulled him down and, out of fear of what others might think, he withdrew from fellowship with the non-Jewish believers. He had fallen into the same trap as the Judaizers, making something other than faith in Christ the basis of gospel fellowship. So, in 'one of the most tense and dramatic episodes in the New Testament,'[1] Paul 'opposed [Peter] to his face' (2:11), because his actions were a denial of the gospel and hugely damaging to the stability of the church at Antioch, taking even Barnabas off course.

Paul presses home his attack on the Judaizers' false teaching *by defending the gospel* (3:1–4:31). The Galatians were denying the reality of their own experience (3:1–5). They did not receive the Holy Spirit by observing the law but by believing the gospel Paul preached to them. They were also being duped by views that ran counter to the clear teaching of the Old Testament (3:6–9). Abraham was justified by faith alone and not by being circumcised. They were also missing the whole point of Jesus' death (3:10–14). In order to be justified by law-keeping, we have to obey the law perfectly. Since no one can do so, everyone is under the law's curse. But Jesus bore the curse for us in his death.

The Galatians betrayed a fundamental misunderstanding of the nature of God's promise (3:15–18). The law, coming much later, could not displace God's promise to Abraham, on which his justification rested. They had also misread the law's purpose (3:19–24). The law does not lay out a way of salvation, but shows us our need of a Saviour and drives us to him. It is the difference between a road map and a mirror. A road map tells us how to get from A to B, while a mirror shows us what we are like. The Judaizers were teaching that God's law is a road

[1] John R. W. Stott *The Message of Galatians* (Leicester: Inter-Varsity Press, 1968), p. 49.

map; but even one of the Jerusalem apostles, to whom the Judaizers looked up, taught that it is a mirror, not a road map (*James* 1:22–25).

By allowing themselves to be taken in by the Judaizers, the Galatian Christians were not moving forward in their Christian experience but going backwards. They were trading freedom for slavery (4:1–11). The Old Testament was the time of minority, when freedom was curbed by all kinds of restrictions, but the New Testament is the time of majority, when the restrictions are lifted and the full rights of sonship enjoyed. Paul reminds them, too, that their actions were, in reality, downplaying his ministry among them (4:12–20). He concludes his defence of the gospel by telling the Galatian Christians that they were actually failing to hear the law's message (4:21–31). In a rare New Testament example, Paul allegorizes the story of Genesis 21:1–21 to show that those who follow the Judaizers' false teaching are like Ishmael – still in slavery. But those who are justified by faith alone are like Isaac – free and inheritors of all God's promises.

Paul ends his attack on the Judaizers' teaching *by defending Christian freedom* (5:1–6:10). The Galatians must stand firm in the freedom Christ has bought for them. To seek to be justified by the law is to make Christ of no value. It is to lose his benefits altogether (5:1–12). The Christian life is not a matter of beginning by grace and then continuing by obeying rules: it is all grace from start to finish. When some Christians today hear that, they swing to the other extreme, thinking that freedom is living as they please. But that is not the Christian view of freedom, for Paul makes it clear that Christian freedom is not licence (5:13). It is the sinful nature that causes licence (5:16–21), not God's grace.

Christian freedom produces righteous living, for the purpose of Christian liberty 'is that . . . we might serve the Lord without fear, in holiness and righteousness before him, all the days of our life'.[1] It leads to serving others in love (5:13–15), produces the fruit of the Spirit (5:22–23), curbs self-centred pride, self-assertion and envy (5:25–26), generates a meek and gentle attitude towards the erring (6:1–5), creates loving generosity towards those who teach in the church (6:6), and brings about expectation and hope in Christian living and service (6:7–10).

[1] *Westminster Confession of Faith,* Chapter 20, Section 3.

As he concludes (6:11–18), Paul contrasts his motives with those of the false teachers and asks a blessing on God's people, the true Israel, who have the same faith as Abraham and share in God's promises (6:16).

THE QUESTIONS OF GALATIANS

Galatians raises several questions, and one of them is that of *authority*. The voices in the church clamouring to be heard are deafening. The church growth experts, the pop psychologists, the charismatic prophets and visionaries, the traditionalists, the mystics: all are seeking our agreement and support. Who do we listen to? We only listen to the Lord, speaking through his authorized apostles in Scripture. Because of its memorable answer, many Christians know or have heard of the first question and answer in the *Shorter Catechism*. But are you familiar with the second question? It asks, 'What rule has God given to direct us how to glorify and enjoy him?' The answer given is, 'The Word of God, which is contained in the Scriptures of the Old and New Testaments, is the only rule to direct us how we may glorify and enjoy him.'[1] This is our authority: the Bible, and nothing but the Bible.

Galatians also raises the whole question of *salvation*. How are people put right with God? Galatians is clear: salvation is only on the basis of God's grace as expressed in the atoning, curse-bearing substitutionary death of Jesus on the cross. It cannot be earned. Nor is it a matter of God doing his part and us doing ours, or of getting in by grace and staying in by works. Salvation is by grace from beginning to end. It is only experienced by faith, not through participation in sacraments and church rituals. We are justified by grace alone through faith alone in Christ alone. Anything else is not just another way of looking at things, or a new perspective on what Paul says: it is 'another gospel', which is not the gospel at all. Increasing sections of the church have taken their eye off the ball in this matter: we must not.

Galatians also raises the question of *holiness*. Holiness stems from a clear understanding of Christian freedom. It is not a legalism in which spirituality is defined in terms of codes of dress, behaviour and speech, determined more by church culture than the Bible's teaching. Nor

---

[1] *The Shorter Catechism*, Q. and A. 2.

is it the opposite extreme in which the slogan, 'under grace, and not under law', seems to justify all kinds of loose behaviour. The holiness which stems from Christian freedom is neither legalism nor licence but increasing conformity to Christ. He is the embodiment of true Christian freedom. When did anyone ever serve others in love, produce the fruit of the Spirit, show an absence of self-centred pride, self-assertion and envy, or display a meek and gentle attitude towards the erring, more than Jesus did?

Finally, Galatians raises the question of *church membership*. If the false teachers had succeeded the church would have become totally Jewish, or, at best, split into Jewish and Gentile churches. Church growth gurus tell us that the 'Homogeneous Unit Principle' is one of the best ways to grow a congregation. If a congregation is basically made up of the same type of people it will grow, because birds of a feather flock together. But Paul says something completely different. The church is made up of all sorts of people (3:26–28), and congregational membership should reflect this. If a congregation is made up of the same type of people, whether in age, social class, educational standing or ethnicity, it is unhealthy, no matter what plaudits are heaped on it, because the church embraces all age groups, all cultures, all races, and all classes.

Galatians deals with some very contemporary issues in the church. No wonder it has become a theological war zone. The devil wants to undermine the biblical truths taught in it so as to create confusion in the church. When you get into Galatians, you should, as well as praying for the Spirit's illumination and strength to understand and obey it, put on your helmet and flak jacket, in a spiritual sense, because you are stepping on to a battlefield.

49

Ephesians

Ephesus, the principal city of the Roman province of Asia (modern western Turkey), was a vibrant commercial centre with extensive road and river links to the surrounding area. It was also the meeting place for different religious ideas. As Acts 19:19 indicates, it was a centre for occult practices. Many members of the church in Ephesus had been deeply involved, but when they became Christians they burnt their books of magic. The value of the books was reckoned at 50,000 drachmas. Since a drachma was a day's wages, in today's terms this is not far short of £3 million. Ephesus was also a focal point for the Imperial Cult which Augustus, the first Roman Emperor, encouraged. He saw Emperor worship as a way of uniting the different racial groups within his empire. Not to be involved in it was regarded as treason, and this put tremendous strain on Christians in Ephesus, who wanted to be loyal citizens of God's Kingdom and loyal citizens of the Roman Empire. But Ephesus' main claim to religious fame was as a centre for the worship of Artemis, or Diana (*Acts* 19:23–41). The Temple of Artemis in Ephesus was the largest building in the ancient world, nearly four times larger than the more famous Parthenon in Athens. It was adorned with beautiful sculptures and paintings, and was regarded as one of the 'Seven Wonders of the World'.

Paul lived in Ephesus for three years (*Acts* 20:31), the longest he remained in any one place. At the end of Acts 19:9, manuscripts of the 'Western Text' include a phrase that is omitted from almost all translations. It says that this teaching took place 'from the fifth to the tenth hour', that is, from 11:00 am to 4:00 pm. Public life in the Greek cities began very early, usually around daybreak, but from the fifth to the tenth hour everyone rested till the day was cooler. If this detail is reliable, when the city stopped work and rested, Paul began his teaching. Since this went on for two years, his teaching must have been very thorough indeed. The result was that 'all the Jews and Greeks who lived in the province of Asia heard the word of the Lord' (*Acts* 19:10). We know that Christian congregations were formed in other Asian cities like Colosse, Sardis, Hierapolis, Smyrna, Pergamum, Thyatira, Philadelphia and Laodicea. Paul never visited these places, yet the gospel message cascaded out from Ephesus to them.

Paul probably wrote Ephesians from prison in Rome around AD 62, while he waited for his appeal to Caesar (see *Acts* 25:11) to be heard by the Emperor. It is the first of his 'Prison Letters'.

The Characteristics of Ephesians

Ephesians is *general in its style*. It does not seem to be addressing a specific issue in a specific setting, but deals with the general difficulties that Christians anywhere and at any time face in living for Christ in a non-Christian society.

Ephesians is also *broad in its scope*. The letter was written with a wide range of recipients in mind: husbands and wives, children and parents, and slaves and free (5:22–6:9). It deals with issues that have a far-reaching time-frame. It speaks of eternity past (1:4), then moves seamlessly into the present time, then shifts effortlessly into dealing with eternity to come (3:10–11).

It is *covenantal in its arrangement*, that is, it first explains what God has done for us (1–3), and only then outlines how God wants us to live (4–6). Christianity never operates on the basis of trying to get God to accept us because we obey him. God accepts us on the basis of what he has done in his Son. We obey him because of his grace.

The Structure of Ephesians

The theme of *God's salvation* is dominant in the first three chapters, and the theme of *the Christian's calling* in the last three chapters.

As he writes about GOD'S SALVATION (1–3), Paul begins by outlining all *God's gracious blessings* (1:3–14). While modern versions break down this section into as many as seven sentences, it is actually one sentence in Greek, running for two hundred and two words and gathering momentum as it does so. The sentence's flow is broken once by the phrase 'to the praise of his glorious grace' (1:6) and twice by the phrase 'to the praise of his glory' (1:12, 14), which gives the section a trinitarian structure. God the Father has blessed us by choosing us to be his from before time began (1:2); adopting us into his family (1:5); and accepting us (1:6). By his death, God the Son has redeemed us (1:7), setting us free from sin's control over our lives; securing our forgiveness (1:7); and giving us an insight into God's plan (1:9–10). God the Holy Spirit assures us that we will receive our inheritance. We are sealed by the Spirit (1:13), which marks us out as permanently belonging to God, and he also acts as a first instalment, guaranteeing that we will receive the full payment of our inheritance in heaven (1:14). These are wide-ranging blessings: adoption and acceptance relate to our present, redemption and forgiveness to our past, and inheritance to our future. Expressions like 'love', 'grace', 'freely given' and 'in him' remind us that these are gracious blessings which we did not earn or deserve. With such gracious and glorious blessings, it is little wonder that Paul, without appearing to draw breath, praises and praises and praises the God of our salvation!

It is possible to be materially rich and not to know it, and it is also possible for Christians not to realize how spiritually rich they are, especially if they live in a society which is constantly putting them down as irrelevant and marginalizing them. Paul therefore *prays for understanding* (1:15–23), asking that, through the activity of the Holy Spirit, we might grasp the richness of our deepening relationship with God (1:17). More specifically, Paul prays that we might understand our hope (1:18), take in how fabulously rich our inheritance is (1:18), and experience the intensity of God's great power operating in and through us (1:19–23).

Then Paul returns to his theme to write about *God's transforming salvation* (2:1–22). God's salvation has transformed our lives so that we have experienced a spiritual resurrection (2:1–10). We were spiritually dead (2:1–3) because we wanted to go our own way and because we were in slavery to the world, the flesh and the devil, all of which exposed us to God's just anger. We were oblivious of God and unable to have any sort of relationship with him. But God has made us spiritually alive (2:4–9) so that now we can live for him and please him (2:10). Paul also depicts this transformation in terms of reconciliation (2:11–22). Once we were far away and alienated from God (2:11–12), but God took the initiative and, on the basis of the death of Christ on the cross, he has ended the alienation, bringing us back to himself (2:12) and to each other (2:14–22).

Personal references are rare in Ephesians, but Paul makes a few in speaking of *God's inclusive salvation* (3:1–13). He explains that the scope of what God is doing includes both Jews and Gentiles, as God makes them joint inheritors of his salvation (3:6). He calls this a 'mystery', which is a technical term in Scripture for a truth that would have remained hidden had not God revealed it. Paul was granted insight into this great hidden purpose of God. It was this that motivated him to travel widely with the gospel (3:7–9) and to suffer as a result (3:13; *Acts* 22:21–22).

Paul concludes what he has to say about God's salvation with *another prayer for understanding* (3:14–21). He approaches God with a perfect balance of reverence and intimacy, acknowledging his fatherhood and sovereignty (3:14–15), and prays that Christians might be inwardly strengthened with God's might (3:16), grasp the greatness of the love of Christ for them (3:18), and be filled to capacity with God's grace (3:19). He concludes this prayer with a magnificent doxology (3:20–21), which fills us with solid confidence about God's willingness and ability to answer prayer. Using what has been called a 'super-superlative' within an ascending series of ideas, Paul reminds us that 'our ability to ask, indeed our ability to conceive what we might ask, cannot stretch to the limits of what God can actually accomplish'.[1]

The focus of Ephesians shifts as Paul begins to write about THE CHRISTIAN'S CALLING (4–6). God's salvation does not drop out of the picture. but is always there in the background, providing the motivation and the power for us to live in a way that is in line with the

---

[1] Sinclair B. Ferguson, *Let's Study Ephesians* (Edinburgh: Banner of Truth, 2005), p. 95.

gospel (4:1). In the light of all that God has done for us, we are called to *be united in the church* (4:1–16). This passage disposes of two current myths. The first is that unity means uniformity. This would mean that there will be no true unity until everyone is the same. The other myth is the converse of the first: that diversity means division, so that, again, everyone must be forced to be the same. Christians have the triune God in common and share in his unity (4:4–6), but that unity is not uniformity because, as a result of his triumph over his enemies, the Lord gives everyone in the church different gifts (4:7–10). Paul concentrates on the Word-based gifts, given to build up the church quantitatively and qualitatively (4:10–16). But it remains true that Christians must work hard at maintaining the unity which already exists, so Paul explains what unity-maintaining qualities need to be seen in our lives (4:2–3).

Paul then moves on to show that, in the light of all that God has done for us, we are called to *be different from the world* (4:17–5:21). Our lives have been changed by God's grace and we are to reflect this by putting off behaviour that belonged to our old way of life and, in its place, putting on behaviour that is appropriate for our new lives (4:17–24). In a section which is, to all intents and purposes, an extended explanation of the second table of the Ten Commandments, Paul spells out what this will mean. In a world of falsehood and lying we are to put on the truth (4:25). In a world of anger we are to put on forgiveness and compassion (4:26–27, 31–32), and in doing so illustrate the nature of God's salvation. In a world of dishonesty and cutting corners, we are to work hard for a living (4:28), refusing to fall for the get-rich-quick mentality that is all around us. In a world of criticism and fault-finding, in which people are constantly undermining others to boost their own egos, we are to put on encouragement (4:29–30). In a world of immorality we are to put on purity (5:3–14). In a world of excess, in which people damage their own health and harm others by their overindulgence, we are to put on sobriety and self-control (5:15–21).

In the light of all that God has done for us, we are called to *be orderly in the home* (5:22–6:9). As the one who established marriage and family life, God has set out how things are to be ordered in the home, and

Christians are to adhere to it. Wives are to submit to their husbands in the same way that they gladly and enthusiastically submit to Christ (5:22–24). Husbands are to be the head of the home and love their wives with the same sacrificial, self-giving and character-developing love that Christ displayed towards them (5:24–33). Children are to obey their parents (6:1–3) because it is right and because they want to obey God. Parents are not to irritate their children but instead to bring them up in God's ways (6:4). Slaves are to do wholeheartedly what their masters say as if they were serving Christ himself (6:5–8). Masters are not to be hard on their slaves, remembering that believing slaves serve the same Master they do (6:9).

Finally, in the light of all that God has done for us, Paul calls on Christians to *stand firm in the fight against Satan* (6:10–20). The devil will be doing all he can to stop Christians fulfilling their responsibilities in the church, in society and in the home, for these are the theatres of war in which we will engage with our enemy. Every Christian is involved in spiritual warfare, and it is fought out in the details of everyday life. If we are to stand firm against the devil's schemes, we must utilize the weapons God has given to us. Paul reminds us of the defensive weapons God has put at our disposal to fight off Satan's attacks. We have God's truth (6:14) to help us combat Satan's lies; Christ's righteousness (6:14) to repel any attacks on our assurance; peace with God secured by Christ's death (6:15) to give us stability; faith – which is taking God at his word by accepting his teaching, obeying his commands, heeding his warnings and resting upon his promises – shields us from Satan's assaults and frustrates his most ferocious attacks (6:16); and God's salvation, and especially the future aspect of that salvation with its certain prospect of heaven, will give us confidence in the battle (6:17).

Although there is no need for us to be defeated, Paul wants us to think in terms of advance. So he also writes about two offensive weapons. We have the powerful weapons of God's Word (6:17) and prayer (6:18–20), with which we can take the battle to Satan.

Paul is not drawing his inspiration for the picture of the Christian soldier from the Roman soldiers who were guarding him, as many commentators suggest, but from his regular source of ideas – the Old

Testament. In reality, what God gives us to help us fight against Satan is the Lord himself (*Isa.* 59:15–17). With him on our side, our prospect of winning and being more than conquerors is absolutely guaranteed (*Rom.* 8:31).

This great letter ends where it began – with a reference to God's grace. He prays that God's grace, which he has praised so enthusiastically and written about so passionately, might be the experience of all who love our Lord Jesus Christ, the personification of God's grace.

50

Philippians

Philippi was the most important city of a region of northern Greece known as Macedonia (*Acts* 16:12). It was founded in the middle of the fourth century BC and named after Philip II of Macedon, Alexander the Great's father. The Romans conquered it in the middle of the second century BC, but the most significant thing that happened to Philippi occurred in 42 BC when it was given the status of a Roman colony (*Acts* 16:12). Contrary to later ideas of colonial status, this was seen as something to be proud of (*Acts* 16:20-21). A Roman colony was to be a miniature Rome. It was controlled by Roman law, and its citizens were to copy the lifestyle of the Romans. Paul takes this idea and applies it to the church in Philippi, saying that the Christians are to live like citizens of heaven (1:27). Just as people should know what Rome is like by coming to Philippi, so non-Christians should know what heaven is like by coming into a Christian congregation. In 3:20 Paul reminds the Philippians that, just as the behaviour of the people of Philippi was to show that they were Roman citizens, so Christians' behaviour should show that they are heaven's citizens.

The story of Paul's visit to Philippi is recorded in Acts 16:6–40. Paul Silas, Timothy and Luke arrived in Philippi during Paul's second missionary journey as a result of some extraordinary circumstances (*Acts* 16:6–10). The mission had an unpromising beginning. There was no synagogue, but Paul made use of what was there and Lydia was converted (*Acts* 16:13–15). Paul and Silas fell foul of the civic authorities and were beaten and thrown into prison (*Acts* 16:16–24). Once again God overruled the situation and the jailer who was guarding them was converted (*Acts* 16:25–34). After the authorities had been reminded by Paul that they had acted contrary to Roman law, Paul and Silas were asked to leave Philippi, which they did (*Acts* 16:25–40). In spite of a very modest beginning and much opposition, the first church on European soil was established.

THE PURPOSE OF PHILIPPIANS

This letter was written several years after Paul's initial visit to Philippi. References to the 'palace guard' (1:13) and 'Caesar's household' (4:22) support the view that Paul wrote it during his period of house arrest in Rome as he waited for his appeal to the Roman Emperor to be heard (*Acts* 28:30–31), and this would date Philippians sometime between 61 and 64.

Paul tells us in several places why he wrote. He wanted to tell the Christians in Philippi about his circumstances (1:12), and to express his appreciation for their support (1:3–5) and the gift they sent him (4:14–20). He also wanted to assure them that Epaphroditus, the person who had brought their gifts from Philippi to Rome, had recovered from his serious illness and was well enough to return home (2:25–30).

But Paul also had some pastoral reasons for writing. Epaphroditus had told Paul about an undercurrent of tension among the Christians at Philippi, which had shown itself openly in a very public personality clash between Euodia and Syntyche (4:2–3). So Paul appeals to them to stay united (1:27–2:18). He also writes to warn them about the danger of false teaching, whether the extreme of self-righteous legalism (3:1–11), or the other extreme of self-indulgent licence (3:12–4:1).

THE STYLE OF PHILIPPIANS

Philippians is characterized by warmth. It is obvious from what is written that Paul and the Philippians loved each other (1:7–8; 2:12; 4:1). It is also characterized by gentleness. Even when he has to reprove them, Paul does so very gently (1:27; 2:1–11; 4:2–3). Joy also characterizes Philippians: the words 'joy' and 'rejoice' occur twelve times in this short letter.

However, the most striking feature of Philippians is how focused it is on the Lord Jesus Christ. There are sixty-one references to him, including pronouns, in its one hundred and four verses. The centre-piece of the letter is 2:5–11, which directs our attention to who he is and what he did. Paul may be quoting here from an early Christian hymn. Whether this is so or not, everything Paul says in Philippians stems from this passage. Unity flows from having the Lord's humble, self-giving attitude of mind (2:1–5), and Paul pleads with Euodia and Syntyche to 'agree with each other in the Lord' (4:2). Timothy and Epaphroditus are commended (2:19–30) because they model his servant leadership. The source of our joy as Christians is what the Lord Jesus has done, and not our circumstances (3:1, 3; 4:4, 10). Even when Paul warns of error (3:2–3), it is because Christ's honour is at stake.

THE STRUCTURE OF PHILIPPIANS

As is often the case, the structure of Philippians does not correspond with the chapter divisions in our English translations. But there is a structure to what Paul wrote. After a standard introduction (1:1–2), he expresses his thanks for the Philippians' support and gives them some information about his circumstances (1:3–26). Then, based on what Epaphroditus had told him, he appeals for unity (1:27–2:30). After warning them about the false teaching of legalism and licence (3:1–4:1), Paul ends with words of exhortation and encouragement, some greetings, and a prayer (4:2–23).

THE HUB OF PHILIPPIANS

Just as a wheel revolves around its hub, so Philippians revolves around 2:6–11. It is impossible to understand what Paul is saying without getting to grips with this passage. By calling Jesus 'Lord' (2:11), and by applying to him a text applied to God in the Old Testament (2:10–11; *Isa.* 45:22–23), as well as by anticipating for Jesus worship which the Old Testament stipulated should be given to God alone (2:9–11), Paul is declaring that Jesus Christ is truly God, equal in divinity, power and glory with the Father and the Holy Spirit. Paul also asserts with equal vigour that Jesus is truly human. While retaining his full deity, Jesus laid aside the outward trappings of his glory when he came to earth, joining human nature to his divine person (2:6–7). He was not immune from the harsh realities of life but endured all that goes along with true humanity, with the one exception that he never sinned (*Heb.* 4:15). In 1098, Anselm, the Archbishop of Canterbury, wrote a book called *Cur Deus Homo? – Why did God become Man?* Paul gives a two-track answer to Anselm's question. The Son of God became man to give us an example to follow (2:5). In the rest of Philippians, Paul sets his example before us in all kinds of ways. But we need more than an example: we need a Saviour to deal with our sin. So Paul also informs us that, in obedience to his Father's will, Jesus came to lay down his life for sinners (2:8).

But if Jesus stooped infinitely low, he is also raised infinitely high. 'No passage of Scripture more beautifully portrays the depth of condescension and the height of exaltation experienced by Jesus Christ than does Philippians 2:6-11.'[1] His enemies had lifted him up on a cross to humiliate him, but God raised his Son up to heaven's throne, giving him universal and supreme authority and, as a consequence, fulfilling Isaiah 53:12 and Psalm 2:6–9.

THE CHALLENGES OF PHILIPPIANS

The warmth of this letter should not make us think that it is not going to challenge us deeply. The process of secularization, which squeezes religion to the periphery of life, and the sapping influence of self-indulgence, in which personal comfort and security are the most important things in the world, have crept into the church, and many Christians, especially in the West, have yielded to the temptation of taming the gospel. We want a gospel which will bring us personal benefits, but not a gospel that calls us to serious, holy living. So we go after 'a domesticated version of the gospel . . . Not too much – just enough to make me happy, but not so much that I get addicted.'[2] Philippians challenges this sinful tendency.

Paul calls on us *to put the gospel first* (1:1–26). When this happens, many areas in our lives will be affected. Fellowship between Christians will be transformed. The depth in the relationship between Paul and the Philippians, which is evident right from the start of the letter (1:3–4),

[1] John MacArthur, *Philippians* (Chicago: Moody Press, 2001), pp. 137–8.
[2] D. A. Carson, *Basics for Believers* (Leicester: Inter-Varsity Press, 2004), p. 9.

was due to their common passion for the gospel, their 'partnership in the gospel' (1:4). Here is the answer to the longing among Christians today for fellowship that moves beyond the superficial. If everyone were to put the gospel first, this would generate a depth in our relationships which would both build up the church and attract non-Christians to the Saviour. It would also take our prayers to a new level, weaning us away from continually focusing on personal matters and giving our prayers a consistent spiritual centre. In 1:9-11, Paul prays that the gospel might advance in the Philippians' lives so that they would be able to discern what is best, as opposed to what is merely good. Praying for other Christians in that way would transform our prayer lives.

Paul's devotion to the gospel prevented him from becoming resentful on account of the harsh treatment he received. He saw it all as advancing the gospel (1:12). Through his imprisonment, the usually unreachable Praetorian Guard, the Emperor's personal bodyguard, had been evangelized (1:13), and backbone had been put into some normally timid Christians to speak up for the Lord (1:14). He was not even troubled by those whose motives were mixed, because they were preaching Christ, and that was far more important to Paul than what was being said about him (1:18). Our resentment at tough circumstances may be due to the fact that our lives are centred on our own comfort and reputation rather than the gospel. Amazingly, Paul tells us that he would prefer a negative outcome to his appeal because, even though this would lead to his execution, he would be with Christ in heaven (1:23). However, because he believes that there is still work for him to do, Paul is prepared to set his personal preferences aside in order to be of continued use for the gospel (1:22, 24–25). Sadly, this self-denial, motivated by concern for the advance of the gospel, is a rare commodity in the contemporary church.

Paul also wants us *to make the cross the focus of our Christian calling* (1:27–2:18). The gravitational pull of the hub passage is experienced most keenly in this section of the letter. If the cross was the focus of Christ's calling, then it must be the focus of ours, otherwise our claim to be his genuine followers will be a sham. But making the cross the focus of our Christian calling has far-reaching practical implications. It will involve us in suffering (1:27–30). And yet this prospect is actually a great encouragement to us. It is a sign that we will be saved (1:28). If we suffer as a result of our loyalty to Christ (1:30), that shows that we genuinely belong to him (*Matt.* 5:11). Just as our ability to believe is God's gracious gift to us, so is our suffering (1:29) because it is the way to glory, just as the Lord's suffering was the way to glory for him.

Making the cross the focus of our Christian calling will lead to harmony among Christians. In 2:1–11, Paul tackles the low-level friction that existed in the Philippian congregation, informing us, especially in 2:3–4, how to promote unity. This is not just moral advice since the cross demands that we behave in this way towards other Christians. Christ Jesus humbly set aside his own interests (2:6) in order to look out for our interests by dying for us (2:7–8). If we make his death the pattern for our lives, harmony among Christians will blossom. The weeds of selfish ambition, self-interest, and obsession with our own reputation will wither, giving unity room to flourish.

If the cross is the focus of our lives then we will be committed to the kind of long-term obedience outlined in 2:12–13. If we want to obey God over the long haul with passion and joy, then we need to imitate our Saviour and make the cross the focus of our Christian calling.

Paul also challenges us *to imitate godly Christian leaders* (2:19–4:1). As he writes about Timothy and Epaphroditus, neither of whom was a stranger to the Philippians (1:1; 2:25; 4:18), Paul stresses how like Christ they were: Timothy, in that he was totally concerned with others' well-being rather than his own (2:5–8, 20–21); Epaphroditus, in that he was prepared to leave his comforts and make sacrifices for others (2:6, 30). Paul says that Epaphroditus was prepared to take huge risks in terms of his own health, safety and convenience to help Paul. The apostle is challenging us to imitate Christian leaders, not for their abilities or personal charisma, but for their Christlikeness.

Paul then challenges us to imitate Christian leaders whose confidence is in Christ Jesus alone (3:1–9). He warns us to have nothing to do with those who distort the gospel by teaching, in subtle and not so subtle ways, that it is possible to contribute to our own salvation (3:2). In an intensely autobiographical passage, Paul states that, if anyone could make a case for earning his salvation, he could (3:4–6). But he came to see that everything he viewed as an asset was actually a liability, and his confidence shifted decisively from trusting in himself to trusting in Christ alone. When he did this, Paul discovered the righteous standing before God for which he was desperately searching (3:7–9).

However, his spiritual experience was not static but dynamic. Using the picture of an athlete who wants to run faster, jump higher and throw further (3:12–16), Paul states his desire to know Christ better (3:10). He is challenging us to imitate Christian leaders who are not stagnant in their relationship with Christ but are moving forward to become more like him. Paul's final challenge in this section is for us to avoid those who claim to be spiritual but who are locked into a materialistic mindset (3:18–19), but to copy those who eagerly await a Saviour from heaven (3:20–21). In all this Paul is setting before us the best examples, those who are most like the Lord Jesus Christ himself (2:5).

Instead of domesticating the gospel, Paul appeals to us *to live out a lifestyle which is thoroughly distinctive* (4:2–23). This is the theme that links together what might seem a series of random instructions. In a society which is so fragmented and swamped with broken relationships, we are to get on with each other (4:2–3). Euodia and Syntyche were to get on with each other, not in some vague way but 'in the Lord', reflecting the agreement existing between the Father, the Son and the Holy Spirit. In a society in which people base happiness on their circumstances, we are to rejoice in the Lord (4:4), building our joy upon God's unwavering love for us. In a society which panders to the assertive and aggressive, we are to be known for our gentleness (4:5). In a society that runs on anxiety and adrenalin, we are not to be stressed about anything. Instead we are to commit ourselves and our circumstances into our sovereign Saviour's hands and to have confidence in him (4:6–7). In a society obsessed with the trivial and vulgar, we are constantly to be filling our thinking with the honourable and the important (4:8–9). In a society in which the power of advertising has made greed and acquisition the order of the day, and 'retail therapy' the cure for all ills – until the credit card bill arrives – we are to learn the art of contentment (4:10–13), recognizing that our wise God knows what our real needs are and, in keeping with his promise in Psalm 34:8–10, will meet them. In a society in which gratitude and basic politeness are becoming exceedingly scarce, we are to develop the virtues of thankfulness and courtesy (4:14–19). This thoroughly distinctive lifestyle will result in an exalted regard for God's honour and glory (4:20).

But we do not have in ourselves the resources needed to live like this, and, because we do not, Paul ends Philippians with a prayer that we might constantly experience the grace of our Lord Jesus Christ with our spirits (4:23).

51

Colossians

We need to know a little about Colosse's location because it forms an important backdrop to Paul's letter. Colosse was located about one hundred miles inland on the River Lycus, a tributary of the River Meander. This river was one of the main trade routes linking the interior of the Roman province of Asia, Ephesus, its main city, and Miletus, the port for Ephesus. Many travellers and traders passed along these routes through Colosse, and some made it their home. The town became an ethnic melting pot where native Phrygians rubbed shoulders with Greeks, Romans and Jews. Not only did these cultures live side by side but each had its own brand of spirituality.

The church in Colosse partly owed its existence to the town's location on a major trading route. It was started by Epaphras (1:7) who seems to have been converted at Ephesus during Paul's three-year ministry there. In Acts 19:10, Luke tells us that 'all the Jews and Greeks who lived in the province of Asia heard the word of the Lord' during Paul's residence there. Among them was Epaphras, who perhaps travelled from Colosse to Ephesus, heard Paul preach, was converted, went back home to Colosse, and organized the church there.

THE PURPOSE OF COLOSSIANS

Although he had never personally evangelized Colosse (2:1), Paul felt spiritually responsible for the church there because it owed its existence indirectly to him. So, probably around AD 60–61, he wrote a letter from prison in Rome to the Christians in Colosse. This was around the same time he wrote Ephesians, and there are similarities between the two letters. Both have the same basic structure of doctrine followed by practice, and, in the practical section, many of the same themes and ideas occur. One example is the 'Put Off / Put On' pattern for sanctification which he gives (3:1–17; *Eph.* 4:17–29). But there are differences. 'While Ephesians focuses on the church of Christ, Colossians focuses on the Christ of the church. . . . The former focuses on the body, while the latter focuses on the head.'[1]

Epaphras visited Paul in prison and told him about the situation in Colosse. The Colossians were making good spiritual progress, but the church was under threat from some travelling teachers who had recently arrived in Colosse and were teaching ideas that were wide of the mark. Colossians is Paul's response to Epaphras' information. In the letter, Paul expresses his delight at the Colossians' spiritual progress (1:3), encourages them to stand up for the truth in the face of the false teaching that is being peddled by these itinerant preachers (2:6), and outlines the nature of true Christian behaviour (3:1).

THE STRUCTURE OF COLOSSIANS

We should note that Colossians has a very clear covenantal structure: first a doctrinal section (1–2), then a practical section (3–4). Paul explains what God has done for us in Christ before outlining how we should live in response. With the exception of biblical Christianity, the basic idea of all religious belief systems is that, if we do our best, God will accept us and see we come to no real harm in the end, for, after all, what more can he ask from us? This is the framework of works righteousness. It is not good news at all. In fact, it is the worst possible news because we can never know if our best is good enough, and will always live with a dark cloud of uncertainty over us, wondering if we have made the grade. The good news is that God accepts us, not because of anything in us or done by us, but solely on the basis of what Christ has done for sinners. Our behaviour flows out of our acceptance, and not from a hope of earning salvation by our works. We cannot be reminded too often that this is the basic teaching of the Christian gospel. We need, as Martin Luther said, to beat this truth into our heads on a daily, even hourly, basis.

[1] Roger Ellsworth, *The Bible Book by Book* (Darlington: Evangelical Press, 2002), pp. 342–3.

Colossians begins with *a personal section* (1:1–14), in which Paul expresses his delight at the Colossians' spiritual progress. He first greets the church (1:1–2). Notice that he refers to the 'faithful brothers in Christ' (verse 2). The Colossian Christians are feeling the heat and need to hear this emphasis on loyalty to the Lord. Paul then expresses his thanks to God for them (1:3–8), praising God for their faith, love and hope, and for the transforming impact the gospel has had on their lives. Paul ends this personal section by praying for the Colossians (1:9–14). He has two specific requests: that they may know God's will (1:9), and that they may live a life worthy of the Lord and pleasing to him (1:10–11). By God's will he means his general will for all believers revealed in Scripture, rather than his specific will for each individual Christian. The kind of life Paul prays for is not one of spectacular spiritual experiences, but rather one of patient endurance, faithfulness to Christ, and joyful thankfulness to God for all he has done in Christ.

There follows *a doctrinal section* (1:15–2:23), in which Paul begins to tackle the false teaching being peddled in Colosse. He does not say exactly what this teaching was, but from what he writes we can work out some elements of what was being taught.

Ideas were being put forward that undermined the person and sufficiency of Christ. He was not God, it was said, and so not supreme; and good as he was, more was needed in order to be saved. What was needed, not surprisingly, was just what these preachers were bringing. So Paul goes on the offensive by painting a magnificent picture of Jesus' supremacy and sufficiency (1:15–2:7).

Jesus is the image of God (1:15) in that he is the exact representation of God. If we want to know what God is like, we only need to know the Lord Jesus Christ. He is supreme in authority and majesty. The term 'firstborn' in 1:15 refers to precedence in status rather than precedence in time. He is the Creator (1:16). Everything was made by him and for him. There may well be plants and animals in deserts and rainforests which, even today, no human eye has seen. But the Lord Jesus sees them, and they bring him delight. His glory is so great that it takes the vast canvas of the universe to begin to display it. He is pre-existent (1:17): there never was a time when he did not exist in the magnificent splendour of his glory, in perfect fellowship with the Father and the Holy Spirit. He sustains everything (1:17; *Heb.* 1:3). Without his constant activity, the universe would disintegrate. We must not think that, after he created the universe, God stepped back from it and left it to run itself. Every moment of every day, the Lord Jesus is actively sustaining the universe. We could not even draw our next breath unless he gave us the ability to do so.

He is also king of the church (1:18) by virtue of his resurrection. Because he has been raised from the dead, he is pre-eminent among his people. Jesus is God (1:19; 2:9). He is the 'fulness' of God. In Greece today, that same Greek word is used in lifts to indicate their maximum capacity. The Lord Jesus cannot be any more God than he is. He is the Redeemer (1:20–23): his death is the only way by which God and sinful human beings can be reconciled.

By painting this magnificent picture of Jesus' supremacy and sufficiency, Paul is dismissing the false teachers' claim that he was not God and that what he did on the cross was not good enough to save sinners. It is as if Paul is saying to these travelling preachers: 'Do you have any idea who Jesus really is? Do you have any grasp of what he has actually achieved?' By refuting their ideas, Paul is cutting the ground from under their feet.

Paul keeps up his offensive by exposing the bankruptcy of error (2:8–23), and here we get an inkling of what the 'Colossian Heresy' was like. It seems to have combined many different ideas. The false teachers put in a little Greek philosophy (2:8–15), which Paul says is useless because it is based on flawed, sinful human wisdom that sounds impressive but is mere hot air (2:8). Moreover it cannot deal with the problem of sin (2:11–15). They added some Jewish legalism (2:16–17), emphasizing the importance of food laws and observing sacred days, which Paul says are only of value in that they were pointers to Christ (2:17). Then some angel worship was thrown into the mix (2:18–19). They seem to have taught that angels played an important role as go-betweens in dealings between God and human beings. Their mixture of ideas was topped off with a large helping of asceticism (2:20–23). The Greeks believed that matter was evil and only the spirit was good.

How then did 'spiritual' people deal with their material bodies and what they did through them? There were two schools of thought. One favoured 'licence'. Because the body is not important, people should just live as they please. Nothing they do can affect them spiritually. The second school of thought was 'asceticism'. It said that, since the body is evil, it has to be kept in check with all kinds of harsh self-disciplinary measures. The first school of thought reigned supreme in Corinth, while in Colosse the second dominated. The false preachers blended these ideas together in a spiritually poisonous concoction. Paul warns the Colossian Christians not to put it anywhere near their lips.

Paul's approach to heresy in Colossians is quite different from his approach in Galatians. In Galatians he tackles it head on, while in Colossians his approach is the more subtle one of showing the bankruptcy and insufficiency of false teaching. This variety highlights the need for our defence of the faith to take account of the nature of the error we are combatting.

The next part of Colossians is *a practical section* (3:1–4:1). In this section Paul shows the difference the grace of Christ makes to our behaviour. All cults and false religions want to regulate the behaviour of their adherents, usually by setting out a long lists of dos and don'ts (especially don'ts). The false teachers in Colosse were no different. The behaviour they wanted to see was based on externals (2:21), and, although these external rules appeared to be wise, they had no real value (2:23). Rules and regulations cannot control people's sinful inner desires. They may curb them, but they cannot deal with them. Law cannot control or change: only the grace Christ gives can do that.

Christian behaviour is not based on regulations; instead it is an outworking in practice of what happened to us when we were converted and of our new status as God's people (3:1–4, 12). Paul first describes sanctification in terms of putting off behaviour that belonged to our old way of life (3:7–8), and, in its place, putting on new behaviour that is in line with our new life in Christ (3:12). He then describes it in terms of being what we are. We are God's chosen people, different from the world. This is what we are, so we are to behave differently from the world, not in the sense of living by strange rules and regulations, but in the sense that, in a world of friction, revenge, pride, sensuality and falsehood, we are to be people of love, forgiveness, humility, purity and integrity. Sadly, reacting to the legalism of a past generation, many Christians today have gone to the opposite extreme, so that there is no difference between their behaviour and the world's behaviour. We are not to be legalists, but we are to be different, because we *are* different. This should be seen in our lives (3:5–17); in place of the various sins mentioned in 3:5–11, we are to put on love (3:12–14), the peace of Christ (3:15), the word of Christ (3:16), and the name of Christ (3:17). It is also to be seen in our homes (3:18–4:1), in those relationships in which our sin tends to surface most quickly and be seen most clearly.

In his *conclusion* (4:2–18), Paul asks the Colossians to pray for him (4:2–4), encourages them to be concerned for outsiders (4:5–6), and sends greetings to and from several individuals (4:7–18).

The Relevance of Colossians

Our 'modern' outlook is not very different from that of Colosse in the middle of the first century. People take a little bit of this religion and a little bit of that belief system and combine them all together in a smorgasbord of ideas which they then adopt as their own personal religion. It does not matter whether or not it is coherent, as long as it makes them feel good, because, in today's religious marketplace, experience is all that matters. The result of all this religious pluralism is that the Lord Jesus Christ is devalued because he is treated as one among many religious leaders, and his work is downgraded because it needs to be supplemented by other ways of 'salvation'.

We need to listen again to Paul's message about the supremacy and sufficiency of the Lord Jesus. There is no one like him. No one else can save lost sinners. No one is greater; therefore no one can offer a more perfect salvation. All the fulness of God dwells in him bodily; therefore only in him is there life in all its fulness. And if our stand for his uniqueness stirs up anger and opposition from those within the ranks of organized religion, as well as those in secular society – as it inevitably will – then let us ask for God's power to endure patiently and remain loyal to Christ, the supreme Lord and all-sufficient Saviour.

52

1 Thessalonians

Paul does not seem to have chosen where to evangelize at random. Instead, under the Holy Spirit's direction (*Acts* 16:6–10), he visited strategic places where the gospel, to all appearances, could make the greatest impact. This is why he went to Thessalonica, a bustling city of around one hundred thousand inhabitants, the capital and administrative centre of the Roman province of Macedonia in northern Greece. It was a major trading centre situated on one of the best natural harbours in the northern Aegean Sea and at the intersection of four main roads, the most important of which was the Via Egnatia, the main land route connecting Rome in the west, via an Adriatic Sea crossing, with Byzantium (now Istanbul) in the east. As well as the native Greek and colonial Roman population there was a significant Jewish community.

Paul and his companions Silas and Timothy arrived in Thessalonica during Paul's second missionary journey. Their short and turbulent visit is recorded in Acts 17:1–10a. Paul made straight for the synagogue, knowing that, as in Pisidian Antioch (*Acts* 13:15), he would be invited to speak. For three Sabbaths, Paul preached Jesus' death and resurrection from the Old Testament Scriptures (*Acts* 17:2–3). Some Jewish men, along with many interested Greeks and prominent women, believed and a church was formed, probably meeting initially in the home of Jason. But the Jews were extremely annoyed by this defection and they stirred up trouble for Paul and the new Christians. With the help of some local ruffians, they started a riot (*Acts* 17:5), and went to look for Paul at Jason's house. Failing to find him, they hauled Jason and some other Christians before Thessalonica's city officials, accusing them of treason and harbouring traitors (*Acts* 17:6–7). This was not a trivial

[370]

charge but a very serious matter. In a city which practised Emperor worship, to say that there was another king called Jesus amounted to treason. No wonder the place was in turmoil. If the authorities in Rome got even a hint of rebellion in Thessalonica, they would come down very hard on the city. Jason and the others were released on bail, and the Christians decided that Paul should leave. So under cover of darkness, they smuggled him out of the city (*Acts* 17:10a). Paul then made his way, via Berea, to Athens, sending Timothy back to Thessalonica to get news of the church (3:1–2). When Timothy arrived back from Thessalonica, Paul had moved on to Corinth, from where he wrote the letter to them which we now call 1 Thessalonians. It was written around AD 50, making it one of the earliest New Testament documents – probably the third after James and Galatians.

THE PURPOSE OF 1 THESSALONIANS

Paul had a personal reason for writing 1 Thessalonians. His opponents were suggesting that he did not really care about the Thessalonian Christians, and that his night time escape proved this. So Paul wrote to assure them of his continuing concern for them, telling them of his unsuccessful attempts to get back to see them again.

Paul also had a pastoral reason for writing. The Jews in Thessalonica continued to make mischief for the young church (2:14–16), but Timothy had brought Paul the encouraging news that the Thessalonian Christians were not simply hanging on by the skin of their teeth, but were, in spite of severe pressure, actually making significant spiritual progress (1:3). Paul wrote to express his delight at this news. However, Timothy also brought Paul less encouraging news about muddled thinking and puzzling behaviour among the Christians. Paul therefore wrote to instruct them about these matters.

THE STRUCTURE OF 1 THESSALONIANS

Paul first focuses on the past and writes words of *explanation* to the Thessalonian Christians. He reminds them of their conversion (1:1–10). Then, to dispel the reports about him, he defends his conduct during his time in Thessalonica (2:1–16) and since (2:17–3:13).

The second part of the letter (4:1–5:28) concentrates on the present: Paul writes words of *encouragement* to the Thessalonian Christians, urging them to live in a certain way. They are to be sexually self-controlled (4:1–8); to love each other (4:9–10); to get on quietly with their own lives (4:11–12); to be hopeful in the face of death (4:13–18); to live righteous lives in the light of the Lord's return (5:1–11); and to order their church life and worship in an appropriate way (5:12–28).

THE THEME OF 1 THESSALONIANS

In this letter, under the Holy Spirit's inspiration, Paul writes about the interaction between the gospel and the church in five different areas. The first is *Christian evangelism* (1:1–10). This section shows how the gospel brings the church into existence. There is debate as to how long Paul's mission in Thessalonica lasted. Luke refers to Paul preaching in the synagogue for three Sabbaths (*Acts* 17:2), and, on that basis, some think that Paul's time in Thessalonica was brief. Others suggest that a church could not possibly have been formed, organized, and taught to the extent the Thessalonians had been in only three to four weeks. But why not? These were revival times, and God works in revival times in a much more rapid way than in more 'normal' times.

Irrespective of how long or how short a time he spent there, when Paul arrived in Thessalonica there was no church, and when he left there was a church. How did this happen? From one angle, the church came into existence because of God's electing love (1:5). Before time began, the Father, the Son, and the Holy Spirit decided there would be a church in Thessalonica, and so there was. From another angle, the church existed because Paul preached the gospel in Thessalonica (1:5) and the Thessalonian Christians responded positively to it (1:6 and 9–10). As Paul preached, he was conscious that the Holy Spirit was using his words to affect his hearers' consciences, minds and wills. As they listened to Paul, the Thessalonian Christians became aware that they were not simply listening to a human being but that they were hearing God himself speak (2:13). In Christian evangelism, there should always be this harmonious and vigorous interaction between God's sovereign purposes and power on the one hand, and man's preaching of the gospel and response to it on the other. God's sovereignty and human responsibility do not compete in Christian evangelism but always work in tandem and in harmony. How the gospel brought the church in Thessalonica into existence illustrates this.

Paul then moves on to write about *Christian ministry* (2:1–3:13), and how ministers serve both the gospel and the church. The easiest way to discredit the message is to discredit the messenger, and this is how Paul's detractors operated. In defending his ministry, he gives us four pictures of a Christian minister. He is, in the first place, a *steward* (2:3–4). (The word 'steward' is not used but the concept of stewardship is clearly in Paul's mind.) God has entrusted the gospel to his ministers. They are to declare his message, not their own opinions. One day they will give an account of how they have exercised that trust (*2 Tim.* 4:1; *1 Pet.* 5:4). For this reason ministers' actions should be above reproach. There should be no sharp practice or flattering words (2:3, 5). The Christian minister is also like a *mother* (2:5–8). Paul was gentle, caring, loving and self-sacrificial towards the Thessalonians. As far as he was concerned, the Thessalonian Christians, though out of sight, were never out of mind. In a world where communication was not so instant as it is today, he still made every effort to keep in touch with them (2:17–3:13). The third picture of the Christian minister is that of a *father* (2:9–12). Paul was accused of being just like the travelling preachers who criss-crossed the Roman Empire, making a living from their gifts of eloquence and gaining a reputation for dishonesty. But Paul asserts that his willingness to support himself and not to be a drain on the Thessalonians' meagre resources was evidence that he was not out to line his own pockets. Instead, like a good father, he encouraged, comforted and exhorted the Thessalonian Christians. The final picture is that of a *herald* (2:13–16) who announces God's message, and does not make up his own message. He is to say what God says, neither more nor less.

These four images show how the balance between the gospel and the church operates in the Christian ministry. Christian ministers, as stewards and heralds, are servants of the gospel, and, at the same time, as mothers and fathers, servants of the people. How these two are to be kept in balance was memorably stated by W. E. Sangster, a Methodist minister. When he took up his first pastoral charge, near the beginning of the twentieth century, he reminded the congregation that, while he was their servant, the Lord Jesus – and not they – was his Master.

In 4:1–12, Paul deals with *Christian behaviour*, or how the church must live out the gospel. The key idea in this section is that Christians should be obviously different from non-Christians (4:3a). That is the main emphasis in the Bible's teaching about sanctification. Rather than living to please ourselves and others, we are to please God (4:1). Our behaviour is to be determined, not by our own desires and instincts, nor by the attitudes of the people around us, but by the authoritative teaching of the Scriptures (4:2). Rather than being out of control, we are to be self-controlled. Paul highlights the area of sexual morality as illustrating Christian self-control (4:3–8). In Paul's world, as in ours, homosexual and lesbian encounters, and sexual liaisons both before and outside marriage, were common and allowed. But everything Paul writes about this subject shows heterosexual marriage to be the only God-given context for sexual relations. He also teaches that honour, and not selfish personal gratification, is the God-given style for sexual relations within heterosexual marriage. Then, rather than using and exploiting each other, we are to love each other (4:9–10). Finally, rather than being lazy and adopting our culture's 'money-for-nothing' mindset, we are to work hard and honestly for our money (4:11–12).

In the penultimate section of the letter, Paul speaks about *Christian hope* (4:13–5:11). The gospel should inspire us with hope in the face of death. Some Thessalonian Christians feared that their dead relatives might be at some disadvantage or even miss out completely when Jesus returned. So Paul explained the certainty of the resurrection of Christians (4:14). Christians grieve because – like everyone else – they are affected by death's severing of relationships. But Christians grieve in a context of hope, and this rests firmly on the rock-solid historical fact of Jesus' bodily resurrection. We will rise just as surely as he rose, and share in his victory over death. Paul brings the Thessalonian Christians further reassurance by reminding them of the events surrounding the Lord's return (4:15–17). The same Jesus who was born, lived, died, and rose again will come from heaven. When he does, those Christians who have already died will rise from the dead first. They will be joined by Christians who are still alive, and together all will go out to meet the Lord. The picture is taken from Psalm 24:7–10, where the inhabitants of a city run out to welcome home their conquering king and his army, and then escort them with great joy and celebration back into the city. So the Lord's people will go out to meet him when he returns in all the splendour of his power and glory, and then they will come back to earth with him as he sets up his judgment throne. They will not disappear quietly off into heaven but remain with the Lord for ever. Inexplicably some use this passage to teach a 'secret rapture', in which the church will be secretly spirited away to heaven while non-Christians are left behind. This idea of a secret rapture bristles with problems. Not least is the fact that there is nothing secret about any of the events that take place in connection with Jesus' return as outlined in 4:15–17.

The gospel will also bring stability in the light of Christ's return (5:1–11). Teaching on the Second Coming always seems to lead to speculation about its timing. Paul warns that it will be unexpected, like a house-breaker, and inevitable, like labour at the end of a pregnancy. Instead of being curious about the chronology of the Second Coming, we should be ready, living in a godly way, remaining wide awake, so that we are not taken by surprise.

In the final section, in a series of short exhortations, Paul deals with *Christian community life* (5:12–28), and how a gospel church should function. Within the church there is a God-established authority structure, and he calls on men to fill these positions of leadership. Christians are to respect those in authority because of their hard work (5:12–13). They are to care for other members of the fellowship (5:14–15). By doing so, they will embody God's love in an attractive way. There is also to be order in worship (5:16–22), so that it is characterized by joy, prayer and attentive listening to God's Word.

This is the kind of interaction Paul envisages between the gospel and the church. The gospel creates the church, and the gospel, rather than the latest fads and trends, is to shape and define the church's beliefs, behaviour, structures and life. This is why the gospel must be rightly understood, and why it must be right at the centre of church life.

53

2 *Thessalonians*

This letter is obviously the sequel to 1 Thessalonians. It was written by Paul (1:1) from Corinth (*Acts* 18:5), probably in AD 50, to the Christians in the northern Greek city of Thessalonica who not long before had received 1 Thessalonians.

THE PURPOSE OF 2 THESSALONIANS

The reason Paul wrote another letter to the Thessalonians so hot on the heels of the first is that, in the few short months since he wrote, significant things had happened to which he needed to respond. Three groups of people were having an unsettling effect on the Thessalonian Christians. The first group were *persecutors* outside the church. In the short time between the two letters, Paul learned that the persecution faced by the Thessalonian Christians had worsened. So he wrote to bring encouragement to those undergoing it. The comfort he brought was centred on the return of the Lord Jesus (1:3–12).

The second group were *rumour-mongers* within the church who were passing on teaching, allegedly from Paul, to the effect that the Lord had already returned. Paul tackles this error head on, explaining that certain events must happen before that tremendous event can take place (2:1–17). The prophecy, report or letter, supposedly from Paul, was false, and not from God. As Christians we are not to be gullible and think that everything that claims to be from God is actually from him. Satan can disguise himself as an angel of light, quote the Bible, and even perform miracles. How then can we know whether someone who claims to speak from God is genuine? Paul expected everything to be judged against the standard of apostolic teaching (2:5). If it was in line with apostolic teaching, it was to be accepted and obeyed (2:15). If not, it was to be rejected. The final group were *idlers* within the church who were not working but scrounging from other Christians. Paul has some sharp words for them (3:6–15).

THE STRUCTURE OF 2 THESSALONIANS

After a brief introduction (1:1–2), the structure of the letter is determined by Paul's response to each of the three groups just mentioned.

He begins by addressing the persecution the church was facing, and writes about *the revelation of the Lord Jesus* (1:3–12). The Thessalonian Christians were under continuing pressure simply because of their loyalty to the Lord and the gospel (1:3). But even though they had only been Christians for a short time, they were persevering and refusing to give up (1:4). What keeps Christians loyal to the Lord in such challenging circumstances? It is the hope that one day justice will be done, and be seen to be done. Paul reminds the Thessalonians that the day is coming when God will punish those who persecute his people and bring relief to the persecuted (1:6–7a). This will take place when the Lord Jesus is revealed (1:7b). The Minor Prophets had announced that, one day, God would intervene in history to punish his people's enemies and rescue his people. They called it 'The Day of the Lord', and Paul applies this concept to Jesus' return. When he comes back to wind up history, Jesus will bring in judgment upon those who are not his people (1:8–9), and give deliverance to his people (1:10). On that day, all wrongs will be righted and Christians will be seen to be who they really are – God's children.

In writing about the prophet Zechariah we mentioned that Christian living has an 'already, but not yet' shape to it. We are already heirs of heaven, but we have not yet entered into our inheritance. Great swathes of the contemporary church marginalize the Bible's 'already, but not yet' principle, claiming with swaggering self-confidence that Christians can and should experience the blessings of heaven right now. If Christians do not experience total fulfilment, total happiness, ecstatic worship, an absence of pain, sickness, and temptation – then there is something seriously wrong with their Christian lives. But when these things fail to happen, these Christians, who are poorly taught and led astray, are disillusioned and confused. They do not realize that their pain, illness, disappointments, tears, frustration, and ordinariness are meant to cause them to look forward to heaven where these things will have passed away and where everything will be joy and light.

The emphasis in this section is on Jesus' glory. The idea is repeated again and again. The apostle uses the term 'apocalypse', meaning 'unveiling', to describe the Lord's coming. As when the curtains are pulled back on a sunny morning and the sunlight streams in, so, when the veil is torn away, will the Lord be seen in all his awesome splendour. Then everyone will grasp exactly who the Lord Jesus is, so fulfilling Isaiah 40:5. The Lord will also be glorified in his people (1:10). Christians will be glorified when he returns because, when we see him, we will be changed to be like him (1 John 3:2). But there will be a double glorification: 'By transforming us into his own image, [Jesus] himself will be seen, admired and adored in us.'[1] We must not have a man-centred view of heaven as simply a place where we will enjoy all the benefits of salvation in their fulness. The essence of heaven will be our preoccupation for all eternity with the Lord and his glory.

Paul goes on to remind us that the Lord Jesus will exclude from his glory all who have rejected him (1:8–9). Those who do not turn from their sin and place their trust exclusively in Christ will be punished with exclusion from his glorious presence for all eternity in hell. Some who claim to hold to what the Bible teaches find this doctrine too hard to stomach. They want to dilute what Paul says, claiming that the word 'destruction' (1:9) could imply that those who refuse to believe in the Lord Jesus will at some stage experience annihilation. However, there is no biblical data to support this idea. In spite of the ridicule we will have to suffer, we have no choice but to fall into line behind Jesus and his apostles who taught hell to be a real place of everlasting punishment. Meanwhile, Jesus must begin to be glorified in us (1:12). In the light of his return, Christians are to live in a certain way. We are to prepare for the day when he will be glorified by beginning to glorify him now in the way we live (1:11).

[1] John Stott, *The Message of Thessalonians* (Leicester: Inter-Varsity Press, 1991), p. 152.

This is what kept the Thessalonian Christians going in the face of stiff opposition. They looked forward to the day when Jesus would return. On that day, justice would be done, all wrongs would be righted, and all evil would be punished. They would be saved and rescued. Christ would be glorified, and they would go to share in his glory.

Paul then moves on to deal with the false teaching being circulated by writing about *the rebellion of Antichrist* (2:1–12). The rumour being circulated was that Jesus had already returned. But Paul reminds them that that could not happen until certain things had first come to pass. Specifically, Paul states that Jesus will not come back until a certain event, the Great Rebellion, has taken place, and a certain person, Antichrist, has appeared (2:3).

The Bible teaches two truths about the Second Coming that we need to hold together. Jesus' return will be unexpected (*1 Thess.* 5:2–3). But before he comes back, certain things must happen. Apart from what is mentioned here, the good news about Jesus will spread worldwide (*Matt.* 24:14) and ethnic Israel's rejection of her Messiah will come to an end and large numbers of Jewish people be converted (*Rom.* 11:25–29). The two strands of thought counterbalance each other, and we need to hold both if we are to remain biblical.

What Paul says about the Great Rebellion and Antichrist's appearance is probably less than our sinful curiosity would like, though what Paul tells us is all we need to know to live as Christians (*Deut.* 29:29). However, he does make certain things clear. One of these concerns the leader of the Great Rebellion (2:3b–5). He will be against any authority other than his own, and against God and his rule, demanding obedience and worship for himself. Totalitarianism, not anarchy, is what he stands for. Who is he? Many candidates, some more plausible than others, have been put forward down the years. So far, the simple answer is that we do not know who he is, since the person Paul is referring to has not yet appeared on the scene of history. But when he does, we will know for sure, because the verb related to the noun 'apocalypse', used of Jesus' second appearing, is also used of him in 2:3. Just as, when Jesus is revealed, everyone will know, so when Antichrist is revealed, all God's people will recognize him for who he is.

We are also informed of the nature of the Great Rebellion (2:6–8). The word Paul uses to describe the Great Rebellion (*apostasia*, 2:3) is used in the Septuagint, the Greek translation of the Old Testament, to describe Israel's spiritual and moral defection from God. This will be a time of widespread falling away from God and truth. But something is holding the Great Rebellion back (2:6–7). Some have suggested this means the Holy Spirit and the church, and others the preaching of the gospel, but most think it means the power of the state and good government. Human government is based on the creation ordinances which God established before the Fall and so they are universal in all humanity. These include the inviolability of life, the sanctity of marriage, the importance of the family, the right to property, and the need to maintain justice. When these are openly destroyed, then we are in the Great Rebellion.

Paul also speaks of the dynamics of the Great Rebellion (2:9–12). The driving force will be Antichrist. He will perform counterfeit miracles (2:9), using them to deceive the masses, so that they will naïvely follow him as he aggressively propagates error (2:11). But his rebellion will be mercifully short, and Jesus will come and destroy him (2:8). This will not be a long war of attrition, but victory will come quickly and decisively.

There are many different interpretations of history today. Some see it as a series of meaningless, unconnected, random events. Others look on history as circular, so that there is no real beginning or end. The Bible views history as linear, with a starting point and an end point. In this section, Paul has been giving us an overview of history from the Bible's perspective. It is a drama of three acts. The first act is a time of restraint when lawlessness is held in check. During this period, Christ's kingdom makes great advances as both Jews and Gentiles become his followers. The second act is a time of rebellion when the restraint of law is removed and Antichrist is revealed. Satan's kingdom will make a final attempt to gain the upper hand and exert itself with frantic ferocity. The final act of the unfolding drama of history is a time of retribution when Jesus returns, defeats Antichrist, winds up history, and judges the living and the dead.

In the final section of the letter, Paul turns his attention to the idlers and their destabilizing effects by reminding the Thessalonians of *the responsibility of Christians* (2:13–3:15). Although Paul has been concentrating on the future, his teaching about the Second Coming has practical implications for life in the present. One of the greatest social reformers in British history was Anthony Ashley Cooper, the seventh Earl of Shaftesbury. Against huge odds, he drove through Parliament social reforms that we take for granted today such as limits on the hours people can work, protection of women and children in factories, and the humane treatment of the insane. What kept Lord Shaftesbury going? It was the thought of the Lord's return. His favourite Bible verse was Revelation 22:20, and towards the end of his life he said, 'I do not think that in the last forty years I have lived one conscious hour that was not influenced by the thought of our Lord's return.' God probably will not call on us to be great social reformers like Lord Shaftesbury, but he does call on us to live in a certain way in the here and now in the light of Jesus' return.

In the light of Christ's return, we should *stand firm* (2:15). Others may follow lies and worship idols, but we are to press on in following the truth and worshipping the Lord Jesus. The key to standing firm in hard times is prayer. This is why 1 and 2 Thessalonians are full of prayers uttered by Paul on behalf of the Thessalonian Christians (for example, 2:16–17). Again, if the Lord is coming back, we should *spread the Word* (3:1–5). Evangelism will be a high priority for those who look forward to his coming. And if Jesus is coming back, we should *work hard* (3:6–15). Paul is not thinking here of specifically Christian service but of ordinary work, which some among the Thessalonian Christians were avoiding. Nor does he mean those who cannot work because of advancing age or ill health, or who cannot find employment due to the economic situation, but those who refuse to work. They probably tried to justify their conduct by appealing to the fact that the Lord was coming soon, or perhaps they considered work beneath them, being free men, not slaves. Paul has some strong words for people like this (3:10, 12). They are to work and earn their own bread, in order to support their families and give to those in genuine need.

The apostle rounds off the letter with a conclusion in which he commends the Thessalonian Christians to God and his peace and grace (3:16-18).

THE CHALLENGE OF 2 THESSALONIANS

It is very easy to miss the challenge of this letter. Both 1 and 2 Thessalonians are highly significant in relation to the Bible's teaching on the Second Coming, but it would be a serious mistake to imagine that that great event is the *only* concern of these letters. When we read what Paul writes – specially what he says about the Great Rebellion and Antichrist – questions crowd into our minds, and it is easy to get sidetracked into fanciful and idle speculation about the Lord's return and miss the point of the letter. Its main thrust is *how to live for the Lord and be loyal to him in a hard situation.* The Lord himself gives us practical instructions about how to do this through his authorized apostolic spokesman, and we must give heed to these and obey them. Paul's teaching about the Lord's return is meant to give us the motivation to do so, and must always be seen in that context.

In Luke 18:8, Jesus asks the question. 'When the Son of Man comes, will he find faith on the earth?' When he returns, will he find us busy doing what he told us to do? Will we be standing firm, loyal to the truth and to him? Or will He find us seduced by error and giving our worship to other things and people? Will we be spreading the Word, or will he find us silent? Will we be getting on with the ordinary business of living for him in our daily circumstances, or will he find us being disruptive? This is the challenge of 2 Thessalonians, not speculation about when the Great Rebellion will occur, or who the Antichrist will be.

54

1 Timothy

We come now to a distinct sub-section of the New Testament, historically known as 'The Pastoral Epistles' – 1 and 2 Timothy and Titus. They are called this because they are addressed to individuals with pastoral oversight of churches and discuss issues of doctrine, life and leadership. Paul was aware that his life was coming to its end (2 *Tim*. 4:6–8). In fact, 'his approaching death looms behind all three . . . letters.'[1] So he gave instructions to Timothy and Titus, his two most trusted associates, concerning how the church was to function when he was gone.

THE RECIPIENT OF 1 TIMOTHY

Paul wrote four letters to individuals, the three 'pastoral epistles' and Philemon. Timothy, the recipient of the first of these, was from Lystra in the Roman province of Galatia, now south-central Turkey. He was converted during Paul's first missionary journey (*Acts* 13–14), and this is why Paul often refers to Timothy as his spiritual 'son' (1:2, 18). He was raised in a spiritually-divided home. Eunice, his mother, was Jewish and had become a Christian, while his father was Greek and does not appear to have been a Christian (*Acts* 16:1; 2 *Tim*. 1:5).

When Paul returned to Lystra, Timothy had made such strides as a Christian that Paul took him with him on his journey. Over time, Timothy progressed from being Paul's apprentice (*Phil*. 2:22) to being a co-worker and colleague (*Rom*. 16:21) and one of his most trusted associates. He often acted as a special assistant to Paul. For example, when Paul was forced to leave Berea, he left Timothy behind to

---

[1] John R. W. Stott, *The Message of 1 Timothy and Titus*, (Leicester: Inter-Varsity Press, 1996), p. 122.

consolidate the work there and in Thessalonica (*Acts* 17:14; 1 *Thess.* 3:2). Paul also sent Timothy to Corinth to find out what was happening there (1 *Cor.* 4:17; 16:10). When Paul could not go somewhere in person, for whatever reason, he often sent Timothy as his representative, and Timothy was acting in this role when Paul wrote 1 Timothy.

THE PURPOSE OF 1 TIMOTHY

While Paul was in Macedonia (northern Greece) on a mission trip, he left Timothy in Ephesus to sort out some problems in that church (1:3). Paul knew how tricky this assignment would be, so he wrote to help and encourage Timothy. He was concerned that Christians should believe distinctive truths and behave in a distinctive way (3:14–16). Timothy was to convey Paul's concerns to the church and seek to bring their belief and behaviour into line with Paul's instructions.

THE STRUCTURE OF 1 TIMOTHY

The letter begins with a standard *introduction* (1:1–2), in which Paul underlines his apostleship (1:1) and Timothy's role as Paul's authorized representative (1:2a). If Timothy was challenged in the Ephesian church, he would be able to reply, 'I am not giving you my own personal opinions but speaking as Paul's authorized representative.' If Paul's right to tell them how to behave and what to believe was challenged, Timothy would be able to remind them that Paul himself was not giving his own ideas but writing as the Lord Jesus' authorized apostle.

Paul then writes about the *challenge* facing Timothy (1:3–20), which was to counter the false teaching that was corrupting the Ephesian church (1:3b). These false teachers were within the church, and probably elders. When he took his leave of the elders of the Ephesian church, Paul warned them that some of their own number would arise and teach error, so creating confusion in the church (*Acts* 20:29–30). This seems to have come true already. The ringleader appears to have been a man called Hymenaeus (1:20), mentioned twice in the Pastoral Letters (1:20; 2 *Tim.* 2:17). In those references, his name is always put first, suggesting that he was the ringleader. He is always referred to in a negative way, indicating that he was teaching heresy. Timothy was to command Hymenaeus and his associates to cease spreading error. In the light of some of the firm things Paul says about the younger widows in the Ephesian church (5:11–15; 2 *Tim.* 3:6–7), it seems possible that Hymenaeus and his followers were gaining a hearing among these women and using their homes as a base from which to spread their falsehoods.

The false teaching was in fact very weak (1:4a). It seems to have consisted of a mixture of Jewish and Greek ideas that sounded impressive on the surface. When analysed, however, it amounted to nothing more than far-fetched superstition. Moreover, it was spiritually useless (1:4b-6), and even morally damaging (1:7–10a), in that it misused God's law, the true function of which is to curb sin and lead to Christ (*Gal.* 3:24).

The worst feature of the false teaching was that it led away from 'the sound doctrine that conforms to the glorious gospel' (1:10b-11). When Paul wrote the Pastoral Letters there was a growing consensus in the church as to what constituted accepted Christian doctrine. These letters are strewn with references to 'the faith', 'doctrine', 'the gospel', 'the truth' 'teaching' and 'instruction'. There are no statements of doctrine as such, but there are five 'trustworthy sayings', three of which are found in 1 Timothy (1:15; 3:1; 4:9), and two quotations which may be from early hymns or creedal statements (3:16; 2 *Tim.* 2:11–13). In contrast to the false teaching of Hymenaeus and his followers, the truth is intellectually robust, spiritually effective and morally transforming, and Paul gives his own experience as proof of the gospel's power (1:12–17). Timothy's task was to counter the false teaching, not just by exposing its inherent weakness, but also by promoting the life-transforming power of the true apostolic gospel.

Normally when there was a problem in a church, Paul wrote to the church as a whole, sending a letter which was to be read out to the whole congregation. But this may have been impossible in this case, because of the strong influence of Hymenaeus and his associates. So Paul made sure his apostolic voice was heard by writing to Timothy, his representative, and telling him what he was to say to the church. The core of the letter is therefore *instructions* (2:1–6:10) to the church about how it was to behave, and to Timothy concerning the conduct of his ministry in Ephesus.

Paul places a high premium on the place of public worship in the life of the congregation, so he begins his instructions with directions about what is to happen when the church meets together for worship. Since Paul begins with this, we must ask ourselves whether we value public worship as highly as Paul did. His specific instructions concern prayer (2:1–7), the conduct of men and women (2:8–9), what women should do and not do in public worship (2:9; 11–14), and what women should be primarily concerned about (2:9a; 10; 15). The principle underlying all Paul's specifics is that worship should be characterized by prayer and harmony. There should be a focus on God and on being inwardly transformed. When people come into church ostentatiously dressed, or in all the latest styles, they are saying, 'Look at me!' But the focus should be on God, not on us. For this reason Paul wants us to be taken up with listening to God's Word, taught by those with a divine calling, not on one another and outward appearances.

Normally the spiritual health of a congregation cannot rise above that of its leaders. This was certainly true in Ephesus: the congregation was in difficulty because of the poor quality of its leaders. This is why Paul spends time dealing with the congregation's leadership and with different kinds of leader (3:1–4:16). There are overseers or elders (3:1–7) – in the New Testament the two terms seem to mean the same. Within the eldership, there are ruling elders and elders who teach as well as rule (5:17). In many churches, ruling elders are called simply 'elders', while the term 'minister' is reserved for elders who also teach. On another level, below the elders, there are also deacons and deaconesses who care for practical needs (3:8–13). The task of teaching and ruling elders is to teach God's Word, give spiritual leadership to the congregation, promote discipleship, exercise discipline, and provide spiritual counsel.

Paul also deals with the qualifications for leadership. Both types of eldership are open only to males (2:12–14). The reason for this is neither cultural nor limited to the situation of the time in Ephesus, but goes back to the creation and how God established male/female relationships before the Fall. The creation pattern is that leadership with its teaching and ruling responsibilities is always male. Redemption does not overturn the created order; in fact, it strengthens and restores it to its original intent and beauty. The diaconate is open to both men and women. However, not all men can be elders and not all men and women can be deacons. Certain criteria, based on character, have to be met. Leadership in the church is more about what leaders *are* rather than what they *can do*. It is this that sets Christian leadership apart from secular leadership. It is not those with the greatest ability and skills who should be in positions of Christian leadership, but those who are most godly.

Another contentious issue in Ephesus was the acceptance of leadership. Hymenaeus and his friends would not be eager to accept Timothy's authority, and Timothy's age was also against him (4:12). He was to gain acceptance for his leadership, not by being dictatorial or insisting on his position, but by living a godly, Christlike life (4:7–8, 11–12, 16), in a way which could function as an example to others. It is the quality of a leader's life that secures acceptance for his leadership.

Paul explains how various groups in the church are to be treated (5:1–6:2). Everyone is to be treated with respect (5:1–2). Widows who are in genuine need and who are behaving appropriately are to be supported (5:3–16). There was no welfare system in Paul's day, and widows were in a very uncertain situation. Some were not behaving appropriately (5:6, 13), and they were to be brought into line. Younger widows were encouraged to remarry. They would then be independent of church support and be free to carry out their God-given calling (5:14; 2:15). Elders were to be honoured (5:17–20), and slaves were to work hard and not to provoke their masters (6:1–2).

Definite instructions are given about the congregation's priorities (6:3–10). Hymenaeus and his followers were giving the gospel a bad name by seeking to make money by their false teaching (6:3–5). Paul therefore issues a warning about making money our priority. Drawing on Job 1:21, Paul reminds us that we brought nothing into the world and will take nothing out of it. Echoing Mark 4:18–19, he reminds us that many people have experienced spiritual disaster through making the pursuit of wealth their priority. Godliness is to be our main priority. Then we will gain something far more beneficial and lasting than wealth (6:6).

Paul's final *counsel* to Timothy concerns the conduct of his ministry (6:11–21). He is to pursue godliness (6:11) with relentless tenacity. He is to fight for the truth (6:12). There are matters worth fighting for, and one of them is the truth of the gospel. If we lose the truth, we have nothing left, and will ourselves be lost. When the truth of the gospel is at stake, if we abandon it and fail to fight for it, we deserve to be shot as deserters! He is to take a stand for what is right (6:13–16), following and being strengthened by the Lord's example. Like a Yeoman Warder ('Beefeater') at the Tower of London, watching over the Crown Jewels, Timothy is to guard the gospel (6:20), not allowing anyone to tamper with something so priceless. This was a daunting task, and to someone with Timothy's timid personality it must have seemed beyond his power. But Paul's last word is a reminder of the grace of God that will help him (6:21b).

THE CHRIST OF 1 TIMOTHY

In some well-known statements, 1 Timothy presents us with a wonderful picture of who the Lord Jesus is. He is the one who came into the world to save sinners (1:15). If he saved Paul, he can save anyone. He is the only Saviour (2:5–6), because, in the dispute between God and men, the perfect mediator has to be able to represent both parties perfectly. Only Jesus is perfectly God and perfectly man: two natures in one person. Therefore he is the one mediator and the only Saviour. This is one of the areas in which we will have to fight increasingly for the truth of the gospel in our pluralistic society. There is only one Saviour, and if people do not believe in the Lord Jesus alone, no matter how good and nice they are, and no matter how devoutly they adhere to their own religions, they will be lost forever. Jesus is also the universal Saviour (4:9–10). The false teachers in Ephesus seemed to be restricting salvation to a small elite, but Paul reminds us that God's salvation is offered freely to all, irrespective of who they are or what they have done or failed to do.

However the dominant picture of Jesus in 1 Timothy is that he is king of the church, ruling his people through his Word. How did this Word come to the church? In Paul's time, during the period when the apostles were still alive, it was heard through his authorized apostles. Since that time and down to today, it is heard through the faithful teaching of the apostolic message. Here is the chain of command: the Lord Jesus, the king, by his Spirit, taught the apostles (*John* 14:26), who taught people like Timothy (*2 Tim.* 3:14), who taught other qualified teachers (*2 Tim.* 2:2). 'The true apostolic succession is a continuity not of order but of doctrine, namely the teaching of the apostles handed on from generation to generation. And what makes this doctrinal succession possible is that the teaching of the apostles was written down and has now been bequeathed to us in the New Testament.'[1] The church is not a democracy, in which every citizen has the right to say what should happen, but it is a theocracy, ruled by King Jesus, whose authoritative voice is heard today in the faithful preaching of the Bible, his supreme and final Word to us.

[1] *Ibid.*, p. 12.

55

2 Timothy

Although 2 Timothy comes before Titus and Philemon in the New Testament it was, in fact, written after them. It was Paul's last letter, written near the end of his life (4:6) from prison in Rome (1:8, 16–17). Paul was probably executed during the persecution of Christians instigated by the Emperor Nero. For Nero, the Christians were convenient scapegoats, on whom he could lay the blame for all the economic, social and political problems that flared up in the Empire during his disastrous reign. Nero was killed in 68, so it is reasonable to assume that 2 Timothy was written in either 66 or 67.

Paul wrote 2 Timothy for two reasons. There was a personal and short-term reason. He wanted Timothy to visit him in prison in Rome before his death, and to bring along some clothes, books, and scrolls which would make prison life more bearable (4:9, 13, 21). Although we do not know for certain, many believe that this was Paul's second imprisonment, and that the journeys which are implied in the Pastoral Letters and Philemon took place between his release and his re-arrest. He was awaiting his full trial, but he was not expecting to be set free; death appeared inevitable (4:6).

But the second reason is kingdom-focused and long-term. He is about to die and he wants the kingdom to advance after his departure, so he instructs Timothy to remain faithful and to take steps to ensure that the truth is passed on to others, who will in turn pass it on to yet others (2:1–2). As in a relay race, Timothy is to take the baton of the gospel from Paul and to run with it as strongly as he can. Then he is to hand it on to qualified men, who will run with it before passing it on to their successors. Thus the long-term future of the kingdom will be secure. This is why Paul writes with such passion. Just reading this letter aloud is a very moving experience, because it is an emotional document. One commentator said that he could not read 2 Timothy 'without finding something like a mist gathering in the eyes'.[1] All his Christian life, Paul has been passionate about the advance of God's Kingdom and the glory of Christ. That is why he has been prepared to suffer and sacrifice so much (2:8–10). And this was his passion right to the end of his life. With great solemnity he commands Timothy to make sure that he holds firmly to the truth and ensures that it is passed on down the generations. In this way God's kingdom will continue to advance and the Lord continue to be glorified.

THE STRUCTURE OF 2 TIMOTHY

Paul's *introduction* (1:1–7) is much more than a standard introduction to a letter from an older man to a younger. Paul is aware that what he will ask Timothy to do is very difficult, and that Timothy's timid personality will make it even more challenging. So Paul reminds Timothy of all the things he has in his favour. There was Timothy's family background (1:5). Lois, his grandmother, and Eunice, his mother, were Christians, and he could rely on their prayers and support. Then there was Timothy's friendship with Paul. Paul had trained him and was also praying for him. There was also the gift Timothy had received (1:6). Paul recognized that God had given Timothy certain spiritual gifts, in spite of his retiring personality, which would enable him to serve God effectively. Paul tells Timothy to use these, letting them burst into life in God's service. Most significantly there is the Holy Spirit's help (1:7). Timothy is encouraged to rely on the Holy Spirit for strength. Ultimately this would be the crucial factor in determining success or failure in his mission.

After the expanded introduction, Paul gives Timothy instructions about what he is to do with the gospel (1:14; 2:2; 3:13–14; 4:1–2). These directives give the letter its shape. In the first place, Timothy is to *guard the gospel* (1:8–18). Paul uses two expressions to describe the gospel in

---

[1] Handley C. G. Moule, *The Second Epistle to Timothy*, (Religious Tract Society, 1905), p. 16.

this section, the first being 'the pattern of sound teaching' (1:13). This expression confirms the existence of a growing consensus among Christians as to the content of the gospel. 2 Timothy contains the fourth of the five 'Trustworthy Sayings' found in the Pastoral Letters (2:11–13). The way this is formatted in modern versions reflects the belief that it was an early hymn or creedal statement. The Greek word for 'sound' means 'health giving'. Timothy is to keep to this pattern, following it, modelling his life on it and not straying from it. The second expression is 'the good deposit' (1:14), for the gospel is something incalculably valuable that has been entrusted to us by God. Timothy is to guard it, making sure that it is not tampered with or altered in any way.

Timothy is to do this all the more tenaciously in the light of what was happening around him. There was state persecution of the church (1:8, 12a), making it extremely dangerous to be a Christian. Prominent men like Demas (4:10), had turned back. Then there was desertion from inside the church (1:15). Hymenaeus and his allies had refused to obey Paul's instructions through Timothy, and continued to spread error in the church. Prominent Christians like Phygelus and Hermogenes had gone along with the error. The truth was being damaged and distorted. Timothy must make sure he mounts a strong guard over the gospel.

The second instruction Paul gives is to *pass on the gospel* (2:1–26). Others might see persecution and defection from the truth as excuses to keep their heads down and to delay carrying out their responsibilities, but Timothy was to see these things as all the more reason to pass on the gospel to others (2:2). In this section, Paul gives six pictures of the gospel minister – the sort of man who can be trusted with the truth and relied on to pass it on to others uncontaminated.

The gospel minister is to be like *a loyal soldier* – totally focused on the cause in spite of the fact that he knows this will mean hardship (2:3–4). Loyalty, a total focus on the cause and hardship are all things that come with the territory for a soldier. The gospel minister is to be like *an athlete who obeys the rules* (2:5). Today there are strict rules about not taking performance-enhancing drugs, and any who do are stripped of their medals. God has set out in his Word, not only the work he wants done, but also the methods to be used in doing his work.

The gospel minister should always comply with the rules and do God's work in God's way. The gospel minister is to be like *a hardworking farmer* (2:6). Particularly in the days before mechanized agriculture, the harder the farmer worked the more prosperous he generally was. If a gospel minister wants to see people converted and maturing in their faith, then he has to work hard. The gospel minister is to be like *an unashamed workman* (2:14–19). The crucial factor in determining whether or not a gospel minister need be ashamed of his work is how he treats God's Word (2:15). A good workman understands and interprets the Bible accurately and correctly, and then passes it on to others simply, clearly and passionately. The gospel minister is to be like *a clean utensil* (2:20–22). If a gospel minister is to be useful to God, he has to be clean (2:21). That is why Paul tells Timothy to go after holiness (2:22). Perhaps Robert Murray M'Cheyne was thinking about these verses when he wrote these challenging words to a friend who was about to be ordained as a gospel minister: 'It is not great talents God blesses so much as great likeness to Jesus.' The gospel minister is to be *the Lord's servant* (2:23–26), the main characteristic of whose life is his gentleness (2:24–25a).

Underlying all these metaphors is the idea of self-discipline. Multitudes of things demand the minister's attention, and multitudes of people are ready to tell him what he should be doing. To be focused on pleasing the Lord calls for self-discipline, and involves saying the word that is hardest to say – 'No!' When things are slow, hard, and apparently going nowhere in God's service, it is tempting to jump on the latest bandwagon and adopt non-biblical fads. It takes a great deal of self-discipline to keep on doing God's work in God's way, knowing that this will not bring him the instant success he might like and others demand. Because ministers have no-one checking up on them, self-discipline is needed to work hard and not drift into lazy ways.

Sermon preparation is hard work, taking time and effort. It takes self-discipline not to cut corners and just throw anything together. If ministers are to be unashamed workmen, they need to get to grips with the Bible text, give the sermon a structure and shape, choose helpful words in which to state the truth, find relevant illustrations to illuminate the truth, and, as if all that was not hard enough, engage in the labour of praying over the sermon.

Today people do not usually connect being good at one's job and character. I do not stop to ask whether the engineer who built the bridge I travel over every day was an upright family man who was kind to old ladies. I only ask if he was good at his job, so that the bridge will not fall into the river. It is so easy for the church to take up this outlook and think that effectiveness in God's work has to do with methods. Ministers who insist on linking effectiveness and character usually suffer the ultimate humiliation in our society of being labelled 'unsuccessful'. It takes huge self-discipline to be gentle in a society which applauds the idea of might being right, and in a church which rewards those who shout the loudest or complain the most vocally. Throughout this section, Paul is showing Timothy that, if he is to be a good minister who passes on the truth to others so that the gospel advances, he needs to take himself firmly in hand.

Then Timothy is reminded to *continue in the gospel* (3:1–17). Paul was completely open with him about the context in which his work would be done (3:1). Notice that Paul describes the time in which he was writing as 'the last days'. In the Bible, this phrase does not mean the time immediately before the Second Coming, but the time since the Lord's first coming (*Acts* 2:14–17; *Heb.* 1:1–2). Paul was living in the last days, and so are we. They will be characterized by a focus on self (3:2a); an obsession with materialism (3:2a); a moral collapse in society (3:2b–4a); an obsession with pleasure and entertainment (3:4b); and a lack of power in the church, allowing leaders to peddle their error unchecked and exploit people for their own ends (3:5–9).

Timothy was not to be swept away by this landslide but to stand firm against it by continuing to hold on to the gospel (3:14a). He is to do so for two reasons. Firstly, he knows that he learned the gospel from Paul (3:14b), and that Paul bears all the hallmarks of a genuine apostle, especially that of suffering for the gospel (3:10–12). Secondly, and more importantly, he has experienced the power of the gospel in his own life. In 3:15–17, Paul reminds Timothy of this. The Bible is God's Word because it is entirely from him (3:16a). Through the Holy Spirit's influence, the Bible is able to bring about conversions (3:15); to change people's thinking, as it teaches and corrects; to transform behaviour, as it rebukes and trains in righteousness (3:16b); and to equip men for God's service (3:17). Because he knows the truth and has experienced the power of the gospel, Timothy is to continue in it and not be overwhelmed by all that is happening around him.

So far, much of what Paul has told Timothy to do concerns defending the gospel. But Paul knows that the best form of defence is attack, so he calls on Timothy to go on the offensive and *proclaim the gospel* (4:1–8). Timothy is to speak what God has spoken in his Word.

Timothy's preaching is to be *urgent* (4:2). The gospel is a life-or-death message. Eternal destinies are at stake. 'You cannot break men's hearts by jesting with them, or telling them a smooth tale, or by speaking flowery words. Men will not cast away their dearest pleasures upon a drowsy request of one who seems not to mean what he speaks, or to care much whether his request be granted' (Richard Baxter, *The Reformed Pastor*, p. 145). He was to be consistent in his proclamation (4:2). There are times when ministers love to preach and there are times when that is the last thing they want to do. No matter how he feels, Timothy is consistently and constantly to proclaim God's Word, seizing every opportunity to do so. He is also to be *relevant* (4:2). Timothy is to take account of where people are spiritually. Some will be broken and needing to be healed. The word 'correct' (4:2) is used in Greek medical manuals of setting a broken limb so that it heals properly. Some will have fallen into sin and need to be rebuked. Some will have fears and doubts and need to be encouraged.

He is to be *patient* in proclamation (4:2). Proclaiming is a long-haul activity. It is like sowing seed: seed does not germinate and grow instantly. And he will need great patience, in the light of how people will react to a Bible-preaching ministry (4:3–4). They will only want to listen to preachers who say what they want to hear and who say nice things about them. They do not want to hear an explanation and application of the Bible, but want to be entertained with stories. Timothy is to be patient when this happens. He is not to lose his nerve and take up the latest craze but patiently do what he has been taught to do

(4:5). He is to be *intelligent* as he preaches (4:2). The preaching ministry is a teaching ministry, because the way to people's hearts, according to the Bible, is not through their emotions and feelings but through their minds. Finally, Timothy is to be aware of how great a *responsibility* it is to preach. This is why Paul begins his instruction to Timothy to proclaim the gospel in a very solemn way (4:1). Timothy is to realize that one day he will answer to God for how he has conducted his ministry. Paul knows that he is reaching the end of his ministry, and he wants Timothy to be able to say the kind of things he is able to say (4:7–8) when he comes to the end of his.

Tucked away among Paul's *final personal remarks* about his circumstances (4:9–22) are two phrases which sum up his life (4:18b, 22b). Paul's Christian life was dominated by a passion for proclaiming God's grace so that glory might be brought to the Lord for ever.

THE RELEVANCE OF 2 TIMOTHY

At the risk of being melodramatic, these are dark days for Bible-believing Christians. Not that there is open persecution of Christians by the state in most Western countries; and some leading politicians in the United Kingdom and the United States claim to be Christians; but it is becoming increasingly uncomfortable for Christians to operate in the public arena. The low-level opposition to Christians that exists in many places will become more openly hostile as we refuse to accept society's pluralistic and politically-correct agenda. The last 150 years have also witnessed, from within the church itself, a concerted attack on all the major truths of the Bible. People from within the professing church have not only questioned but have almost fallen over themselves to reject great biblical truths such as God's sovereignty, Jesus' deity, the Bible's authority, inerrancy and sufficiency, justification by grace alone through faith alone in Christ alone, Jesus' uniqueness as the only way to God, and the penal substitutionary nature of his death. This rejection of Bible truth within the church has led, not just to people who claim to be Christians believing anything and everything, but to a collapse of right behaviour in the professing church. When it comes to matters like human sexuality, attitudes to money and possessions, the conduct of business, work, and family life, there is often little or no difference between Christians and non-Christians. Social pundits are predicting the inevitable disappearance of Christianity in its Western European guise, if things go on in the way they are going at present.

What are we to do? We are to look at what Paul says to Timothy, because 2 Timothy was written in a similar situation. The state persecution and the widespread defection from the truth that existed when Paul wrote 2 Timothy led one commentator to write, 'Christianity ... trembled, humanly speaking, on the verge of annihilation.'[1] We are not to go with the flow and give in to all the latest trends. We are to guard the gospel and continue in it. No-one finds this easy, but just as Timothy was promised the help and grace of Christ, so are we (1:7; 2:1; 4:17, 4:22). We are not to be afraid. Even if we have to suffer for the gospel, we know that our suffering is a sign that we are genuine Christians for godliness and suffering are inseparable (2:19; 3:12). And even if we have to face death for our loyalty to Jesus, we know that death is not the end because he, our Saviour, has defeated death (1:9–10; 2:11–12; 4:6–8). However, we are not to retreat into a bunker and shut the door. We are to go on the attack and proclaim the gospel. As we do so, we have confidence in the Bible's sufficiency (3:15–17). Without any props, add-ons, or gimmicks, God's Word has the power, in itself, to save sinners, to transform lives, and to equip Christians for active service.

[1] *Ibid.*, p. 18.

56
Titus

The time when the Pastoral Letters were written was crucial to the continued advance of the gospel. Paul was about to be removed by death (*2 Tim.* 4:6). He recognized that he must pass the truth of the gospel on to others. They in their turn would pass it on to still others. The picture, as we have seen, is that of a relay race (*2 Tim.* 2:1–2).

Titus is very similar in many ways to 1 Timothy. The problems Titus faced in Crete were very similar to those Timothy faced in Ephesus. The two letters were probably written at roughly the same time, around AD 63, when Paul was in Nicopolis (3:12) on Macedonia's east coast.

TITUS AND HIS MISSION

All we know about Titus we learn from Paul's letters. He is not mentioned in Acts. The first time we meet him is during the first major theological controversy to engulf the Early Church. This revolved around the issue of whether or not Gentiles had to submit to the rite of circumcision –virtually becoming Jews – in order to be true Christians. Paul asserted strongly that salvation was received by faith alone, and, in Galatians 2:1–4, he referred to Titus to prove his case. Titus was a Greek who was converted through Paul. This is why Paul calls him 'my true son' in 1:4. But Titus was not compelled to be circumcised, proving that non-Jews could be genuine Christians without having to become Jews first. About this time, Titus seems to have become one of Paul's trusted travelling companions.

From what Paul says about him in various letters, it seems that Titus became Paul's problem-solver. An example of this was the important role he played in healing the rift between Paul and the church in Corinth. When the Corinthian Christians rejected Paul's authority, Titus was sent with a letter in which Paul rebuked the Corinthians for their sinful behaviour. What was in the letter and Titus' gracious demeanour seem to have worked together to restore fellowship betwen Paul and the Corinthians (*2 Cor.* 7:13–16). Then Paul entrusted Titus with a second mission to Corinth. Titus was given the delicate task of persuading the non-Jewish Corinthian church to support Paul's collection for the poorer Jewish churches in Judea (*2 Cor.* 8:6, 16–17, 23–24).

In the letter addressed to him, Titus is still solving problems among the Christians of the island of Crete (1:5a). His mission is to establish sound belief and right behaviour among them. This is illustrated in 1:1, where Paul links 'the knowledge of the truth' with 'godliness'. The words for 'sound' and 'soundness' occur five times in the letter (1:9, 13; 2:1, 2, 2:8), and the phrase 'what is good' appears seven times (1:8; 2:3, 7, 14; 3:1, 8, 14). The similarity between Titus' mission and Timothy's in Ephesus accounts for the resemblances between the two letters.

THE STRUCTURE OF TITUS

In the *introduction* (1:1–4), Paul's words to Titus go well beyond a conventional opening in that Paul sets out the main theme of the letter – the unbreakable connection between belief and behaviour. The apostolic gospel concerning the grace of God in Christ is the great determining and motivating factor in what we think, do and say (1:1b–3).

The first issue Paul deals with is *the church's leadership* (1:5–16). The most fundamental matter Titus must deal with is to make sure that the church has good leaders. That is why straightening things out and appointing elders are mentioned in the same breath (1:5). These things are inseparable, because no church can rise above its leaders.

Paul spells out what kind of elders Titus is to appoint. The elder has to have an obvious Christian spirituality. The umbrella term Paul uses is that he must be 'blameless'. He says this twice (1:6, 7). Paul cannot possibly mean that he must be perfect: that would exclude everyone! It is a legal term which means that, if he was put on trial for a crime, the weight of evidence would acquit him. Today we would probably say he must have 'integrity'. This great overriding aspect of the elder's character is to be clear to all. But even here Paul does not let us define what blamelessness is as we wish: he tells us what it means. He explains the concept negatively (1:7), mentioning a list of defects that an elder must not have. But he also sets out the positive side (1:8), showing what commendable qualities elders should consistently display. Added to these is the characteristic of faithfulness, for the elder is to be 'the husband of but one wife' (1:6). Great efforts have been made to unpack the meaning of this phrase, but essentially the point being made is that an elder must be a man of conspicuous faithfulness to his wife, completely free from sexual misconduct.

Although he concentrates on what an elder *is*, Paul also says that an elder must be able to *do* certain things. He must have the kind of abilities that are seen in the way he runs his home and organizes his family's life (1:6). In that context, he will show if he has the skills of decision making, delegation, encouraging others to work together in a common cause, and disciplining others in love. He must also have communication skills, a clear understanding of the gospel, the ability to teach the truth, and the knowledge to refute those who teach error (1:9).

Having explained what the church's leaders should be like in 1:5–9, Paul shows why they must be like this in 1:10–16. The first reason is that there are many unruly people in the church (1:10a, 12, 16b). The Cretans had a bad reputation in this regard. Whoever took on a leadership role in the church in Crete needed to be able to deal with people who could be disruptive and hard to handle. The second reason is the presence of false teachers (1:10a, 11, 13–16a) who had to be silenced because they were ruining people's lives (1:11). Just as 'the knowledge of the truth . . . leads to godliness' (1:1), so false teaching leads to wrong behaviour. It must therefore be challenged and refuted, but the gospel must also be promoted.

Having started with the church's leadership, Paul extends his remarks to focus on *the church's lifestyle* (2:1–15). Once right beliefs have been re-established in the church, Titus is to teach them the kind of behaviour that is in accordance with this right belief (2:1). The pattern here is the same as in the previous section: Paul first explains the 'what', and then explains the 'why'.

Titus is not to allow Christian behaviour to be a free-for-all. There are certain ways in which Christians should behave, and this behaviour prevents the gospel being brought into disrepute (2:5b). It also promotes the gospel, making it attractive and appealing to others (2:10b). Titus is to explain this right behaviour to the various groups in the Christian community in Crete – the older men (2:2), the older women (2:3), the young women (2:4–5), the young men (2:6–8) and slaves (2:9–10). Not everyone will be happy with what Titus teaches. It will rule out a more 'flexible' approach to Christian behaviour, but Titus is not to be deterred. He is to teach these things clearly and courageously (2:15).

In 2:11–14, Paul gives the reason for all he had just said. It is all related to God's salvation in the Lord Jesus. Paul speaks of the two appearings of the Lord. The first is the past event mentioned in 2:11, when he appeared on the scene of history to be born, live, die, rise again and ascend to his Father's throne. The second appearing is the future event mentioned in 2:13, when the Lord will appear again on the stage of time to wind up history, judge the living and the dead, and take his people home to heaven. As a result of the first appearing, we were set free from sin's destructive control over our lives (2:14a) and cleansed from the guilt of our sin (2:14b). The language Paul uses in 2:14 echoes that of the Old Testament sacrificial system in which people were redeemed and their guilt removed by means of a sacrifice. When the Lord appears a second and final time, our salvation will be complete because we will be free from the very presence of sin forever.

Both appearings impact the way Christians live now. Being set free from sin's guilt and destructive control enables us to say 'No' to ungodliness and worldly passions (2:12a). The hope of Christ's second appearing promotes holy and godly living until he comes (2:12b). Paul is reminding us that Christian living is not following a set of rules but living out the implications of our salvation. The better our grasp of salvation, the better equipped we will be to live out its implications. Once again we see the unbreakable connection between belief and behaviour.

Paul now turns to looks outwards as he highlights *the church's witness* (3:1–8). In 2:1–16, he spoke of doing good within the church. Now in 3:1–2, he deals with doing good in secular society. It is striking how unspectacular his description is. It is not about mounting campaigns and protests; just getting on with our lives in an unassuming way (3:1–2). That is how the church makes a difference in society.

Paul explains why we should live in this way, and once again it all has to do with God's salvation. The description of unconverted people is true not only of the anti-social and disruptive Cretans but of all men in their natural state. But then something amazing happened to them: the triune God saved them. The source of their salvation was the Father's kindness, love and mercy (3:4–5a). It was achieved by the justifying grace of Jesus Christ our Saviour on the cross (3:6b–7a). And it was made real in the Cretans' experience by the Holy Spirit's activity (3:5b). As a result of the work of Father, Son and Holy Spirit they had become something they were not before. They are therefore to be what they have now become, and live out what God has done in and for them.

Paul finishes his letter to Titus with personal words of encouragement and instruction (3:9–15).

The Message of Titus

Like all the Pastoral Letters, Titus reminds us of *the kingship of Christ over the church*. The Lord rules through the apostolic Word. From his earliest to his latest letters, Paul is very conscious of the apostolic authority committed to him. To question, modify or reject the apostles' teaching is really the same as questioning, modifying or rejecting the teaching of the Lord Jesus Christ. We are to do what the apostles say because in doing so we are fulfilling what the Lord wants. At the end of the day, pleasing him is the only thing that really matters.

Titus also reminds us of *the grace of Christ in the church*. For such a short letter, Titus has a great deal to say about grace. It highlights our need for grace, because we are rebels against God. Contrary to popular opinion, we are not good people, but bad people (3:3). If God were to condemn us to hell for all eternity, no one could accuse him of unfairness. But in his grace, he gave us what we did not deserve and saved us (3:4–5a). God demonstrated his grace by taking our human nature and coming in the person of his Son. While his birth was a display of God's grace (2:11), the supreme demonstration of grace was his death as our substitute, bearing our condemnation, punishment and curse (2:14a). As a result of what he did, our lives are radically transformed. We are set free from sin's control (2:14a), cleansed from sin's guilt (2:14b), given a new life (3:5b), and provided with a righteous standing before God and his justice (3:7a).

But as a result we are to live in a way that is in line with the radical transformation his grace has brought about in us. We are to be what we are, 'eager to do what is good' (2:14b), and 'devote[d] . . . to doing what is good' (3:8b). And our motivation in this is also God's grace. This is clear from the structure of Titus, especially in the second and third chapters. Paul does not just tell us *what* to do: he also tells us *why* we should do so, and the 'why' always has to do with God's grace (2:11; 3:4). We do not begin by grace, and then try to continue by our own efforts. It is grace that motivates and empowers us every day of our Christian lives.

The message of Titus is very clear: it is the unbreakable connection between belief and behaviour, with the apostolic gospel concerning God's grace in Christ as the great determining and motivating factor in all we think, do, and say.

57

Philemon

Paul wrote thirteen letters which the Holy Spirit has preserved for us in the New Testament, nine to churches and four to individuals. Philemon is the shortest of all, containing only 355 Greek words, and its size explains why it is the last of Paul's letters in the New Testament. There are many links between Philemon and Colossians. Philemon himself was one of the leading figures in the church at Colosse. The church met in his house (2). The letter was also written at the same time as Colossians, around AD 60, when Paul was under house arrest in Rome. There he wrote Philippians, Ephesians, Colossians and Philemon – known as 'The Prison Letters'.

THE MESSAGE OF PHILEMON

The theme of the letter is forgiveness for a wrong done. To understand this we must look at Paul, the *writer* of the letter, Philemon, the *recipient* of the letter, and Onesimus, the *subject* of the letter.

If we look at them in reverse order, we meet *Onesimus, the man who needed forgiveness*. We can reconstruct his story from what Paul writes. The first part concerns Onesimus the fugitive. In New Testament times, there were huge numbers of slaves – perhaps as many as one in every five or six people was a slave. They were right at the bottom of the social order and were reckoned the property of their owners. Onesimus was one of Philemon's household slaves (16), and, for reasons we are not told, he ran off to Rome. Running away was a crime punishable by crucifixion and many recaptured slaves were crucified by their masters as a deterrent to others. But if that was not enough, Onesimus seems also to have stolen some property from Philemon. Paul may be alluding to this in verse 18.

Part two of the story concerns Onesimus the convert. God had better plans for Onesimus than a life on the run, for while in Rome, in a way we are not told, he met Paul, whom God used to bring him to faith in Christ. Paul twice refers to Onesimus as 'my son' (verse 10), meaning he had been used to bring him to the Lord. After his conversion, Onesimus became very dear to Paul. In verse 12, Paul says something very striking: 'I am sending him back to you, sending my very heart' (ESV). Then in verse 16, Paul says Onesimus is 'very dear' to him. Sadly some people profess conversion to get themselves out of a mess, and then, when the crisis is over, they go back to their old ways, showing that their profession was false. But Paul was convinced this was not the case with Onesimus. He brings this out using a play on words in verse 11. Onesimus' name means 'useful', but, as far as Philemon was concerned, he was the very opposite. But now, because he has become a new man in Christ, Onesimus *is* useful. The complete change in him proves that his conversion is real.

Part three is the return of Onesimus. Becoming a Christian would not make the mess he had made of his life just vanish as if nothing had happened. There were human consequences of his sin that could only be sorted out by going back to Colosse and to Philemon. In one sense, Paul *had* to send Onesimus back to Philemon. Harbouring a runaway slave was a crime. But Onesimus himself needed to return to seek Philemon's forgiveness. The relationship between them needed to be restored, especially now that they were both Christians. But in addition Onesimus needed to return to make restitution. He seems to have stolen from Philemon, and he had also robbed Philemon of his labour. Conversion does not free us from the human consequences of our sins. Ultimately God has dealt with our offences. But we must do everything in our power to right the wrongs we have done to human beings. Can you imagine the scene as Onesimus turns up at Philemon's house with nothing but a letter from Paul in his hand and perhaps Tychicus at his side for moral support? He deserves punishment. He needs forgiveness.

The recipient of the letter is *Philemon, the man in a position to show forgiveness.* What Paul was asking of Philemon was no small thing. He was to welcome Onesimus back (17) in the same way he would welcome Paul himself. He was also to send the bill for Onesimus' debt to Paul (18). Paul did not say to Philemon, 'That is all in the past. Just forgive and forget.' There were real issues of restitution that needed to be dealt with, and Paul wants Philemon to transfer the debt to his account.

It would not be easy to welcome back into his house a man who had stolen from him and then abandoned him. Could he be trusted? Will Philemon have to count the silverware every day? And was not Paul's request to charge the debt to him just another way of saying, 'Philemon, write off the debt'? In Philemon's culture, forgiving Onesimus would have been a sign of weakness. His neighbours would be horrified. They would see such leniency as a green light to other slaves to follow Onesimus' example, and it might encourage Onesimus to minimize the seriousness of what he had done. The pressure from his culture to bring the full rigour of Roman law down upon Onesimus would have been huge.

But despite all this, it was Philemon's Christian responsibility to forgive Onesimus. He was a leader in the Colossian church. It met in his house (2). His actions had to provide a positive example to the other Christians. Besides, forgiving Onesimus would be spiritually beneficial to Philemon. He would understand more clearly what God had done for him. Look at what Paul says to him in verse 6. Paul is not talking here about speaking to non-Christians about Jesus; he is talking about expressing Christian forgiveness to another Christian. When he forgave Onesimus, who owed him everything and deserved only punishment, Philemon would see more clearly how God had acted towards him. Under Roman law, as a master, Philemon had the right to punish Onesimus, but Paul was calling on him to set aside his rights. The Lord Jesus is the supreme example of someone setting aside his rights in order to forgive. He is the eternal Son of God, equal in power and glory with the Father and the Spirit, but he set aside his rights and in overwhelming grace, kindness and love, came to earth, taking on true humanity in order to die on the cross to secure our forgiveness. Paul is calling on Philemon to be a Christian, to follow Christ's example, to walk as he walked and, in doing so, to become more like him.

The other main player is, of course, *Paul, the man who encouraged forgiveness*. Paul's great desire to see Philemon and Onesimus reconciled is striking. He was not afraid to put a church leader like Philemon on the spot and openly challenge him to step outside the norms of his culture in forgiving Onesimus. And he also pushes the boundaries of what we would regard as acceptable in appealing to Philemon to forgive Onesimus. Although in verse 8 he says that he is not going to order Philemon to forgive, Paul comes pretty close to it! He shamelessly appeals to all the favours Philemon owes him. Philemon owed his conversion to Paul (19b). Although he would have loved to have helped Paul when he was in prison, he could not. But Onesimus, Philemon's slave, had done so, thus paying back part of the debt Philemon owed Paul (13). Forgiving Onesimus would see the debt settled. Paul was also willing to make sacrifices to see that reconciliation really took place. Coming to visit Colosse (22) would involve considerable inconvenience and expense.

Did the letter work? Did Philemon forgive Onesimus? Surely the answer is 'Yes'. It is hard to imagine the letter being included in the New Testament if its purpose had failed. In addition there is a mention in a letter of Ignatius, who lived just after the New Testament period, of a bishop named Onesimus in Ephesus. Although we do not know for sure, tradition has it that this is the same man. He had lived up to his name – useful – and become useful, not just to Philemon but to the wider Christian community in the region.

THE CHALLENGE OF PHILEMON

Philemon challenges us *to practise Christian subversion*. Paul's appeal to Philemon simply to forgive Onesimus and take him back, instead of ordering him to give all his slaves their freedom immediately, is seen by some as tacit support for the *status quo*, of which the institution of slavery was very much a part. But we need to look closer. Paul was not propping up the establishment. A frontal assault on slavery was an impossibility. The Roman authorities would have viewed an order to Christians to give slaves their freedom as rebellion. It would have brought social and economic chaos on the Roman Empire. The authorities would have come down hard on the church. Instead Paul chose to subvert the institution of slavery. In Philemon, Paul puts in place the great spiritual principle that would eventually bring slavery down: master and slave were spiritually equal because both belonged to Christ (15–16). Nowhere does the New Testament attack slavery directly. Instead it subverts and undermines it by calling for a change of heart in both masters and slaves.

How do we change the evils in our culture? Philemon tells us that we do so, not by organizing rallies and petitions and holding demonstrations, but by practising Christian subversion. Only when people's hearts are changed will real change come about.

Philemon also challenges us *to practise Christian forgiveness*. Are we like Onesimus, in need of someone's forgiveness? It is not enough to say 'Sorry'. The offended person is not really interested in how we feel. We need to say, 'I was wrong. I have no excuses to make. Please forgive me.' We may also have to make restitution to the person.

Are we like Philemon, with the opportunity to forgive someone? He has done something really bad, but he is repentant and comes asking for our forgiveness. We do not really have any choice: we must forgive him. His sin against us is insignificant compared with our sin against God. What a difference this would make to relationships among Christians!

Are we like Paul, encouraging forgiveness? When we see two Christians at loggerheads, are we prepared to go out of our way to bring about reconciliation? There is something particularly Christlike in seeking to make peace. Jesus was the world's greatest peacemaker. He went out of his way to make peace between God and us. When we encourage forgiveness and seek to bring about reconciliation, we are simply following him.

It may be one of the shortest books in the Bible, but Philemon has a weighty message and challenges us at a deep and practical level about what it means to follow the Lord.

58
Hebrews

During the autumn of 1941 Winston Churchill visited Harrow, his old school, and made a speech in the course of which he said, 'Never give in. Never give in. Never, never, never, never – in nothing, great or small, large or petty – never give in . . .' In some ways this is also the message of Hebrews to Christian believers.

THE WRITER OF HEBREWS

We do not know with any certainty who wrote Hebrews. The style and thought patterns do not seem to be Paul's, and some have suggested Barnabas, Apollos or Timothy as possible authors. But there are some things we can say about the writer. Though Hebrews 2:3 seems to suggest he was not an apostle, he must have been closely associated with the apostles or his book would not have been included in the New Testament canon. We know he was closely associated with Timothy (13:23). He knew the Old Testament intimately and had thought deeply about the relationship between Christianity and Judaism. But he was not a native of Judea. Greek, not Hebrew, was his first language. He was a Greek-speaking or Hellenistic Jew, writing very polished Greek, and quoting from the Septuagint, the Greek translation of the Old Testament, not from the Hebrew text. He was also an able communicator, organizing his material well and making his points forcefully.

THE RECIPIENTS OF HEBREWS

We are almost as much in the dark about the recipients as about the author, but they seem to have lived in Italy (13:24), probably in Rome. The letter's very distinct Jewish flavour suggests that it was written to ethnically-Jewish people who had been converted to Christianity, hence the title, Hebrews. The writer assumes a good working knowledge of the Old Testament Scriptures and the Old Testament religious system with its priests and sacrifices. The recipients had been Christians for some time, as we can see from the writer's charge that their understanding of the truth ought to be greater, given the time they had been converted (5:12).

They were facing persecution. References to opposition and suffering are found throughout the final chapters (10:32b–34; 11:34b–38; 13:3). Persecution might be their lot either as Christians or as Jews. Nero, the Roman Emperor, made the minority Christian community scapegoats for a disastrous fire, and thousands died between AD 64 and Nero's death in 68. Then in 66 Judea revolted against Roman rule. Nero sent the legions to put down the rebellion. Jerusalem was finally captured in 70. The Temple was destroyed and the sacrifices ceased. All this suggests that Hebrews was probably written between 64 and 70. Persecution of Christians began in 64 and ended in 68 with Nero's death. But the letter cannot have been written after 70, since the author writes about the sacrifices as if they were still taking place.

THE PURPOSE OF HEBREWS

The Hebrew Christians were under pressure to give up following Jesus the Messiah from three different directions. One was the persecution of Christians instigated by Nero. No doubt many of their friends had died grisly deaths, and they were tempted to think that renouncing their Christian faith might be the best survival option. A second source of pressure came from their ethnicity as Jews. The rebellion in Judea had raised Jewish nationalism to fever pitch. Continuing to reject Judaism seemed a betrayal of their national and cultural identity. The temptation to turn back to Judaism arose because nationalism was becoming more important to them than the gospel. The third source of pressure lay in the nature of Christianity. Christians were a small minority within the Roman Empire. Churches were small, compared with the numbers flocking to the Temple in Jerusalem and the synagogues throughout the Roman Empire. Christian worship was very plain and simple compared with Jewish worship at the Temple which was dramatic and appealed to all the senses. In the face of these multiple pressures the writer charges the Hebrews never, never to give up following the Lord Jesus Christ, but rather to persevere to the end in their faith in the one who had endured so much for their salvation.

THE STRUCTURE OF HEBREWS

The book is a mixture of instruction and warning. The writer sets out Jesus' supremacy, showing not only that he is incomparably greater and better than anything in Judaism, but also that he is actually the fulfilment of everything in Judaism. It was the shadow but he is the reality. But he also warns them from numerous Old Testament examples that to go back to Judaism would be a spiritual disaster for them. They would lose everything.

JESUS' SUPERIORITY: The writer relentlessly drives home the message that the Son of God is incomparably better than anything in Judaism. He is *superior to the prophets* (1:1–2). God had truly spoken through the Old Testament prophets, but their message was not his final word because they spoke of one who was still to come, and also because their prophecies could not contain the full picture. Now, in Christ, God's message to us is final. He is the one who was to come, and he gives us the full picture. There is nothing more to come. Jesus is also *superior to angels* (1:3–14). In the Judaism of that time there was an emphasis on, almost an obsession with, angels. They were viewed as intermediaries between God and men. In this section Jesus is presented as God's true and only mediator because he is superior to the angels. He is the Son (1:5), while angels are servants (1:7); he is eternal (1:8), while they are created; and he is the one who is to be worshipped (1:13), while the angels are to worship him (1:6). And the Son is *superior to angels despite his humiliation* (2:5–18). The writer anticipates a question: How can Jesus be superior if he was a man and died? Do not his humanity and death nullify his supremacy? The author directs us to Psalm 8:4–6. Jesus humbled himself and voluntarily became for a while lower than the angels by taking on real humanity (2:14), but he did so in order to identify himself fully with us in every way (2:17–18), and in order to secure our salvation through his death (2:14–15). This is far more than any angel has ever done. So, even in his humiliation, Jesus is superior to the angels. Jesus is even *superior to Moses* (3:1–6). Along with Abraham and David, Moses was the Jews' great hero. Surely no one can be greater? Yes, just as the person who builds the house is superior to the house itself (3:3). Moses is only a servant – a faithful servant, but a servant nevertheless – while Jesus is the Son (3:5–6a).

As the centrepiece of his encouragement to his readers to remain faithful to Christ the writer shows that he is *superior in his priesthood and sacrifice* (4:14–10:18). On the surface, Judaism's sacrifices and priesthood might seem more exciting and dynamic than Christian worship, but Jesus' sacrifice and priesthood are the fulfilment of all Judaism's ritual. He is also from a better order of priests (7:1–28). Long before Levi, Abraham – Levi's great-grandfather – paid homage to Melchizedek (7:4–10, *Gen.* 14:1–20). Christ's priesthood is eternal (7:3, 23–25).

Jesus mediates a better covenant than Judaism's priests (8:1–13). When the author of Hebrews writes about a new covenant, he means a better one. The old covenant, mediated by the Levitical priests, was from God and was good, as far as it went, but the new covenant, which Jesus mediates, is better than the old. The writer presents three reasons why this is so. Firstly, it is administered by a superior High Priest (8:1–2). Then it is administered from a better place (8:3–5). The Temple sanctuary, from which Judaism's priests administer the old covenant, is not the real thing: it is a copy of the real Temple, which is in heaven. Thirdly, the new covenant is based on better promises (8:6–13). The new covenant promises what every human being needs: forgiveness for the past (8:12; see *Jer.* 31:34b), and power to live for God in the present (8:10–11; see *Jer.* 31:33–34a).

The worship of the tabernacle was only figurative and could not really take away sins (9:1–15), but Christ's sacrifice is real and effective. Its superiority is proved in many ways (9:16–10:18). It is superior because of the nature of his sacrifice. He did not offer up animals, but he offered himself. But it is the finality of the offering that really shows its superiority. Five times in Hebrews, the writer underlines the 'once for all' nature of Jesus' sacrifice (7:7, 9:12, 9:26, 10:2, 10:10). This stands in marked contrast to the continuous nature of the sacrifices in the Temple. Day after day, month after month, and year after year, sacrifices were offered, but animal sacrifices were insufficient. However, Jesus' sacrifice really dealt with sin (9:26, 10:10). The writer states four times that Jesus 'sat down' at God's right hand (1:3, 8:1, 10:12, 12:2). Judaism's priests never sat down because their work was never completed. You only sit down when you have finished what you are doing. Jesus sat down because he had completed his work: his death had dealt radically and effectively with sin.

In all these ways the writer is saying to his readers, 'Look at what you are thinking of going back to and look at what you are thinking of giving up! You are thinking of giving up the superior to go back to the inferior; the reality to go back to the shadows; the effective to go back to what has failed. Surely this cannot be the right path.'

A less dominant but still vital line of reasoning in the writer's positive argument is THE CALL TO KEEP FOLLOWING JESUS. In 11:1–40, we find *an argument to keep going*. It is the 'Roll of Honour' of men and women in the Old Testament who, by faith, remained true to God in spite of great difficulties. The God who enabled these heroes to stand firm in the past will also help his people in the present (12:1). Then, in 12:1–11, we see *the way to keep going*. How do we actually keep going? By a combination of self-discipline and God's discipline. As far as self-discipline is concerned, we keep going by fixing our eyes on Jesus (12:2), who did not give up, even when faced with the prospect of the cross, because there was something huge to be gained by going through the pain, namely, his people's salvation. We are to have the same attitude, to attain heaven and glory. We keep going by throwing off everything that might hinder us, even if the things are not bad in themselves. We keep going by dropping the sin that entangles us, and by running the race with perseverance (12:1), realizing that the Christian life is not a sprint but a long-distance race. As for God's discipline, we keep going through things which God sends into our lives which test our faith. They are often painful, but they are a sign of his love for us (12:5–10). God's discipline is designed for our good (12:11). Finally, in 13:1–17, there is *our duty as we keep going*. Too often Christians can use difficulties

and times of pressure as an excuse not to do what they should do as
Christians. The writer reminds his readers that they are still to show
practical kindness to those in need (13:1–5); to be content (13:4–5); to
be grateful for what God has done for them (13:15); to do good (13:16);
and to be submissive to their leaders (13:17).

Not everything in Hebrews is presented in a positive light. The writer
has some very negative things to say, and we need to take seriously
THE WARNINGS ABOUT TURNING BACK which are scattered among the
more positive parts of the letter. He warns them of traps and dangers.
One trap is *ignoring what God has done in his Son* (2:1–4). Not paying
attention to what the Lord says in his Word causes Christians to drift
away from him (2:1, 3a). Another is *not believing God* (3:7–4:13). Our
hearing of the Word must be more than a mere intellectual exercise
(3:12). We need to love the Word and allow it to move us to obedience.
Our emotions must be stirred and our wills moved. There is also the
trap of *ceasing to grow* (5:11–6:20). The writer laments that, although
they have been Christians for years, they are still immature (5:11–14).
A fourth trap is *not persevering in holiness* (10:19–39). God is deadly
serious about holiness (12:14b) and those who do not pursue it are in
great danger. Finally, they are to make sure that they do not fall into
the trap of *refusing to heed God's warnings* (12:12–29), which are not to
be taken lightly. If we heed warnings from mere mortals because we
know that they are protecting us from physical and temporal danger,
how much more should we heed warnings from God, who is protecting us from spiritual and eternal danger (12:25)?

Some of the warnings in Hebrews are so strong that people imagine
that they teach that Christians can lose their salvation. However, the
Bible, which does not contradict itself, marshals formidable evidence
to show that Christians cannot lose their salvation. This teaching is
known as 'The Perseverance of the Saints'. However, the flip side of this
doctrine is that the saints are people who persevere, and it is this that
the writer of Hebrews is stressing. It is as Christians pay attention to
what the Lord has done, and receive the Word in faith – so that they
grow spiritually and progress in holiness – that they are strengthened
to keep on following the Lord.

THE RELEVANCE OF HEBREWS

We are told today that, in the interests of tolerance and social cohesion, we must treat all religious systems as equal with Christianity. But we cannot, because the Lord Jesus Christ is in a class of his own. He, and not Moses, Mohammed or the Buddha, is God's great and concluding Prophet. God has spoken finally in his Son to show us what he is like, because his Son alone is 'the radiance of God's glory, the exact representation of his being' (1:3). In him God has said all he has to say. He is God's great and final Priest, who offered himself as the decisive sacrifice which dealt effectively with sin. God showed his approval of his Son's work in death by raising him from the dead, something that did not happen to Moses, Mohammed or the Buddha. He is the great and ultimate King who has sat down on heaven's throne beside his Father. One day Moses, Mohammed, the Buddha, and everyone who has ever lived will bow down before him and acknowledge him as King. In our pluralistic society we must be tolerant of others who differ from us and do all we can to promote social cohesion. But we must also state humbly and firmly that Jesus is supreme and that no other religious leader can be compared with him.

Our society is becoming an increasingly hostile place for people who hold to the truth. If we modify the truth and water it down to suit the prevailing philosophies of our society, we will be accepted. But if we stand firm on the gospel, we will find our society an increasingly inhospitable place. What are we to do? Are we to give up following the Christ of the Bible, who is unique, and turn back to adopt a wishy-washy, watered-down version of Christianity which stands for nothing and is not different from what everyone else thinks? Of course not! Here is what we are to do: 'Therefore, since we are surrounded by such a great cloud of witnesses, let us throw off everything that hinders and the sin that so easily entangles, and let us run with perseverance the race marked out for us. Let us fix our eyes on Jesus, the author and perfecter of our faith, who for the joy set before him endured the cross, scorning its shame, and sat down at the right hand of the throne of God. Consider him, who endured such opposition from sinful men, so that you will not grow weary and lose heart' (12:1–3).

59

James

As we come to James we start the last lap of our journey through the Bible. James is the first of a group of letters known as the 'General Letters', or, if you prefer the traditional term, the 'Catholic Epistles'. Apart from the book of Revelation, which stands by itself, the General Letters are the last main section of the Bible. They consist of James, 1 and 2 Peter, 1, 2 and 3 John and Jude, and they are addressed to Christians in general rather than to specific congregations or individuals.

THE WRITER OF JAMES

There was only one James whose name would have been instantly recognized among the first Christians, and that was the half-brother of Jesus (*Mark* 6:3). Before the cross, James had not believed Jesus' claim to be the Son of God (*John* 7:5), but, after the resurrection, he came to see the validity of his claims and placed his trust in him as his Lord and Saviour (2:1). James became the leader of the church based in Jerusalem, and rose to prominence as the chairman of the Council of Jerusalem (see the notes on Acts and on Galatians). His closing address to the Council clinched the argument in favour of salvation by faith alone in Christ alone (*Acts* 15:13–21). An indication that this James was the writer of the letter known as James is that 230 words in this letter are also found in his address to the Council.

THE RECIPIENTS OF JAMES

As leader of the church based in Jerusalem, James had a special interest in Christians from a Jewish background, and, although this letter is written to Christians in general, it has a distinctly Jewish flavour. Christians are described in a distinctive Old Testament way (1:1).

Typically Jewish terms are used throughout the letter. For example, in 2:2, the word translated 'meeting' is actually 'synagogue'. The letter contains references to Old Testament characters, such as Abraham, Isaac, Rahab, Job and Elijah. James assumes that his readers are familiar with these people and their stories.

This Jewish flavour has led to the view that it was written quite early, sometime between 45 and 50, while the church was still in the main Jewish in its outlook. Because of the reference to the recipients being 'scattered among the nations' (1:1), it is thought that James wrote to the Jewish Christians who had to flee Jerusalem because of the persecution that flared up in the aftermath of Stephen's death (*Acts* 8:1) and became refugees as far away as Phoenicia (modern-day Lebanon), Antioch (modern-day Syria) and Cyprus (*Acts* 11:9).

The Style of James

James' style stands firmly in the tradition of the Wisdom Literature of the Old Testament and of the Sermon on the Mount. There are many echoes of Matthew 5–7 in James (compare *Matt.* 7:7 and 1:5; *Matt.* 7:11 and 1:17; *Matt.* 7:23 and 1:22; *Matt.* 5:3 and 2:5; *Matt.* 7:12 and 2:8; *Matt.* 5:7 and 2:13; *Matt.* 7:16 and 3:12; *Matt.* 5:9 and 3:18; *Matt.* 7:1 and 4:11; *Matt.* 6:19 and 5:2.) James is adopting the same style as Jesus did when he preached the Sermon on the Mount, namely that of the Wisdom Literature.

One of the characteristics of Wisdom Literature is the use of parallel statements where the thought of the second line contrasts with that of the first (for example, *Prov.* 16:25). James uses this technique of contrasts throughout. One example is 3:13–18 where he contrasts two kinds of wisdom. Wisdom Literature uses many rhetorical questions, and James' letter abounds with these (2:3–7, 2:14, 2:21, 3:11–12, 3:13, 4:1, 4:5). It is generally accepted that 'James is the New Testament counterpart of the [Old Testament] Wisdom tradition.'[1]

This means that, though there is a structure to his letter, James does not write in the same logical way as Paul does. Paul has a theme, which he develops in a logical linear fashion, moving steadily from A to B to

[1] Gordon D. Fee and Douglas Stuart, *How to Read the Bible Book by Book* (Grand Rapids, Michigan: Zondervan 2002), p. 401.

C. James is totally different. He has themes, but he does not develop them in a linear fashion. He typically adopts a theme and looks at it from various angles. We cannot analyse the structure of James as we would that of a Pauline letter.

The Purpose of James

The idea that James and Paul are at loggerheads is often brought forward by sceptics who want to attack the reliability of the Bible as often as possible. In particular, James 2:24 is used to contradict justification by faith alone. Even some of the Bible's greatest friends, such as Martin Luther, have wondered whether James and Paul are contradicting each other.

But those who think this way have forgotten James' decisive defence of justification by faith alone in Acts 15. We must allow James some basic consistency in his thinking. Objectors have also forgotten James' style of writing. The purpose of Wisdom Literature is not doctrinal but practical. James is not writing about the doctrine of justification. He takes that for granted. He is concerned with how those who have been justified should live – not to explain how we get right with God, but to tell those who are already right with God how to live uprightly.

The Structure of James

James is concerned to dismiss three myths about practical Christian living. The first is that *difficulties are always bad for us.* The instinct for self-preservation looms large within our psyche, so we try to avoid difficulties, seeing them as working against our best interests. But James wants us to revise this assessment. He says something very arresting: difficulties are reasons for joy (1:2). He does not mean we should invite pain, but he assures us that difficulties are the way to maturity for Christians (1:3–4). We see the value of testing in some areas, such as the development of drugs; but in the development of our faith we imagine that the absence of testing is best for us. James shocks us by telling us the exact opposite: difficulties are stepping stones to Christian maturity; the path God takes us along when he wants to improve our faith (1:3–4).

While we are still reeling from what he has just said, James informs us that difficulties are a big spiritual benefit because they force us to depend on God (1:5–8). They shatter our self-confidence and force us to seek God in prayer. We cry, 'I cannot handle this in my own strength. Please help me.' This is why James follows up what he has just said about difficulties producing maturity by speaking of God's generosity in answering prayer (1:5). In his severe kindness, God places us in circumstances in which we must depend on him and cry out to him for help. When we do this, we grow.

James presses on by reminding us that difficulties are passing (1:9–12). When we experience difficulties, it is easy to envy those for whom life is easy, especially if they are non-Christians. We start to feel resentful towards God and convince ourselves that following the Lord is a waste of time. But James reminds us that wealth, security and ease are all temporal and passing (1:11). He calls on us to focus on what is of eternal value (1:12).

James is a realist. He is aware that difficulties are spiritually dangerous times for us (1:13–18). The crucial factor is our reaction to difficulties. If we can see them in terms of the testing of our faith to make it stronger, they are beneficial. But James knows that the devil seeks to exploit our difficulties, making us resentful of God's dealings. The end result of this, if not checked, is departure from God and spiritual death (1:13–15).

James therefore challenges us to reject the received wisdom that difficulties are spiritually bad for us and to adopt God's wisdom which sees them as driving us to depend on God more for what we cannot immediately see.

The second myth James dismisses is that *faith is what I think, or what I feel*. As leader of the Jerusalem church, James had a bird's-eye view of what was going on in the wider church, and two groups of people were causing him concern. One group understood faith to mean simply giving mental assent to the truth. If you believed the right things, all was well. The other group argued that people needed to have an experience of the truth. For them faith consisted essentially in having spiritual experiences. These two types of people are still to be found in the church today.

James argues strongly in 2:14–26, that both viewpoints are wrong. When it comes to true faith, the most important thing is not what we think or how we feel: it is what we do. He has already hinted at this in 1:19–25 where he stated the importance of actually putting God's Word into practice, not merely listening to it (1:22). In 2:14–26, James spells things out clearly by describing three kinds of faith. The first is dead faith (2:14–18). This believes all the right things but is not lived out in actual practice. 'Faith that is not acted out is not faith at all.'[1] The second type is demonic faith (2:19). James tells us that the demons believe the right things: they are totally orthodox. They also have moving experiences associated with the truth. It makes them 'shudder' – a very strong word. But their experience does not cause them to do what is right, namely, to submit in humility to God's rule. The third kind is dynamic faith (2:20–26). James presents Abraham and Rahab as models of this true faith. Both of them believed right things about God. Both of them had moving experiences in connection with what they believed about God. But both of them – and this is the crucial factor – did something: Abraham was prepared to offer up Isaac (2:21) and Rahab protected the spies who had come to spy out Jericho (2:25). They showed their faith by what they did, not simply by what they believed and felt. Their wills were moved, as well as their minds and their emotions.

We are not to measure our faith by what we think or how we feel. Our actions are the measure of whether we have true faith (2:26). Our good works cannot save us, as James had already argued strongly at the Council of Jerusalem. However, our good works show that we have saving faith. James would have endorsed the view that says that we are saved by faith alone, but that the faith that saves us is not alone.

There is one more myth that James wants to see deleted from the way Christians think: the idea that *religion is a private matter*. One hears this frequently, especially from people who do not want to talk about their faith – probably because they have no faith to talk about. It is true that faith is a very personal matter. In fact it has to be personal if it is genuine. But James is constantly emphasizing the point that it is

[1] Mark Dever, *Promises Kept: The Message of the New Testament*, (Wheaton, Illinois: Crossway Books, 2005), p. 433.

anything but private. It is very public, because the reality of our faith is seen in what we do in the public arena. Is not this the point he was hinting at in 1:27 and making so forcefully in 2:14–26?

More specifically, true religion is shown in our dealings with others. This is important because James seems to have been writing to people who had problems relating to each other. Throughout the letter there is evidence of friction. Some were boasting about their future prospects, perhaps in comparison with those of other Christians (4:13–17). They were quick to become angry with each other and quick to use hurtful words (1:19). They were cursing one another (3:9–10). They were slandering one another (4:11–12). They were grumbling about each other (5:9). Rich Christians were demeaning poorer ones (5:1–6). Their meetings showed the horrible signs of favouritism, with the rich receiving preferential treatment (2:1–13). All the ugly signs of disharmony were there.

The superficial reason for this tension is that they could not control their tongues but were constantly stirring up disharmony. This is why James has some strong words to say about the control of the tongue (1:26 and 3:1–12). However, there were more fundamental deep-seated problems. For a start these people were selfish, and James twice exposes this as the cause of their divisions (3:14–16; 4:1–3). Coupled with their selfishness was their pride. They had adopted the proud attitude of the society around them. This is why James accuses them of playing fast and loose in their relationship with God (4:4–7).

However, like the good pastor he was, James did not want to leave his readers wallowing hopelessly in their sin. He explained to them how their divisions could be healed. They were to adopt the biblical pattern of putting off the bad and putting on the good. Instead of pride, they were to humble themselves before God (4:7–10). Instead of selfishness, they were to adopt heavenly wisdom and love peace (3:17–18). This would produce a change in their words. They would now promote harmony and build up good relationships. They would use their tongues to pray for the sick (5:14), confess their sins to one another (5:16a), persist in prayer for each other (5:16b–18), and bring back those who had wandered off from God (5:19–20).

Religion is not a private matter. It is very personal, but it is also very public, showing itself in our life together with other people.

'Although James is sometimes read in contrast to Paul, both James and Paul are, in fact, absolutely together at the crucial point made by James throughout his letter, namely, that the first thing [we do] with [our] faith is to live [it out]'¹ in the details of everyday life. Nothing could be more practical than the issues James highlights – how to react to life's inevitable difficulties, how to live out our faith, and how to relate to those around us.

¹ Fee and Stuart, *How to Read the Bible Book by Book*, p. 401.

60

1 Peter

In spite of the massive contribution Christianity has made to our nation's heritage, our society is rapidly becoming a hostile place to those who want to follow Jesus. How are we to live in a society which, under a smokescreen of tolerance, is becoming increasingly anti-Christian? This letter gives us the answer, because its theme is how to live as a Christian in a hostile world.

The Background to 1 Peter

Before we look at what this letter actually says, let us review the background, an understanding of which is vital to working out why Peter said what he did. Like all the other General Letters, 1 Peter is named after *its author*, and, although sceptics have dismissed the idea that it was written by Peter, the former Galilean fisherman, the evidence for his authorship is still strong, not least from what the letter itself says. For example, in 5:1–4, when he instructs the elders to be shepherds of God's people, surely he is thinking of how, after his resurrection, Jesus restored him and gave him the task of feeding his sheep. Or again, in 5:5–9, when he tells the young men to calm down, to be humble and to be on the lookout for Satan's temptations, surely he is thinking about how hot-headed and proud he used to be and how this led to him to collapse spiritually when he denied Jesus. Peter acknowledges that he received help from Silas in writing the letter (5:12). The phrase can mean that Silas was the courier who brought the letter to its recipients, or that Peter dictated the letter to Silas, who wrote it down, or that Peter asked Silas to read it over before sending it on.

1 Peter was *written from Rome*, because, in 5:13, Peter tells us that, when he put pen to paper, he was 'in Babylon'. He is not referring to

the literal place in what is now Iraq, because, even in Peter's day, it was a ruin. 'Babylon' was code for Rome (*Rev.* 16:19; 17:5; 18:2). In New Testament times, Rome was the great nemesis of the church, just as Babylon was in Old Testament times. If Peter was writing from Rome, this dates his letter in the early 60s because he is thought to have been killed in the persecution of the church instigated by Nero, and this did not happen until after the great fire of Rome, AD 64. The letter was written *to Christians in what is now Turkey*, since Pontus, Galatia, Cappadocia, Asia and Bithynia, the areas where the recipients lived, make up most of modern-day Turkey.

As he writes, Peter *draws heavily on the Old Testament*, with around sixty Old Testament verses or passages quoted or alluded to. Eleven per cent of the letter is made up of nine direct quotations from the Old Testament. There are references to Old Testament characters, such as Sarah and Abraham (3:6) and Noah (3:20–21), and to Old Testament events, such as the Passover (1:18–20). Many of the terms Peter uses have their roots in Old Testament imagery. For example, in 1:4, Peter speaks about our 'inheritance'. When we think of our inheritance, we do so in concrete terms; it is a place called heaven. But, according to its Old Testament roots, inheritance has more to do with a person, God himself, than with a place. In 1:2, Christians are described, once again in very Old Testament terms, as priests, and, according to the Old Testament, the priests' inheritance was not land, because they received none when Canaan was divided up, but God himself (*Num.* 18:20). Peter probably intends us to see the Lord Jesus himself as the inheritance of New Testament priests like us. Hence we look forward to being with the Lord forever in heaven. Again, in 2:4–5, Peter uses the Old Testament imagery of the Temple to describe the church. Again, in 2:9–10, Peter draws on the Old Testament Scriptures to find categories with which to describe the church (*Exod.*19:6; *Deut.* 7:7–8; *Isa.* 43:21; *Hos.* 1:2–2:1). This extensive use of the Old Testament has caused some to think that the people to whom he was writing were from a Jewish background, but that is assuming too much. Paul's letters were also steeped in the Old Testament, but he wrote to Christians who were mainly from a non-Jewish background. By making the Old Testament background so prominent in his letter Peter is saying that, if we want to understand the New Testament properly, we need to see it as the fulfilment of the Old Testament.

1 Peter was written as *a pastoral letter*. The people to whom Peter was writing were facing a severe challenge. They were suffering for their faith. From time to time, what we might call state-sponsored persecution of Christians took place. An example was the systematic persecution of Christians set in motion by Nero from 64 to 68. This persecution claimed the lives of thousands of Christians throughout the Roman Empire, including, according to tradition, Paul and Peter. But Christians also faced low-level, localized persecution, and it was probably this kind of opposition that the people Peter was writing to were facing. He writes a pastoral letter to help them deal with their suffering, and to help them make sense of it.

THE THEMES OF 1 PETER

The main themes of 1 Peter are not hard to identify if we read the text carefully. One of its great themes is *salvation*, because we have references to it both at the beginning and at the end of the letter (1:2; 5:12). The expression 'dear friends', which Peter uses infrequently (2:11; 4:12), marks out places where the theme is *suffering*. If we look for words that are repeated, we will discover that the verb *submit* is used five times (2:13, 18; 3:1, 5; 5:5), indicating that a third theme is submission.

As he develops the theme of *salvation*, Peter is posing the question, 'What has happened to you?' The answer, in a nutshell, is that God has saved them. Peter reminds us that the stream of salvation must be traced to its source in God. This is why Peter begins 1:3–12, a section in which he outlines God's salvation, by giving praise to God (1:3). More specifically, the source is God's grace, and Peter mentions grace seven times in the letter (1:2, 10, 13; 4:10; 5:5, 10, 12). Then Peter draws our attention to the focus of salvation, Jesus Christ, especially his death, which Peter describes in four ways. Jesus' death was a sacrifice that enables us to approach God (1:2). The phrase 'sprinkling by his blood' is taken from Old Testament sacrificial language. Just as the purpose of an Old Testament sacrifice was to make it possible for the worshipper to approach God, so Jesus' death brings us into God's presence. Jesus' death secured our redemption (1:18–19). He is the fulfilment of the Passover lamb, whose death spared the Israelites from the destruction of all the firstborn in Egypt. By his death, the Lord Jesus has set us free from a slavery worse than any in Egypt: our slavery to sin and its tyrannical control over our lives. His death turns away God's anger from us (2:24). In Jesus' death, the wrath of God against us has been exhausted in the Substitute. It is all tied up in the phrase 'on the tree'. Anyone who hung on a tree was dying under God's judgment (*Deut.* 21:23), and, as our Substitute, Jesus died under God's judgment, bearing his wrath. Jesus' death restores friendship between God and us (3:18). Now that the great barrier which separated us from God has been dealt with, we can be reconciled to God. Intimacy, freedom, friendship and reconciliation are all concepts that Peter uses to describe the benefits of salvation. Peter moves on to explain how God's salvation, secured by Jesus' death, becomes real in our lives. We experience that salvation as we are born again (1:23); as we believe in Christ (1:8, 1:21, 2:7); as – in a clear reference to Psalm 34:8 – we taste how good the Lord is (2:3); and as we come to Christ, the living stone (2:4). Finally, Peter writes about the result of salvation, and in particular how it brings us hope. Christians who are suffering need hope, and this idea recurs five times (1:3, 13, 21; 3:5, 15).

We can see that *suffering* is a major theme of 1 Peter from the way the words 'suffer' or 'suffering' recur nine times. Peter is helping these Christians make sense of their present experience. In echoes of Jesus' statement in Matthew 5:11, Peter emphasizes that he is speaking of suffering for being a Christian, not suffering for our faults (2:19–20). He reminds us that suffering strengthens our faith (1:6–7). Just as fire removes the impurities from gold, so suffering purifies our faith, and will bring glory to God when the Lord comes again. If we follow a Saviour who suffered, suffering must be seen as part of our Christian calling (2:18–25). When we suffer unfairly and unjustly, we are to follow the example of non-retaliation that Jesus set us. Suffering gives opportunities for witness (3:8–18), which do not arise if things are going well for us. When we suffer for being Christians and doing what is right, we should not be frightened. Instead we should always be ready to give an answer to anyone who asks the reason for our hope. Suffering gives us the privilege of sharing in Jesus' sufferings (4:12–19), and it is the path to glory (5:10–11). It was the path to glory for the Lord Jesus. Why should it be any different for us? Suffering is not something we like to contemplate, but it is part and parcel of being a Christian in many countries in the world and may yet be in ours. We need to hear Peter's instruction so that if it comes our way, we may be ready.

My parents worked in Africa for ten years, where they stood out as being different from the locals, not just in the colour of their skin but in their lifestyle. Christians are 'strangers in the world' (1:2) and 'aliens' (2:11). We do not really belong here, because we are different from the non-Christians around us (2:9–10). Because we live in a very rights-conscious and rights-assertive culture, one of the ways in which we can show the difference concerns the idea of *submission*. In an increasingly anti-authority society, the Christian lifestyle is to be characterized by submission and proper respect to those in authority (2:13–17). In a workplace environment where workers' rights are being asserted, often so that workers can have more pay and benefits for less productivity, we are to submit to our employers (2:18–25), even when they are not what they should be. In a culture which urges women to be assertive and to stand up aggressively for their rights, Peter calls on wives to submit to their husbands (3:1–6), even to those who are not Christians. The cultivation of inward graces may be the means God uses to bring unbelieving husbands face to face with the transforming power of the gospel. Instead of copying the stereotype of the macho male, husbands are to submit to God's purpose for a husband and love their wives (3:7). Rather than buying into a self-focused and self-serving style of leadership, which is so rife in our world, elders are to submit to God's purpose for them (5:1–4) and to be servant-leaders, copying the Lord Jesus by caring for, serving and being examples to God's people. Younger men might think that they could do things differently or more quickly, but they are not to be impetuous. Instead they are to submit to the church's leadership (5:5–9).

There is nothing extraordinary in the advice Peter gives. But though it is unspectacular, it is precisely how God wants us to behave in difficult times. We are not to get increasingly excited, mounting this protest and that. We are just to get on with living for the Lord, in the way God instructs us to do in his Word.

What will happen if we live out our salvation, even in the context of suffering, by displaying this submissive lifestyle? Glory will be brought to the Lord Jesus (2:12) and his name will not be brought into disrepute (3:16).

61

2 Peter

The Christians to whom Peter wrote were doubly exposed to danger. They were facing an external threat, as a small minority in an increasingly hostile environment. The civil authorities were becoming more intolerant, and the storm clouds of state-sponsored persecution were gathering on the horizon. But they were also facing danger from among their own number. False teachers had infiltrated the church and were undermining the faith of these vulnerable Christians. Peter dealt with the external threat in 1 Peter, and he deals with the internal threat in 2 Peter.

The letter was written shortly before Peter's death (1:14–15), between AD 64 and 66, to the same group of Christians to whom he had written 1 Peter (3:1). Right at the end of the letter he restates its two main themes: false teaching, which will destabilize our Christian lives if we are not on our guard against it (3:17), and Christian growth, which we are to pursue with vigour (3:18).

THE NATURE OF CHRISTIAN GROWTH (1:3–11)

Having prayed that his readers might grow spiritually (1:2), Peter elaborates on several aspects of growth in grace. He explains *the aim of Christian growth* (1:3–4). We are familiar with the saying, 'If you aim at nothing, you will be sure to hit it.' Peter does not want us to live directionless lives, so he tells us to aim at knowing God better, displaying godliness, and keeping ourselves pure, as we reject the standards, values and attitudes of secular society. This is excellent advice, but how can it be done? Peter reminds us of *the resources for Christian growth* (also in 1:3–4). God has given us power. We can never say that it is impossible to be what God wants us to be. And God has also given us promises in his Word. As Christians we have the great twin resources of the Bible and prayer. In the Bible we learn how God wants us to live, and through prayer we obtain the power to live in that way.

But how does Christian growth actually happen? Peter does not leave us in the dark but tells us about *the method of Christian growth* (1:5a). We cannot grow without making the effort. The Greek word translated 'add' comes from the world of Greek theatre, in which it described the actions of a wealthy citizen who footed the bill to make sure that the play went ahead. It carries with it the idea of sparing no expense. The lives of growing Christians are characterized by vigorous activity and strenuous effort. Growing Christians are never lazy Christians.

Peter moves on to write about *the direction of Christian growth* (1:5b–7). In relation to God, we are to display goodness and knowledge; in relation to ourselves, self-control and perseverance; and in relation to others, godliness, brotherly kindness and love.

Why should we make the effort to display these qualities in our lives? In answer to this question, Peter gives us *incentives for Christian growth* (1:8–11). Christian growth makes us effective in our Christian lives (1:8). There is an unbreakable link between our spiritual growth and our effectiveness as Christians (2 *Tim.* 3:16–17). Earlier (p. 393) we noted Robert Murray M'Cheyne's comment, 'It is not great talents God blesses so much as great likeness to Jesus.' Christian growth will show that we understand what the Christian life is all about (1:9). Christians who are not growing are suffering from two problems: spiritual short-sighted-ness, in that they have forgotten what the ultimate aim of the Christian life is, and spiritual amnesia in that they have forgotten the purpose for which they were saved (*Titus* 2:4). However, growing Christians do not suffer from these spiritual diseases. Christian growth will also increase our assurance of salvation (1:10). Although we receive salva-tion from God as a gift (1:1), we know we have received that gift when we display the fruits of salvation. Finally, Christian growth will give us a glorious end to our lives (1:11). Peter's logic is obvious. If we start the Christian life in the right way and continue it in the right way, we will also end it in the right way, receiving a rich welcome into heaven from our Lord and Saviour (*Matt.* 25:34).

THE FOUNDATION FOR CHRISTIAN GROWTH (1:12–21)

We cannot grow as Christians without the help of Scripture, and Peter makes this point by constantly linking the concept of knowledge with that of Christian growth (1:2, 1:5, 1:8, 3:18). But the Bible, and in particular the Bible's trustworthiness, was under attack from false teachers. So in this section of his letter Peter gives reasons to trust the Scriptures and the apostolic testimony to Christ. The Bible is trustworthy because it is *based on historical facts*. Some people think that Bible stories should be prefaced with the phrase, 'Once upon a time . . .' and should be placed in the 'Myths and Fairy Tales' section of the library. 'The Bible might contain truths for living,' they say rather patronisingly, 'but they are not based on historical fact.' But, says Peter, what we have told you is true. We, the apostles, were there and saw for ourselves what happened (1:16a). He gives Jesus' transfiguration as an example of an event he witnessed (1:17–18). He saw with his own eyes Jesus' glory and heard with his own ears the Father's voice. His defence amounts to this: 'We were there!'

The Bible is also trustworthy because *its teaching has been confirmed* (1:19a). When he writes, 'We have the word of the prophets made more certain,' he is obviously making a comparison, but what two things is he comparing? It seems to me he is comparing the 'word of the prophets' as it was given in the past with the self same 'word of the prophets', seen in the light of what has happened. The historical events surrounding Jesus' birth, life, death, resurrection and ascension, of which the apostles were eyewitnesses, have confirmed the trustworthiness of the Scriptures. Certain things were foretold, and they have happened.

Another factor confirming the Bible's trustworthiness is that *it comes from a trustworthy God* (1:20–21). Where did the Bible come from? In one sense, we have to say that men wrote it, for 'men spoke' (1:21). However – and this is the point Peter wants to underline – they wrote under the control of the Holy Spirit, for 'men spoke from God' (1:21). The Holy Spirit so controlled the human authors that they wrote down God's words without error (1:21). The Bible has its origin in God, and not in the fertile imagination of any human being (1:20). If God is trustworthy, then the Bible, which came from him, must be trustworthy. The truth of the Bible, which Francis Schaeffer labelled 'true truth' – that is, what is absolutely and not just relatively true – is the product of a God who cannot lie.

Notice *two asides,* as we might call them, which Peter makes in connection with the Bible. In 3:16, he recognizes Paul's letters as part of what is called the canon of Scripture. Even before all the books of the New Testament were written, Paul's apostolic letters were recognized as being just as divinely inspired as the Old Testament Scriptures: part of the Bible, which came from God. Then, in 1:19, Peter reminds us that, if the Bible is trustworthy, we need to pay attention to it and do what it says.

An Unmasking of False Teachers (2:1–22)

If the trustworthy truth of the Bible plays a strategic role in Christian growth, then the threat of false teaching which takes people away from it should cause Christians concern. It certainly caused Peter concern, and, in a section that is not for the faint-hearted, he launches into what has been called 'a colourful diatribe'[1] in which he unmasks the false teachers. Peter tells us that *false teachers teach false ideas.* This may sound too obvious to state, but it is the criterion by which they can be detected. One of the truths these false teachers denied was the sovereign lordship of Christ (2:1). We are not told exactly how they did this but, whatever their precise teaching was, they downgraded him from his rightful position as sovereign Lord of all. However, Peter does inform us that the basis for their ideas was their own fertile imaginations, rather than the truth of Scripture (2:3a).

Then he explains that *false teachers live false lives.* Peter exposes the way in which these false teachers used religion as an opportunity for immorality – mentioning this in 2:2 where he talks about 'their shameful ways' and then spelling it out in more detail in 2:13–14a. They also exhibited greed, exploiting those who followed their falsehoods and enriching themselves at their expense. He mentions this in 2:3 and then, using the example of Balaam, spells it out in more detail in 2:14b–16.

[1] Dick Lucas and Christopher Green, *The Message of 2 Peter and Jude* (Leicester: Inter-Varsity Press, 1995), p. 17.

Peter highlights the fact that *false teachers make false promises*. They promise the earth but they cannot deliver what they promise (2:17–20). This is why Peter calls their teaching 'destructive' in 2:1. They destroy people's hopes by making promises they cannot possibly keep.

However, he points out that *false teachers will be condemned*. In 2:3–6, Peter gives three examples of God's judgment on sin. If God judged the rebellious angels, the world at the time of Noah, and Sodom and Gomorrah, then there is no escape for such false teachers as these.

But what will happen to Christians when false teachers are at large? Peter reassures us by informing us that *true believers will be kept safe*. In a world in which error and evil prevailed, God protected Noah (2:5), and rescued Lot (2:7–8). When false teaching and sin are rampant, we are not to be afraid. We are to look to God and ask him to fulfil the Lord Jesus' request in John 17:15.

A REBUTTAL OF FALSE TEACHING (3:3–15)

A major biblical truth that the false teachers were challenging was the Second Coming of Christ. They had to challenge this truth if they were to continue to live lives of error and sin. I have to admit that when I was at school I did as little as possible, and the only reason I did as much as I did was that there was an exam at the end of term. Had there been no exam, no judgment day, no day of reckoning, I would have done even less. The thought of being held accountable can keep people's behaviour in check. Remove this accountability and the end result is chaos. To live disobedient lives in which they did and thought as they pleased, the false teachers had to remove the idea of judgment.

The way in which they set about this was to question the reliability of God's promise (3:4). They said, in effect, 'Jesus promised that he would return, but nothing cataclysmic has happened. The world has just gone on in the usual way. Is Jesus' promise as reliable as you say it is?' But Peter points out that, in the first place, they have forgotten their history (3:5–7). God warned of a flood in Noah's time, but nothing seemed to happen. The world went on as usual until, with shocking suddenness, the flood arrived. So it will be when Christ returns. Peter also says that they have forgotten that God is never in a hurry (3:8).

Alluding to Psalm 90:4, Peter reminds us that God's perspective on time is completely different from ours. What appears to us to be a delay is no delay to him. But most significantly, Peter shows that they have forgotten that God is patient (3:9). God is not slow to keep his promise, but he is patient and is allowing time for repentance.

But Peter underlines the fact that the day of the Lord will come. The Lord Jesus' return will bring about the end of history and of the world (3:10). But, like the rest of the Bible, Peter is particularly concerned about the practical effect of these truths on our lives (3:11a). The fact of the Lord's return should not be an occasion for idle speculation but an incentive to right living. As we remember that he will return, we should be living holy and godly lives (3:11b–12b), and so we should be growing spiritually (3:18). In a sense, the letter has come full circle. Peter's first exhortation was about Christian growth (1:5), and so is his last (3:18). By growing spiritually, we will counteract the destabilizing effects of false teaching (3:17). We will also bring glory to God (3:18b), which is where the letter began.

62

1 John

In 1858, the *Austria*, a steamship heading for the United States, caught fire and sank, killing around 400 people. One survivor told how five Christian friends stood trapped with the fire behind them and the ocean in front of them. They agreed that they would jump from the ship together; but before they did so, they prayed, expressing their confidence that in just a few moments they would all meet again in heaven. John's first letter was written so that its readers might enjoy the same humble confidence those men had. From 5:13 we discover that the recipients of this letter were Christians who lacked assurance. The letter was written so that they might know they had eternal life. But before we consider this theme, we must look at other issues surrounding this short letter.

THE WRITER OF 1 JOHN

The writer of 1 John does not identify himself, but the only likely author is John. The connection between 1 John and John's Gospel in terms of vocabulary, sentence structure and ideas is very strong. To take chapter 1 alone, both begin by talking about 'the beginning' (1:1 and *John* 1:1), both stress eyewitness testimony (1:1–2 and *John* 1:7, 15a), both refer to eternal life (1:2 and *John* 1:4), and both affirm that Jesus is the Son of God (1:7 and *John* 1:14, 18).

John had a prominent role in the inner circle of Jesus' disciples along with Peter and his brother James, and there are hints that he had a special place in Jesus' heart. John was also prominent in the early days of the Christian church. With Peter, he had an important role in confirming the success of Philip's mission in Samaria as the gospel began to break out of its Jewish confines (*Acts* 8:14–25). Paul tells us that John was present at the Council of Jerusalem (*Gal.* 2:9). After that, John disappears from the record for a time. But now, right at the end of the New Testament, he reappears as the author of three short letters and the lengthy book of Revelation.

Irenaeus, a leader in the church who lived in the early part of the first century, tells us that John moved to Ephesus and continued to exercise his apostolic ministry there until sometime in the reign of the Roman Emperor Trajan, who ruled from 98 to 117. This would mean that John lived to a very old age, and if he wrote 1 John in Ephesus, it would be one of the last New Testament letters to be written, probably during the decade 85 to 95.

The Background to 1 John

Ephesus was a great trading centre. It was not just a marketplace for goods of all kinds, but also a marketplace for ideas. To it came people, who claimed to be Christian, but also claimed to have special knowledge (*gnosis*) that ordinary Christians did not have and would not understand. Most commentators believe that John was dealing with this early form of Gnosticism in his first letter. The false teachers also maintained the unbiblical idea that matter was inherently evil and massively inferior to knowledge and the spirit.

This false teaching had devastating consequences. It divided the church between the 'spiritual' – those in the know – and the 'unspiritual'. Things became so bad that the 'spiritual' split from the church (2:19), so that they could enjoy their advanced and superior form of spirituality. Even more serious was the way that the false teachers distorted the truth about the person of the Lord Jesus. They denied that he had become a real man (2:22; 4:2–3). Their teaching was that the divine Christ did not really become man; he only seemed to have a body. This view is known as 'docetism', from the Greek word *dokeo*, to seem. They held that the Jesus who was born was not divine. He only became God when the divine Christ united with the earthly Jesus at his baptism. Then, just before his death, the divine Christ withdrew from the earthly Jesus. It is against this background of embryonic Gnosticism that 1 John's emphases make sense.

THE STRUCTURE OF 1 JOHN

John seldom argues a case in a logical and linear way. He writes about his three themes of truth, love and obedience (or holiness), and then he returns to them more than once, looking at them in a different order and from a different angle each time.

After an *introduction* (1:1–2:2), in which John throws down the gauntlet to these false teachers and begins to challenge their ideas, the bulk of the letter is taken up with *three cycles of teaching* (2:3–5:5), in which John elaborates on the themes of truth, love and obedience. The first cycle runs from 2:3–27. In it John focuses on obedience (2:3–6), love (2:7–11) and truth (2:18–27). In the second cycle which runs from 2:28 to 4:6, the same three themes are dealt with in the same order: obedience (2:28–3:10), love (3:11–18) and truth (4:1–6). The third and final cycle of teaching is from 4:7 to 5:5, and the pattern alters slightly as John writes about love (4:7–12), then truth (4:13–21) and finally obedience (4:21–5:5). In a *conclusion* (5:6–21), John reassures his readers that, in spite of all that is being said about them by the false teachers, they are genuine Christians.

The following way of visualizing 1 John has been suggested: 'For myself I have found the image of a spiral staircase . . . helpful. As you climb the central staircase in a stately home, you see the same objects or paintings from a different angle, often with a new appreciation of their beauty. It is rather like that with the great [themes] John is concerned to state and revisit in his letter.'[1]

THE THEMES OF 1 JOHN

The false teachers had a hugely destabilizing effect on the ordinary Christians. As they listened to the false teachers expound what it meant to be 'spiritual' and realized that they did not have this 'knowledge', they began to wonder if they were really Christians at all. And as they listened to what the false teachers had to say about Jesus, they began to wonder if the one in whom they had trusted for their salvation was the real Saviour. John writes to bring the ordinary Christians the assurance

[1] David Jackman, *The Message of John's Letters* (Leicester: Inter-Varsity Press, 1988), p. 18.

that they really are Christians. 'His first concern is not to confound the false teachers . . . but to protect his readers . . . and to establish them in their Christian faith.'¹ So he outlines three types of test that people can apply to their lives to see whether they truly are Christians.

The Moral Test: Do We Obey God's Commands?

John does not fudge the issue: one of the indications that we are Christians is that we do what God says in his Word (2:3). But though he is authoritative, John is not authoritarian. He explains why obedience is the way we show we are Christians, and his explanation centres on who God is.

God is holy. Using the picture of light, John describes God's holiness in a positive and a negative way. Positively God is transparently pure, and negatively he is flawlessly holy with no twilight zones, no darkness, in his character (1:5). In contrast, John uses the picture of darkness to describe those who take a distorted view of sin. People are in darkness when they deny that they are sinful by nature, claiming that they are basically good (1:8). People are also in darkness when they deny that they actually sin, so minimizing sin that it is no longer called 'sin' (1:9). To have this distorted view of sin is to be in darkness, and, in echoes of Habakkuk 1:13, John clearly points out that God, who is light, can have nothing to do with darkness, and that anyone who thinks light and darkness can co-exist is perverse (1:6, 8, 10).

God is also our Father. In 2:28–3:10, John's thinking shifts from the contrast between light and darkness to the contrast between the children of God and the children of the devil. John says some things which have caused many Christians a great deal of anxiety through the years. However, although some of the details of what he writes may be hard to understand, the general thrust of what he is saying is clear. God's children are against what God their Father is against, and God is against sin because it is breaking his law (3:4). God's children will also try to imitate the example of their righteous Father (3:7b).

We know that we are Christians because we obey God's commands, but we also know that we often fail, and so does John. This is why he

¹ John Stott, *The Epistles of John* (Leicester: Inter-Varsity Press, 1964), p. 41.

writes 2:1–2. God's purpose is that we live holy lives. But John is a realist. He is aware that Christians sin. So he points us to Jesus Christ and his death. He tells us that Jesus has died in order to deal with God's anger against our sin and to offer up that sacrifice which brings acceptance with God. When we sin, we are not to try and cover our sin by minimizing it or denying it. Instead we are to bring it out into the open and confess it to God. Then, on the basis of what Jesus has done, God will forgive us (1:9).

The Social Test: Do We Love God's People?

Another indication that we are Christians is that we love God's people (3:14). Once again, John gives reasons for this. With Jesus' words in John 13:34 as his backdrop, John informs us that, if we do not love other Christians, we are disobeying Jesus' express command (2:7; 3:23; 4:21). To love just a few favourite people is to be in open rebellion against the Lord. Also, if we do not love other Christians, we are narrowing the focus of the Saviour's death. Jesus died for the world (2:2; 4:14). In John's thinking, the term 'world' does not mean the planet spinning in space or everyone who has ever lived or ever will live on that planet but those in rebellion against God and his rule. In other words, Jesus died for sinners, and sinners of all shapes and sizes. John is emphasizing the breadth of Jesus' death. We are to love all those for whom Jesus died. If we love only a select few, we are actually narrowing the focus of the Lord's death.

If we do not love other Christians, we are refusing to imitate God our Father. Twice John tells us that God is love (4:8, 16). If we really are his children, we will imitate our Father by loving other Christians in a practical way (3:18) just as he has loved us in a practical way (4:9). If we say that we love God but do not love other Christians, we are frauds (4:20a). If we do not love other Christians, we are displaying spiritual naïvety (4:20b). To claim that we love God, whom we cannot see, and yet not love other Christians, whom we can see, would be laughable, if it were not so serious (3:17). If we do not love other Christians, we are actually showing that we are not Christians. That is how bluntly John puts it (2:9; 3:14b).

The Doctrinal Test: Do We Hold to the Truth about Jesus?

The truth that we are to hold to is that Jesus is God come in human flesh, so that he is fully God and fully man in the same person. Once more John is pretty blunt: if we do not believe this about Jesus, we are not Christians. He puts it negatively (2:22; 4:3) and positively (4:2, 14; 5:1). There is to be no nonsense about Jesus only seeming to be a man, or about the divine Christ coming upon the human Jesus at his baptism and leaving him just before his death. In the incarnation, the eternal Son of God took full humanity into union with himself. The Son became something he had not been until then, and he has never divested himself of our nature, so that, even in heaven, he 'continues to be God and man in two distinct natures and one person forever.'[1]

This is not an in-house argument between competing theological camps. It is absolutely vital to hold that Jesus Christ is God himself come in human flesh because he came to save. He came to be a pro-pitiatory sacrifice for us, to turn aside God's justified anger against us (2:2; 4:10) and to give us eternal life (4:9). He did this by giving up his life for us. In a statement which is a distinct reference back to Genesis 3:15 we are told that he came to overturn the devil's work (3:8). This salvation could only be accomplished by one who was both God and man. The one who saved us had to be God because only God had the power to achieve salvation. But the one who saved us also had to be man because it was human beings who had sinned, who were respon-sible for their sin and who had to make amends for it. This is why John insists so strongly on Jesus' real deity and real humanity. Without both he cannot save.

Many people today find this doctrinal test distasteful. They want to be flexible in what they believe and to have the option of modifying their views. They say, 'It is faith in Jesus that saves and not faith in propositions about Jesus.' But like all sound-bites this has its problems. It is faith in Jesus that saves, but who is he? If people have faith in a Jesus of their own making, they have a salvation of their own making. It is only faith in the Jesus of the Bible that saves. That is why we must have clear, precise views of him.

[1] *The Shorter Catechism*, Q. & A. 21.

If we can humbly affirm that we do obey God's commands, love his people, and hold to the truth about Jesus, even if people say we are not really spiritual or try to make us feel unspiritual, we can be absolutely sure that we are true Christians. Our obedience to God's commands may not be all that it should be. Our love for other Christians may not be as deep as it should be. Our loyalty to the truth may not be as firm as we would like it to be. But if obedience, love and loyalty to the truth are there to some degree, it is enough.

John Newton once said, 'I am not what I ought to be. I am not what I wish to be. I am not what I hope to be. But I can truly say I am not what I once was.' If we can say the same, we have eternal life and are on the path to eternal glory.

63

2 John

Have you heard the prayer, 'Lord, make the sound people loving, and the loving people sound'? The person who uttered it was clearly concerned that some Christians were more interested in truth than in love, while others had swung to the opposite extreme and were more interested in love than in truth. 2 John has a similar concern. John put pen to paper for a second time to show the proper balanced relationship that ought to exist between truth and love.

The Writer of 2 John

Like all the 'General Letters', 2 John is named after its author. There is continuing debate about whether or not John, the last surviving apostle and the author of 1 John, is 'the elder' mentioned in verse 1. But the similarities between the content and vocabulary of 1 John and 2 John point to John being the writer.

The Recipient of 2 John

John was clearly on good terms with the recipient. The thought of visiting her filled him with keen anticipation (12). But who was she? There is debate over this question. It was written to 'the chosen lady and her children' (1), but was there an actual 'lady', or is this a veiled reference to a local congregation? The older commentators tend to go for the individual option and more recent commentators for the corporate option. I believe John was writing to a local congregation. The structure and language of the Greek text, with a mixture of 'you' singular and 'you' plural, point to a metaphorical use of the term 'chosen lady'. So does the fact that this metaphor is used elsewhere in the New Testament for a local congregation (1 Pet. 5:13).

The Backdrop to 2 John

Like 1 John, 2 John was written against the backdrop of emerging Gnosticism. At the time it was written, perhaps as late as the early 90s, the Roman Empire had become infested with all sorts of weird and wonderful religious ideas, many of which came from the East. In the next century, these would develop into what is called 'Gnosticism', but when John wrote, this was only in its embryonic stages. Although its beliefs are hard to pin down, Gnosticism did deny many of the accepted truths of the gospel as taught by the apostles, especially the truth that Jesus Christ was a real man, and it led to divisions between those claiming superior enlightenment and knowledge, and those whom this elite group deemed ignorant and unspiritual.

When John, in verses 5–6, reminds his readers about the importance of Christians loving each other, his words must be seen against the background of the loveless divisions with which incipient Gnosticism was already blighting the church. And when, in verse 7, he writes about those deceivers who said that Jesus Christ did not come as a real human being, it is clear that their error was already infiltrating the church. This teaching was one of the central planks of Gnosticism. It stemmed from the belief that physical matter was essentially evil. The thought of God – pure spirit – contaminating himself by taking on human flesh was abhorrent to these deceived men.

The Message of 2 John

John highlights two priorities: the first is that of *keeping a right balance between truth and love* (1–6). In the best-selling book, *Men Are from Mars, Women Are from Venus*, by John Gray, the main premise is that men are more concerned about problem solving and truth, while women are more concerned about empathy and loving relationships. While this may be a sweeping over-generalization, it does reflect the view of many today that there is little or no connection between truth and love. Love is viewed as merely an emotion, while truth is a reality perceived by the mind. There is no real connection between them. But John highlights four connections between truth and love and shows that the two need to be kept in balance.

Firstly, both truth and love have their source in God. This has already been shown in 1 John. 'God is light' (*1 John* 1:5). Just as the property of light is to shine, so it is characteristic of God to reveal truth. Yet, at the same time, 'God is love' (*1 John* 4:16). Truth and love cannot be divorced because both come from God.

Secondly, truth creates relationships of real love. For many, truth is the biggest barrier to love and unity, but not for John. It is obvious from verse 12 that there was a relationship of love between John and this local congregation. But he tells us that this relationship of love and harmony was created and fostered by a common love of the truth (1a and 2). 'If Christian love is founded upon Christian truth, we shall never increase the love which exists between us by diminishing the truth we hold in common.'[1]

Thirdly, truth defines how love is to be expressed. Is love all we need, as the Beatles used to sing? No. Love is important (5), but we need truth too. Love is expressed in doing what Jesus Christ, who is the truth, says (6a). The idea of walking is mentioned three times in verses 4 and 6. This implies that the Christian life is a road along which we walk. It is the 'Road of Love' (6b), the 'Road of Obedience' (6a) and the 'Road of Truth' (4a). These are not three different roads, but the same road with three different names.Love's activities are to be regulated by obedience to the truth. 'Your love is not blind. Truth should make your love discriminating.'[2]

The fourth connection is that it is love which should provide the motivation for living out the truth. This is what John is getting at in 6a. Jesus' commands are commands of love, and if we love him, we will want to keep his commands. Love for Jesus lies at the centre of our lives of obedience.

How do we keep the right balance between truth and love? First of all, by taking care that our love does not wander outside the limits of truth. The moment the way we express love steps outside the limits of the truth, our love is perverted and quickly degenerates into selfishness. And secondly, by making sure that our love for the truth does not

[1] John Stott, *The Epistles of John* (Leicester: Inter-Varsity Press, 1964), p. 203.
[2] *Ibid*, p. 204.

lose touch with a heart of love. We must have a firm grasp of the truth, but we must hold to the truth in love. 'Your love for others is not to undermine your loyalty to the truth. On the other hand, you must never champion the truth in a harsh or bitter spirit. . . . Christians should be marked equally by love and truth, and you are to avoid the dangerous tendency of extremism, pursuing either at the expense of the other. Your love grows soft if it is not strengthened by truth, and your truth grows hard if it is not softened by love. You need to live according to Scripture, which commands you both to love others in the truth and to hold the truth in love.'[1]

The second priority is that of *resisting error* (7–13). John was planning to visit these people and talk to them face to face (12), but there was one matter which just could not wait. The issue that was burning in John's heart was the threat these Christians faced from false teachers who were travelling from place to place peddling their error. So he warns them of the danger, and then he gives instructions on how to deal with false teachers and their error.

Error is dangerous. It destroys loving Christian fellowship. In verses 1–6, John has shown that truth creates and fosters love. If truth and love are interwoven and inseparable, then error (see verse 7) undermines love and destroys fellowship. Error is against Christ. False teachers are 'anti-Christ'. Their Gnostic ideas misrepresented and dishonoured Christ, and so were against him. Error cuts people off from God (8). When true Christians are seduced by error, they are robbed of their joy, their enjoyment of God's peace, and their fellowship with God, because error strangles spiritual life. Error robs people of salvation (9). John is not saying that true Christians can be lost. What he is saying is that only the real Saviour can bring a real salvation. The problem with error is that it gives people an imaginary Saviour, which means that they have an imaginary salvation. At the end of the day, this cannot save them.

John shows that error must be resisted. In those days, the way ideas were spread was through people travelling from place to place and talking to others. They relied on being given hospitality in someone's home

[1] *Ibid*, pp. 204–5.

and using this as a base from which to spread their message. The way to nip the spread of error in the bud was to refuse to give false teachers hospitality. This is what John tells these Christians to do (10–11).

John shows that error can be resisted, but we must be aware of the possibility of being led astray. When John says to us, 'Watch out' (8a), he is telling us not to presume, either by overestimating ourselves or by underestimating the power of error. We can also guard against error by being clear about what we believe. Before he became a pastor, Stuart Briscoe worked in a bank. His first job was in the section that dealt with counterfeit money. When he asked a more experienced colleague the best way to detect counterfeits, he was told, 'Handle the real stuff. The more familiar you are with legal money, the easier you will spot counterfeit money.' The best antidote to error is the truth. The clearer we are about who the Lord Jesus is, the better protected we will be from error. Another way of keeping ourselves safe from error is to make full use of the sound teaching and loving fellowship of the church.

Verses 12–13 are not a postscript to the letter but an integral part of it. John wants to come and visit these people in order to have fellowship with them and to teach them face to face. Apostolic teaching within the context of a loving Christian fellowship keeps our Christian lives on track. Error cannot thrive in the environment of sound teaching and loving fellowship.

How can our desire that the sound people should be loving and the loving people sound become a reality? By listening to and practising what John teaches in 2 John about keeping truth and love in the right balance.

64

3 John

In 2 John, the apostle *told* us about the balance between truth and love, but now, in 3 John, he *shows* us the balance between truth and love.

The Connections between 2 John and 3 John

In both letters John introduces himself as 'the elder' (1; *2 John* 1). They are also very similar in size. Both could have been easily written on a single sheet of papyrus but 3 John is slightly shorter (by 25 Greek words). The letters have a common vocabulary and a shared theme, namely, the relationship between truth and love. Both were written around the same time, probably in the early 90s. The similarities between them suggest that they could have been written on the same day. Both letters are concerned about the attitude of Christians towards travelling teachers. In the ancient world, this was the way ideas were spread.

The Differences between 2 John and 3 John

The most obvious difference is that 3 John was written to an individual, to John's 'dear friend Gaius' (1). But another subtle difference concerns the attitude of Christians to travelling teachers. In 2 John, there is a warning about welcoming false teachers, but in 3 John there is a warning about refusing to welcome true teachers from within the church who were preaching the apostolic message (9 and 10b). 'The possible abuse of hospitality by the heretics is not to become an excuse for failing to show hospitality to true and faithful Christian preachers.'[1]

[1] David Jackman, *The Message of John's Letters* (Leicester: Inter-Varsity Press, 1988), p. 190.

THE STRUCTURE OF 3 JOHN

The structure of this short letter is built around the four people mentioned in it: Gaius, Diotrephes, Demetrius and John. After a conventional opening (1–2) which mentions the name of the sender, the name of the recipient and a greeting or prayer, 3 John refers to *Gaius, who received the letter* (3–8). He is commended for his loyalty to the truth of the gospel. John repeatedly mentions how he is walking in the truth (3–4). John also applauds his faithfulness in showing hospitality to preachers of the gospel. In our culture, visiting preachers are generally invited to stay in the minister's house or manse, but in the first century travelling preachers were put up in people's homes. Gaius opened his home to travelling gospel preachers, and his hospitality was greatly appreciated (5–8).

We are next introduced to *Diotrephes, who provoked the letter* (9–11). He was a selfish, self-assertive bully who wanted to be pre-eminent in the church. He was in the habit of slandering those who were in spiritual authority over him (9b–10a), because the cheapest and easiest way to boost one's own ego is to pull down others. He also refused faithful preachers opportunities to speak in the church (10b), and threatened to excommunicate anyone who gave them hospitality (10c). Diotrephes was treating those teaching apostolic truth in a way that should have been reserved for those teaching error, and it was his flagrant challenge to apostolic authority that forced John to write to Gaius.

Then we meet *Demetrius, who carried the letter* (12). John commends him warmly, asking that he be welcomed and given hospitality.

Finally, there is *John, who wrote the letter* (13–14). He expresses his desire to visit Gaius in order to talk at greater depth about the issues raised in his letter.

THE MESSAGE OF 3 JOHN

When an antiques expert is asked to value silverware, he or she will look for the hallmark which shows whether the article is genuine silver, or just silver plate. John now describes the hallmarks of truth and love in harmony. In 2 John he told us to keep truth and love in a proper balance. Now he shows us what that proper balance is like.

Having truth and love in the right balance involves *having no greater delight than the spiritual success of others.* John was thrilled to see Gaius' spiritual progress, and he was not afraid to tell him so (3). John had what today might be called a holistic outlook on life because he was also concerned about Gaius' health and general well-being (2a), but it was his spiritual progress that delighted him most (4). How do we feel when we see another Christian doing well spiritually? Do we genuinely rejoice, or do we feel a twinge of jealousy because we wish that God was blessing us in that way? If truth and love are in balance in our lives, we will be genuinely delighted when others are going on with the Lord, regardless of our own situation.

The second hallmark of having truth and love in the right balance is *generosity towards those engaged in the Lord's work.* Gaius, who loved the gospel and wanted to see it advancing, was generous towards those who travelled from place to place preaching the truth (5, 7–8). Even though he had never met them before, Gaius welcomed them, because he loved the truth, and they were preaching the truth. He gave them hospitality in his home, fed them, and gave them a bed for the night. He then did all he could to assist them in their preaching tour and allowed them to use his home as a base for spreading the gospel. When these preachers met John again, they could not speak highly enough of Gaius' practical generosity (6). This generosity was costly in more ways than one: it was costly in monetary terms, but he was also going out on a limb to support these preachers because Diotrephes was not only aggressively discouraging people in the church from supporting them, but was actually threatening to excommunicate anyone who did so (10b). Gaius was showing a great deal of courage in doing what he did. If we have a love for the truth and a love for others, we will want to see the gospel spread. So we will be generous towards those engaged in doing just that. We will be generous in our giving. We will support them in our prayers, because those engaged in the Lord's work often feel isolated. To know that others are praying for them gives them a big boost. And we will be generous in our praise, because those engaged in the Lord's work can become discouraged, and a little generous praise goes a long way to lift their spirits.

Another hallmark of having truth and love in the right balance is *the imitation of good examples*. Imitating others is something that runs deep in our make-up as human beings. Children imitate their parents, though when they grow up to be teenagers, they imitate anyone but their parents. Even adults, who like to think that they are strong and independent, imitate others. We are all influenced in this way. The only question is, whose example will we follow? The strongest personality around us, or those who excel in grace? John tells us to imitate what is good (11). If we have truth and love in balance in our lives, we will not want to be influenced by anything but truth and love.

The fourth hallmark of having truth and love in the right balance is *a genuine concern for all Christians*. Gaius and the people among whom he worshipped were not statistics to John. He loved them because they loved the same truth he did. So he sends each of them personal greetings. He wants Gaius to greet them individually for him (14b). John had these ordinary Christians on his heart and, no doubt, in his prayers.

The last hallmark is a negative one because Diotrephes' activities introduce a dark side to an otherwise bright letter. He had truth and love out of balance. But we can turn what John says about him around, transforming a negative into a positive, and say that the fifth hallmark of having truth and love in the right balance is *a healthy congregational life*. Diotrephes had broken the partnership between truth and love, and it had disastrous consequences for the congregation. The congregation was starved of God's Word. The New Testament canon had not been completed, and God was continuing to speak either directly through John, the last surviving apostle, or indirectly through those John had taught. But Diotrephes refused to have anything to do with John (9b) or the teachers whom he had instructed (10b). Diotrephes loved the sound of his own voice so much that he silenced the sound of the Lord's voice speaking through his apostles, and so starved the congregation of God's Word. Also the congregation was divided because Diotrephes was vocal in his attacks on John (10a). His slander of John and his associates forced people to take sides. Were they with Diotrephes or with John? Thus the congregation was bullied and browbeaten into submission.

However, if we turn these negatives into positives, we can see that keeping a right balance between truth and love produces a healthy congregation. God's Word is heard because the truth is loved. God's people are built up because only words that are beneficial and encouraging are spoken. And even when difficult things have to be said, the truth is still spoken in love. God's church is secure because people know that their leaders genuinely love them and are not using them to bolster their own egos.

In all that he has written, is not John simply telling us to be more like the Lord Jesus, more full of grace and truth (*John* 1:14)? This is the great challenge that this letter sets before us. That great result will only be achieved when, by God's grace, we keep truth and love in their right and proper balance in our lives.

65
Jude

I t seems that Jude started out to write one kind of letter and ended up writing a completely different kind of letter. His original inten- tion was to write about the Christian faith; instead he wrote about *contending for* the Christian faith (3).

THE WRITER OF JUDE
Jude is the last of the New Testament 'General Letters', and, like the others, it is named after its writer. Jude tells us that he is James' brother (1). In the church at that time the only James whose name would have been instantly recognizable would have been James, the Lord's half- brother (*Mark* 6:3), the writer of the letter of James and a leader in the Jerusalem church. Though Jude was not an apostle, his connections with the apostles no doubt qualified his letter for inclusion in the New Testament canon.

THE PURPOSE OF JUDE
Jude tells us why he abandoned his original plan to write about God's salvation. False teachers had infiltrated the church and were pushing their errors among God's people. Jude wrote to warn Christians about this danger and to challenge them to stand up for the truth (3–4a).

THE RECIPIENTS OF JUDE
We are not told exactly who the people to whom Jude wrote were, but we can deduce some things about them.

They were from *a Jewish background*. Jude is full of references to Old Testament people, places and events – the Exodus period (5); the angelic rebellion against God (6); Sodom and Gomorrah's destruction (7); the archangel Michael and Moses (9); Cain, Balaam and Korah (11); and Enoch and Adam (14). These would have been very familiar to anyone from a Jewish background, but a little obscure to others.

They were also *special to God*. Although he does not name the people to whom he wrote, Jude gives a stunning description of them. They were called, loved and kept by the Father and the Son (1). The Holy Spirit had called them to trust in Christ and they had responded believingly. In echoes of Jeremiah 31:3, they are loved by God the Father with an everlasting love. They are kept safe by the Lord Jesus Christ.

THE STYLE OF JUDE

Jude seems to have loved *triads*. His threefold description of the people to whom he wrote is one of many threes in his letter. There is the triple blessing of verse 1b; the three examples of God's judgment in 5–7; and the terrible triad of false teachers in verse 11.

Another feature of Jude's style is his *reliance on 2 Peter*. Apart from the common theme of an attack on false teachers, there are parallels between verse 4 and 2 Peter 2:1. Then 2 Peter 3:3 is quoted in verse 18. Finally, in verse 4, the Lord is described as 'Sovereign'. The only other time this Greek word is used in relation to Jesus is in 2 Peter 2:1. The connections between Jude and 2 Peter are so close that the two letters are often considered together.

However, although the letter has links with 2 Peter, Jude does not slavishly copy Peter: the letter has *its own peculiar features*. One of these is its references to angels. There are four separate references in twenty-five verses (6, 8, 9, 14). Another feature is its allusions to books outside the Bible. In verse 9 Jude quotes from a book called 'The Assumption of Moses', and, in verses 14–15, he alludes to 'The Book of Enoch'.

Another striking feature is what we might call Jude's *political incorrectness*. There is 'the faith . . . once for all entrusted to the saints' (3b), and anything that deviates from it is to be labelled 'error'. Our relativistic society wants to say that there is no such thing as black and white: everything is a shade of grey. Jude says the exact opposite: there is black and white, right and wrong, truth and error, the faith and false teaching.

Jude instructs us to be intolerant towards error, which is anything out of line with the apostles' teaching. He does not accept the contemporary received wisdom that we must regard contradictory views as equally valid ways of looking at the truth. Instead he challenges us to contend for the faith, and reminds us that this will involve opposing, not receiving, error.

Jude strongly affirms Jesus' uniqueness. Jesus is the 'only Sovereign' (4b). There is only one way to God – Jesus Christ and him alone. But he has not yet reached the limit of his political incorrectness. He makes it very clear that sexual immorality and perversion – and from the reference in the context to Sodom and Gomorrah he clearly means homosexual acts – lead directly to God's judgment (7). He does not say that homosexuality is a valid lifestyle choice, acceptable on equal terms with heterosexual marriage. It goes against God's creation order (*Gen.* 2:24) and Jesus' teaching (*Mark* 10:6–9), and this rebellion will incur God's judgment.

The Shape of Jude

The letter begins in a conventional way with the writer's name, a description of the recipients, and a greeting (1–2). Then he states the danger facing the church (3–4). False teachers, in a very cunning way, were trying to turn the Bible's belief system and behavioural norms upside down. In the light of this, Jude outlines our responsibility (5–23). We are to oppose the error (5–19), while, at the same time, making sure we are developing our own relationship with God (20–23). As we do this, Jude tells us to have confidence (24–25). This note is sounded throughout the letter, as Jude reminds us that the chances of God ignoring error and letting false teachers get away with what they are doing are non-existent. However, the note of confidence reaches its crescendo with the great praise-statement in the last two verses of the letter.

The Message of Jude

Jude tells us that, when error creeps into the church, we are to adopt a twin-track approach. On the one hand, we are to contend for the faith (3b), and, at the same time, we are to continue in the faith (20a).

We are to contend for the faith.

Jude issues a call to arms, informing us how to spot the enemy and how to fight him. False teachers are subtle and plausible. We must saturate our minds with apostolic teaching (17). Then, when false teaching arises, even though it causes us great pain, we will not be surprised, because the Bible told us to expect it (18). And because our minds are full of the Bible, when we listen to false teachers we will almost instinctively know that what they are saying is not quite right. Many of us are not musically trained, but we have listened to enough good music to be able to say almost without thinking, 'That sounds a bit off key and flat.'

Then, as we look more closely at what is being said, our initial suspicions are confirmed because our Bible-attuned minds detect other problems with what is being taught. We notice problems in the false teacher's relationship to the Bible. Jude calls these false teachers 'dreamers' (8). They were claiming direct revelation from God in the form of dreams, and these soon became a more important source of authority than the Bible. False teachers always make their own opinions and ideas superior to the Bible's authority. We also see that false teachers have problems when it comes to the Lord Jesus. They deny his uniqueness as the only Saviour (4b). Again false teachers are always trying to downgrade and domesticate him.

Then we become aware of the way false teachers take advantage of God's people. Jude is damning in his criticism of them in this respect. He condemns the fact that they are not really interested in God's people but are only interested in themselves. Again and again he highlights their self-obsession (12, 16). Jude also condemns them for the way they fail to help God's people. They promise a great deal but they cannot deliver. When the land is parched and badly in need of rain to revitalize it, the sight of a cloud brings the hope of refreshing rain. But these false teachers are 'clouds without rain' (12b). When a farmer goes out to his orchard in the autumn, he expects to see a crop of fruit growing on his trees. But these false teachers are like 'autumn trees without fruit' (12b). False teachers always do this to God's people: they exploit them, and they also disappoint them.

We sense the false teachers' uneasiness with the gospel. The gospel is a gospel of grace, but Jude exposes how they have distorted the gospel in order to live immorally. The purpose of the gospel is to teach us to say 'No' to sin (*Titus* 2:11–12), but these men have turned the gospel on its head (4b). 'It does not matter how you live,' they say. 'God will forgive you no matter what you do.'

Having identified the enemy, Jude spells out how we are to fight. We are to fight *with humility*. He was not contending for the faith in order to boost his reputation as a great rooter-out of heresy. Jude was a humble man. That is seen in the way he describes himself. If he had wanted to enhance his own personal standing in the church, he could have reminded us that he was Jesus' half-brother. Instead he chose to describe himself as 'a servant of Jesus Christ' (2). It was not personal ambition that made him contend for the faith.

We are to fight *with reluctance*. In verse 3 we can sense the tension Jude felt between his personal desires and his Christian duty. He was a hesitant controversialist, contending for the faith, not because he wanted to, but because he had to.

We are to fight *with vigour*. However reluctant Jude was to contend for the faith, when he did lock horns with the false teachers, he opposed them vigorously. His language is robust. He does not mince his words. The Lord's honour and the church's well-being were at stake, so Jude does not fight half-heartedly.

We are to fight *with thoughtfulness*. Jude's attack on the false teachers is not so much a blanket nuclear strike as a series of pinpoint dagger thrusts that go straight to the heart of their falsehoods. This is the reason he refers to the non-biblical books, 'The Assumption of Moses' and 'The Book of Enoch'. The false teachers were using these books to bolster their ideas. If Jude had simply said that their teaching was out of line with the Bible, that would have made little impression on those introducing error. The Bible's authority was not final to them – their exciting and vivid dreams were much more thrilling than words on the pages of a musty book. So what Jude does is to take the very books the false teachers thought so important and use them to contradict their teaching and behaviour.

We are to fight *with confidence*. Nowhere does Jude even hint that the false teaching would destroy the church. He has confidence that God will deal with error. In the past God judged those who rebelled against him – the Israelites, the fallen angels, and Sodom and Gomorrah (5–7) – and those who promoted error for their own selfish ends – Cain, Balaam and Korah (11). Jude is confident that God will do the same with these self-obsessed teachers. Jude also has confidence that God will protect his people from the false teaching. This is the reason for the wonderful doxology of 24–25, which stresses God's keeping power.

Simultaneously, we are to continue in the faith.
Being faithful to the truth is not an excuse for neglecting our own relationship with God. If we do, we will be like a man who is faithful to his wife but never shows her any love. 'What God wants from us is not only doctrinal faithfulness, but our love day by day.'[1] This is why Jude tells us to develop our faith, to pray, to continue to bask in God's love, and to be full of hope (20–21). He reminds us to look out for others too (22–23) because love for God and love for others are inextricably linked together. Some people struggle with error, wondering if it might be true. Some are enticed to dabble in it. We are to show mercy to these people and win them back through love (22). One of the reasons people drift into error is that false teachers seem more interested in them and loving towards them than Christians who believe all the right things. Jude is telling us to out-love false teachers. But in seeking lovingly to bring back those who have been seduced by error to the Lord and the truth, we are not to be over-confident. We are to 'show mercy mixed with fear' (23). Sometimes in helping people and rescuing them, we have to go pretty close to the fire.

This is the great challenge of Jude – *contending for* the faith, and, at the same time, *continuing in* the faith. That is very hard to do because we are weak, and very prone to go to one extreme or the other. Apart from the Lord himself, the great historical example of contending for the faith and at the same time continuing in the faith is a man called

[1] Francis Schaeffer, *The Church at the End of the Twentieth Century*, p. 129.

Athanasius. A heresy called Arianism, which taught that Jesus is not God but only the highest created being, was sweeping through the church in the fourth century. Often it seemed that Athanasius was the only person fighting against this Christ-dishonouring error. Someone said to him, 'Athanasius, the world is against you.' To which he replied, 'Then Athanasius is against the world!' Often he suffered for his stand for the truth. His life was constantly in danger, and five times he was dismissed as Bishop of Alexandria and sent into exile. But he refused to give up, and eventually Arianism was condemned and cast out of the church as heresy. Athanasius was a formidable defender of the truth, but he was also extremely godly, combining rock-solid orthodoxy with deep-rooted holiness.

Jude may be a small letter, but it punches well above its weight. It challenges us to be like Athanasius, not only contending for the faith, but also continuing in the faith.

66

Revelation

Members of an Internet discussion group were asked to summarize their favourite book very briefly. Here is part of someone's summary of the Bible: 'Great start . . . Cracking ending that is open to many interpretations.' Our last chapter deals with the Bible's 'cracking ending' – the book of Revelation.

SOME COMMON GROUND

Although some dispute it, most agree that John wrote Revelation (1:1). The Greek in which the book was written suggests that Aramaic or Hebrew was the writer's first language. This would be consistent with John being the writer. All agree that Revelation was written on Patmos, a small barren island in the Aegean Sea about 40 miles off the coast of modern-day Turkey. Today part of it is a UNESCO World Heritage Site, but in John's time it was not a holiday destination but a prison island. John had been banished to Patmos because of his loyalty to the Lord Jesus (1:9), and there, 'on the Lord's day', he was given the vision which we call 'Revelation' (1:10). Another point of agreement is that the recipients of Revelation were seven congregations in the Roman province of Asia (1:11). A final point of general agreement is that the source of Revelation's symbols and pictures is the Old Testament. Although there are no direct quotations from the Old Testament, 'no other New Testament writer alludes to the Old Testament as much as John . . . He seems consciously to have modelled what he says on the Old Testament.'[1] The stronger our grasp of the Old Testament, the easier we will find it to work out what Revelation is saying.

[1] Simon Jones, *Discovering the New Testament* (Leicester: Crossway Books, 2001), p. 141.

THE MAIN INTERPRETATIONS OF REVELATION

One major interpretation is known as *Futurism*. This regards most of Revelation as a description of events that will take place in the future. Revelation 4:1 is a key verse in this interpretation. The main problem with this view is that it makes Revelation largely irrelevant to its original readers. Why did John bother sending it to the seven churches in Asia if, apart from chapters 2 and 3, it was not really for them?

Another major interpretation is *Preterism*. This sees Revelation as a highly symbolic description of the events surrounding the fall of Jerusalem to the Romans in AD 70. This gives rise to disputes over the dating of Revelation. Most think Revelation was written around 95, making it the last New Testament book to be written. This date coincides with the severe persecution of Christians by the Roman Emperor Domitian and would explain why John was on Patmos. But Preterists date Revelation before 70, arguing that if the fall of Jerusalem had taken place, John would have alluded to it in Revelation. The fact that he did not shows that it had not yet taken place. Preterists think that the persecution John is referring to was the one during Nero's reign in the mid-60s. The problem with this is that Nero's persecution was restricted to Rome and Italy and did not spread as far as Asia, where John was.

The third main interpretation of Revelation is *Historicism*. This sees Revelation as charting the historical events which will take place throughout the course of history from Jesus' first coming to his scond coming. So according to this view, Revelation contains a message for Christians of all ages, as well as an element of prediction.

The final way of interpreting Revelation is *Idealism*. This sees Revelation as entirely symbolic. It does not refer to any specific events but instead outlines principles and patterns of spiritual life and warfare that will operate from Jesus' first coming to his second coming. These principles will be seen at work in the world at many times and in different settings. Revelation therefore speaks not just to people in the past, and not just to people in the future, but to people in every time and place.

KEYS THAT UNLOCK THE MEANING OF REVELATION

Revelation's main theme

Revelation is all about Jesus Christ (1:1). This implies that any book or sermon based on Revelation that does not have Christ as its focal point has misinterpreted Revelation. Revelation tells us about the victory of the Lamb (17:14). More specifically, it tells us that the Lamb has achieved his victory by means of his death and resurrection (1:18) and that his victory will be consummated at his return (11:15). His victory march has begun, but it has not yet reached its completion.

Revelation's structure

Revelation does not have the logical flow of, say, one of Paul's letters. Neither does it have the chronological sequence of, say, the book of Acts. Like parts of Daniel and Zechariah, Revelation belongs to a category of Bible literature known as 'Apocalyptic'. Apocalyptic literature has a structure, but it is not a logical one or a sequential one. The structure of Revelation is one of *progressive parallelism*.

Revelation has seven parallel sections. Each covers the same period, the period between the two comings of Christ, but looks at it from a different angle, rather as the replay of a brilliant goal is shown from various camera angles. The seven sections are Jesus among the seven golden lampstands (1–3); the book with the seven seals (4–7); the seven trumpets (8–11); the attack by the dragon and his agents – the beasts and the harlot – on the woman and her child (12–14); the seven bowls (15–16); the fall of the harlot and the beasts (17–19); and the judgment of the dragon and the new heavens and new earth (20–22).

There is progression within the parallelism. Each vision has four common themes: the Lord's triumph, the church's struggles on earth, God's judgment on evil, and the joy and security of heaven. The earlier visions concentrate on the first two themes, briefly mentioning the others. In the later visions, more weight is given to the last two themes. For example, in Vision 4 (12–14), the breakdown is as follows: the Lord's triumph (12:1–16) is 29.5% of the total vision; the church's struggles (12:17–13:18), 33.4%; heaven (14:1–5), 9.4%; and God's final judgment (14:6–20), 27.7%. But, in Vision 7 (20–22), the breakdown is completely different. the Lord's triumph (20:1–6) is 12.75% of the total vision; the church's struggles (20:7–9), 6.4%; God's final judgment (20:10–15), 12.75%; and heaven (21:1–22:5), an overwhelming 68.1%.

How Revelation's symbolism operates

The most striking feature of apocalyptic literature is its use of symbolism. Revelation uses vivid, terrifying and grotesque images, and representative numbers. But how does this symbolism operate? Sometimes different symbols can run into each other and refer to the same thing. In Revelation the devil has three agents – the beast out of the sea, which represents state opposition and persecution of the church; the beast out of the earth, which represents false religion; and the harlot, which represents worldly seduction. They symbolize Satan's attack on the bodies, minds and hearts of God's people. But very often all three can manifest themselves in the same thing. In our society the institutions of government, religion and business are distinct, but in many societies throughout history the three have been rolled into one.

Also the symbols refer to principles of human behaviour and God's activity throughout the period between the two comings, not specific events. Take, for example, the 'Four Horsemen of the Apocalypse' in 6:1–8. The rider on the white horse (6:1–2) represents Christ and the conquering power of the gospel. The rider on the red horse (6:3–4) represents war; the rider on the black horse (6:5–6) famine; and the rider on the pale horse (6:7–8) death. This is not about a specific war, famine, or time of death, but a principle that operates throughout history. Between the two comings, two things will happen: Jesus' kingdom will advance, and Satan's kingdom will retaliate with frantic ferocity.

Again, the numbers are not literal but symbolic. The main numbers in Revelation are *three*, which represents God; *four*, which represents the creation; *seven*, which represents perfection; *ten*, which represents completeness; and *twenty-four*, which represents the church. Then there are all the various combinations of the main numbers. Take, for example, the famous '666' of 13:18. What is that number saying? The answer is not complicated. In Revelation, seven is the number of perfection. What is the number six? It is perfection minus one. This symbolic number is telling us that everything contrary to God, and

666 comes up in the vision of the two beasts who oppose God, is less than perfect, and so is doomed to failure.

THE MILLENNIUM

Every point about the interpretation of Revelation is contested, but none is more so than the Millennium, the one thousand years of 20:2. There are three main interpretations. First of all, there is *Premillennialism*. Premillennialists believe that the one thousand years must be taken literally and that Jesus will come before they begin. Although there are different types of premillennialism, the most popular version teaches that Jesus will come for his people and secretly rapture them away to heaven. Then there will be seven years of satanic activity, which they label, 'The Tribulation'. At the end of this period, Jesus will openly come back with his people and literally reign on earth for one thousand years. At the end of the Millennium, Satan will rebel in what is called his 'Little Season', which Jesus will bring to an end. After that comes the judgment at the Great White Throne and the inauguration of the new heaven and new earth.

The second view is *Amillennialism*. Amillennialists believe that there will be no literal one thousand years. The number is symbolic, referring to the whole age. Satan has been bound as a result of Jesus' first coming (*Mark* 3:27; *Col.* 2:15). He is still active but he cannot stop the spread of the gospel throughout the world (20:3). Just before Jesus returns, Satan will have his final rebellion, but it will be brought to an end by Jesus' return, which will usher in the Final Judgment and the new heaven and new earth.

The third interpretation is *Postmillenialism*. Postmillennialists believe mostly the same things as Amillennialists, with one major difference. They believe that before Christ returns the gospel will make substantial progress and transform society more and more.

Each position has its problems, but Premillennialism has most.

THE SIGNIFICANCE OF REVELATION

Revelation is the Bible's final book. All the great themes reach their conclusion here, especially in the description of heaven in 21–22.

In Revelation we see that *the kingdom has come*. God's people (21:3) are in God's place (21:1) under God's rule (21:5). We also see that *the curse has been reversed*. When Adam sinned, God cursed the world (*Gen.* 3:14–24). But in heaven all the sorrow, sadness and death are removed (21:4; 22:3a). Again we see that *paradise has been restored*. John's description of God's city, the new Jerusalem (22:1–2) refers back to the Garden of Eden (*Gen.* 2:9–14). The paradise that was lost through the first Adam's disobedience has been restored through the last Adam's obedience, the obedience that took him to the cross.

Again we see that *the covenant has been fulfilled*. God's covenant with Abraham promised a people, protection, God's presence and a place (*Gen.* 12:2–3). In Revelation all these covenant promises are fulfilled to perfection. Through Jesus 'all peoples on earth will be blessed'. In 7:9 we see the great crowd no one can count (*Gen.* 15:5; 22:16–18), made up of those with the same faith in Christ that Abraham had, worshipping together in heaven. Heaven is the place to which Abraham ultimately looked forward (*Heb.* 12:16). It is the essential place of protection. The Lord completely shields us from anything that might harm us (7:16–17). Heaven will be continually and eternally filled with God's presence (21:3; 22:5). Everything has come full circle. Everything is complete.

THE CHALLENGE OF REVELATION

Revelation is not there for us to fight over or speculate about, but to help us to live. In 2–3, the Lord Jesus addresses seven congregations in Asia, and what he says to them indicates how he wants us to live. He wants us to love him because he warns the church at Ephesus that it has lost its first love for him (2:1–7). He wants us to be faithful to him, even in the teeth of strong opposition, because he praises the church at Smyrna for doing just that (2:8–11). He wants us to be holy because he admonishes the church at Pergamum for slackness towards those who oppose holiness (2:12–17). He wants us to be intolerant of error because he reprimands the church at Thyatira for its accommodation of a false teacher (2:18–29). He wants us to be vital and real in our relationship with him because he rebukes the church at Sardis for its deadness and living on past glories (3:1–6). He wants us to be involved